A·N·N·U·A·L E·D·I·T·I·O·N·S

Business Ethics   01/02

Thirteenth Edition

EDITOR

John E. Richardson
Pepperdine University

Dr. John E. Richardson is professor of marketing in the George L. Graziadio School of Business and Management at Pepperdine University. He is president of his own consulting firm and has consulted with organizations such as Bell and Howell, Dayton-Hudson, Epson, and the U.S. Navy, as well as with various service, nonprofit, and franchise organizations. Dr. Richardson is a member of the American Management Association, the American Marketing Association, the Society for Business Ethics, and Beta Gamma Sigma honorary business fraternity.

McGraw-Hill/Dushkin
530 Old Whitfield Street, Guilford, Connecticut 06437

Visit us on the Internet
http://www.dushkin.com

Credits

1. Ethics, Values, and Social Responsibility in Business
Unit photo—© 2001 by PhotoDisc, Inc.
2. Ethical Issues and Dilemmas in the Workplace
Unit photo—Courtesy of Digital Stock.
3. Business and Society: Contemporary Ethical, Social, and Environmental Issues
Unit photo—© 2001 by Sweet By & By/Cindy Brown.
4. Ethics and Social Responsibility in the Marketplace
Unit photo—Courtesy of Tom Way/IBM Microelectronics.
5. Developing the Future Ethos and Social Responsibility of Business
Unit photo—© 2001 by PhotoDisc, Inc.

Cataloging in Publication Data
Main entry under title: Annual Editions: Business Ethics. 2001/2002.
1. Business ethics—Periodicals. I. Richardson, John E., *comp.* II. Title: Business ethics.
ISBN 0–07–243354–X   658.408   91–649227   ISSN 1055–5455

Thirteenth Edition

Cover image © 2001 by PhotoDisc, Inc.

Printed in the United States of America   1234567890BAHBAH54321   Printed on Recycled Paper iii

To the Reader

In publishing ANNUAL EDITIONS we recognize the enormous role played by the magazines, newspapers, and journals of the public press in providing current, first-rate educational information in a broad spectrum of interest areas. Many of these articles are appropriate for students, researchers, and professionals seeking accurate, current material to help bridge the gap between principles and theories and the real world. These articles, however, become more useful for study when those of lasting value are carefully collected, organized, indexed, and reproduced in a low-cost format, which provides easy and permanent access when the material is needed. That is the role played by ANNUAL EDITIONS.

Recent events have brought ethics to the forefront as a topic of discussion throughout our nation. And, undoubtedly, the area of society that is getting the closest scrutiny regarding its ethical practices is the business sector. Both the print and broadcast media have offered a constant stream of facts and opinions concerning recent unethical goings-on in the business world. Insider trading scandals on Wall Street, the marketing of unsafe products, money laundering, and questionable contracting practices are just a few examples of events that have recently tarnished the image of business.

As corporate America struggles to find its ethical identity in a business environment that grows increasingly complex, managers are confronted with some poignant questions that have definite ethical ramifications. Does a company have any obligation to help solve social problems such as poverty, pollution, and urban decay? What ethical responsibilities should a multinational corporation assume in foreign countries? What obligation does a manufacturer have to the consumer with respect to product defects and safety?

These are just a few of the issues that make the study of business ethics important and challenging. A significant goal of *Annual Editions: Business Ethics 01/02* is to present some different perspectives on understanding basic concepts and concerns of business ethics and to provide ideas on how to incorporate these concepts into the policies and decision-making processes of businesses. The articles reprinted in this publication have been carefully chosen from a variety of public press sources to furnish current information on business ethics.

This volume contains a number of features designed to make it useful for students, researchers, and professionals. These include a *topic guide* for locating articles on specific subjects related to business ethics, the *table of contents* with summaries of each article and key concepts in italics, and a comprehensive *index*. Also included in this edition are selected *World Wide Web* sites that can be used to further explore article topics. These sites are cross-referenced by number in the *topic guide*.

The articles are organized into five units. Selections that focus on similar issues are concentrated into subsections within the broader units. Each unit is preceded by an overview which provides background for informed reading of the articles, emphasizes critical issues, and presents key points to consider that focus on major themes running through the selections.

Your comments, opinions, and recommendations about *Annual Editions: Business Ethics 01/02* will be greatly appreciated and will help shape future editions. Please take a moment to complete and return the postage-paid *article rating form* on the last page of this book. Any book can be improved, and with your help this one will continue to be.

John E. Richardson

John E. Richardson
Editor

Contents

UNIT 1

Ethics, Values, and Social Responsibility in Business

Six selections provide an introduction to business ethics and social responsibility.

The concepts in bold italics are developed in the article. For further expansion please refer to the Topic Guide and the Index.

UNIT 2

Ethical Issues and Dilemmas in the Workplace

Eighteen selections organized within seven subsections examine crucial employee-related issues and their ethical implications for management's decision-making practices and policies.

The concepts in bold italics are developed in the article. For further expansion please refer to the Topic Guide and the Index.

The concepts in bold italics are developed in the article. For further expansion please refer to the Topic Guide and the Index.

UNIT 3

**Business
and Society:
Contemporary,
Ethical, Social,
and Environ-
mental Issues**

Eleven articles organized within
three subsections provide an analysis
of important ethical, social, and
environmental issues affecting both
domestic and global workplaces.

The concepts in bold italics are developed in the article. For further expansion please refer to the Topic Guide and the Index.

UNIT 4

Ethics and Social Responsibility in the Marketplace

Eight selections organized within two subsections describe the practice of incorporating ethics into the marketplace.

The concepts in bold italics are developed in the article. For further expansion please refer to the Topic Guide and the Index.

UNIT 5

Developing the Future Ethos and Social Responsibility of Business

Six selections consider guidelines and principles for developing the future ethos and social responsibility of business.

The concepts in bold italics are developed in the article. For further expansion please refer to the Topic Guide and the Index.

1

Topic Guide

This topic guide suggests how the selections in this book relate to the subjects covered in your course.

The Web icon (◎) under the topic articles easily identifies the relevant Web sites, which are numbered and annotated on the next two pages. By linking the articles and the Web sites by topic, this ANNUAL EDITIONS reader becomes a powerful learning and research tool.

TOPIC AREA	TREATED IN	TOPIC AREA	TREATED IN
Codes of Ethics (Codes of Conduct)	2. Sears Lectureship in Business Ehtics 4. Doing Well by Doing Good 31. Values in Tension 32. Global Standards, Local Problems 33. Environment of Ethics in Global Business 34. Caux Round Table 35. Sweatshops: No More Excuses 39. Managing for Organizational Integrity 43. Winery With a Mission ◎ *1, 3, 5, 10, 19*		48. New Workforce ◎ *3, 5, 19, 20, 24, 25*
		Environmental Disregard and Pollution	4. Doing Well by Doing Good 5. Ford-Firestone Lesson: Heed the Moment of Truth 7. Is Your Office Killing You? 23. 3M's Big Cleanup 26. Greening of Corporate America 27. Elephant at the Environmental Cocktail Party 28. Trust in the Marketplace 31. Values in Tension 32. Global Standards, Local Problems 33. Environment of Ethics in Global Business 34. Caux Round Table 39. Managing for Organizational Integrity 42. 100 Best Corporate Citizens 43. Winery With a Mission 46. Profits From Principle ◎ *20, 24*
Conflicts of Interest	3. Defining Moments 17. Sorrow and Guilt 24. Parable of the Sadhu 26. Greening of Corporate America 27. Elephant at the Environmental Cocktail Party 28. Trust in the Marketplace 31. Values in Tension 49. Start-Up of Her Own ◎ *1, 3, 5, 6, 7, 8, 10, 13, 14, 19, 32*		
Discrimination	15. What Minority Employees Really Want 16. Silver Lining 17. Sorrow and Guilt 28. Trust in the Marketplace 31. Values in Tension 35. Sweatshops: No More Excuses 48. New Workforce 49. Start-Up of Her Own ◎ *12, 13, 16, 22*	**Equal Employment Opportunities**	13. Harassment Grows More Complex 15. What Minority Employees Really Want 16. Silver Lining ◎ *4, 12, 16, 18, 21, 22*
		Ethical Training	1. Thinking Ethically 2. Ethics: The Way to Do Business 4. Doing Well by Doing Good 6. Why Character Counts 11. Anatomy of Fraudulent Behavior 13. Harassment Grows More Complex 22. Motivating Moral Corporate Behavior 26. Greening of Corporate America 29. Virtual Morality 36. Companies Are Discovering the Value of Ethics 37. Ethics in the Public Eye 41. Mission Driven, Values Centered ◎ *1, 3, 5, 6, 8, 10, 12*
Downsizing	17. Sorrow and Guilt 18. Alternatives to Downsizing 46. Profits From Principle ◎ *4, 12, 13, 18*		
Employee Conduct and Responsibility	10. Cyber Crime 20. Columbia/HCA Whistle-Blowers to Fight for Gold 29. Virtual Morality 40. When Good People Do Bad Things at Work ◎ *13, 17, 22*		
Employee Rights, Health, and Safety	1. Thinking Ethically 3. Defining Moments 7. Is Your Office Killing You? 8. Electronic Communication in the Workplace 9. Religion in the Workplace 15. What Minority Employees Really Want 17. Sorrow and Guilt 19. Blowing Whistles, Blowing Smoke 20. Columbia/HCA Whistle-Blowers to Fight for Gold 23. 3M's Big Cleanup 25. Work & Family 29. Virtual Morality 32. Global Standards, Local Problems 33. Environment of Ethics in Global Business 34. Caux Round Table 35. Sweatshops: No More Excuses 38. Company Simply Refused to Pay 40. When Good People Do Bad Things at Work 42. 100 Best Corporate Citizens 43. Winery With a Mission 46. Profits From Principle	**Legal and Legislative Environment**	2. Ethics: The Way to Do Business 4. Doing Well by Doing Good 7. Is Your Office Killing You? 8. Electronic Communication in the Workplace 13. Harassment Grows More Complex 14. Tales From the Front Line of Sexual Harassment 19. Blowing Whistles, Blowing Smoke 20. Columbia/HCA Whistle-Blowers to Fight for Gold 22. Motivating Moral Corporate Behavior 27. Elephant at the Environmental Cocktail Party 28. Trust in the Marketplace 29. Virtual Morality 30. Online Privacy 32. Global Standards, Local Problems 34. Caux Round Table 37. Ethics in the Public Eye 38. Company Simply Refused to Pay 39. Managing for Organizational Integrity 44. Ethical Challenges for Business in the New Millennium 48. New Workforce ◎ *1, 3, 5, 6, 8, 10, 12, 19, 24, 27*

2

● AE: Business Ethics

The following World Wide Web sites have been carefully researched and selected to support the articles found in this reader. The sites are cross-referenced by number and the Web icon (●) in the topic guide. In addition, it is possible to link directly to these Web sites through our DUSHKIN ONLINE support site at *http://www.dushkin.com/online/*.

The following sites were available at the time of publication. Visit our Web site—we update DUSHKIN ONLINE regularly to reflect any changes.

General Sources

1. Center for the Study of Ethics in the Professions
http://www.iit.edu/departments/csep/
Sponsored by the Illinois Institute of Technology, this site links to a number of world business ethics centers.

2. Harvard Business School (HBS)
http://www.hbs.edu/educators.html
Surf through the many valuable links attached to this Educators and Research News site to preview upcoming issues of the *Harvard Business Review*.

3. Murray G. Bacon Center for Ethics in Business
http://www.public.iastate.edu/~BACON_CENTER/ homepage.html
This Iowa State University site was developed to aid businesses to understand and come to grips with ethical dilemmas.

4. U.S. Department of Labor
http://www.dol.gov
Browsing through this site will lead you to a vast array of labor-related data and discussions of issues affecting employees and managers, such as the minimum wage.

5. Wharton Ethics Program
http://rider.wharton.upenn.edu/~ethics/#Objectives/
The Wharton School of the University of Pennsylvania provides an independently managed site that offers links to research, cases, and other business ethics centers.

Ethics, Values, and Social Responsibility in Business

6. Association for Moral Education (AME)
http://www.wittenberg.edu/AME/
AME is dedicated to fostering communication, cooperation, training, and research that links moral theory with educational practices. From here it is possible to connect to several sites of relevance in the study of business ethics.

7. Business Policy and Strategy
http://www.aom.pace.edu/bps/bps.html
This site of the Business Policy and Strategy Division of the Academy of Management is full of information about various topics in business theory and practice.

8. Ethics Updates/Lawrence Hinman
http://ethics.acusd.edu
This site provides both simple concept definitions and complex analysis of ethics, original treatises, and sophisticated search engine capability. Subject matter covers the gamut, from ethical theory to applied ethical venues.

9. National Center for Policy Analysis
http://www.public-policy.org/~ncpa/pd/pdindex.html
This organization's archive links lead you to interesting materials on a variety of topics that affect managers, from immigration issues, to affirmative action, to regulatory policy.

10. Online Journal of Ethics/Institute for Business and Professional Ethics
http://condor.depaul.edu/ethics/ethg1.html
This journal describes itself as "an online journal of cutting edge research in the field of business and professional ethics." Search the site for article archives and many valuable ethics and professional resources.

11. Organization and Management Theory
http://www.nbs.ntu.ac.uk/DEPTS/HRM/Index.htm
This is part of Ray Lye's Human Resource Management Resources on the Internet. It provides annotated links to an array of documents, studies, and other resources on the theory and practice of the learning organization.

Employees and the Workplace: Ethical Issues and Dilemmas in the Workplace

12. American Civil Liberties Union
http://www.aclu.org/issues/worker/campaign.html
The ACLU provides this page in its "Campaign for Fairness in the Workplace." Papers on cover such privacy issues as lifestyle discrimination, drug testing, and electronic monitoring.

13. American Psychological Association
http://www.apa.org/books/homepage.html
Search this site to find references and discussion of important ethics issues for the workplace of the 1990s, including the impact of restructuring and revitalization of businesses.

14. Annenberg Washington Program in Communications Policy Studies of Northwestern University
http://www.annenberg.nwu.edu/pubs/downside/
Is your employer snooping on you? Stephen Bates discusses the National Information Infrastructure (NII). View this page for issues regarding privacy rights in the workplace.

15. Fortune
http://www.pathfinder.com/fortune/bestcompanies/ intro.html
What features make a company a desirable employer? *Fortune* magazine discusses the characteristics of the "100 Best Companies to Work For." This page leads to many other *Fortune* articles and resources and a list of the 100 best companies.

16. International Labour Organization (ILO)
http://www.ilo.org
ILO's home page leads you to links that describe the goals of the organization and summarizes international labor standards and human rights. Its official UN Web site locater can point you to many other useful resources.

17. What You Can Do in Your Workplace
http://www.connectforkids.org/info-url1564/ info-url_list.htm?section=Workplace
Browse here for useful hints and guidelines about how employees, employees' families, management, and society can help a company become more family-friendly.

18. U.S. Equal Employment Opportunity Commission (EEOC)

http://www.eeoc.gov

The EEOC's mission "is to ensure equality of opportunity by vigorously enforcing federal legislation prohibiting discrimination in employment." Consult this site for facts about employment discrimination, enforcement, and litigation.

Business and Society: Contemporary, Ethical, Social, and Environmental Issues

19. CIBERWeb

http://ciber.centers.purdue.edu

This site of the Centers for International Business Education and Research is useful for exploring issues related to business ethics in the international marketplace.

20. Communications for a Sustainable Future

http://csf.colorado.edu

This site leads you to information on topics in international environmental sustainability. It features the political economics of protecting the environment.

21. National Immigrant Forum

http://www.immigrationforum.org

The pro-immigrant organization offers this page to examine the effects of immigration on the U.S. economy and society. Click on the links to underground and immigrant economies.

22. Sympatico: Workplace

http://www.ntl.sympatico.ca/Contents/Careers/

This Canadian site provides an electronic network with a GripeVine for complaining about work and finding solutions to everyday work problems, and a HomeBase for learning how to work from home effectively.

23. Stockholm University

http://www.psychology.su.se/units/ao/ao.html

Explore topics related to job design and other business organizational concerns through this site presented by the Division of Work and Organizational Psychology.

24. United Nations Environment Programme (UNEP)

http://www.unep.ch

Consult this UNEP site for links to topics such as the impact of trade on the environment. It will direct you to useful databases and global resource information.

25. United States Trade Representative (USTR)

http://www.ustr.gov

This home page of the U.S. Trade Representative provides links to many U.S. government resources for those interested in ethics in international business.

Ethics and Social Responsibility in the Marketplace

26. Edwin B. Dean

http://mijuno.larc.nasa.gov/dfc/whatsnew.html

Read the many articles, consider the various points of view, and click on the links in this site to explore important business-related theories and issues such as cost management and living systems theory and design.

27. Kitchener Business Self-Help Office: Seven Steps to Exporting

http://www.city.kitchener.on.ca/departments/economic_ development/Kitchener_import_export.html

This site describes seven steps to exporting, from selecting an export market to actually beginning to export. It addresses such critical topics as distribution, pricing, and subsidiaries.

28. Total Quality Management Sites

http://www.nku.edu/~lindsay/qualhttp.html

This site points you to a variety of interesting Internet sources to aid in the study and application of Total Quality Management principles.

29. U.S. Navy

http://www.navy.mil

Start at this U.S. Navy page for access to a plethora of interesting stories and analyses related to Total Quality Leadership. It addresses such concerns as how TQL can improve customer service and affect utilization of information technology.

Developing the Future Ethos and Social Responsibility of Business

30. MELNET

http://www.bradford.ac.uk/acad/mancen/melnet/ index.html

MELNET is a "virtual cooperative" for people looking to improve the way they do business. Through this interactive site, learn about the course of management in the twenty-first century.

31. Sheffield University Management School

http://www.shef.ac.uk/uni/academic/I-M/mgt/ research/research.html

The Current Research page of this British school will lead you to information on a broad array of real-world management issues for now and in the future.

32. Trinity College/Computer Science Course

http://www.cs.tcd.ie/courses/2ba6/best967/dukej/ index.html

This page, Innovation in the Workplace, provides insight into what the future holds for employers and employees.

We highly recommend that you review our Web site for expanded information and our other product lines. We are continually updating and adding links to our Web site in order to offer you the most usable and useful information that will support and expand the value of your Annual Editions. You can reach us at: *http://www.dushkin. com/annualeditions/.*

www.dushkin.com/online/

Unit Selections

1. **Thinking Ethically: A Framework for Moral Decision Making,** Manuel Velasquez, Claire Andre, Thomas Shanks, and Michael J. Meyer
2. **The Sears Lectureship in Business Ethics at Bentley College—Ethics: The Way to Do Business,** Nicholas G. Moore
3. **Defining Moments: When Managers Must Choose Between Right and Right,** Joseph L. Badaracco Jr.
4. **Doing Well by Doing Good,** *The Economist*
5. **Ford-Firestone Lesson: Heed the Moment of Truth,** Marianne M. Jennings
6. **Why Character Counts,** Stephen R. Covey

Key Points to Consider

❖ Do you believe that corporations are more socially responsible today than they were 10 years ago? Why or why not?

❖ In what specific ways do you see companies practicing social responsibility? Do you think most companies are overt or covert in their social responsibility activities? Explain your answer.

❖ What are the economic and social implications of "management accountability" as part of the decision-making process? Does a company have any obligation to help remedy social problems, such as poverty, urban decay, and pollution? Defend your response.

❖ From an organizational perspective, what do you think are the major arguments for and against social responsibility?

 **Links**   **www.dushkin.com/online/**

These sites are annotated on pages 4 and 5.

Ethical decision making in an organization does not occur in a vacuum. As individuals and as managers, we formulate our ethics (that is, the standards of "right" and "wrong" behavior that we set for ourselves) based upon family, peer, and religious influences, our past experiences, and our own unique value systems. When we make ethical decisions within the organizational context, many times there are situational factors and potential conflicts of interest that further complicate the process.

Decisions do not only have personal ramifications—they also have social consequences. Social responsibility is really ethics at the organizational level, since it refers to the obligation that an organization has to make choices and to take actions that will contribute to the good of society as well as the good of the organization. Authentic social responsibility is not initiated because of forced compliance to specific laws and regulations. In contrast to legal responsibility, social responsibility involves a voluntary response from an organization that is above and beyond what is specified by the law.

The six selections in this unit provide an overview of the interrelationships of ethics, values, and social responsibility in business. The first two essays offer practical and insightful principles and suggestions to managers, enabling them to approach the subject of business ethics with more confidence. The next three selections point out the complexity and the significance of making ethical decisions. The last essay discusses the importance of implementing exemplary character in personal and organizational decision making.

thinking ethically

A FRAMEWORK FOR MORAL DECISION MAKING

DEVELOPED BY MANUEL VELASQUEZ, CLAIRE ANDRE, THOMAS SHANKS, S.J., AND MICHAEL J. MEYER

Moral issues greet us each morning in the newspaper, confront us in the memos on our desks, nag us from our children's soccer fields, and bid us good night on the evening news. We are bombarded daily with questions about the justice of our foreign policy, the morality of medical technologies that can prolong our lives, the rights of the homeless, the fairness of our children's teachers to the diverse students in their classrooms.

Dealing with these moral issues is often perplexing. How, exactly, should we think through an ethical issue? What questions should we ask? What factors should we consider?

The first step in analyzing moral issues is obvious but not always easy: Get the facts.

The first step in analyzing moral issues is obvious but not always easy: Get the facts. Some moral issues create controversies simply because we do not bother to check the facts. This first step, although obvious, is also among the most important and the most frequently overlooked.

But having the facts is not enough. Facts by themselves only tell us what *is;* they do not tell us what *ought* to be. In addition to getting the facts, resolving an ethical issue also requires an appeal to values. Philosophers have developed five different approaches to values to deal with moral issues.

The Utilitarian Approach

Utilitarianism was conceived in the 19th century by Jeremy Bentham and John Stuart Mill to help legislators determine which laws were morally best. Both Bentham and Mill suggested that ethical actions are those that provide the greatest balance of good over evil.

To analyze an issue using the utilitarian approach, we first identify the various courses of action available to us. Second, we ask who will be affected by each action and what benefits or harms will be derived from each. And third, we choose the action that will produce the greatest benefits and the least harm. The ethical action is the one that provides the greatest good for the greatest number.

The Rights Approach

The second important approach to ethics has its roots in the philosophy of the 18th-century thinker Immanuel Kant and others like him, who focused on the individual's right to choose for herself or himself. According to these philosophers, what makes human beings different from mere things is that people have dignity based on their ability to choose freely what they will do with their lives, and they have a fundamental moral right to have these choices respected. People are not objects to be manipulated; it is a violation of human dignity to use people in ways they do not freely choose.

Of course, many different, but related, rights exist besides this basic one. These other rights (an incomplete list below) can be thought of as different aspects of the basic right to be treated as we choose.

From *Issues in Ethics,* Winter 1996, pp. 2–5. © 1996 by the Markkula Center for Applied Ethics. Reprinted by permission.

the case of
maria elena

Maria Elena has cleaned your house each week for more than a year. You agree with your friend who recommended her that she does an excellent job and is well worth the $30 cash you pay her for three hours' work. You've also come to like her, and you think she likes you, especially as her English has become better and you've been able to have some pleasant conversations.

Over the past three weeks, however, you've noticed Maria Elena becoming more and more distracted. One day, you ask her if something is wrong, and she tells you she really needs to make additional money. She hastens to say she is not asking you for a raise, becomes upset, and begins to cry. When she calms down a little, she tells you her story:

She came to the United States six years ago from Mexico with her child, Miguel, who is now 7 years old. They entered the country on a visitor's visa that has expired, and Maria Elena now uses a Social Security number she made up.

Her common-law husband, Luis, came to the United States first. He entered the country illegally, after paying smugglers $500 to hide him under piles of grass cuttings for a six-hour truck ride across the border. When he had made enough money from low-paying day jobs, he sent for Maria Elena. Using a false green card, Luis now works as a busboy for a restaurant, which withholds part of his salary for taxes. When Maria Elena comes to work at your house, she takes the bus and Luis baby-sits.

In Mexico, Maria Elena and Luis lived in a small village where it was impossible to earn more than $3 a day. Both had sixth-grade educations, common in their village. Life was difficult, but they did not decide to leave until they realized the future would be bleak for their child and for the other children they wanted to have. Luis had a cousin in San Jose who visited and told Luis and Maria Elena how

well his life was going. After his visit, Luis and Maria Elena decided to come to the United States.

Luis quickly discovered, as did Maria Elena, that life in San Jose was not the way they had heard. The cousin did not tell them they would be able to afford to live only in a run-down three-room apartment with two other couples and their children. He did not tell them they would always live in fear of INS raids.

After they entered the United States, Maria Elena and Luis had a second child, Jose, who is 5 years old. The birth was difficult because she didn't use the health-care system or welfare for fear of being discovered as undocumented. But, she tells you, she is willing to put up with anything so that her children can have a better life. "All the money we make is for Miguel and Jose," she tells you. "We work hard for their education and their future."

Now, however, her mother in Mexico is dying, and Maria Elena must return home, leaving Luis and the children. She does not want to leave them because she might not be able to get back into the United States, but she is pretty sure she can find a way to return if she has enough money. That is her problem: She doesn't have enough money to make certain she can get back.

After she tells you her story, she becomes too distraught to continue talking. You now know she is an undocumented immigrant, working in your home. What is the ethical thing for you to do?

This case was developed by Tom Shanks, S.J., director of the Markkula Center for Applied Ethics. Maria Elena is a composite drawn from several real people, and her story represents some of the ethical dilemmas behind the immigration issue.

This case can be accessed through the Ethics Center home page on the World Wide Web: http://www.scu.edu/Ethics/. You can also contact us by e-mail, ethics@scu.edu, or regular mail: Markkula Center for Applied Ethics, Santa Clara University, Santa Clara, CA 95053. Our voice mail number is (408) 554-7898. We have also posted on our homepage a new case involving managed health care.

- *The right to the truth:* We have a right to be told the truth and to be informed about matters that significantly affect our choices.
- *The right of privacy:* We have the right to do, believe, and say whatever we choose in our personal lives so long as we do not violate the rights of others.
- *The right not to be injured:* We have the right not to be harmed or injured unless we freely and knowingly do something to deserve punishment or we freely and knowingly choose to risk such injuries.
- *The right to what is agreed:* We have a right to what has been promised by those with whom we have freely entered into a contract or agreement.

In deciding whether an action is moral or immoral using this second approach, then, we must ask, Does the action respect the moral rights of everyone? Actions are wrong

to the extent that they violate the rights of individuals; the more serious the violation, the more wrongful the action.

The Fairness or Justice Approach

The fairness or justice approach to ethics has its roots in the teachings of the ancient Greek philosopher Aristotle, who said that "equals should be treated equally and unequals unequally." The basic moral question in this approach is: How fair is an action? Does it treat everyone in the same way, or does it show favoritism and discrimination?

Favoritism gives benefits to some people without a justifiable reason for singling them out; discrimination imposes burdens on people who are no different from those on whom burdens are not imposed. Both favoritism and discrimination are unjust and wrong.

The Common-Good Approach

This approach to ethics presents a vision of society as a community whose members are joined in the shared pursuit of values and goals they hold in common. This community comprises individuals whose own good is inextricably bound to the good of the whole.

The common good is a notion that originated more than 2,000 years ago in the writings of Plato, Aristotle, and Cicero. More recently, contemporary ethicist John Rawls defined the common good as "certain general conditions that are . . . equally to everyone's advantage."

In this approach, we focus on ensuring that the social policies, social systems, institutions, and environments on which we depend are beneficial to all. Examples of goods common to all include affordable health care, effective public safety, peace among nations, a just legal system, and an unpolluted environment.

Appeals to the common good urge us to view ourselves as members of the same community, reflecting on broad questions concerning the kind of society we want to become and how we are to achieve that society. While respecting and valuing the freedom of individuals to pursue their own goals, the common-good approach challenges us also to recognize and further those goals we share in common.

The Virtue Approach

The virtue approach to ethics assumes that there are certain ideals toward which we should strive, which provide for the full development of our humanity. These ideals are discovered through thoughtful reflection on what kind of people we have the potential to become.

Virtues are attitudes or character traits that enable us to be and to act in ways that develop our highest potential. They enable us to pursue the ideals we have adopted.

Honesty, courage, compassion, generosity, fidelity, integrity, fairness, self-control, and prudence are all examples of virtues.

Virtues are like habits; that is, once acquired, they become characteristic of a person. Moreover, a person who has developed virtues will be naturally disposed to act in ways consistent with moral principles. The virtuous person is the ethical person.

In dealing with an ethical problem using the virtue approach, we might ask, What kind of person should I be? What will promote the development of character within myself and my community?

Ethical Problem Solving

These five approaches suggest that once we have ascertained the facts, we should ask ourselves five questions when trying to resolve a moral issue:

- What benefits and what harms will each course of action produce, and which alternative will lead to the best overall consequences?
- What moral rights do the affected parties have, and which course of action best respects those rights?
- Which course of action treats everyone the same, except where there is a morally justifiable reason not to, and does not show favoritism or discrimination?
- Which course of action advances the common good?
- Which course of action develops moral virtues?

This method, of course, does not provide an automatic solution to moral problems. It is not meant to. The method is merely meant to help identify most of the important ethical considerations. In the end, we must deliberate on moral issues for ourselves, keeping a careful eye on both the facts and on the ethical considerations involved.

This article updates several previous pieces from Issues in Ethics *by Manuel Velasquez—Dirksen Professor of Business Ethics at SCU and former Center director—and Claire Andre, associate Center director. "Thinking Ethically" is based on a framework developed by the authors in collaboration with Center Director Thomas Shanks, S.J., Presidential Professor of Ethics and the Common Good Michael J. Meyer, and others. The framework is used as the basis for many Center programs and presentations.*

FOR FURTHER READING

Frankena, William. *Ethics,* 2nd ed. (Englewood Cliffs, N.J.: Prentice Hall, 1973).

Halberstam, Joshua. *Everyday Ethics: Inspired Solutions to Real Life Dilemmas* (New York: Penguin Books, 1993).

Martin, Michael. *Everyday Morality* (Belmont, Calif: Wadsworth, 1995).

Rachels, James. *The Elements of Moral Philosophy,* 2nd ed. (New York: McGraw-Hill, 1993).

Velasquez, Manuel. *Business Ethics: Concepts and Cases,* 3rd ed. (Englewood Cliffs, N.J.: Prentice Hall, 1992) 2–110.

The Sears Lectureship in Business Ethics at Bentley College

Ethics: The Way to Do Business

NICHOLAS G. MOORE

Nicholas G. Moore is chairman of PricewaterhouseCoopers and senior partner of the U.S. firm of Pricewaterhouse-Coopers LLP. He became chairman and CEO of Coopers & Lybrand L.L.P. in 1994 and chairman of Coopers & Lybrand International in 1997. PricewaterhouseCoopers, with about 140,000 people and offices in more than 150 countries, is the world's largest provider of professional services.

Some people would characterize ethics as a relatively soft concept. This is 1998. Competition is fierce. The winnings go to those who are the quickest. But we view ethics as a hard-core value. Because the values that are the product of consistent ethical behavior are what hold widely distributed organizations together. And that's one of the most compelling reasons for a firm like ours to have an ethics program in place. We are widely distributed. We're all over the world. And having resources that people can use every day is very important. You can't legislate moral behavior; you've got to have principles, values, and standards by which people can make decisions.

Companies used to be defined almost exclusively by the products they produced or the services they rendered. That's all changed. We're now defined by the way we provide our products and services. Our behavior defines how we're perceived in the marketplace in ways that products never really could.

So ethical behavior is good business. Now that may be contrary to prevailing public perception. Our attitudes are shaped not only by our experience, but also by the press and the media. I happen to be blessed with four children: three out of college, just barely, and one in college. I have some sense of how their attitudes have been shaped, not only by me, but by other forces. And I think there is a perception out there that ethical behavior doesn't

necessarily coincide with business. I have to tell you that everything in my experience suggests just the opposite.

I spent most of my career in Silicon Valley. I can tell you, even with the smallest high-technology companies, the product had to be good, the market had to be good, the people had to be good. But the one thing that was checked out most extensively by venture capitalists was the integrity of the management team. And if integrity wasn't there, it didn't matter how good the product was, how good the market was—they weren't funded. That taught me a lesson and, since then, I have observed nothing to change my conclusion: Companies that operate ethically have a competitive edge over those that do not.

There are short-term costs to operating ethically. We all know that. You can lose a customer over an ethical issue. You can lose market share. But the consequences of ethical failure are even greater—and they are long term. The cost of ethical failure can be very high, and not just in financial penalties. There can be a loss of trust, and trust is important to all constituencies of a business: employees, shareholders, and customers.

People who want to participate in an environment that's congruent with their own value system will leave an unethical organization. So sound ethical behavior is a competitive advantage. In our business, trust is everything. Our clients depend on us for unquestioned integrity, objectivity, and independence. If you think about what we do—and we are in lots of businesses these days—without trust we are really out of business. Ethical behavior is our franchise.

We're also part of something that's very powerful right now, and that's globalization. As companies globalize, as they continue to look overseas for growth, they can experience cultural confusion about what they should do on the ethics side. There's the saying "When in Rome, do as the Romans do." But we can't simply do as the Romans do. We need to ask the questions that will help us make decisions that are culturally sensitive. When is different just different and when is different wrong? The answer to that kind of question—and our people face it day in and day out, both within our organization and on the client side—is not clear. Some cases are black and white: corrupt business practices, bribery. Obviously, clearly wrong. Also, often very illegal. There can be violations of the Foreign Corrupt Practices Act. Other laws that govern international business can result in fines, criminal penalties, and all the other things associated with illegal or unethical behavior.

But the gray areas are tougher to deal with. Think about the issues we deal with here in the United States, and then transplant them to foreign soil. Issues like diversity, the environment, child labor. We are much more sensitive to these issues. Still, the answers are very, very gray. And if they're gray here, they are really murky overseas. They require clear thinking and organizational support. I want to talk a little bit about how we think we provide that to our people, and to our clients, through our ethics program.

Ethics is at the heart of our success. You can look across our lines of business. You can look at what our strategies are. But what really drives our business is our people. The people we have out there on the line, making professional judgments, rendering opinions, every single day. The choices they make set precedents for us. They create expectations on the part of our clients. They define the values of our organization.

If you think about our number of people around the world, it's not an organization where legislation works. You really have to have some glue to hold things together. So we created resources to help our people make ethical decisions as they experience them. These include:

- A policy statement that defines the letter and spirit of our commitment;
- A code of conduct on the way we do business;
- Ethics training to shed light on the day-to-day problems that our people face;
- A confidential, toll-free Helpline; and
- A confidential mailbox.

The program really is about facilitating clear decision-making. We all know that ethical questions don't always have clear-cut answers. But every answer can be well thought out. We have the mechanisms in place, and a consultative culture in place, to allow people to enjoy the benefits of a well-thought-out answer. People are entitled to the support of their organization, and that's what we think we're providing.

Before we get to the Q&A, let me conclude by making a couple of comments. First, when it comes to ethics, everyone wins. Companies win, because people make better decisions. And people win because their companies support them. This allows everyone to move for- ward with confidence. When companies stand up for what's right, day in and day out, it has a positive impact. Positive in terms of who it attracts, because good people want to work in ethical environments. It simplifies decision-making. We know what we won't even think about doing. And, in the process, we earn the respect of our competitors, our clients, and our people. In the long term, that's very, very important. So ethical behavior is at the core of the way we do business, and it's the only way we're going to do business. These resources already exist in the United States and will be extended to all PricewaterhouseCoopers personnel worldwide.

QUESTIONS

Below are a few highlights from Nicholas Moore's question and answer session with some 250 Bentley College students, faculty, and guests.

Mr. Moore, I'm an independent director currently serving as a chairman of the audit committee which, as you know, hires and fires the auditors. Under what circumstances have or would you ever fire a client for an ethical issue?

You may be surprised, but we fire clients all the time. We have a very strict client acceptance process and a very strict client continuation policy. Every year, a partner is required to participate in that process, answer a lot of hard questions, and arrive at a decision about whether we should continue with that client.

A lot of this is risk management. It's almost like an underwriting decision. If people feel there is any possibility in a client environment that the people who are responsible for making decisions might be inclined to make an unethical decision, or a decision premised on lack of integrity, we don't waste any time. We verify what the situation is, and we're out of there very quickly.

I'm an international student here at Bently College. I'm concerned about firms in the U.S. that globalize, and the guidelines they have constructed for ethics exchanges, especially in Third World countries. I would like to hear your point of view.

I think that the big professional services firms are mechanisms for elevating accounting standards and maybe even other standards around the world. And we're fully prepared to exercise that capability. And I can tell you that the regulators, particularly those here in the United States, are interested in these issues because right now there is a march going on from all corners of the world to the U.S. capital markets for money. And the ability to issue securities, to raise money in the United States, is highly dependent upon the reliability of the financial statements and other representations made by management. We believe that we can play a big part in making that happen.

Defining Moments:
WHEN MANAGERS MUST CHOOSE BETWEEN

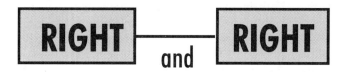

RIGHT — and — RIGHT

By Joseph L. Badaracco Jr.

THOUGHTFUL MANAGERS SOMETIMES face business problems that raise difficult, deeply personal questions. In these situations, managers find themselves wondering: Do I have to leave some of my values at home when I go to work? How much of myself—and of what I really care about—do I have to sacrifice to get ahead? When I get to the office, who am I?

Difficult questions like these are often matters of right versus right, not right versus wrong. Sometimes, a manager faces a tough problem and must choose between two ways of resolving it. Each alternative is the right thing to do, but there is no way to do both. There are three basic types of right-versus-right problems: those that raise questions about personal integrity and moral identity; conflicts between responsibilities for others and important personal values; and, perhaps the most challenging, those involving responsibilities that a company shares with other groups in society.

Most companies are now enmeshed in networks of ongoing relationships. Strategic alliances link organizations with their customers and suppliers, and even competitors. Many companies also have complicated dealings with the media, government regulators, local communities and various interest groups. These networks of relationships are also networks of managerial responsibility. Taken together, a company's business partners and stakeholders have a wide range of legitimate claims, but no company can satisfy all of them. At times, stakeholder responsibilities conflict with managers' personal and organizational obligations. When these conflicts occur, managers confront this third type of right-versus-right problem.

A particularly stark example of this occurred in the pharmaceutical industry nearly a decade ago. Late in 1988, the senior management of Paris-based Roussel-Uclaf had to decide where and how to market a new drug, called RU 486. Early tests had shown that the drug was 90 to 95 percent effective in causing a miscarriage during the first five weeks of pregnancy. The drug came to be known as "the French abortion pill,"

and Roussel-Uclaf and its managers found themselves at the vortex of the abortion controversy.

The chairman of Roussel-Uclaf, Edouard Sakiz, was a physician with a longstanding personal commitment to RU 486. He would make the final decisions on introducing the drug. Earlier in his career, while working as a medical researcher, Dr. Sakiz had helped develop the chemical compound on which RU 486 was based. He believed strongly that the drug could help thousands of women, particularly in poor countries, avoid injury or death from botched abortions. In the developed world, he believed, RU 486 would provide women and physicians with a valuable alternative to surgical abortions.

But Dr. Sakiz couldn't base his decision on RU 486 solely on his personal values. As the head of a company, he had other important obligations. Some were to his shareholders; from this perspective, RU 486 was a serious problem. Revenues from the drug were likely to be quite small, particularly in the early years. Yet, during this period, antiabortion groups would mount an international boycott of products made by Roussel-Uclaf and Hoechst, the German chemical giant that was Roussel-Uclaf's largest shareholder. A successful boycott would cost the two companies far more than they would earn from RU 486. At worst, a boycott could imperil Roussel-Uclaf's survival, for it was a relatively small company with weak profits.

Like any executive, Dr. Sakiz also had responsibilities for the people in his company. He had to assess the seriousness of the threats of violence against Roussel-Uclaf and its employees.

At a personal level, Dr. Sakiz faced a version of the question, Who am I? Was he, first and foremost, a medical doctor, a scientific researcher, an advocate of women's rights, or a corporate executive with responsibilities to shareholders and employees? In addition, his decision on RU 486 would commit his company to some values rather than others, thereby answering the organizational question, Who are we?

The prospect of introducing RU 486 placed Dr. Sakiz at the center of a network of responsibilities to important groups and institutions outside Roussel-Uclaf. Among these were the French Government, which owned 36 percent of Roussel-Uclaf, and the French Ministry of Health, which closely regulated the company, thus shaping its business opportunities.

Hoechst, which owned 55 percent of Roussel-Uclaf, also made strong ethical claims on the company. Its chairman was a devout Roman Catholic, who opposed abortion on moral grounds and had repeatedly stated his position in public. Moreover, Hoechst had a mission statement committing the company to lofty goals, which was put in place partly in reaction to its role in producing a poison gas used at Auschwitz.

China was another powerful actor in the drama. It wanted access to RU 486 for population control. The moral ground for China's position was avoiding the misery and risks of starvation resulting from its surging population.

Roussel-Uclaf's network of relationships and responsibilities raised extremely difficult questions for Dr. Sakiz and his company. What, in fact, were the company's obligations to women? To the Government laboratory that helped develop the steroid molecule on which RU 486 was based? To the larger medical and research communities? Were the unborn a stakeholder group? Could Roussel-Uclaf introduce the drug both in the West, citing a woman's right to choose, and in China, where women had apparently been coerced into abortions, even near the end of their pregnancies?

Dr. Sakiz's decision would define his company's role in society and its relationships with stakeholders. Everyone was watching him intently because his actions would be decisive, for RU 486 and for the company. In addition, he would be revealing, testing and in some ways shaping his own ethics. In short, Dr. Sakiz also had to make a personal choice that would become an important part of his life and career.

In late October 1988, a month after the French Government approved RU 486, Dr. Sakiz met with the executive committee of Roussel-Uclaf. Dr. Sakiz asked for a discussion of RU 486. After several hours, he called for a vote. When he raised his own hand in favor of suspending distribution of RU 486, it was clear that the pill was doomed.

The company's decision, and Dr. Sakiz's role in it, sparked astonishment and anger. The company and its leadership, some critics charged, had doomed a promising public health tool and set an example of cowardice. Other critics suggested sarcastically that the decision was no surprise, because Roussel-Uclaf had decided, in the face of controversy during the 1960's, not to produce contraceptive pills.

Three days after Roussel-Uclaf announced that it would suspend distribution, the French Minister of Health summoned the company's vice chairman to his office and said that if it did not resume distribution, the Government would transfer the patent to a company that would. After the meeting, Roussel-Uclaf announced that it would distribute RU 486 after all.

These events suggest that the RU 486 episode was something considerably less than a profile in courage. Edouard Sakiz seemed to have protected his job by sacrificing his convictions. There was, to be sure, strong opposition to RU 486, both inside and outside the company, but Dr. Sakiz made no effort to mobilize and lead his allies. He gave up without a fight. At a defining moment for the company, Dr. Sakiz's message seemed to place political caution and returns to shareholders above research and "the service of Life," as the company's mission statement put it.

But the surprising reversal of Roussel-Uclaf's original decision caused suspicion among some observers, who began to ask whether Dr. Sakiz had figured out a way to get what he wanted with a minimum of damage to himself and his company. Indeed, some wondered if the company and the Government had choreographed the entire episode. Others noted that Government science and health officials and Roussel-Uclaf managers and researchers had worked together for years—on RU 486, on other products and on many other regulatory issues—making it easy for them to anticipate each other's reactions.

What had Dr. Sakiz accomplished? More specifically, had he protected and advanced his own position? Had he contributed to the strength and security of his company? And had he defined its role in society in a creative way?

In personal terms, Dr. Sakiz succeeded in making good on his own commitment to RU 486—Roussel-Uclaf would distribute the drug. At the same time, he protected his job against the chairman of Hoechst. Be-

> ## ARISTOTLE COUNSELS MODERATION AND CAUTION PRECISELY BECAUSE HE IS GIVING ADVICE FOR SITUATIONS IN WHICH IMPORTANT ETHICAL CLAIMS STAND IN OPPOSITION.

cause the French Government had effectively ordered Roussel-Uclaf to distribute the drug, Hoechst would accomplish little by replacing Dr. Sakiz with an opponent of RU 486. For Roussel-Uclaf employees, the period of uncertainty and speculation was over, and the company decision was clear.

Dr. Sakiz seems to have defined Roussel-Uclaf's role in society in a remarkable, perhaps even daring way. It would be a political activist and catalyst. The company worked to stimulate and then shape media coverage; it invited its allies to mobilize after dismaying them by suspending distribution; it acceded to Government intervention that it may have encouraged or even arranged; and it tried to blur responsibility for the introduction of RU 486.

Roussel-Uclaf was committed to "the service of Life" following an original, complex and audacious strategy. Roussel-Uclaf would distribute RU 486, first in France and then elsewhere, but neither Dr. Sakiz nor his company had volunteered for martyrdom.

Clearly, there is an urgent need to find other lessons for managers who face choices like Dr. Sakiz's. The writings of Aristotle, who developed the foremost theory of human virtue, are an excellent place to find such lessons. Aristotle counsels moderation and caution precisely because he is giving advice for situations in which important ethical claims stand in opposition. He wants to discourage men and women who find tension or conflict among their duties, commitments, responsibilities and virtues from veering too sharply in one direction or another and trampling on some fundamental human values as they pursue others. This is why Stuart Hampshire has written that, for Aristotle, "balance represents a deep moral idea in a world of inescapable conflicts."

The ideal of balance provides valuable guidance for managers who must resolve right-versus-right conflicts—especially those like Edouard Sakiz's, that pit so many important values and responsibilities against each other. Aristotle's question for managers would be this: Have you done all you can to strike a balance, both morally and practically? By Aristotle's standard of balance, Dr. Sakiz performed quite well.

Joseph L. Badaracco Jr. is the John Shad Professor of Business Ethics at the Harvard Business School. He has taught courses on strategy, general management, business-government relations and business ethics in the school's M.B.A. and executive programs. Mr. Badaracco is a graduate of St. Louis University, Oxford University, where he was a Rhodes scholar, and the Harvard Business School, where he earned his M.B.A. and doctorate.

Doing well by doing good

Anti-globalisation protesters see companies as unethical as well as exploitative. Firms demur, of course, but face an awkward question: Does virtue pay?

TO MANY people the very concepts of "business" and "ethics" sit uneasily together. Business ethics, to them, is an oxymoron—or, as an American journalist once put it, "a contradiction in terms, like jumbo shrimp." And yet, in America and other western countries, companies increasingly wonder what constitutes ethical corporate behaviour, and how to get their employees to observe it. Management schools teach courses on the subject to their students. Business ethics is suddenly all the rage.

Fashionable perhaps—but also vague. Protesters in Washington, DC, were this week railing against corporate immorality as well as the IMF. But plenty of people retort that companies should not be in the business of ethics at all—let alone worrying about social responsibility, morals or the environment. If society wants companies to put any of these ahead of the pursuit of shareholder value, then governments should regulate them accordingly. Thirty years ago Milton Friedman, doyen of market economics, summed up this view by arguing that "there is one and only one social responsibility of business—to use its resources and engage in activities designed to increase its profits."

Even those who think companies do have wider responsibilities argue about the best way to pursue them. Ulrich Steger, who teaches environmental management at the International Institute for Management Development in Lausanne, says that companies cannot possibly hope to pursue a single abstract set of ethical principles and should not try. No universal set of ethical principles exists; most are too woolly to be helpful; and the decisions that companies face every day rarely present themselves as ethics versus economics in any case. He says that companies should aim instead for "responsible shareholder-value optimisation": their first priority should be shareholders' long-term interests, but, within that constraint, they should seek to meet whatever social or environmental goals the public expects of them.

Certainly companies, which increasingly try to include their ethical principles in corporate codes, stumble over how to write in something about the need for profitability. Or, to put the dilemma more crudely: when money and morality clash, what should a company do? Most firms try to resolve this with the consoling belief that such clashes are more imagined than real, and that virtue will pay in the end. Yet they cannot always be right.

Indeed, companies face more ethical quandaries than ever before. Technological change brings new debates, on issues ranging from genetically modified organisms to privacy on the Internet. Globalisation brings companies into contact with other countries that do business by different rules. Competitive pressures force firms to treat their staff in ways that depart from past practice. Add

unprecedented scrutiny from outside, led by non-governmental organisations (NGOs), and it is not surprising that dealing with ethical issues has become part of every manager's job.

Don't lie, don't cheat, don't steal

In America, companies have a special incentive to pursue virtue: the desire to avoid legal penalties. The first attempts to build ethical principles into the corporate bureaucracy began in the defence industry in the mid-1980s, a time when the business was awash with kickbacks and $500 screwdrivers. The first corporate-ethics office was created in 1985 by General Dynamics, which was being investigated by the government for pricing scams. Under pressure from the Defence Department, a group of 60 or so defence companies then launched an initiative to set up guidelines and compliance programmes. In 1991, federal sentencing rules extended the incentive to other industries: judges were empowered to reduce fines in cases involving companies that had rules in place to promote ethical behaviour, and to increase them for those that did not.

But the law is not the only motivator. Fear of embarrassment at the hands of NGOs and the media has given business ethics an even bigger push. Companies have learnt the hard way that they live in a CNN world, in which bad behaviour in one country can be seized on by local campaigners and beamed on the evening television news to customers back home. As non-governmental groups vie with each other for publicity and membership, big companies are especially vulnerable to hostile campaigns.

One victim was Shell, which in 1995 suffered two blows to its reputation: one from its attempted disposal of the Brent Spar oil rig in the North Sea, and the other over the company's failure to oppose the Nigerian government's execution of Ken Saro-Wiwa, a human-rights activist in a part of Nigeria where Shell had extensive operations. Since then, Shell has rewritten its business principles, created an elaborate mechanism to implement them, and worked harder to improve its relations with NGOs.

Remarkably, Shell's efforts had no clear legal or financial pressure behind them. Neither of the 1995 rows, says Robin Aram, the man in charge of Shell's policy development, did lasting damage to the company's share price or sales—although the Brent Spar spat brought a brief dip in its market share in Germany, thanks to a consumer boycott. But, he adds, "we weren't confident that there would be no long-term impact, given the growing interest of the investment community in these softer issues." And he also concedes that there was "a sense of deep discomfort from our own people." People seem happier working for organisations they regard as ethical. In a booming jobs market, that can become a powerful incentive to do the right thing.

The quest for virtue

In America there is now a veritable ethics industry, complete with consultancies, conferences, journals and "corporate conscience" awards. Accountancy firms such as PricewaterhouseCoopers offer to "audit" the ethical performance of companies. Corporate-ethics officers, who barely existed a decade ago, have become

de rigueur, at least for big companies. The Ethics Officer Association, which began with a dozen members in 1992, has 650 today. As many as one in five big firms has a full-time office devoted to the subject. Some are mighty empires: at United Technologies, for example, Pat Gnazzo presides over an international network of 160 business-ethics officers who distribute a code of ethics, in 24 languages, to people who work for this defence and engineering giant all round the world.

For academic philosophers, once lonely and contemplative creatures, the business ethics boom has been a bonanza. They are employed by companies to run "ethics workshops" and are consulted on thorny moral questions. They also act as expert witnesses in civil lawsuits "where lawyers usually want to be able to tell the judge that their client's behaviour was reasonable. So you are usually working for the defendants. They want absolution," says Kirk Hanson, a professor at Stanford Business School.

Outside America, few companies have an ethics bureaucracy. To some extent, observes IMD's Mr Steger, this reflects the fact that the state and organised labour both still play a bigger part in corporate life. In Germany, for example, workers' councils often deal with issues such as sexual equality, race relations and workers' rights, all of which might be seen as ethical issues in America.

In developing a formal ethics policy, companies usually begin by trying to sum up their philosophy in a code. That alone can raise awkward questions. The chairman of a large British firm recalls how his company secretary (general counsel) decided to draft an ethics code with appropriately lofty standards. "You do realise", said the chairman, "that if we publish this, we will be expected to follow it. Otherwise our staff and customers may ask questions." Dismayed, the lawyer went off to produce something more closely attuned to reality.

Not surprisingly, codes are often too broad to capture the ethical issues that actually confront companies, which range from handling their own staff to big global questions of policy on the environment, bribery and human rights. Some companies use the Internet to try to add precision to general injunctions. Boeing, for instance, tries to guide staff through the whole gamut of moral quandaries, offering an online quiz (with answers) on how to deal with everything from staff who fiddle their expenses on business trips to suppliers who ask for kickbacks.

The best corporate codes, says Robert Solomon of the University of Texas, are those that describe the way everybody in the company already behaves and feels. The worst are those where senior executives mandate a list of principles—especially if they then fail to "walk the talk" themselves. However, he says, "companies debate their values for many months, but they always turn out to have similar lists." There is usually something about integrity; something about respect for the individual; and something about honouring the customer.

The ethical issues that actually create most problems in companies often seem rather mundane to outsiders. Such as? "When an individual who is a wonderful producer and brings in multiple dollars doesn't adhere to the company's values," suggests Mr Gnazzo of United Technologies: in other words, when a company has to decide whether to sack an employee who is productive but naughty. "When an employee who you know is about to be let go is buying a new house, and you're honour-bound not to say anything," says Mr Solomon. "Or, what do you do when your boss lies to you? That's a big one."

Issues such as trust and human relations become harder to handle as companies intrude into the lives of their employees. A company with thousands of employees in South-East Asia has been firing employees who have AIDS, but giving them no explanation. It now wonders whether this is ethical. Several companies in America scan their employees' e-mail for unpleasant or disloyal material, or test them to see if they have been taking drugs. Is that right?

Even more complicated are issues driven by conflicts of interest. Edward Petry, head of the Ethics Officer Association, says the most recent issue taxing his members comes from the fad for Internet flotations. If a company is spinning off a booming e-commerce division, which employees should be allowed on to the lucrative "friends-and-family" list of share buyers?

Indeed, the revolution in communications technologies has created all sorts of new ethical dilemmas—just as technological change in medicine spurred interest in medical ethics in the 1970s. Because it is mainly businesses that develop and spread new technologies, businesses also tend to face the first questions about how to use them. So companies stumble into such questions as data protection and customer privacy. They know more than ever before about their customers' tastes, but few have a clear view on what uses of that knowledge are unethical.

Foreigners are different

Some of the most publicised debates about corporate ethics have been driven by globalisation. When companies operate abroad, they run up against all sorts of new moral issues. And one big problem is that ethical standards differ among countries.

Reams of research, says Denis Collins in an article for the *Journal of Business Ethics,* have been devoted to comparing ethical sensitivities of people from different countries. As most of this work has been North American, it is perhaps not surprising that it concluded that American business people are more "ethically sensitive" than their counterparts from Greece, Hong Kong, Taiwan, New Zealand, Ukraine and Britain. They were more sensitive than Australians about lavish entertainment

and conflicts of interest; than French and Germans over corporate social responsibility; than Chinese in matters of bribery and confidential information; and than Singaporeans on software piracy. Given such moral superiority, it is surprising that American companies seem to turn up in ethical scandals at least as often as those from other rich countries.

Many companies first confronted the moral dilemmas of globalisation when they had to decide whether to meet only local environmental standards, even if these were lower than ones back home. This debate came to public attention with the Bhopal disaster in 1984, when an explosion at a Union Carbide plant in India killed at least 8,000 people. Most large multinationals now have global minimum standards for health, safety and the environment.

These may, however, be hard to enforce. BP Amoco describes in a recent environmental and social report a huge joint venture in inland China. "Concerns remain around the cultural and regulatory differences in risk assessment and open reporting of safety incidents," the report admits. "For instance, deference to older and more senior members of staff has occasionally inhibited open challenging of unsafe practices." BP Amoco thinks it better to stay in the venture and try to raise standards. But Shell claims to have withdrawn from one joint venture because it was dissatisfied with its partner's approach. Most companies rarely talk about these cases, creating the suspicion that such withdrawals are rare.

Bribery and corruption have also been thorny issues. American companies have been bound since 1977 by the Foreign Corrupt Practices Act. Now all OECD countries have agreed to a convention to end bribery. But many companies turn a blind eye when intermediaries make such payments. Only a few, such as Motorola, have accounting systems that try to spot kickbacks by noting differences between what the cus-

tomer pays and what a vendor receives.

Some corruption is inevitable, say companies such as Shell, which work in some of the world's nastiest places. "If someone sticks a Kalashnikov through the window of your car and asks for 20 naira, we don't say that you shouldn't pay," says Mr Aram. "We say, it should be recorded." United Technologies' Mr Gnazzo takes a similar view: "We say, employees must report a gift so that everybody can see it's a gift to the company, and we can choose to refuse it. Every year we write to vendors, saying that we don't want gifts, we want good service."

Rights and wrongs

Human rights are a newer and trickier problem. Shell has written a primer on the subject, in consultation with Amnesty International. It agonises over such issues as what companies should do if they have a large investment in a country where human rights deteriorate; and whether companies should operate in countries that forbid outsiders to scrutinise their record on human rights (yes, but only if the company takes no advantage of such secrecy and is a "force for good").

The force-for-good argument also crops up when companies are accused of underpaying workers in poor countries, or of using suppliers who underpay. Such problems arise more often when there are lots of small suppliers. At Nike, a sporting-goods firm, Dusty Kidd, director of labour practices, has to deal with almost 600 supplier-factories around the world. The relationship is delicate: "They are independent businesses, but we take responsibility," says Mr Kidd. When, last year, Nike insisted on a rise in the minimum wage paid by its Indonesian suppliers, it claims to have absorbed much of the cost.

NGO s have berated firms such as Nike for failing to ensure that workers are paid a "living wage". But that can be hard, even in America.

"I once asked a university president, do you pay a living wage on your campus?" recalls Mr Kidd. "He said that was different. But it isn't." In developing countries, the dilemma may be even greater: "In Vietnam, our workers are paid more than doctors. What's the social cost if a doctor leaves his practice and goes to work for us? That's starting to happen."

Stung by attacks on their behaviour in the past, companies such as Shell and Nike have begun to see it as part of their corporate mission to raise standards not just within their company, but in the countries where they work. Mr Kidd, for instance, would like Nike's factories to be places where workers' health actually improves, through better education and care, and where the status of women is raised. Such ideals would have sounded familiar to some businessmen of the 19th century: Quaker companies such as Cadbury and Rowntree, for instance, were founded on the principle that a company should improve its workers' health and education. In today's more cynical and competitive world, though, corporate virtue no longer seems a goal in its own right.

When, in the late 1980s, companies devoted lots of effort to worrying about the environment, they told themselves that being clean and green was also a route to being profitable. In the same way, they now hope that virtue will bring financial, as well as spiritual, rewards. Environmental controls can, for instance, often be installed more cheaply than companies expect. Ed Freeman, who teaches ethics at the Darden Business School at the University of Virginia, recalls how the senior executive of a big chemical company announced that he wanted "zero pollution". His engineers were horrified. Three weeks later, they returned to admit that they could end pollution and save money. "The conflict between ethics and business may be a lot less than we think," he argues.

Most academic studies of the association between responsible corporate ethics and profitability suggest that the two will often go together. Researchers have managed to show that more ethically sensitive sales staff perform better (at least in America; the opposite appears to be the case in Taiwan); that share prices decline after reports of unethical conduct; and that companies which state an ethical commitment to stakeholders in their annual reports do better financially. But proving a causal link is well-nigh impossible.

What of the growing band of ethical investors? "I don't know of a single one of these funds which looks at the effectiveness of a company's internal ethics programme," says the EOA's Mr Petry, sadly. So a defence firm scores bad marks for being in a nasty industry, but no offsetting good marks for having an elaborate compliance programme.

And then there is the impact on employees. It may be true that they like working for ethically responsible companies. But, says Stanford's Mr Hanson, "I see a lot of my graduate students leaving jobs in not-for-profits to go and work for dot.coms." Few dot.coms would know a corporate ethics code if it fell on their heads. Small firms, in particular, pay far less attention than bigger rivals to normalising ethical issues and to worrying about their social responsibilities. Yet employment is growing in small companies and falling in big ones.

There may still be two good reasons for companies to worry about their ethical reputation. One is anticipation: bad behaviour, once it stirs up a public fuss, may provoke legislation that companies will find more irksome than self-restraint. The other, more crucial, is trust. A company that is not trusted by its employees, partners and customers will suffer. In an electronic world, where businesses are geographically far from their customers, a reputation for trust may become even more important. Ultimately, though, companies may have to accept that virtue is sometimes its own reward. One of the eternal truths of morality has been that the bad do not always do badly and the good do not always do well.

Ford-Firestone Lesson: Heed the Moment of Truth

Manager's Journal

By Marianne M. Jennings

My students know one fundamental principle of business ethics that Ford and Firestone forgot. That principle was not culled from years of research or modeled through an Excel spreadsheet. Rather, it is the most basic of precepts: The truth always gets out.

Such wisdom would have served both companies well in averting the current public-relations crisis that will soon ripen into class-action lawsuits managed by lawyers who have been lying idle since hogtying the tobacco companies.

There was a moment of truth for every company that passed through the public spanking lines of the media, Congress and courts that Ford and Firestone now face. That moment of truth comes when those within the company realize something is awry with their product, practices, earnings statements or culture. The moment usually comes when things are peachy in sales and earnings and its truth is ignored in the name of saving face and, perhaps, earnings.

Knowing the inevitable outcome—for truth does percolate—why do bright and experienced people ignore it? For even if the truth is known only within the confines of the company, it will out. Circumstances beyond even the best manager's control take over once the chance has passed to act on the moment of truth.

Johns Manville learned of the "crunching" lungs of asbestos workers in the 1930s, as reflected in the minutes of its board meetings. Instead of working on product development, warnings or even safety equipment, the company forged onward with a strategy of trying to keep the scientific community from disclosing its findings and of limiting the increasing numbers of plaintiffs by settlements for silence.

Dow Corning didn't deserve its bankruptcy or the multibillion-dollar settlements for its silicone implants because the science didn't support the alleged damages. However, there was a moment of truth when those implants, placed on a blotter, left a stain. The company could have disclosed the possible leakage, researched the risk, and warned doctors and patients. Given the congressional testimony on the implants, many women would have chosen them despite the risk. Instead, they sued because they were not warned.

Beech-Nut's crisis was a chemical concoction instead of apple juice in its baby food products. Executives there ignored an in-house chemist who tried to tell them they were selling adulterated products. Kidder-Peabody fell despite warnings from employees about a glitch in its accounting system that was reporting bond swaps as sales and income.

These cases all have several things in common. First, their moments of truth came and went while the companies took no action. Second, employees who raised the issue were ignored, or, in some cases, fired. Third, there were lawyers along for the ride, as they have been with Ford and Firestone.

Never rely on a lawyer in these moments of truth. Lawyers give controlling legal authority but are not particularly good at controlling damage. Lawyers shouldn't make business decisions; moments of truth require managers. More importantly, moments of truth require managers with strong ethics who will do more than the law requires and less than the law allows.

As a now infamous memo reveals, Ford and Firestone did not feel obligated to reveal to the U.S. Transportation Department that certain tires were being recalled in overseas markets. The companies should have realized that it was not a question of whether the recall would be reported, but by whom.

Do businesses ever face the moment of truth wisely? One great example is James Burke, CEO of Johnson & Johnson at the time of the 1982 Tylenol capsule scare. The minute Tylenol was linked to the cyanide poisonings, Johnson & Johnson recalled and destroyed 31 million bottles of the product, at a cost of $100 million, and Mr. Burke bent over backward to deal openly and forthrightly with the media and public. The result was one of the best crisis-management performances in history; the company won back nearly all its customers.

Perhaps the best example of an industry willing to use the truth to set itself free was the electric utility sector. During the 1980s, the media went hysterical over electromagnetic fields. These EMF, located in areas near electrical power lines, spawned litigation for cancer among those living nearby and produced claims of reduced property values.

In response to these unfounded fears, utilities went to their customers with monthly bill inserts discussing EMF. They funded studies, disclosed studies and encouraged all to study the issue. They took steps of "prudent avoidance," placing power lines sufficient distances away from properties.

The result? The EMF scare, which might have been the utility industry's asbestos, disappeared. Even sympathetic cases involving child plaintiffs did not sway juries; the causal connection was simply not there. EMF was managed with ethics and an attitude: If EMF is a problem, we manage it early and make it right. If it's a false alarm, we have the credibility and trust earned with voluntary action and disclosure at the moment of truth.

Unfortunately, Ford CEO Jacques Nasser and Bridgestone/Firestone CEO Masatoshi Ono did not heed their own moment of truth early enough. They are now paying the price.

Ms. Jennings is a professor of legal and ethical studies at Arizona State University.

Why Character Counts

Without it, you'll never truly succeed

By STEPHEN R. COVEY

SOME TIME AGO I was asked to consult for a bank that was having a problem with employee morale. "I don't know what's wrong," bemoaned their young president. Bright and charismatic, he'd risen through the ranks only to see his institution faltering. Productivity and profits were down. He blamed his employees. "No matter what incentives I provide," he said, "they won't shake off this gloom and doom."

He was right. The atmosphere seemed poisoned with suspicion and lack of trust. For two months I ran workshops, but nothing helped. I was stumped.

"How can anyone trust what's happening here?" was a typical refrain of employee. But no one would tell me the source of this distrust.

Finally, in more casual conversation, the truth emerged. The boss, who was married, was having an affair with an employee. And everyone knew it.

It was obvious now that the company's poor performance was caused by his conduct. But the greatest damage this man was doing was to himself. He was thinking only of his own gratification, disregarding long-term consequences. Moreover, he had violated a sacred trust with his wife.

In a word, his failing was one of *character.*

What Really Matters

Today it is out of vogue to speak in terms of character. But there is no more essential aspect of any person.

Character is made up of those principles and values that give your life direction, meaning and depth. These constitute your inner sense of what's right and wrong based not on laws or rules of conduct but on *who you are.* They include such traits as integrity, honesty, courage, fairness and generosity—which arise from the hard choices we have to make in life. So wrong is simply in doing wrong, not in getting caught.

Yet, some people wonder if our inner values matter anymore. After all, hasn't our noted bank executive succeeded in every visible way, despite his transgressions?

This question demonstrates a quandary of our modern life. Many have come to believe that the only things we need for success are talent, energy and personality. But history has taught us that over the long haul, who we are is more important than who we appear to be.

During the nation's first century and a half, almost everything in the literature of success and self-help focused on what could be called the character ethic. Such eminent figures as Benjamin Franklin and Thomas Jefferson made clear their belief that we can only experience true success and happiness by making character the bedrock of our lives.

After we moved into the industrial age and after World War I, the basic view of success shifted to what we could call the personality ethic. Success became more a function of charm, skills and techniques that, at least on the surface, lubricate the process of human interaction. Rather than struggle with thorny issues of right and wrong, we turned to making things run smoothly.

Some of that philosophy expressed itself with harmless but superficial maxims such as "smiling wins more friends than frowning." Other ideas were clearly manipulative or even deceptive—faking interest in others' hobbies so they will like you, for instance.

With a value system based solely on skill and personality, we find heroes in athletes, musicians and in powerful business executives. But despite the admiration we feel for these achievers, we shouldn't necessarily look upon them as role models. While skill is certainly needed for success, it can never guarantee happiness and fulfillment. These come from developing character.

From the Inside Out

You can begin to build character at any age. The key is learning how to look within—to work *inside out.*

With the inside-out approach, private victories precede public victories. These private victories are simply promises you make to yourself and others and then keep. They don't have to be profound or life-altering, like a career change. They can be as mundane as a commitment to exercise every day.

A promise like this may sound inconsequential, but it represents the hard choices we face in everyday life. The first step toward building character is to tackle a hard choice, commit to change and stay with it.

Day by day, as you make and keep increasingly challenging promises, you will be making deposits in your "character account." What begins as great effort will eventually become habit. And as you get into the habit of building character in the smaller areas of your life, your ability to develop character strength in more important spheres will grow.

Private victories therefore lead to our larger public victories. For instance, to gain more latitude in your job, you must first be a more responsible employee. To create a happy marriage, first be the kind of person who generates love, generosity, dependability and trust.

There's no more essential ingredient for character growth than trust. Whether it's trust we earn from colleagues or a spouse, it is built slowly over time in an infinite variety of circumstances.

One of the most commonly overlooked ways to build trust is to be loyal to those who are not present. Suppose you and I were criticizing our boss behind his back. What will happen if you and I later have a falling out? You know my nature—I'll bad-mouth you. You've seen me do it.

Now suppose you were to start criticizing the boss and I suggest we go to him and explore how things might be improved. You'd likely assume that I'd act with equal respect if someone were to criticize you.

Start at Home

Another way to build character is to admit your mistakes. Character is revealed in how we handle things that go wrong.

Years ago I had to choose someone to organize a huge meeting. I gave an untested employee a chance, and he bombed it big time. "It was all my fault," he told me. "But if you give me another chance, you have no idea how far I'll go to make the next one succeed."

Listen. Empathize. Appreciate. It's your choice. Are you willing to do that?

He displayed such courage in admitting his failure that I did give him another chance. And I've never regretted it. He performed so superbly that my estimation of his character was higher than if he'd done it right the first time.

The best opportunities to build character, however, are within our families, where we are constantly tested—and most vulnerable to lapses. True character begins at home.

Often we sense that we can get away with things around those who know us best, who will love us regardless of our conduct. This can end up subverting our character and our relationships. How often have we heard of someone who is a gem of an employee but treats his or her spouse like a piece of the woodwork?

Perhaps even more common is the following scenario: At one seminar, after I'd spoken on the importance of demonstrating character within the family, a man came up and said, "I like what you're saying, but my wife and I just don't have the same feelings for each other that we used to. I guess we don't love each other anymore. What can I do?"

"Love her," I replied.

He looked puzzled. "How do you love when you don't feel love?"

"My friend," I responded, "love is a verb. The *feeling* of love is the fruit of love. So love your wife. You did it once, you can do it again. Listen. Empathize. Appreciate. It's your choice. Are you willing to do that?"

Of course, I was asking this man if he was willing to search within himself for the character required to make his marriage work. All our relationships follow the contours of life; they have ups and downs. This is why our families provide a critical measure of our character—and the opportunity, again and again, to nurture it.

WHAT BECAME of the bank president who was involved sexually with an employee? When I confided to him what I knew of his affair and the effect it was having on his staff, he ran his fingers through his hair. "I don't know where to begin," he said.

"Is it over?"

He looked me squarely in the eye. "Yes. Absolutely."

"Then begin by talking with your wife," I answered.

He told his wife, who forgave him. Then he called a meeting of his staff and addressed their morale problem. "I have found the cause of the problem," he said. "It is me. I am asking you to give me another chance."

It took time, but eventually employee morale—a sense of openness, optimism and trust—improved. In the end, however, the executive was doing himself the greatest favor. He was finding his own path to character.

STEPHEN R. COVEY is author of the bestseller *The 7 Habits of Highly Effective Families*. This is his first article written for The Digest.

Unit Selections

Key Points to Consider

❖ Ethical dilemmas occur when a manager or an employee is faced with two or more conflicting ethical choices. In your opinion, what ethical dilemmas do managers face most frequently? What ethical dilemmas do employees face most often?

❖ What forms of gender and minority discrimination are most prevalent in today's workplace? In what particular job situations or occupations is discrimination more widespread and conspicuous? Why?

❖ Whistle-blowing occurs when an employee discloses illegal, immoral, or illegitimate organizational practices or activities. Under what circumstances do you believe whistle-blowing is appropriate? Why?

❖ In "The Parable of the Sadhu," a major problem was the lack of a mechanism for developing consensus on dealing with the sadhu. Given the complexities of an organization, where an ethical dilemma often cannot be optimally resolved by one person alone, how can an individual secure the support of the group and help it to reach a consensus as to the appropriate resolution of the dilemma?

 **Links** **www.dushkin.com/online/**

These sites are annotated on pages 4 and 5.

LaRue Tone Hosmer, in *The Ethics of Management,* lucidly states that ethical problems in business are truly managerial dilemmas because they represent a conflict, or at least the possibility of a conflict, between the *economic performance* of an organization and its *social performance.* Whereas the economic performance is measured by revenues, costs, and profits, the social performance is judged by the fulfillment of obligations to persons both within and outside the organization.

Units 2 to 4 discuss some of the critical ethical dilemmas that management faces in making decisions in the workplace, in the marketplace, and within the global society. This unit focuses on the relationships and obligations of employers and employees to each other.

Organizational decision makers are ethical when they act with equity, fairness, and impartiality, treating with respect the rights of their employees. An organization's hiring and firing practices, treatment of women and minorities, allowance of employees' privacy, and wages and working conditions are areas in which it has ethical responsibilities.

The employee also has ethical obligations in his or her relationship to the employer. A conflict of interest can occur when an employee allows a gratuity or favor to sway him or her in selecting a contract or purchasing a piece of equipment, making a choice that may not be in the best interests of the organization. Other possible ethical dilemmas for employees include espionage and the betrayal of secrets (especially to competitors), the theft of equipment, and the abuse of expense accounts.

The articles in this unit are broken down into seven sections representing various types of ethical dilemmas in the workplace. "Is Your Office Killing You?" begins the first section by revealing that one out of every three workers may be spending time in a workplace that is making them sick. "Electronic Communication in the Workplace—Something's Got to Give" reflects the ongoing battle over rights and privacy issues of e-mail at the office. In the next article, "Religion in the Workplace," there is a coverage of how many organizations are

acknowledging the significance of workers who bring their religious beliefs to the job.

In the subsection entitled *Employee Crime,* three articles explore cyber crime, insider trading, S&L rip-offs, bond scandals, and illegitimate global wire transfers.

The two selections under the subsection *Sexual Treatment of Employees* take a close look at the sexual treatment of employees in the workplace and examine how recent court decisions are attempting to clarify sexual harassment.

The two readings in the *Discriminatory and Prejudicial Employment Practices* subsection scrutinize key ingredients that minority employees desire in a company and explore the importance of using older workers to their fullest potential.

In the next subsection, *Downsizing of the Work Force,* two articles suggest the importance of management's seriously thinking about the specific reasons for considering layoffs, creative alternatives to downsizing, and possible strategies to be used in assisting survivors of downsizings.

The two selections included under the heading *Whistle-Blowing in the Organization* analyze the ethical dilemma and possible ramifications of whistle-blowing.

The articles "Leaders as Value Shapers" and "Motivating Moral Corporate Behavior," which open the last subsection, *Handling Ethical Dilemmas at Work,* delineate the importance of managers and employees fully understanding their values as they face serious ethical dilemmas at work. "3M's Big Cleanup" delves into the reasoning behind 3M's decision to recall a top product. The last unit article, "The Parable of the Sadhu," presents a real-world ethical dilemma for the reader to ponder.

Ethical Issues and Dilemmas in the Workplace

IS YOUR OFFICE KILLING YOU?

Sick buildings are seething with molds, monoxide—and worse

BY MICHELLE CONLIN

Everything was running perfectly that spring afternoon at the courtyard-style Best Western Springdale in the suburbs of Cincinnati. Room service was humming along at a reliable clip. The floral-patterned comforters were getting fluffed. Kids were splashing in the pool. Then, suddenly, General Manager Jim Crane got an emergency call about a leak that was turning Room 529 into a virtual waterfall. Within minutes, he and the hotel's burly engineer were ripping apart the room's walls. Inside, they found something out of a B-grade horror movie: a deathly smelling mold so gooey and hairy it seemed like it was breathing.

Crane soon discovered that, like the Blob, the Aspergillus strain of mold was everywhere: swarming through bathrooms, sprouting out of ceilings, and creeping through the ventilation and vending machine areas. This was May, 1998, and for the next year Crane worked to rid the hotel of the mounds of black growth. He knew they were a disaster for guest relations, but what he didn't realize was that each time he

took a breath, he was inhaling the mold's toxic fungal spores. These bioaerosols landed on the delicate mucous membranes of his airways and lungs, causing chronic inflammation and eventually leading to a medical diagnosis of hypersensitivity pneumonitis. The condition further scarred his lungs and eventually progressed into pulmonary fibrosis, a disease that is painful, debilitating, and sometimes even fatal. Slowly and invisibly, his workplace was killing him.

Today, Crane wheezes on his living room sofa—paying bills with his retirement savings and taking 17 different drugs each day. He filed a lawsuit in January against the hotel's owners, Laks Enterprises, which wouldn't comment on the suit. They lost the hotel through foreclosure to Bank of America in September after spending more than $2 million on an exhaustive remediation, and "the hotel is now safe," says the hotel's director of sales, Karen Sullivan. Already, though, Crane has lost half of his lung capacity. Says Crane's physician, Dr. Eckardt Johanning, medical director of Eastern New York Occupational & Environmental Health

LUNG DISEASE

Jim Crane, former manager, Best Western, Cincinnati, Ohio.

Crane takes 17 different drugs daily for pulmonary fibrosis after a toxic mold invaded the hotel he managed

Center in Albany: "Lack of proper protection and maintenance in that building caused this tragedy."

NO STANDARD. Crane's case may be an extreme example of what can happen when you work in a sick building, but he is hardly alone. Employees at Levi Strauss, US West, BP Amoco, even the Environmental Protection Agency, have claimed they suffered sick-building-related illnesses. Cases like these happen so often, in fact, that the World Health Organization estimates that one out of every three workers may be toiling away in a workplace that is making them sick.

The culprit: a stew of largely undetected dangers—from the carbon monoxide and other contaminants sucked into a building when air-intake vents overhang exhaust-filled loading docks and parking garages, to the volatile organic chemicals (VOCs) seeping out of building materials, furniture, office equipment, carpet, paint, and pesticides, to the molds and bacteria funneled through muck-filled heating, ventilation, and cooling systems (HVACS). Even the smoke from those puffing away at entrances gets sucked back into the building, chimney-style, because of the suction from revolving doors (what engineers call "the stack effect").

Putting in workaholic hours amid these contaminants is bad enough, but what makes it even worse is that, unlike at home, most of us can't even crack open a window at the office. Instead, we breathe yesterday's air and work in monotonous, uniform spaces under a forest of fluorescents, which can cause boredom, eyestrain, and lethargy. For those with robust immune systems, this may not matter much. But for 20% to 30% of the office population, the problems can range from the mild—headaches, nausea, dizziness, short-term memory loss, irritability, and itchy eyes and throats—to possible damage to the nervous and respiratory systems. Doctors also link the doubling of asthma rates since 1980 to bad indoor air.

Associated with sick-building syndrome is a controversial disease called multiple chemical sensitivity (MCS), which can make people allergic to almost anything containing a man-made chemical. This condition can sideline sufferers into surreal, boy-in-the-plastic-bubble worlds: Don Paladin, a former teacher, got MCS from pesticides sprayed at his school and is now forced to spend most of his time in his aluminum-sided "sanctuary." Other MCS victims say they are forced to live outside or sport medical masks wherever they go. No wonder the EPA calls indoor

DIAGNOSING A SICK OFFICE

1. Interview people with symptoms—and review records of past complaints to determine possible causes. Is the HVAC system dirty? Has the bathroom recently flooded? Is there a renovation being done on the floor below?

2. Ask your building operator to conduct an investigation and give you records of past complaints.

3. Hire your own outside specialist in indoor air quality/HVAC, and compare results with the building operator's. This will protect you against a building operator who is trying to hide something.

4. Share all information with employees—secrecy breeds fear.

5. Monitor results.

air quality one of the top five environmental health risks of our time.

But even as the evidence mounts that sick-building illnesses are on the rise, the extent of the problem has been almost impossible to measure. Amazingly, the federal government has no effective standards for indoor air quality in offices. The Occupational Safety & Health Administration (OSHA) has standards that are supposed to protect workers against individual contaminants such as benzene and formaldehyde, both carcinogens. But those standards were set for industrial workplaces and have been force-fit to apply to white-collar offices. "The OSHA standards don't always protect you from all kinds of exposures that people are having at the office," says Elissa Feldman, EPA's associate director of the Indoor Environments Div. "There is no federally guaranteed protection from exposure to unhealthy air indoors."

What's more, the chemical soup swirling through office air "is a complex mixture that we just don't know that much about and no one has set standards for," adds Feld-

man. "We're not [always] sure of the health effects." This, despite the fact that we spend 90% of our time inside—and more than half of that at work. What's also scary is that pollutant levels indoors are two to five times, and on occasion 100 times, more concentrated than outdoors, according to the EPA. "There are offices in America that I've been in that were probably more dangerous to my health than a Superfund site," says William McDonough, former dean of the University of Virginia School of Architecture.

WORKER CLAIMS. Twenty years ago, sick-building complaints were often written off as the psychosomatic rantings of the disaffected—or just the whining of lazy boss-haters. Rare cases—like the shocking outbreak in 1976 of a mysterious lung ailment during an American Legion convention (now known as Legionnaires' Disease)—were considered medical aberrations that couldn't become commonplace. Today, those attitudes are fading in the face of new research buttressing the validity of sick-building syndrome, including new studies linking symptoms to buildings that are damp or freshly renovated.

Experts who study illnesses caused by buildings divide them into two categories. The first—building-related illness—is when readily identifiable microbes or fungi give people actual diseases, like the Legionnaire's outbreak in April from bacteria blown out of the Melbourne aquarium's air-conditioning system that killed four people and infected 99 others. The second—sick-building syndrome—is when people report symptoms that can't be traced to one cause. Local governments are now starting to legitimize these sick-building-related illnesses as a condition for social benefits. Nearly a dozen states from New Mexico to Maryland now recognize MCS as a bona fide claim for workers' compensation. MCS is also covered—on a case-by-case basis—under the Americans with Disabilities Act, obliging

DO YOU WORK IN A TOXIN FACTORY?

The modern office is home to as many as 350 different volatile organic chemicals released by building materials, furnishings, and office equipment. That's not to mention the molds and bad indoor air that often flourish in these sealed-up environments. Some of the biggest offenders:

Printers and fax machines
They all ooze ozone. Scientists have yet to figure out definitively what happens when that ozone mixes with the workplace's other volatile organic chemicals.

Smoking
When people in your office sneak a smoke—even if it's behind closed doors—the second-hand stuff funnels through the ventilation system to the rest of the office.

Exterminators
It doesn't help that exterminators spray pesticides that may contain carcinogens over your workspace.

What fresh air?
Believe it or not, many fresh air vents are located over loading docks and parking garages, sucking in carbon monoxide and other contaminants.

Sealed windows
Most people now work in enclosed offices. Not being able to crack open a window means that you're relying on building managers to pump through enough fresh air—something they don't always do.

Carcinogenic cleaning products
There are 70,000 chemical cleaning products on the market, many of which are used to clean up your office. Some of these products may contain carcinogens.

Copy machines
They also emit ozone. What's worse, they are not always next to vents, so their emissions stay trapped in the office air.

The office bathroom—the modern mold machine
Who hasn't seen a clogged toilet? Flooded bathrooms can create molds.

The stack effect
Co-workers who smoke may think they are doing you a favor by taking it outside. But experts say this can be even worse. When you open the revolving door, the building sucks in the second-hand smoke like a chimney.

Renovations
Working in a building—especially those with sealed windows—can cause workers to inhale paint fumes, construction dust, and odors from new furnishings that can irritate skin, eyes, and airways.

Hidden Dangers: A Glossary
HVACs Heating, ventilation, and air-conditioning systems. Often they circulate contaminated air.
VOCs Volatile organic chemicals. They're emitted by furnishings, cleaning products, and equipment.
MCS Multiple chemical sensitivity. Sufferers are hypersensitive to chemicals.
CCP Carbonless copy paper. Found in credit-card and bank receipts. It contains known and probable carcinogens.

---

employers to make accommodations for sufferers.

U.S. companies could save as much as $58 billion annually by preventing sick-building illnesses and an additional $200 billion in worker performance improvements by creating offices with better indoor air, say researchers William J. Fisk and Arthur H. Rosenfeld of the Lawrence Berkeley National Laboratory in Berkeley, Calif. The researchers also found that the financial benefits of improving office climates can be 8 to 17 times larger than the costs of making those improvements. And the same VOCs that affect people can also harm expensive equipment. They create a film that covers computer circuit boards and telephone switches, causing them to blink or conk out, say Telcordia Technologies Inc. senior scientists Charles J. Weschler and Helen Shields. Just fixing those faulty phone wires has cost telecommunications companies more than $100 million over the past 10 years, they say.

Legal heat is also focusing attention on the issue. Last year, in a landmark case, the Ohio State Supreme Court awarded Joann Taylor an unprecedented $400,000 jury award from her former employer Centerior Energy Corp., now a part

MULTIPLE CHEMICAL SENSITIVITY

Don Paladin, MCS sufferer, Bellingham, Wash.

After pesticides were sprayed at the school where he taught, Paladin became allergic to chemicals. He takes refuge in an aluminum-sided "sanctuary"

*The EPA says that indoor air is one of the top **five** environmental health **risks** of our time*

of First Energy. The charge: She was forced to keep working in her newly renovated office even after she had been rushed to the hospital with chest pains and vomiting from the chemical fumes in the new carpet. First Energy says no other employees had complaints and that Taylor had to keep working in that building in order to perform her job.

SKYLIGHTS. Indeed, sick-building cases are becoming more and more common—and are often filed against building owner/operators. While there were only a few such cases five years ago, today "there are hundreds," says New York environmental consultant Wayne Tusa. It all adds up to indoor air becoming the next big environmental target, just as awareness of outdoor pollution led to the landmark Clean Air Act of 1970. Indeed, compared with European building standards, the U.S. seems stuck in the environmental Dark Ages.

But despite this growing climate of recognition, sick-building syndrome remains controversial. Many employers and building owner-operators say workers exaggerate illnesses. Doctors are often split on the issue, one camp dismissing many of the claims as hysterical, while the other sees them as the tip of the iceberg, foreshadowing a kind of chemical AIDS they say could be the scourge of the 21st century.

Even a company that does the right thing by being honest with employees about a building's dangers can be trapped in a legal quagmire. That's what happened to BP Amoco PLC after the company discovered a cancer cluster at its Naperville (Ill.) lab.

But a few businesses are taking action long before they get into trouble. At its Zeeland (Mich.) factory, furniture maker Herman Miller has created a virtual California.

RESPIRATORY AILMENTS

Rosie Gies and Juanita Johnson, former telephone operator and clerk; US West office, Walla Walla, Wash.

They suffered from nosebleeds and dizziness when vents weren't covered in a renovation

Workers sport Hawaiian shirts and blast the Beach Boys while working in an office that has 100% fresh air and daylight. After the factory opened, productivity improved by 1.5%, enough to pay off the building's $15 million mortgage. The place is so popular that 16 workers who quit last year for better-paying jobs all returned within two weeks because they said that they couldn't stand working in the dark. The U.S. Postal Service saw an even higher productivity gain—a stunning 16% jump—by simply installing skylights and improved lighting at its Reno (Nev.) postal sorting office. "If any CEOS have half a brain, they would start to pay attention to the fact that their employees are their main cost-and-benefit center," says McDonough, now a consultant with Herman Miller and Steelcase. "They can't afford not to do this."

Blame the prevalence of sick buildings, in part, on the energy crisis of the 1970s. That's when office buildings began to be built as tight as tin cans, padded heavily with money-saving layers of insulation and equipped with hyperefficient HVACS. In many cases, these systems, run by operators looking to shave

costs, suck in only five cubic feet of fresh air per minute per person. "That is almost enough to keep people alive," quips New York architect Robert F. Fox Jr., whose firm designs environmentally friendly skyscrapers. Indeed, to save money, some operators shut down the fresh-air intakes altogether. The American Society of Heating, Refrigerating & Air Conditioning Engineers recommends that HVACS pump in 20 cubic feet of fresh air per minute per person—a level below which symptoms increase. But there is nothing compelling building operators to do so, says Mark J. Mendell, team leader for the indoor-air-quality research effort at the National Institute of Occupational Safety & Health (NIOSH).

Stagnant office air also circulates the residue of as many as 350 VOCs that are emitted by building materials, furnishings, and office machines. For example, most office paints contain solvents that can cause everything from eye, nose, and throat irritation to digestive and central nervous system damage. Carpeting sometimes contains PVCs that give off the carcinogen dioxin. Furniture is often made of particle board that is bonded with resins made with carcinogen-containing formaldehyde. That's not to mention the pesticides and cleaning products swabbed over offices that, according to the EPA, may also contain carcinogens that can be discharged into the office air.

No surprise, then, that sick-building-related symptoms are on the rise. Across the country, doctors who treat patients with sick-building-related illnesses say caseloads have mushroomed 40% in the past decade. "There are more and more chemicals being introduced into the office environment through synthetic products, and ventilation systems have not caught up with being able to deliver fresh air," says sick-building specialist Dr. John B. Sullivan Jr. of the University of Arizona College of Medicine.

What makes it difficult for sufferers seeking remedies is that OSHA has no exposure limits for groups of

Some buildings suck in only 5 cubic feet of fresh air per person per minute—"almost enough to keep people alive"

chemicals that researchers believe might act synergistically. OSHA standards for acceptable amounts of benzene, for example, don't take into account the mixture of VOCs reacting with one another. This could be making building air even more dangerous, but because scientists don't yet know for certain how to measure for these combinations, the problems may be going undetected. That could also help explain, scientists say, why some buildings that are making people sick are getting clean bills of health. Or it may be that where standards do exist, OSHA's permissible exposure levels, which are often influenced heavily by politics and industry, are just too high. "These exposure limits don't have

THE "DETOX" DOC

Dr. John Sullivan, Tuscon, Ariz.

"More and more chemicals [are] introduced into the office environment through synthetic products, and ventilation systems have not caught up with being able to deliver fresh air"

any real bearing on what's happening in white-collar office buildings,"

says Alan Hedge, professor of human ecology at Cornell University. "In terms of chemical irritation, we're seeing symptoms at levels way below OSHA's standards."

"DEATH CUBE." An effort to enact sweeping indoor air standards stalled six years ago, when OSHA tried to issue a comprehensive smoking and indoor air-quality rule. The measure would have required all building operators to do basic, routine ventilation checks, change air filters regularly, and avoid using toxic cleaning substances. Not surprisingly, Big Tobacco went into overdrive behind the scenes to torpedo the move since the measure would have required all workplaces to be smoke-free. Shortly thereafter, in 1995, the 104th

WHY THE AIR AND LIGHT ARE SO MUCH BETTER IN PARIS

When the world-renowned architect Jean-Paul Viguier recently won a contract to build a 30-floor Sofitel Hotel in Chicago and a 40-floor office building at La Défense in Paris, the contrast between tough French standards and lax U.S. ones shocked him. French regulations required three times as much ventilation for his Paris tower and twice as much soundproofing as in Chicago—all the while slashing energy consumption to half American levels. By law, each workstation in France needed access to natural light—a scarcity in most U.S. offices. "Europeans are far ahead of Americans in building technology and concern for the environment," Viguier says.

As Americans face an epidemic of sick buildings, they could learn a lot by looking across the ocean. The high cost of energy and tough government regulations have forced European architects and office developers to tackle the problems of bad air and toxic materials. Such improvements aren't uniform throughout the Continent, and they come at a high price: Construction in Europe costs an aver-

age 50% more per square foot than in the U.S. But healthier work environments increase productivity and can actually save money in the long run. A recent Danish study showed that typists increased their output by 6% in offices with cleaner air.

European building regulations begin by stressing the need for fresh air. "In the U.S., most buildings depend on central air-conditioning and sealed windows," says Dan Wood, an American architect working in Rotterdam. Windows open in most European skyscrapers because air-conditioning is controlled room by room. Even if the top floors are sealed, huge ventilation ducts circulate fresh air. And though it's still the case that lots of Europeans puff away in the office, architects are starting to design rooms for smokers that prevent the smoke from infiltrating the entire building. Plus, Europeans use powerful air filters and usually circulate the air three times as frequently as in the U.S.

This helps fight off dangerous bacteria—and keeps deskbound workers from getting sleepy. "Artificial air

causes great fatigue for desk workers," says Pekka Littow, a Paris-based architect. Since artificial light tires people just as much as artificial air, most European building rules require all workers to have access to a window. Because Europeans insist on private offices over cubicles, they usually get superior soundproofing, too.

Cultural differences may prevent U.S. builders from adopting European techniques wholesale. Americans tend to tear down and replace buildings more often than Europeans, who expect them to last generations. But U.S. attitudes may be changing, perhaps because of the wave of anxiety about poor quality and dangerous construction. When he recently won a contract for a Los Angeles-based building, architect Wood, who usually works in Paris and the Netherlands, says he was able to persuade his clients to install individual-room air conditioners. Unfortunately, most U.S. office workers can't even count on that.

By William Echikson in Brussels

*Researchers say **improving** office environments could save companies as much as **$258 billion** annually by averting illnesses and boosting worker productivity*

Congress was ushered in, and it fiercely opposed any new government regulations. The effort was squashed. "Clearly, [sick-building syndrome] is a significant problem—though it is difficult to say how bad it is," says Charles N. Jeffress, Assistant Labor Secretary for Occupational Safety & Health. "And it is very difficult to do something about it." That may be true at the federal level. But as states pass their own laws, Jeffress thinks it may be possible to learn which approaches work and which don't.

Until then, the stories are likely to mount, though they rarely make headlines. At Levi Strauss & Co., for example, internal memos obtained by BUSINESS WEEK show that for eight years, at least 60 employees complained about the air quality at the jeans maker's Stern office building in San Francisco. The workers were especially concerned about smoke from the woodburning oven in the Il Fornaio restaurant on the ground floor. The mesquite-flavored fumes hung so heavy in the air that some employees rigged umbrellas over their desks to protect themselves from falling soot.

At least three people became disabled from acute asthma, severe allergies, and other environmental illnesses as a result of breathing in the carbon monoxide, the memos show. Things got so bad, employees say, that one office even got the grim nickname "the death cube" because three people who occupied it all died of cancer. Levi's took steps to revamp the building's ventilation system over the years, but the complaints persisted. "It proved to be challenging to track the problem down and find the right steps to resolve it," says Linda Butler, Levi's senior manager for communications. Finally, the company raised the air intake vents in 1997 so that the fresh air wasn't commingled with the exhaust from the restaurant, and the problem was fixed, Butler says.

Sometimes, the trouble doesn't stem from an ongoing problem but from one simple renovation project.

In 1991, at a former US West office in Walla Walla, Wash., some construction workers forgot to cover up the air-intake vents when they sprayed industrial-strength petroleum sealant on the building's façade as a part of a roofing and refurbishing project. Workers like clerk Juanita Johnson and telephone operator Rosie Gies, who had had a perfect attendance record during her first six years with the company, began suffering from nosebleeds and dizziness. "I could barely breathe at work because it hurt so much," says Gies, who eventually developed a case of reactive airway disease so debilitating that she says she couldn't lift her 3-year-old daughter. US West closed the office in late 1996 when it consolidated its directory centers. "We did testing by independent consultants and found compounds well below OSHA's permissible exposure limits," says US West Communications Director Dana Smith.

Often, that's exactly what happens. Companies bat away complaints with test results showing that their workspaces meet OSHA standards. But when the standards clearly have been violated, lawsuits such as Celeste Morrell's can follow. Morrell was a case worker in the Social Services Dept. of New York's Onondaga County in 1988 when her department received a new shipment of wooden desks that had a foul, chemical odor. Turns out the double-pedestal desks, like much furniture, was made with particle board consisting of chips of wood glued together with formaldehyde. After breathing in the fumes all day, Morrell, a widowed mother of two, said she felt sick. When investigators scoured the office, they found formaldehyde levels in desk drawers that were up to five times OSHA's standard for short-term exposure. Morrell's physician diagnosed her with formaldehyde poisoning and ordered her not to work within 15 feet of the desks, but she soon developed multiple myeloma, a form of cancer her doctor linked to her of-

fice. Last September, just six months after her suit went to nonjury trial, Morrell died at the age of 51. A judge is still deliberating. "Her desk killed her," says Morrell's attorney, Peter Littman of Ithaca, N.Y. Marc Violette, spokesman for the New York State Attorney General, says the state won't comment on the suit until after the judge has ruled.

HEAVY METAL. To make sure they never end up in court, some building owners, such as New York developer Durst Organization, are taking steps to erect greener and cleaner buildings on their own. Durst's newest building, the rocket-shaped Condé Nast tower, has solar panels, air intakes on every floor, and filters that screen out 85% of the city's contaminants (most buildings have filters that only keep out 35% of impurities). Some manufacturers, such as office furniture makers Steelcase and Herman Miller and office carpet maker Interface, are using materials in office furnishings that are less dangerous—a much needed move since many of the textile trimmings used in office fabrics, for example, are considered hazardous waste, a result of the heavy metal content of the dies and sealants used. Consider the office chair: "Most people are sitting on chairs that are an amalgam of hundreds of chemicals that have never been defined in terms of their effects on human health, and the deeper we look, we find things that are cancer-causing chemicals," says the University of Virginia's McDonough.

Following the lead of these pioneers could well pay off for more companies. Time off from work due to illness can be cut by as much as 30% if workers simply have control over their office air, one study shows. Some states, such as New Jersey and California, are leading the way by enacting some indoor air standards. The EPA is also conducting its first-ever national assessment of the health of the country's office building stock, the biggest such study ever to be performed. Getting a better rating than the norm could

*Experts predict that the 5% to 10% of the population that is **allergic** to chemicals will grow to **60%** by 2020*

be a marketing hook and might allow owners to charge even higher fees in today's helium-filled real estate market.

All this may signal the day when owner-operators make it a priority to choose building materials that are safer, companies demand air-quality reports before signing leases, and employees are as aware of their office's health as their own. Just like stock options and signing bonuses, workers are certain to start demanding fresh air and sunlight once they find out that other employees are getting them. Perhaps one day the office will even have its own annual checkup. If not, many American workers may not be around to complain. They'll be at home—sick.

With John Carey in Washington

IT PAYS TO TELL THE TRUTH

BP Amoco's disclosure of chem-lab risks makes financial sense, too

By Michael Arndt

Trade places for a moment with H. Laurence Fuller, co-chairman of BP Amoco PLC. It's the summer of 1999, and your company is being sued by the families of six scientists stricken with a rare form of brain cancer. All were diagnosed soon after retiring from long careers at BP Amoco's chemical research lab in Naperville, Ill., and five are already dead. You know that because BP Amoco is so big and rich—sales topped $100 billion in 1999—a jury might see Robin Hood justice in socking your company with damages that rival a Lotto jackpot. And now you get this bombshell: The outside medical experts you brought in have concluded the brain-cancer cluster was probably work-related. What do you do? If you're Fuller, you call a press conference and disclose everything.

Although many corporate lawyers would have advised Fuller that his was the dumbest move imaginable, BP Amoco is proving that when it comes to workplace liabilities, honesty is the best policy. By taking the moral high ground, the company deftly upstaged its foes in the court of public opinion, denying them a chance to turn it into another corporate ogre. Now, it is casting itself in the same sympathetic role in a court of law. The company won dismissal last year of a would-be class action. In March, the families of five of the chemists with brain cancer dropped their lawsuits for cash settle-

ments, one for as high as $2.7 million. "Other defendants allow themselves to be put on the defensive," says Victor E. Schwartz, a senior partner at the Washington law firm Crowell & Moring. "BP Amoco broke the vilification."

Candor doesn't come cheap or guarantee absolution. BP Amoco spent millions to hire top-flight medical investigators and specialists and millions more on the recent settlements. Although widespread reports about the mysterious cancers did nothing to hinder British Petroleum Co.'s takeover of Amoco Corp. in 1998, the company's labs, once acclaimed for breakthroughs in polymer research, are today known by potential recruits as causing cancer. Undoubtedly, the company would have suffered regardless of its response. But by stonewalling, it would have lost any chance to mold its image with the public.

NO SECRETS. Frankness has not stopped BP Amoco from getting sued either. In fact, the company may have turned itself into something of a litigation magnet by releasing such incriminating findings. Even with the March settlements, BP Amoco stands accused by an additional two dozen plaintiffs with a variety of seemingly unrelated tumors. But the payoffs will continue if these suits go to trial. After learning of the research-center cancers, BP Amoco shuttered the lab, offered free MRIs to employees, and hired medical experts to comb through medical records of all 1,676 people who had been employed at the "cancer building." Since the company has

owned up to its responsibilities, perhaps the public will think there's less need to slap it with exorbitant damages. That means if BP Amoco loses, it could end up paying less in compensatory and punitive damages, say outside lawyers. Notes Thomas Donaldson, a business professor at the Wharton School and director of its ethics program: "It seems to me that a company that shows it has heart is going to get a better hearing when it comes to the jury box."

With so much to gain by going public, why don't more companies come clean? Often, because corporate lawyers generally instruct clients to hunker down and deny everything. That rote advice does have some logic. Without evidence, plaintiffs may not be able to even bring a case, let alone prove it in court. If no one else knows, they figure, the problem will eventually go away, and the company will have saved itself a public tarring and big-time legal fees.

But as corporate defendants are learning, it is harder and harder to keep secrets today. Bad news can spread on the Internet or a 24-hour cable channel faster than ever before. Once the word gets out, it's usually too late. That's because the act of covering up is criminal in and of itself. "You could try to hide it, and you might get away with it 5 times out of 10, or even 9 times out of 10, but the risk of getting caught even that one time would be severe," observes David E. Van Zandt, dean of

Continued on following page

Northwestern University's law school. "You look like a bad actor."

So far, BP Amoco seems to be avoiding that fate. One of its smartest moves was to hire researchers from Johns Hopkins University and the University of Alabama at Birmingham to construct medical histories of everyone who had ever worked in the Naperville lab. The goal: to uncover an on-the-job link between those with the rare and fatal brain tumors, called gliomas, and the thousands of chemicals the scientists handled since the labs opened in 1970. In the end, the researchers failed to identify a chemical or a combination of chemicals responsible for the cancers. But they found that all six of the cancer victims were white men, assigned to the same building wing at some point in their careers, who had worked at the center for at least 10 years. The glioma rate among this group was 12 times as high as in a normal population, suggesting

BRAIN CANCER

Lawyer Karayannis sued BP Amoco on behalf of his deceased father, Nicholas and two other plaintiffs. Karayannis bears BP Amoco no bitterness, saying: "My father enjoyed working there"

the cluster was related to something in the workplace.

That BP Amoco gets credit for this rankles some plaintiffs' lawyers. They dismiss the study as little more than a publicity stunt crafted to make BP Amoco seem like a good guy. "That's not exactly a news flash—everyone already knew there were too many gliomas," says Tilden Katz of Corboy & Demetrio, a Chicago law firm representing 16 plaintiffs, including the sixth researcher found with brain cancer.

Still, it's hard to argue that BP Amoco didn't do the right thing. Marios N. Karayannis, a partner at Brady & Jensen in Elgin, Ill., sued BP Amoco on behalf of six people who claim they got cancer by working at the lab, including his father, Nicholas, who died in February, 1998. Karayannis settled his father's suit on Mar. 21 for an undisclosed sum. The workplace probably killed his dad, he says. But he adds: "My father enjoyed working there. Becoming bitter would not honor his time there." What company wouldn't want to be regarded like that?

Arndt covers manufacturing from Chicago.

Electronic Communication in the Workplace— Something's Got to Give

Kenneth A. Kovach, Sandra J. Conner, Tamar Livneh,
Kevin M. Scallan, and Roy L. Schwartz

Every day, millions of American workers use their e-mail and Internet systems, confident that their day's transactions are private. But nothing could be further from the truth. According to a major 1997 survey by the American Management Association, 63 percent of large and mid-sized companies acknowledged that they oversee employees through one or more electronic surveillance systems. Almost a quarter of those companies do not let their employees know they are being monitored.

The impact of e-mail has revolutionized the workplace. A poll reported by Kopp (1998) estimates that 90 percent of large companies, 64 percent of mid-sized companies, and 42 percent of small firms currently use e-mail systems. The same poll found that more than 40 million employees correspond via e-mail, and the number is expected to increase by about 20 percent each year. These statistics are indicative of the popularity of electronic communication in today's workplace. E-mail technology has facilitated more efficient interoffice communications, as well as external communications with clients, customers, and other businesses. It has also expedited personal transactions; in many instances, e-mail has effectively replaced the hand- or typewritten note and letter of memorandum.

The unique nature of e-mail as a communication media warrants special consideration regarding privacy. Although it may be used as a substitute for making a telephone call, there is a big difference between the two. The telephone call is transitory—ending when the phone is hung up—whereas an e-mail note is permanent. Moreover, e-mail can much more easily be examined by a third party without the knowledge of the communicating parties.

As technology becomes faster and cheaper, concerns about workplace privacy issues continue to mount. The impressive advancements in computer communications have created many new problems, and in some cases increased the severity of old ones.

Employee privacy is colliding with employer rights in the ongoing battle over e-mail at the office. Who will—and should—win?

It is surprising that despite this growing threat to privacy, there is no legal remedy for employees should their privacy be invaded by their employer. Federal and state courts, for the most part, have upheld employer monitoring, according little or no weight to employee privacy interests—possibly because they do not understand the intrusiveness of the new monitoring technology in the workplace. Neither Congress nor state legislatures have acted to fill the void or provide comprehensive statutory protection for workers. Privacy, ostensibly one of society's most, cherished values, is gradually disappearing from the workplace. According to Fader (1998), "American laws don't protect worker privacy very well. We differ from Europe and most industrialized nations. They stringently limit the employee data companies collect, store, and disseminate. We have no such laws."

LEGAL IMPLICATIONS

The right to privacy in the employment context usually derives from the Fourth Amendment to the U.S. Constitution, which reads:

The right of the people to be secure in their persons, houses, papers and effects, against unreasonable searches and seizures, shall not be violated, and no warrants shall issue but upon probable cause, supported by oath or affirmation, and particularly describing the place to be searched, and the persons or things to be seized.

Because the Constitution applies to actions of the state, public sector workers have the provision of appealing directly to the "reasonable expectation of privacy" standard established by the Supreme Court ruling in *Katz v. United States* (Rodriguez 1998). Private sector employees do not enjoy the same level of privacy protection because actions of private employers rarely constitute "state action," which would open the avenue of appeal directly to the Constitution. Because constitutional rights primarily protect citizens from the government, state action is required before a citizen can invoke such a right. The manner in which a government employer treats its employees is by defi-

---

"In some cases, private sector employees have not been protected against even the most outrageous forms of employer intrusion."

---

nition a state action. The manner in which a private employer treats its employees is not. Because of this dichotomy, public sector employees enjoy far greater privacy rights than those working for private firms.

For the typical private sector employee, then, the only sources of legal protection against intrusive employer surveillance are claims brought under various state statutes or the common law tort "invasion of privacy." The protection provided by these remedies varies widely from jurisdiction to jurisdiction. In some cases, private sector employees have not been protected against even the most outrageous forms of employer intrusion.

To examine the legal implications of e-mail monitoring in the workplace, it is first necessary to consider the circumstances that motivate employers to monitor their workers. One is the ease with which an employer may conduct monitoring. Yet another is the perceived need to curb misuses or abuses of an e-mail system provided and maintained by the employer. Misuse might take the form of wasted time spent sending personal messages to friends, family, or coworkers during business hours. More serious abuses could involve sending harassing messages to coworkers or revealing trade secrets to rival companies.

In the absence of constitutional protection, employees are increasingly looking to Congress and their state legislatures for statutory protection. In response to Congress's perception that abuses associated with

new technologies pose a substantial risk to civil liberties, the Electronic Communications Privacy Act (ECPA) of 1986 was enacted. The ECPA amended Title III of the Omnibus Crime Control and Safe Streets Act of 1968, which merely proscribed the unauthorized *interception* of wire and oral communications. Essentially, it extended Title III's existing prohibitions against the unauthorized interception of electronic communications.

Thus, explains Kopp, Title III and the ECPA together prohibit intentional or willful interception, accession, disclosure, or use of one's oral or electronic communications. The protections extend to cover the intentional interception of communications by unauthorized individuals and third parties, as well as government agents.

However, the ECPA *does not explicitly* offer protection from employers who access or intercept the electronic communications of *their own* employees. Instead, it appears to offer protection only from the unauthorized interception from *outside parties,* or from another employee who has exceeded his authority when accessing, intercepting, or disclosing information on a private corporate system.

Although none of the provisions in the ECPA appear to limit its applicability to employer monitoring of employee e-mail, Kopp discusses three primary exceptions it does contain that may have the same practical effect: the provider exception, the ordinary course of business exception, and the consent exception.

Provider Exception. The provider exception contained in the ECPA generally exempts e-mail service providers from the ECPA prohibitions against interception or accession of e-mail communications in the workplace. A private employer will be exempt from ECPA liability *so long as it is the direct provider of the e-mail system.* This effectively reserves to employers the unrestricted right to monitor employee e-mail. However, the exception may not apply to employers that merely provide e-mail service through a common carrier such as AOL.

Ordinary Course of Business Exception. The ordinary course of business exception to the ECPA, also known as the business extension exception, states in essence that information transmitted in the ordinary course of business is excluded from the definition of "information transmitted by electronic, mechanical, or other devices," as defined in the ECPA. This exception has yet to be applied to e-mail communications in the workplace.

The Consent Exception. The consent exception to the ECPA generally applies in the event that one party to the communication has given prior consent to the interception or accession of the communication. Thus, as long as the communication is intercepted by a person who is either a party to it or has expressly consented to such interception, the prohibitions contained within the ECPA will not apply.

Common Law Torts

Because of the lack of clear constitutional or statutory protection, the primary source of employee privacy protection in the private sector workplace has been state tort law. According to Kopp, tort law recognizes four distinct torts protecting the right of privacy:

1. unreasonable intrusion upon the seclusion of another;

2. appropriation of another's name or likeness;

3. unreasonable publicity given to another's private life; or

4. publicity that unreasonably places another in a false light before the public.

The tort most closely associated with e-mail monitoring in the workplace is the "intrusion upon seclusion" tort. It holds that one who intentionally intrudes, physically or otherwise, on the solitude or seclusion of another, or another's private affairs or concerns, is subject to liability for invasion of privacy if the intrusion would be highly offensive to a reasonable person. In holding that the invasion may be "physical or otherwise," this tort could possibly be extended to protect against e-mail monitoring. It also imposes a standard of objective reasonableness. Thus, in deciding whether the intrusion is into a private matter, courts require not only that the employee have a subjective expectation of privacy, but also that the expectation be objectively reasonable.

The common law tort of invasion of privacy has been applied in two recent cases involving e-mail monitoring in the workplace, both discussed by Kopp. In *Bourke v. Nissan Motor Corp.* (1993), the plaintiffs brought action against their employer for intercepting and reviewing several personal e-mail messages. In rejecting their claim of tortious invasion of privacy, the court held that the employees did not have a reasonable expectation of privacy in their e-mail communications because they had signed a waiver stating that e-mail use was limited to company business. The court also noted that the employees were aware that other coworkers had read their e-mail messages in the past, even though they were not the intended recipients of the messages. Further, the court rejected the plaintiffs' argument that a subjective expectation of privacy existed by virtue of having personal passwords to access the e-mail system, as well as their being told to safeguard their passwords.

The most recent case to address the common law tort of invasion of privacy is *Smyth vs. Pillsbury Co.* (1996), in which an employee brought suit against his employer for wrongful discharge. The employee had

been fired after company executives reviewed the contents of his e-mail messages and found them to contain offensive references toward certain company personnel. He had sent these messages to his supervisor in the knowledge that company policy held that all e-mail communications would remain private and confidential. The plaintiff argued that his termination was against public policy as a violation of his common law right to privacy. The court analyzed his claim under the definition of intrusion upon seclusion and found, first, that the plaintiff could not have a reasonable expectation of privacy in e-mail communications voluntarily made to his supervisor over the company e-mail system. Second, even if he was determined to have a reasonable expectation of privacy in the contents of his e-mail messages, the court would not consider his interception of those communications to be a substantial and highly offensive invasion of privacy, particularly since the e-mail system belonged to the company. The court concluded by adding that any privacy interest of the plaintiff was outweighed by the employer's interest in preventing inappropriate and unprofessional comments over its e-mail system.

As the only cases so far applying common law invasion of privacy to tort e-mail monitoring, *Bourke*

> **"As the only cases so far applying common law invasion of privacy to tort e-mail monitoring, Bourke and Smyth offer a grim outlook for e-mail privacy in the workplace."**

and *Smyth* offer a grim outlook for e-mail privacy in the workplace. The cases suggest that courts will provide a very narrow reading of employees' reasonable expectation of privacy. *Bourke* holds that maintaining a personal password to access the e-mail system does not give rise to an objectively reasonable expectation of privacy. *Smyth* indicates that even an employer's stated policy that employee e-mail is private and confidential will not necessarily give rise to an objectively reasonable expectation of privacy. Thus, the current state of common law with respect to e-mail monitoring clearly favors employers.

It should also be noted that a well-written e-mail policy may not only immunize an employer from liability under the ECPA, but may also immunize it from tort liability for invasion of privacy. In fact, the two cases above strongly support the proposition that a well-written e-mail policy will be sufficient to render unreasonable any expectation of privacy.

New Legislation

The weaknesses of the ECPA combined with increased employee awareness and sensitivity to privacy in the workplace have led to the proposal of new legislation to address the issue of monitoring electronic communications in the workplace. In 1991, the Privacy for Consumers and Workers Act (PCWA) was introduced in Congress, addressing issues of private-sector employee privacy and preserving employee rights. Its provisions would allow a company to monitor employees' e-mail and use the information against them to some extent. However, prior to monitoring, the company would be obligated to inform the employees of the potential, form, and scope of the monitoring, as well as what the data collected might be used for.

The original version of the PCWA failed to pass through Congress. At present, a revised version is still being debated in congressional committee. Meanwhile, the debate over private-sector workplace privacy has been stirred up. The proposal of the PCWA has served to highlight the need for further legislation—beyond the scope of the ECPA—to protect employees' rights to privacy.

BUSINESS RAMIFICATIONS

Driven by the desire to increase productivity and minimize liability, employers have adopted monitoring techniques in an effort to control all aspects of the workplace. They can provide other justifications as well for maintaining these invasive practices, such as the need to evaluate worker performance more efficiently, the need to deter or uncover employee wrongdoing and dishonesty, and even the need to limit tort liability under the respondent superior doctrine.

In 1998, U.S. industry spent half a trillion dollars on computer hardware and software, communications, and training and support. Many companies are now grappling with employees using that technology for purely personal transactions during business hours. This abuse has lowered companies' return on their technological investments. Its cost to employers can only be estimated, but all would agree it is substantial.

Examples of such employee abuse abound. Recently, Salomon Smith Barney terminated two high-ranking stock analysts for using company e-mail systems to share pornography. An analysis of computer logs by Neilsen Media Research found that employees at IBM and Apple together visited Penthouse Magazine's Web site almost 13,000 times in a single month in 1996, using up the equivalent of almost 350 eight-hour days. Another study by SurfWatch Software, a Web filtering company based in Los Altos,

California, found that 24 percent of the on-line traffic at the companies surveyed was not work-related. Sites most commonly visited, reports GaroFalo (1998), were general news, sex, investments, entertainment, and sports. Thus, employers have a legitimate interest in workplace monitoring if they want to limit inappropriate use of company time and maintain or increase productivity.

When it comes to protecting themselves against liability, employers are insisting on the right to monitor communications. They rightfully cite their legitimate interest in running an efficient business and in hiring and retaining honest and productive employees who will perform their jobs in a safe manner. And they fear claims asserting a hostile workplace environment, or harassment lawsuits by workers who happen upon offensive messages. Industry leaders, including Citibank and Morgan Stanley, have been sued by employees over the content of e-mail messages. Recently, a federal court in New York held that a class action race discrimination suit seeking damages of $60 million could proceed against Morgan Stanley, a large Wall Street brokerage firm. The lawsuit stemmed in part from the alleged repeated dissemination of a racist e-mail message through the company's computer system. More and more, cases of sexual harassment and discrimination include allegations that the company e-mail systems were used to transmit inappropriate or offensive material.

Viewing the privacy component of new technology from a different angle, it is possible that increased employee privacy may result in a more efficient workplace. It sends a positive message from the employer to the employees, implicitly trusting them to be responsible for their time and productivity. Such a message could fortify the work relationship between a firm and its workers and infuse personal dignity into the workplace. In contrast, an employer who monitors the workplace daily and is privy to all internal communications may create a workplace filled with distrust. Employees who do not trust their employer have a lower incentive to be efficient, resourceful, and productive.

ETHICAL IMPLICATIONS

There are two main ethical issues regarding privacy in the workplace: employee abuse of company resources and employer abuse of workers' privacy rights. The latter hinges on the notions of human dignity and trust.

In a study reported by GaroFalo, nearly half of the 726 employees surveyed acknowledged that they had engaged in unethical actions using their employers' technology during the previous year. Further, more than one-fourth of those responding stated that they had committed at least one highly unethical or illegal act, including copying company software for home use, using office equipment to search for other jobs, accessing private computer files without permission, visiting pornographic Web sites using office equipment, or sabotaging systems or data of former employers and coworkers.

Americans' respect for privacy has helped creativity and individuality flourish. So the negative effects of reduced individual privacy rights go far beyond simple embarrassment. Loss of privacy often induces conformity to perceived societal norms in order to safeguard personal and professional interests. American culture has been built on diversity and the willingness to accept challenges that test people's creativity. Yet these traits that helped mold our country will suffer if conformity, not privacy, is considered the principle value. Perhaps worst of all, inroads into privacy inhibit personal autonomy and thus individual freedom.

Of course, in addition to the fundamental interest individuals have invested in privacy, they also have a need to obtain and maintain employment. Some employee monitoring is always necessary. Tracking productivity and attendance is done in many, if not most, organizations. It is, however, the seemingly secretive or unexpected nature of certain types of monitoring or surveillance that tend to engender most of the bad feelings that may lead to actionable invasion of privacy claims.

Employers have an obligation to respect the privacy of their employees as well as inform then of monitoring intentions and policies. In addition to buttressing a firm's right to protect its interests, implementing a formal e-mail policy would also reflect an ethical responsibility to protect employees' privacy. One approach is to create a sign-on disclaimer that defines the degree and scope of privacy allowed and reiterates the fact that e-mail is company-owned property. Moreover, employees should be informed that their e-mail communications may be monitored at any time by the company and that, by using the e-mail system, the employee is consenting to be monitored. Finally, users of the e-mail system should be told explicitly not to send inappropriate messages, or they could face disciplinary consequences, up to and including the possibility of discharge.

As workplace technology continues to improve and become more prevalent and more available to employees, so too will the opportunities for employee abuse and, concurrently, the avenues available to firms to monitor and control employee ac-

tivities. Companies must, however, be cognizant of the impact such activities have on the morale of the employees, who feel that their rights are being trampled. They must also beware the possible legal ramifications of overreaching. Employers who engage in monitoring, surveillance, or searches should do so only pursuant to a well-written policy that has been distributed in advance to all employees. Moreover, any such monitoring should be reasonable in nature and strictly for business purposes.

To best address the issue of workplace privacy in light of evolving technology, new federal legislation should be enacted, balancing the rights of employees to privacy with the rights currently afforded to employers. New legislation will also serve to heighten employee awareness of companies' policies regarding the use of workplace technology. The time to embark on such a course of action was yesterday.

References

H. Chase and C.R. Ducat, *The Constitution and What It Means Today,* 13th ed. (Princeton, NJ: Princeton University Press, 1978).

B. Cole-Gomolski, "The Lethal Sting of Forgotten Mail," *Computerworld,* September 8, 1997, pp. 1, 117.

R. Dixon, "Windows Nine to Five: Smyth v. Pillsbury and the Scope of an Employee's Right of Privacy in Employer Communications," *Virginia Journal of Law and Technology,* Fall 1997, pp. 1–26.

S.S. Fader, "Want Some Privacy? Stay at Home," *Chicago Tribune,* May 28, 1998, pp. 1, 3.

W.S. Galkin, "Database Protection: Just the Facts," *The Maryland Bar Journal,* May–June 1993, p. 40.

B. GaroFalo, "Sharing a Middle Ground With Big Brother," *Connecticut Law Tribune,* May 18, 1998, p. 1.

W.S. Hubbartt, *The New Battle Over Workplace Privacy* (New York: AMACOM, 1998).

K.P. Kopp, "Electronic Communications in the Workplace: E-mail Monitoring and the Right of Privacy," *Seton Hall Constitutional Law Journal,* Summer 1998, pp. 1–30.

A. Rodriguez, "All Bark, No Byte: Employee E-Mail Privacy Rights in the Private Sector Workplace," *Emory Law Journal,* Fall 1998, p. 1439.

P. Schnaitman, "Building a Community Through Workplace E-Mail: The New Privacy Frontier," *Michigan Telecommunication and Technology Law Review,* 1998–99, p. 177.

J. Sipior, B.T. Ward, and S.M. Rainone, "Ethical Management of Employee E-Mail Privacy," *Information Systems Management,* Winter 1998, pp. 41–47.

S. Stipe, "Establish E-Mail Policy to Avoid Legal Pitfalls," *Best's Review,* July 1996, pp. 102–103.

S.E. Wilborn, "Revisiting the Public/Private Distinction: Employee Monitoring in the Workplace," *Georgia Law Review,* Spring 1998, pp. 825–887.

N. Wingfield, "More Companies Monitor Employees' E-mail," *Wall Street Journal,* December 2, 1999, p. B5.

Kenneth A. Kovach is a professor of management at George Mason University in Fairfax, Virginia. **Sandra J. Conner, Tamar Livneh, Kevin M. Scallan,** and **Roy L. Schwartz** are MBA students at the University of Maryland, College Park, Maryland.

RELIGION IN THE WORKPLACE

The growing presence of spirituality in Corporate America

BY MICHELLE CONLIN

The big splash at the Young Presidents' Organization powwow in June at Rome's palatial Excelsior Hotel wasn't a ballroom seminar about e-commerce juggernauts or Y2K blowups. Instead, the buzz at this confab of some of the world's youngest and most powerful chief executives was about the shamanic healing journey going on down in the basement. There, in a candlelit room thick with a haze of incense, 17 blindfolded captains of industry lay on towels, breathed deeply, and delved into the "lower world" to the sound of a lone tribal drum. Leading the group was Richard Whiteley, a Harvard business school-educated best-selling author and management consultant who moonlights as an urban shaman. "Envision an entrance into the earth, a well, or a swimming hole," Whiteley half-whispered above the sea of heaving chests. He then instructed the executives how to retrieve from their inner depths their "power animals," who would guide their companies to 21st century success.

Spiritual events like these aren't happening just at exclusive executive enclaves. For the past six years, 300 Xerox Corp. employees—from senior managers to clerks—have participated in "vision quests" as part of the struggling copier company's $400 million project to revolutionize product development. Alone for 24 hours with nothing more than sleeping bags and water jugs in New Mexico's desert or New York's Catskill Mountains, the workers have communed with nature, seeking inspiration and guidance about building Xerox' first digital copier-fax-printer.

One epiphany came when a dozen engineers in northern New Mexico saw a lone, fading Xerox paper carton bobbing in a swamp of old motor oil at the bottom of a pit. They vowed to build a machine that would never end up polluting another dump. Later, at the company's Rochester (N.Y.) design offices, the "quest" continued as co-workers "passed the rock" in Native American talking circles, in which only the person holding the stone can speak. This forced even the loudmouths to listen.

Sure, some of the button-down engineers cracked up over the use of such words as "spirit" and "soul." But, says John F. Elter, the Xerox chief engineer who headed the project, "for almost everyone, this was a real spiritual experience." The eventual result: the design and production of Xerox' hottest seller, the 265DC, a 97%-recyclable machine. Word of the program's success spurred senior executives from companies as diverse as Ford, Nike, and Harley-Davidson to make pilgrimages to Rochester in September to get a firsthand look.

GOD SQUAD. Bottom-rung workers are also getting a sprinkling of the sacred at the workplace. Companies such as Taco Bell, Pizza Hut, and subsidiaries of Wal-Mart Stores are hiring Army-style chaplains who come in any religious flavor requested. Members of these 24-hour God squads visit employees in hospitals, deal with nervous breakdowns, and respond to suicide threats. They'll even say the vows on a worker's wedding day or deliver the eulogy at her funeral.

If America's chief executives had tried any of this 10 years ago, they probably would have inspired ridicule and maybe even ostracism. But today, a spiritual revival is sweeping across Corporate America as executives of all stripes are mixing mysticism into their management, importing into office corridors the lessons usually doled out in churches, temples, and mosques. Gone is the old taboo against talking about God at work. In its place is a new spirituality, evident in the prayer groups at De-

Have you had occasion to talk about your religious faith in the workplace in the past 24 hours? 48% of Americans say yes

DATA: THE UPCOMING BOOK *THE NEXT AMERICAN SPIRITUALITY* BY GEORGE GALLUP JR. AND TIM JONES, GALLUP ORGANIZATION, NATIONAL OPINION RESEARCH CENTER

loitte & Touche and the Talmud studies at New York law firms such as Kaye, Scholer, Fierman, Hays & Haroller.

Across the country, major-league executives are meeting for prayer breakfasts and spiritual conferences. In Minneapolis, 150 business chiefs lunch monthly at a private, ivy-draped club to hear chief executives such as Medtronic Inc.'s William George and Carlson Co.'s Marilyn Carlson Nelson draw business solutions from the Bible. In Silicon Valley, a group of high-powered, high-tech Hindus—including Suhas Patil, founder of Cirrus Logic, Desh Deshpande, founder of Cascade Communications, and Krishan Kalra, founder of BioGenex—are part of a movement to connect technology to spirituality. In Boston, heavy hitters such as retired Raytheon Chairman and CEO Thomas L. Phillips meet at an invitation-only prayer breakfast called First Tuesday, an ecumenical affair long shrouded in secrecy. More publicly, Aetna International Chairman Michael A. Stephen has extolled the benefits of meditation and talked with Aetna employees about using spirituality in their careers.

That's not to mention the 10,000 Bible and prayer groups in workplaces that meet regularly, according to the Fellowship for Companies for Christ International. Just five years ago, there was only one conference on spirituality and the workplace; now there are about 30. Academic endorsement is growing, too: The University of Denver, the University of New Haven, and Minnesota's University of St. Thomas have opened research centers dedicated to the subject. The number of related books hitting the store shelves each year has quadrupled since 1990, to 79 last year. The latest: the Dalai Lama's *Ethics for the New Millennium,* a new business best-seller. Says Laura Nash, a business ethicist at Harvard Divinity School and author of *Believers in Business:* "Spirituality in the workplace is exploding."

In part, what's happening is a reflection of broader trends. People are working the equivalent of over a month more each year than they did a decade ago. No surprise, then, that the workplace—and not churches or town squares—is where American social phenomena are showing up first. The office is where more and more people eat, exercise, date, drop their kids, and even, at architecture firm Gould Evans Goodman Associates in Kansas City, Mo., nap in company-sponsored tents. Plus, the influx of immigrants into the workplace has raised awareness about the vast array of religious belief. All over the country, for example, a growing number of Muslims, such as Milwaukee lawyer Othman Atta, are rolling out their prayer rugs right in the office.

With more people becoming open about their spirituality—95% of Americans say they believe in God or a universal spirit, and 48% say they talked about their religious faith at work that day, according to the Gallup Organization—it would make sense that, along with their briefcases and laptops, people would start bringing their faith to work.

DEEPER MEANING. At the same time, the ultratight labor market has companies tripping over themselves to offer scarce talent any perks and programs that will get them through the door. One recent poll found that American managers want a deeper sense of meaning and fulfillment on the job—even more than they want money and time off. Moreover, the New Economy itself has hot-wired an interest in systems thinking and chaos theory, which have forged some common ground with religion by showing that science is partly about irrational and inexplicable things. The Internet's nonlinear nature is pushing people to take unconventional, intuitive approaches to their work.

But perhaps the largest driver of this trend is the mounting evidence that spiritually minded programs in the workplace not only soothe workers' psyches but also deliver improved productivity. Skeptics who scoff at the use of the words spirituality and Corporate America in the same breath might write this off as just another management fad.

Does modern life leave you too busy to enjoy God or pray as you would like? 51% of Americans say yes

But a recently completed research project by McKinsey & Co. Australia shows that when companies engage in programs that use spiritual techniques for their employees, productivity improves and turnover is greatly reduced. The first empirical study of the issue, *A Spiritual Audit of Corporate America,* published in October by Jossey-Bass, found that employees who work for organizations they consider to be spiritual are less fearful, less likely to compromise their values, and more able to throw themselves into their jobs. Says the book's co-author, University of Southern California Marshall School of Business Professor Ian I. Mitroff: "Spirituality could be the ultimate competitive advantage." Fully 60% of those polled for the book say they believe in the bene-

Do you feel the need in your life to experience spiritual growth? **78%** *of Americans say yes, up from* **20%** *in 1994*

ficial effects of spirituality in the workplace, so long as there's no bully-pulpit promotion of traditional religion.

That's exactly the danger. Even in an era that's more accepting of spirituality, the prospect of religion seeping into secular institutions, especially corporate ones, makes many uneasy. At the fringes, some businesses are running up against the bizarre, such as the maintenance worker who insisted he was the Messiah, the administrative assistant who routinely dropped to her knees outside of people's cubicles to speak in tongues, and the male witch who insisted on having Halloween off. And the more receptive companies are to Bible groups or Buddhist seminars, the more conflicts are erupting. The Equal Employment Opportunity Commission reports a 29% spike since 1992 in the number of religious-based discrimination charges, making those the third-fastest-growing claim, after sexual harassment and disability.

WEBHEADS. But that's no deterrent to spiritually minded CEOs. S. Truett Cathy, an evangelical Christian and chief executive of Chick-fil-A Inc., hosts a hymn-filled prayer service on Monday mornings for those employees of the Atlanta company who want to take part. On Sundays—when McDonald's Corp. and Burger King Corp. are doing a brisk business—Cathy closes his 1,000 fast-food shops because he believes in keeping the Sabbath. For Cathy, it's not so difficult to negotiate the religious differences of his employees because so many of them are evangelical Christians, too.

Shoemaker Timberland Co.'s chief executive, Jeffrey B. Swartz, is in the opposite position. Swartz is one of the few orthodox Jews at the Stratham (N.H.) company. Employees who travel with him on business often razz him about his penchant for pulling out his well-worn prayer book on planes. But he uses his religious beliefs to guide business decisions and, in some instances, company policy, often bouncing work problems off his rabbi. Because community service is such a bulwark of Swartz' faith, all employees at Timberland get 40 hours a year off to volunteer at the charity of their choice.

For Kris Kalra, chief executive of BioGenex, it's the Bhagavad Gita, the Hindu holy text, that offers the best lessons for steering a business out of trouble. Five years ago, Kalra was a hardheaded workaholic who had long missed his kids' baseball games and Brownie troop meetings. He worked holidays and weekends and often expected his 140 employees to do the same, holding his secretary hostage even if one of her kids needed her at home. But as the blowups with his family got worse and his medical-lab technology business stumbled, he had a breakdown. "I realized we were living in a completely material world," Kalra says, referring to the Internet-rich Webheads with their theme houses in the hills. "The higher purpose was being lost."

He dropped out of corporate life for three months, studying the Bhagavad Gita for eight hours a day. After he returned to work, he started listening to other people's ideas and slowly let go of his micromanaging ways. With the approval of 12 patents, Kalra's new products helped increase sales. Instead of putting in those workaholic hours, people on the leafy corporate campus are starting to use flextime.

Employers in old-line industries are also getting in on the trend. Ever since Austaco Inc., the sixth-largest Pizza Hut and Taco Bell franchisee in the U.S., began hiring chaplains in 1992 through a nonprofit called Marketplace Ministries, the company has reduced its annual turnover from 300% to 125%. In fast-food time, that's like having workers stay on for an eternity. The company credits the chaplain program for the drop. Employees such as Taco Bell cashier Kim Park, who has a husband in prison, a daughter in rehab, and two mouths to feed at home, say they wouldn't dream of leaving for another position that didn't have the religious lifeline. "A lot of times I get real depressed, and I have to talk to somebody, or I'll explode," says Park, sitting in a Taco Bell booth just before the lunchtime rush starts. "If I didn't have that support, I don't know what I'd do."

That help comes in the form of her weekly meetings with chaplain Angie Ruiz, who also visits employees at 13 other Taco Bells and Pizza Huts around Austin, Tex. After pulling up to the restaurants in her powder-blue Ford Crown Victoria with the backseat full of Bibles, Ruiz heads straight to the kitchens. She grabs arms and pats backs as she saunters through, quipping about the cashier's stolen junker: "Wanda, we'll have to pray about your car." She checks in on a waitress with a drug-addicted daughter and acts as an interpreter following a dustup between a Mexican busboy and his English-only boss. She even offers a new dishwasher a paperback Bible.

NEW SWIRL. All this may seem counterintuitive at a time of scientific and technological apotheosis. But, just as industrialization gave rise to social liberalism, the New Economy is causing a deep-seated curiosity about the nature of knowledge and life, providing a fertile environment for this new swirl of nonmaterialist ideas. "In this kind of analytical framework," says Harvard's Nash, "suddenly it's O.K. to think about forces larger than yourself, to tap into that as an intuitive source of creative, analytical power." And the Internet's power to blast through old paradigms and create previously impossible connections is inspiring fervent feelings that border on the spiritual. "This new sense of spontaneity has caused even the most literal-minded to say, 'Wow, there's this other force out there,'" says Nash.

60% of Americans say they have absolute trust in God. **79%** of Americans say they believe God exists and have no doubts about it

Spiritual thinking in Corporate America may seem as out of place as a typewriter at a high-tech company. But the warp speed of today's business life is buckling rigid thinking, especially now that the sword-swinging warrior model has become such a loser. Besides, who has time for decision trees and five-year plans anymore? Unlike the marketplace of 20 years ago, today's information and services-dominated economy is all about instantaneous decision-making and building relationships with partners and employees. Often, spiritual approaches can be used to help staffers get better at the long-neglected people side of the equation. It's no wonder high-tech companies are packing nerdy programmers off to corporate charm schools to teach them how to talk to customers and each other. "More and more people are going to spiritual processes for help," says consultant Whiteley, whose clients include Goldman Sachs, Sun Microsystems, and Ford.

Yet as the workplace opens up to such things, "more and more conflicts are going to continue to erupt," says San Francisco-based employment lawyer Howard A. Simon. The clashes split along the same lines the country does. On one side of the divide are evangelical Christians, some of whom want workplace spirituality to focus on a conservative message about Jesus Christ and who think New Age efforts are demonic. On the other are those who fear the movement is a conspiracy to proselytize everyone into thinking alike. Somewhere in between are the skeptics who think it's yet another one of management's fads, exploiting people's faith to make another dollar.

Because of this, many institutions keep away from the issue. Harvard Business School initially turned down a gift from industrial cleaning company ServiceMaster Co. for a religion-and-business lecture two years ago; Harvard officials were nervous about sponsoring anything with religious content. In Silicon Valley, career coach to the high-tech stars Jean Hollands said she had to change her company's name to the Growth & Leadership Center from the Good Life Clinic, lest she scare off clients such as Intel Corp. and Sun Microsystems Inc. "They thought it sounded like a Mormon touchy-feely group," Hollands says. To this day in the Valley's heavily left-brain culture, Hollands says she has to use euphemisms for talking about psychology and spirituality, such as "internal response system" instead of "feelings" and "concerns" instead of "fears." "We're still cautious about putting out that we're holistic, even though we are," she says.

That's why most companies and executives are careful to stick to a cross-denominational, hybrid message that's often referred to as secular spirituality. It focuses on the pluralistic, moral messages common to all the great religions, such as plugging into something larger than yourself, respecting the interconnectedness of all actions and things, and practicing the Golden Rule. But it also puts a premium on free expression and eschews cramming beliefs down other people's throats.

Not everyone sticks to this script, though. Abuses have included everything from management consultants who employees alleged were fronts for the Church of Scientology to cult members who use the workplace as an arena to woo fresh members into their folds. Some lawyers are even getting calls from companies worried about employees who seem to be gripped by a "millennium madness," says Garry G. Mathiason, senior partner at Littler Mendelson, the largest employment law firm in the country. These Y2K zealots often call for violence, and the worry is they'll act out their missions at work.

Generally employers are compelled to make "reasonable accommodations" to employees with religious needs, just as they are required to do for the disabled. Title VII of the Civil Rights Act of 1964 offers broad protections to the religious. However, the courts have been equally strict about not allowing one employee to create a hostile work environment for others by harassing them about what they do or don't believe.

"STEALTH BOMBERS." Jennifer Venters, who used to be a radio dispatcher in the Delphi (Ind.) police department, says she knows this drill from her ex-boss, former police chief, Larry Ives. In a lawsuit filed against Ives, Venters claimed her life changed when he showed up for duty and told her that he had been sent by God to save as many people from damnation as he could. Things got worse, alleges Venters in court documents, when Ives objected to her female roommate, asked her if she had entertained male police officers with pornographic videos, and accused her of having sex with family members and sacrificing animals in Satan's name. According to court documents, Ives capped it all off by suggesting that if she wasn't going to reform her depraved ways, she would be better off just killing herself. Ives, who calls the accusations "totally false," says he did discuss religion with Venters but only when she asked him about his evangelical faith. The Seventh Circuit U.S. Court of Appeals found that Venters had a reasonable basis for a religious harassment claim and ordered that the case go to trial, but it was later settled for $105,000 without any admission of liability.

But not all of these religious disputes are being fought out in the legal arena. Fearing that the rising pluralism in the workplace might lead to the spreading of the "wrong" kinds of religion, some fundamentalist Christians have taken to advising other believers on how to act like "stealth bombers" to perform "religious takeovers" of their organizations and "capture" them for Christ. Some advocated techniques: keeping a Rolodex listing each co-worker's spiritual progress and using Biblical names for e-mail addresses.

All this spiritual revival may have a fin-de-siècle feel—in fact, what's happening now is something of a replay of the spiritual movement that took place at the last turn of the century. The difference is that in those days, workers were considered extensions of machines. Then in the 1930s, the arm-around-the-shoulder theory of management was born. The idea was that bosses need just issue a little praise, and productivity would soar.

Later, in the 1970s and 1980s, thinking shifted toward viewing workers not just as bodies needing sustenance but as people with minds, says University of New Haven Management Professor Judi Neal. Fueling today's trend, too, was the collective revulsion over the greed in the late 1980s. That's when CEOs, determined to rout insider trading and other skulduggery from their organizations, furiously crafted ethics statements as a way to give their employees a new moral compass.

Once words like "virtue," "spirit," and "ethics" got through the corporate door, God wasn't far behind. Bestsellers such as *Jesus, CEO* and *The Seven Habits of Highly Effective People* (one of which is to cultivate spirituality) began to line the oak-paneled bookshelves of America's managers. Seizing the moment, such spiritual gurus as Deepak Chopra and M. Scott Peck began advising corporate chieftains about how they could tie the new secular spirituality into their management techniques. Team-building programs sprouted like mad. So too did the Dilbertian sendups of these efforts, some of which swept through organizations at the same time that downsizing was crushing morale.

Body, emotion, brain. The only thing missing from the equation was spirit. But will this revival amount to anything more than a momentary sensation? No matter how it shakes out, in the wake of the Internet's creative destruction, new rules will have to be made. And the physical and human capital that powered the latter part of the 20th century is likely to be coupled with a new kind of social capital. Perhaps it's already coming.

CYBER CRIME

First Yahoo! Then eBay. The Net's vulnerability threatens e-commerce—and you

The scenario that no one in the computer security field likes to talk about has come to pass: The biggest e-commerce sites on the Net have been falling like dominoes. First it was Yahoo! Inc. On Feb. 6, the portal giant was shut down for three hours. Then retailer Buy.com Inc. was hit the next day, hours after going public. By that evening, eBay, Amazon.com, and CNN had gone dark. And in the morning, the mayhem continued with online broker E*Trade and others having traffic to their sites virtually choked off.

The work of some super hacker? For now, law enforcement officials don't know, or won't say. But what worries experts more than the identity of this particular culprit or outlaw group is how easily these attacks have been orchestrated and executed. Seemingly, someone could be sitting in the warmth of their home and, with a few keystrokes, disrupting electronic commerce around the globe.

DEAD HALT. Experts say it's so easy, it's creepy: The software to do this damage is simple to use and readily available at underground hacker sites throughout the Internet. A tiny program can be downloaded and then planted in computers all over the world. Then, with the push of a button, those PCs are alerted to go into action, sending a simple request for access to a site, again and again and again—indeed, scores or hundreds of times a second. Gridlock. For all the sophisticated work on firewalls, intrusion-detection systems, encryption and computer security, e-businesses are at risk from a relatively simple technique that's akin to dialing a telephone number repeatedly so that everyone else trying to get through will hear a busy signal. "We have not seen anything of this magnitude before—not only at eBay, but across so many sites," says Margaret C. Whitman, CEO of eBay.

No information on a Web site was snatched, no data corrupted, no credit-card numbers stolen—at least so far. Yet it's a deceptively diabolical trick that has temporarily halted commerce on some of the biggest Web sites, raising the question: How soft is the underbelly of the Internet? Could tricks like these jeopardize the explosive growth of the Web, where consumers and businesses are expected to transact nearly $450 billion in business this year? "It's been war out there for some time, but it's been hidden," says James Adams, co-founder of iDEFENSE, an Alexandria, Va., company that specializes in cyber threats. "Now, for the first time, there is a general awareness of our vulnerabilities and the nature of what we have wrought by running helter-skelter down the speed race of the Information Highway."

To be sure, not even the most hardened cyber sleuths are suggesting the Net is going to wither overnight from the misdeeds of these wrongdoers. But the events of recent days are delivering a shrill wake-up

HOW THIS HAPPENED TO YAHOO!, EBAY, AND E*TRADE

Disrupting the Net isn't child's play, but it isn't rocket science, either. And cleaning up the mess takes teamwork.

STEP 1 An individual or group downloads software that is readily available at scores of underground Web sites specializing in hacker tools. The software is easy to use; it's all point-and-click.

STEP 3 They pick a target—Yahoo!, eBay, or Amazon.com—and then sit back in the privacy of their homes and instruct the computers they've hijacked to send requests for information to that site. One or two messages won't do it. But send enough of them at the same time and the resulting congestion clogs networks or brings computer servers and router systems to their knees. It's like constantly dialing a telephone number so that no one else can get through.

STEP 2 They break into scores of computers on the Web and plant a portion of the downloaded program, allowing the hacker to control the machine. Unfortunately, there are plenty of machines on the Net that lack the proper security to stop this.

ILLUSTRATIONS BY RAY VELLA/BW

STEP 4 Responding can take hours. Tracing attackers is hard because they use fake addresses from scores of computers. But as systems administrators sift through the traffic, they can identify the general location—say, an Internet service provider. This takes a coordinated effort involving the company, its ISP, and telecom suppliers. After identifying the machines, the company writes a program to reject the requests—and prays that it doesn't get another flood of messages.

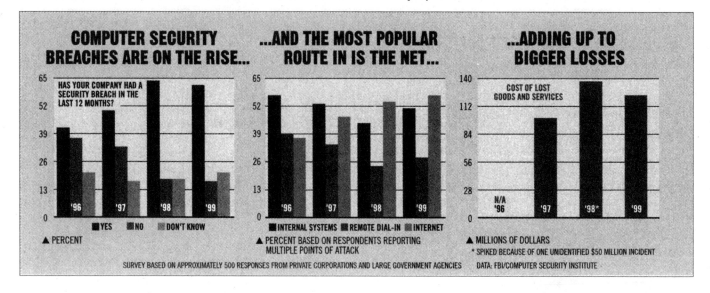

COMPUTER SECURITY BREACHES ARE ON THE RISE...

HAS YOUR COMPANY HAD A SECURITY BREACH IN THE LAST 12 MONTHS?

■ YES ■ NO ■ DON'T KNOW
▲ PERCENT

...AND THE MOST POPULAR ROUTE IN IS THE NET...

■ INTERNAL SYSTEMS ■ REMOTE DIAL-IN ■ INTERNET
▲ PERCENT BASED ON RESPONDENTS REPORTING MULTIPLE POINTS OF ATTACK

...ADDING UP TO BIGGER LOSSES

COST OF LOST GOODS AND SERVICES

▲ MILLIONS OF DOLLARS
* SPIKED BECAUSE OF ONE UNIDENTIFIED $50 MILLION INCIDENT

SURVEY BASED ON APPROXIMATELY 500 RESPONSES FROM PRIVATE CORPORATIONS AND LARGE GOVERNMENT AGENCIES   DATA: FBI/COMPUTER SECURITY INSTITUTE

call to businesses that they need to spend as much time protecting their Web sites and networks as they do linking them with customers, suppliers, contractors—and you. Consider just a quick smattering of recent events: In December, 300,000 credit-card numbers were snatched from online music retailer CD Universe. In March, the Melissa virus caused an estimated $80 million in damage when it swept around the world, paralyzing e-mail systems. That same month, hackers-for-hire pleaded guilty to breaking into phone giants AT&T, GTE, and Sprint, among others, for calling card numbers that eventually made their way to organized crime gangs in Italy. According to the FBI, the phone companies were hit for an estimated $2 million.

Cyber crime is becoming one of the Net's growth businesses. The recent spate of attacks that gummed up Web sites for hours—known as

"denial of service"—is only one type. Today, criminals are doing everything from stealing intellectual property and committing fraud to unleashing viruses and committing acts of cyber terrorism in which political groups or unfriendly governments nab crucial information. Indeed, the tactic used to create mayhem in the past few days is actually one of the more innocuous ones. Cyber thieves have at their fingertips a dozen dangerous tools, from "scans" that ferret out weaknesses in Web site software programs to "sniffers" that snatch passwords. All told, the FBI estimates computer losses at up to $10 billion a year.

As grim as the security picture may appear today, it could actually get worse as broadband connections catch on. Then the Web will go from being the occasional dial-up service to being "always on," much as the phone is. That concept may be nir-

vana to e-tailers, but could pose a real danger to consumers if cyber crooks can come and go into their computer systems at will. Says Bruce Schneier, chief technical officer at Counterpane Internet Security Inc. in San Jose, Calif.: "They'll keep knocking on doors until they find computers that aren't protected."

Sadly, the biggest threat is from within. Law enforcement officials estimate that up to 60% of break-ins are from employees. Take the experience of William C. Boni, a digital detective for PricewaterhouseCoopers in Los Angeles. Last year, he was called in by an entertainment company that was suspicious about an employee. The employee, it turns out, was under some financial pressure and had installed a program called Back Orifice on three of the company's servers. The program, which is widely available on the Internet, allowed him to take over those machines, gaining passwords and all the company's financial data. The employee was terminated before any damage could be done.

The dirty little secret is that computer networks offer ready points of access for disgruntled employees, spies, thieves, sociopaths, and bored teens. Once they're in a corporate network, they can lift intellectual property, destroy data, sabotage operations, even subvert a particular deal or career. "Any business on the Internet is a target as far as I'm concerned," says

---

"We have not seen anything of this magnitude before—not only at eBay but across so many sites. This is probably the single largest denial of service that the Internet has seen"

MARGARET C. WHITMAN

CEO, eBay Inc.

STORMING THE FORTRESS

THE WEAPONS

DENIAL OF SERVICE This is becoming a common networking prank. By hammering a Web site's equipment with too many requests for information, an attacker can effectively clog the system, slowing performance or even crashing the site. This method of overloading computers is sometimes used to cover up an attack.

SCANS Widespread probes of the Internet to determine types of computers, services, and connections. That way the bad guys can take advantage of weaknesses in a particular make of computer or software program.

SNIFFER Programs that covertly search individual packets of data as they pass through the Internet, capturing passwords or the entire contents.

SPOOFING Faking an e-mail address or Web page to trick users into passing along critical information like passwords or credit-card numbers.

TROJAN HORSE A program that, unknown to the user, contains instructions that exploit a known vulnerability in some software.

BACK DOORS In case the original entry point has been detected, having a few hidden ways back makes re-entry easy—and difficult to detect.

MALICIOUS APPLETS Tiny programs, sometimes written in the popular Java computer language, that misuse your computer's resources, modify files on the hard disk, send fake e-mail, or steal passwords.

WAR DIALING Programs that automatically dial thousands of telephone numbers in search of a way in through a modem connection.

LOGIC BOMBS An instruction in a computer program that triggers a malicious act.

BUFFER OVERFLOW A technique for crashing or gaining control of a computer by sending too much data to the buffer in a computer's memory.

PASSWORD CRACKERS Software that can guess passwords.

SOCIAL ENGINEERING A tactic used to gain access to computer systems by talking unsuspecting company employees out of valuable information such as passwords.

DUMPSTER DIVING Sifting through a company's garbage to find information to help break into their computers. Sometimes the information is used to make a stab at social engineering more credible.

THE PLAYERS

WHITE-HAT HACKERS They're the good guys who get turned on the intellectual challenge of tearing apart computer systems to improve computer security.

BLACK-HAT HACKERS Joyriders on the Net. They get a kick out of crashing systems, stealing passwords, and generally wreaking as much havoc as possible.

CRACKERS Hackers for hire who break into computer systems to steal valuable information for their own financial gain.

SCRIPT BUNNIES Wannabe hackers with little technical savvy who download programs—scripts—that automate the job of breaking into computers.

INSIDERS Employees, disgruntled or otherwise, working solo or in concert with outsiders to compromise corporate systems.

Paul Field, a reformed hacker who is now a security consultant.

It's point and click, then stick 'em up. Interested in a little mayhem? Security experts estimate that there are 1,900 Web sites that offer the digital tools—for free—that will let people snoop, crash computers, hijack control of a machine, or retrieve a copy of every keystroke. Steve O'Brien, vice-president for information operation assessments at Info-Ops.com, an Annapolis (Md.)-based company that provides intrusion detection services and security solutions, says the number of ways to hack into computers is rising fast. He tracks potential threats both from hacker groups and from the proliferation of programs. Once a rare find, he now discovers at least three new nasty software programs or vulnerabilities every day. And those tools aren't just for the intellectually curious. "Anyone can get them off the Internet—just point and click away," says Robert N. Weaver, a Secret Service agent in charge of the New York Area Electronic Crimes Task Force.

UNLOCKED DOORS. It's an issue that has crimefighters up in arms. At a hastily called press conference in Washington, D.C., on Feb. 9, Attorney General Janet Reno pledged to battle cyber crime. "We are committed to tracking down those responsible and bringing them to justice" and ensuring "that the Internet remains a secure place to do business," she said. But Ron Dick, chief of the Computer Investigations & Operations Section of the National Infrastructure Protection Center, pointed out that Internet security can't be assured by the government alone. Companies need to vigilantly monitor their computers to ensure that hackers don't surreptitiously install programs from which to launch attacks. "For the Internet to be a safe place, it is incumbent on everyone to remove these tools," he says. Using them, "a 15-year-old could launch an attack."

Make that an 8-year-old, once the Internet is always on via fat broadband connections. There are currently 1.35 million homes in America with fast cable modems, according to market researcher International Data Corp. By 2003, the number will grow to 9 million, and there will be an equal or larger number of digital subscriber line (DSL) connections.

That gives hackers a broad base from which to stage an attack. When a PC is connected to a conventional phone modem, it receives a new Internet address each time the user dials onto the Net. That presents a kind of barrier to hackers hoping to break in and hijack the PC for the kind of assault that crippled eBay, Yahoo, and others. In contrast, cable

Companies are often slow to report crimes and reluctant to reclaim goods

and DSL modems are a welcome mat to hackers. Because these modems are always connected to the Net, they usually have fixed addresses, which can be read from e-mail messages and newsgroup postings. Home security systems known as personal firewalls are widely available for cable and DSL subscribers. But until they reach nearly 100% penetration, they won't prevent intrusions.

In the coming age of information appliances, the situation could get worse. According to many analysts, the U.S. will soon be awash in Web-browsing televisions, networked game consoles, and smart refrigerators and Web phones that download software from the Net. "These devices all have powerful processors, which could be used in an attack, and they're all connected to the Net," Schneier says.

True, broadband customers can switch off their Net connections. But as cool applications come onstream, nobody will want to do that. "There will be streaming music and video, 24-hour news, and all kinds of broadband Web collaboration," says John Corcoran, an Internet analyst with CIBC World Markets. "To take advantage of that, the door will be open 24 hours a day."

Corporations are no better off. There, security is becoming an expensive necessity. "At least 80% of a corporation's intellectual property is in digital form," says Boni. Last year, Corporate America spent $4.4 billion on sales of Internet security software, including firewalls, intrusion-detection programs, digital certificates, and authentication and authorization software, according to International Data. By 2003, those expenditures could hit $8.3 billion.

And still computer crime keeps spreading. When the FBI and the

Computer Security Institute did their third annual survey of 520 companies and institutions, more than 60% reported unauthorized use of computer systems over the past 12 months, up from 50% in 1997. And 57% of all break-ins involved the Internet, up from 45% two years ago.

As big as those numbers sound, no one really knows how pervasive cyber crime is. Almost all attacks go undetected—as many as 60%, according to security experts. What's more, of the attacks that are exposed, maybe 15% are reported to law enforcement agencies. Companies don't want the press. When Russian organized crime used hackers to break into Citibank to steal $10 million—all but $400,000 was recovered—competitors used the news in marketing campaigns against the bank.

That makes the job even tougher for law enforcement. Most companies that have been electronically attacked won't talk to the press. A big concern is loss of public trust and image—not to mention the fear of encouraging copycat hackers. Following the attacks on Feb. 8 and Feb. 9, there was a telling public silence from normally garrulous Internet executives from E*Trade to priceline. com. Those that had not been attacked yet were reluctant to speak for fear of painting a target on their site, while others wanted no more attention.

And even when the data are recovered, companies are sometimes reluctant to claim their property. Secret Service agent Bob Weaver waves a CD-ROM confiscated in a recent investigation. The disk contains intellectual property—software belonging to a large Japanese company. Weaver says he called the company, but got no response.

Thieves and hackers don't even need a computer. In many cases, the physical world is where the bad guys get the information they need for digital break-ins. Dallas FBI agent Mike Morris estimates that in at least a third of the cases he's investigated in his five years tracking computer crime, an individual has been talked out of a critical computer password. In hackerland, that's called "social engineering." Or, the attackers simply go through the garbage—dumpster diving—for important pieces of information that can help crack the computers or convince someone at the company to giving them more access.

"PAGEJACKING." One problem for law enforcement is that hackers seem to be everywhere. In some cases, they're even working for so-called computer security firms. One official recalls sitting in on the selection process for the firm that would do the Web site security software for the White House. As the company's employees set up to make their pitch, one person walked into the room and abruptly walked out. It turns out one of the people in the audience was with law enforcement, and had busted that person for hacking.

It's not just on U.S. shores that law enforcement has to battle cyber criminals. Attacks from overseas, particularly eastern European countries, are on the rise. Indeed, the problem was so bad for America Online Inc., that it cut its connection to Russia in 1996. Nabbing bad guys overseas is a particularly thorny issue. Take Aye.Net, a small Jeffersonville (Ind.)-based Internet service provider. In 1998 intruders broke into the ISP and knocked them off the Net for four days. Steve Hardin, director of systems engineering for the ISP, discovered the hackers and found messages in Russian. He reported it to the FBI, but no one has been able to track down the hackers.

As if worrying about hackers weren't enough, online fraud is also on the rise. The Federal Trade Commission, which responds to consumer complaints about bogus get-rich schemes or auction goods never delivered, says it filed 61 suits last year. How many did it have back in 1994, when the Net was in its infancy? One. So far, the actions have resulted in the collection of more than $20 million in payments to consumers and the end of schemes with annual estimated sales of over $250 million.

The FTC doesn't want to stop there. On Feb. 9, commissioners testified before a Senate panel, seeking an increase in the commission's budget in part, to fund new Internet-related policies and fight cyberfraud. The money is needed to go after ever more creative schemes. In September, for example, the FTC filed a case against individuals in Portugal and Australia who engaged in "pagejacking" and "mousetrapping" when they captured unauthorized copies of U.S.-based Web sites (including those of PaineWebber Inc. and *The Harvard Law Review)* and

produced lookalike versions that were indexed by major search engines. The defendants diverted unsuspecting consumers to a sequence of porno sites that they couldn't exit. The FTC obtained a court order stopping the scheme and suspending the defendants' Web-site registrations.

All of this is not to suggest it's hopeless. Experts say the first step for companies is to secure their systems by searching for hacker programs that might be used in such attacks. They also suggest formal security policies that can be distributed to employees letting them know how often to change passwords or what to do in case of an attack. An added help: Constantly updating software with the latest versions and security patches. Down the road, techniques that can filter and trace malicious software sent over the Web may make it harder to knock businesses off the Net. Says Novell Inc. CEO Eric Schmidt:

"Security is a race between the lock makers and the lock pickers." Regulators say that cybercrime thrives because people accord the Internet far more credibility than it deserves. "You can get a lot of good information from the Internet—95% of what you do there is bona fide," says G. Philip Rutledge, deputy chief counsel of the Pennsylvania Securities Commission. "Unfortunately, that creates openings for fraud."

And other forms of mayhem. That's evident from the attacks that took down some of the biggest companies on the Net. If blackouts and other types of cyber crime are to be avoided, then Net security must be the next growth business.

By Ira Sager in New York, with Steve Hamm and Neil Gross in New York, John Carey in Washington, D.C., and Robert D. Hof in San Mateo, Calif.

The Anatomy of Fraudulent Behavior

John Dunkelberg and Donald P. Robin

Several years ago, a couple of articles appeared in a national newspaper about a young art major from a top ten university who seemed to have a knack for finding under-valued works of art and buying them for later resale at much higher prices. Soon several people had entrusted him with some of their funds to purchase art for them. The results he obtained were outstanding, and additional investors were quickly attracted.

Unfortunately, in a story as old as the original Ponzi scheme, this young man's operation turned out to be a scam. Most of the art he claimed to own had not been purchased and did not exist. In fact, our "art major" had spent most of the funds on his own well-appointed apartment in New York and a lifestyle befitting a wealthy individual. In subsequent articles about the millions of dollars lost in the scam, references to the art major quickly shifted to references of a businessman or an entrepreneur. The metamorphosis from art lover to businessman was sudden and complete.

In the decade from the mid-1980s to the mid-1990s, the American public was beset by insider trading, savings and loan mismanagement, Treasury Bond auctions, and municipal bond scandals. The consensus of most of the articles written about these scandals centered on the lack of acceptable ethical conduct by the people engaged in business in the United States and an opinion on the cause of this lack of ethical behavior. Business schools in particular were singled out and strongly criticized. Numerous anecdotal examples explained how they could improve what was being taught in their curricula.

There was, however, little systematic evidence concerning the background and environment of people who violated acceptable ethical norms. Nor was there much evidence of how education would improve their behavior. Research was needed to find out more about them, with the hope of leading to an understanding of why such unethical activities occur and what, if anything, schools and businesses can do to improve ethical standards.

Running through the articles about both the art scam and the felonious behavior and financial shenanigans of certain individuals in well-known companies is an underlying theme about business and ethical behavior. It seems to indicate that unethical behavior is common in most firms and stems from both a lack of proper ethics training in the B-Schools and the acceptance of such behavior in the competitive business environment. Repeated in countless books, television shows, and movies, the theme seems to imply some general acceptance of the idea that the only way to get ahead is to bend the rules. The relevant question is: Who are these people who break the law, what is their background and training, and why do they do it? Do they think their behavior is acceptable in the business environment? Or are they simply driven by greed and avarice?

THE ETHICAL DILEMMA

Despite many articles written on the dilemmas faced by business managers as they weigh performance goals versus moral obligations,

Reprinted from *Business Horizons*, November/December 1998, pp. 77-82, with permission. © 1998 by the Board of Trustees at Indiana University, Kelley School of Business.

most business decisions are clear-cut between what is legal and illegal. Almost all the individuals in our study were aware of the laws they broke. Almost all those caught profiting from insider trading knew they were breaking the law. No tremendous ethical dilemma was involved; the chance to profit from their insider knowledge was simply greater than the perceived risk of getting caught. What sets these lawbreakers apart from the law-abiding?

To focus our study on business-related crimes, we used the *Wall Street Journal* as the source of information on the individuals to be included. Biographical information was compiled on anyone who either pled guilty or was found guilty of a crime that generated an article in the *WSJ* between January 1, 1990, and December 31, 1997. During this eight-year period, 167 names came up; of this group, complete biographical information was found on 129. This means we were able to find at least eight of our ten variables: age, sex, race, employer, job at the time the crime was committed, type of crime committed, sentence, education, length of service, and functional area of training. In addition, comments were recorded concerning family and work environment in an effort to uncover any factor or factors that may have led to their illegal behavior.

Before examining the demographics of the people profiled in this study, readers should note that this is not a randomly chosen group of criminals. These are individuals who have been found guilty of crimes, usually financial fraud, that are of interest to a national, business-oriented audience. Their criminal activity could be broken into four broad categories: insider trading, savings and loan fraud, government contract fraud, and general fraud.

Demographic Traits of Felons

Several studies have examined the characteristics of people involved in fraudulent activity. The basic purpose of the studies was to try to identify the traits that seem prevalent among those willing to engage in unethical activity and determine whether they are different from the traits of those who are not. The major characteristics examined in these studies included age, education, gender, race, functional area of training, and tenure.

Age. Kelley, Ferrell, and Skinner (1990) found that marketing researchers over 50 generally had higher ethical standards than younger research employees. Several studies have argued that with increasing age comes a preference for established routines (Carlson and Karlsson 1970), an acceptance of formal rule systems (Child 1974), and a more deliberate approach to decision making (Taylor 1975). Daboub, Rasheed, Priem, and Gray (1995) maintain that these traits

Insider trading, S&L rip-offs, bond scandals. . . . Who are these white-collar financial criminals, and why do they think they're above the law?

should lead to a reduced likelihood of illegal corporate acts.

These studies, then, indicate that older people should be less inclined to break the rules. Interestingly, however, in our group the average age was 48 years old, and those over 40 comprised almost 73 percent of the total (see **Table 1**). Wisdom does not seem to have been vested with age among this group.

Table 1

Age of Respondents

Age	Number
20–29	11
30–39	23
40–49	37
50–59	39
60+	16

The image of young professionals willing to cheat to make big money is easy to see in Dennis Levine, 34, a high-profile investment banker with Drexel Burnham; Mark Whitacre, 38, a senior vice president with Archer-Daniels-Midland; or Michael Milken, 42, who headed the high-yield bond department of Drexel Burnham. But how does one explain the crimes of Martin Revson, 83, a director of Revlon? Or Charles Keating, 71, former CEO of Lincoln Savings and Loan?

Education. Education's role in providing—or not providing—a solid moral basis has been cited often as a factor in a person's decision-making. After all, one of education's greatest claims is that it provides students with the ability to reason and think logically and, therefore, make well-informed and honest decisions. Frank, Gilovich, and Regan (1993) found that the percentage of students taking microeconomics who chose unethical options on an honesty test increased dramatically over the course of a semester as compared to a group of students in an astronomy class. Jones, Thomas, Agle, and Ehreth (1990) argued that a positive correlation existed between education and moral development, but that the MBA education seemed to cause a decline in moral development. In contrast, McCabe, Dukerich, and Dutton (1991) found that, rather than the MBA education causing the moral decline, students entering MBA programs seemed to make more unethical decisions than students starting law school.

The evidence presented in **Table 2** does not indicate that higher education has provided a solid moral basis for everyone. Our sample group contained 46 individuals–more than 47 percent of the total–who were members of professions (engineering, accounting, and law) that have a code of ethics. The indication is that these individuals certainly knew what the laws were, but chose to ignore them anyway.

Table 2

Education Received

Education	Number
High School	10
B.A.	20
B.S.	4
Business	4
Engineering	5
Accounting	15
Law	26
MBA	12
Ph.D.	4
TOTAL	97

If the goal of higher education is to provide a solid moral basis, our group failed the course. William Aramony, 68, former president of United Way of America, received his education in social work from well-regarded Clark University. Gary Fairchild, 51, who bilked his firm of $784,000, received a degree from Wheaton College, an outstanding Christian school. Maureen Walsh, 39, had an exclusive private high school education and received degrees from the University of Notre Dame and Northwestern Law School. Despite this background, she bilked her clients of nearly $1.5 million to support a lavish lifestyle.

Gender. Do differences in gender result in different ethical behavior? Studies have been mixed on this subject. Gilligan (1982) argued that males and females have distinctly different moral orientations, attributed to the different socialization of men and women. Her thesis is that women believe they belong to an interpersonal network in which moral questions are handled with care, empathy, and compassion. Men, on the other hand, view moral questions as problems involving rights. A study by Betz, O'Connell, and Shepard (1989), using the responses of 213 busi-

ness school students, found that men were much more competitive and more concerned with money than women and more willing to accept unethical behavior to achieve these goals. Interestingly, a recent study by Mason and Mudrack (1996) surveyed 308 individuals in a classroom setting and found that women scored higher (with more ethical responses) than men among the full-time employed group, but that there was no difference in ethical scores among those students who were not employed.

A number of studies argue that there is little or no gender difference in ethical behavior. In research that examined both managers and students, Hegarty and Sims (1979), Derry (1989), Harris (1990), and White and Dooley (1993) found differences between gender and moral reasoning to be either unrelated or trivial. Robin and Babin (1997) maintain there is little or no difference in behavioral intent between professional males and females.

Regardless of the theory, our group of individuals (see **Table 3**) is almost 94 percent male, with only eight females represented. However, such factors as the "glass ceiling" effect may have contributed to these results. In other words, females may simply not have had as much opportunity to misbehave in a manner that would attract attention from the *WSJ*.

Table 3

Respondents' Gender

Gender	Number
Male	121
Female	8

Race. Similar to Gilligan's argument about the socialization of females, is it not reasonable to posit that different cultures probably socialize their members to different values and so one could expect decisions regarding ethical/unethical behavior to be affected by these values? McCuddy and Peery (1996) argue that racial groups would differ with respect to ethical beliefs; their study of collegians found a significant correlation to support this argument. A study of black and white students by Tsalikis and Nwachukuru (1988) discovered that both groups of students had similar beliefs concerning certain business situations, but dissimilar ethical beliefs in others. Interestingly, Stead, Worrell, Spalding, and Stead (1987) found that race was unrelated to the incidence of unethical decisions.

As with the gender issue, race is a major factor in our group of felons. The entire group is almost all white, containing only three blacks. However, as for women, these results may be explained in part by a lack of opportunity for blacks.

Functional Area of Training. One's functional area of training could be a factor in how one perceives ethical situations. Engineers and accountants are professionals who have acquired a strong code of ethics as part of their training and are perceived as the most ethical type of professional. On the other hand, says Clinard (1983), managers trained in finance are perceived as having a greater propensity to engage in unethical behavior. However, only five individuals in our study were trained in finance, whereas 46 were trained as engineers, accountants, and lawyers.

Tenure. Do people develop a sense of what is acceptable ethical behavior from their work environment? Tyson (1990) found that new managers–those with less than ten years of experience–perceived a greater need to compromise ethical values than those with more experience. Posner and Schmidt (1987) surveyed more than 1,500 managers and found that lower-level managers felt more pressure to compromise personal principles for the goals of the firm than managers who had longer job experience. Moreover, the results of the 1990 study by Kelley et al. indicated that marketing researchers with ten or more years of experience at the same job had a higher ethical standard than those researchers who had been employed in their present position for less than ten years.

Of our group, however, 72 percent had more than ten years in their positions (see **Table 4**), but this tenure did not seem to help them make proper ethical or legal decisions. Thus, the idea that younger people may be more willing to cut ethical or legal corners is not borne out in this study.

Table 4

Number of Years in Position Held

Years in Position	Number
0–10	17
11–20	22
20+	22

Other Variables. An attempt was made to collect data on the religious preferences of the individuals in this sample group, but fairly extensive searches yielded data on fewer than 30 percent of them. From such scant information, very little should be inferred. Nevertheless, several had received excellent religious training from their parents, in parochial schools, and in small liberal arts colleges of a religious denomination. Others were very devoted in their religious practices, but seemed to be able to separate their religious habits from their business practices. Charles Keating gave millions of dollars to Catholic charities, but the money came from his business, not from his own pocket. Interestingly, most of the world's major religions were represented in this group.

Similarly, an attempt was made to determine the marital status of these individuals. But we could not find enough data to make substantial comments. Certainly there were several divorced men with younger second wives, but there were also several who had been married their entire careers and seemed to have a satisfactory family life.

Why People Make Unethical/ Illegal Decisions

The most obvious fact emerging from our study is that, by far, most of these individuals were successful–in terms of position and income–in their careers. Moreover, they were not under competitive pressure to produce, yet they were willing to risk their careers for little additional material gain. How does one explain why an investment banker making over a million dollars a year would risk his job to make an extra few hundred thousand on insider trading? Why would a lawyer earning more than $800,000 per year overcharge expenses to his clients by an average of $10,000 per year?

Ludwig and Longenecker (1993) termed this phenomenon the "Bathsheba Syndrome." They argue that the by-product of success is a leader's unrestrained control of a firm's resources, which can lead to the looting of those resources and an inflated opinion of his ability to control outcomes. This in turn can lead to the belief that he can manipulate events and not have his criminal activity detected.

Our results offer very few ideas on why individuals make poor ethical and illegal decisions. Certainly the stereotypes held by the general public do not seem to fit here. Why, then, do some business people make unethical and illegal decisions that seem irrational and are often personally destructive?

An organization is most influential on the decision making of such individuals when it controls their rewards and punishments. Organizational values and culture can also play an important role. The company may have little impact on criminal behavior when: (1) the employee is effectively an independent operator with little more than profit goals to guide him; (2) the employee is at the top of the organization and personally has considerable control over its values; or (3) for extended periods of time the employee's opportunity for abuse is uncontrolled and unchecked. Most of the cases analyzed here fit one of these three scenarios.

Personal moral values always play an important role in unethical or illegal decision making. The simple fact that the opportunity exists for such behavior does not mean that all or even most people would behave badly. However, some will undoubtedly take advantage of certain situations. For them, egoism dominates their social values and the classic crime-and-punishment issue dominates their decision making.

Saul Gellerman (1986) conducts an interesting discussion of why "good" managers make bad choices. For these people, the desire for money, power, advancement, and/or recognition, along with the perceived probability that a specific action will gain these desired outcomes, is matched against the perceived probability and cost of getting caught. Historically, from the view of crime prevention, increasing the perceived probability is more effective than increasing the cost.

Something besides the traditional crime-and-punishment equation is operating in many cases analyzed in this study. A certain affliction affects those who are most effective and successful at what they do. The disease is called "arrogance" and it is particularly dangerous to those who are highly ambitious and very successful in pursuing their ambitions. Clemons (1987) notes that this disease has been a popular topic for playwrights, from Sophocles to Shakespeare and many others since. Arrogant behavior is not really a desire for more money, power, advancement, or even recognition. Instead, it represents the willingness of individuals to exercise their power when they see the opportunity to do so. Their perception of this power becomes distorted with continued success, and they eventually deem themselves above the rules that apply to others. At this point they are ripe for unethical activity—and for their downfall if they are caught. Ironically, it is not unusual for their downfall to come at the expense of what they would consider a trivial matter, although that is clearly not the only scenario that occurs.

The motivation for our study was to try to discover why some people commit criminal acts in business and to determine whether some commonality existed among such people, particularly concerning their educational background. We found that the typical individual in this group of criminals was white, male, college-educated, in a top management position, and with a tenure in the company of more than 15 years. The surprising characteristic was the large number of people in professions that have a code of ethics. They obviously had the educational background that indicated they knew the difference between the legal and the illegal, but they chose the illegal anyway. Those who broke the law knew what they were doing, but seemed to think they were too smart or too powerful to get caught. Between our group and people who do not cheat, this seemed to be the major difference.

Because the media tend to report exceptions, the public has developed stereotypes of the kinds of individuals involved in business frauds. The sheer volume of articles on high-visibility men like Ivan Boesky and Mike Milken distort the public view of the vast majority of people in management positions. Even our study found articles on only 167 individuals over an eight-year period. This is fewer than two per month—still too high, but not nearly as high as that perceived by the public when hundreds of articles may be written about a single highly visible scandal.

What can be done? Businesses must provide an ethical environment, if for no other reason than that the misbehavior of a single employee within the corporation can be very costly. One man, Nick Leeson, caused the collapse of Barings Bank, an old and highly respected British bank that had loaned the United States the money it needed to finance the Louisiana Purchase. Core organizational values must opt against unethical and illegal practices. Even those at the top must be subjected to a system of checks, perhaps by an outside agency.

Managers willing to use unethical practices must be weeded out early in their tenure with the company. And although trust should be developed with the managers who pass an ethics test, it should be clear that this trust is not absolute. One of the most important precautions a company can take is to manage the ethical core values of its culture as aggressively as it manages for profits. Ethics and profits need not be antagonists; they can readily be made to complement each other.

Universities need to integrate ethics throughout their curricula, not just in business schools. Hard-hitting cases about the effects of hubris on both the individual and the organization would illustrate the negative outcomes from such behavior. Higher education must not miss the opportunity to prepare students for a life that will include opportunities to choose between ethical and unethical, legal and illegal decisions. And although the impact of their programs may not reach everyone, the effort is worth it. Our study focuses on the failures of such programs, not on their more numerous successes that would go unnoticed by the *Wall Street Journal*. Institutions of higher learning must not falter in their efforts to teach ethical values, despite some spectacular failures.

References

M. Betz, L.O. O'Connell, and J.M. Shepard, "Gender Differences in Proclivity for Unethical Behavior," *Journal of Business Ethics, 8* (1989): 321–324.

"Business Bulletin," *Wall Street Journal,* May 31, 1990, p. 1.

R.O. Carlson and K. Karlsson, "Age, Cohorts and the Generation of Generations," *American Sociological Review, 62* (1970): 710-718.

J. Child, "Managerial and Organizational Factors Associated With Company Performance," *Journal of Management Studies, 11* (1974): 175-189.

J.K. Clemons, "Wall Street and the Age-Old Tragic Flaw," *Wall Street Journal,* March 18, 1987, p. 24.

M.B. Clinard, *Corporate Ethics and Crime* (Beverly Hills, CA: Sage, 1983).

A.J. Daboub, A.M.A. Rasheed, R.L. Priem, and D.A. Gray, "Top Management Team Characteristics and Corporate Illegal Activity," *Academy of Management Review, 20,* 1 (1995): 138-170.

R. Derry, "An Empirical Study of Moral Reasoning Among Managers," *Journal of Business Ethics, 8* (1989): 855-862.

R.H. Frank, G.C. Gilovich, and D.T. Regan, "Does Studying Economics Inhibit Cooperation?" *Journal of Economics Perspectives,* Spring 1993, pp. 159-171.

S.W. Gellerman, "Why 'Good' Managers Make Bad Ethical Choices," *Harvard Business Review,* July-August 1986, pp. 85-90.

C. Gilligan, *In A Different Voice* (Cambridge, MA: Harvard University Press, 1982).

J.R. Harris, "Ethical Values of Individuals at Different Levels in the Organizational Hierarchy of a Single Firm," *Journal of Business Ethics, 9* (1990): 741-750.

W.H. Hegarty and H.P. Sims, "Organizational Philosophy, Policies, and Objectives Related to Unethical Decision Behavior: A Laboratory Experiment," *Journal of Applied Psychology, 64* (1979): 331-338.

T.M. Jones, T. Thomas, B. Agle, and J. Ehreth, "Graduate Business Education and the Moral Development of MBA Students: Theory and Preliminary Results," paper presented at the annual meeting of the International Association for Business and Society, San Diego, 1990.

S.W. Kelley, O.C. Ferrell, and S.J. Skinner, "Ethical Behavior Among Marketing Researchers: An Assessment of Selected Demographic Characteristics," *Journal of Business Ethics, 9* (1990): 681-688.

G.R. Ludwig and C.O. Longenecker, "The Bathsheba Syndrome: The Ethical Failure of Successful Leaders," *Journal of Business Ethics, 12* (1993): 265-273.

E.S. Mason and P.E. Mudrack, "Gender and Ethical Orientation: A Test of Gender and Occupational Socialization Theories," *Journal of Business Ethics, 15* (1996): 599-604.

D.L. McCabe, J.M. Dukerich, and J.E. Dutton, "Context, Values and Moral Dilemmas: Comparing the Choices of Business and Law School Students," *Journal of Business Ethics, 10* (1991): 952-960.

M.K. McCuddy and B.L. Peery, "Selected Individual Differences and Collegians' Ethical Beliefs," *Journal of Business Ethics, 15* (1996): 261-272.

B.Z. Posner and W.H. Schmidt, "Ethics in American Companies: A Managerial Perspective," *Journal of Business Ethics, 6* (1987): 383-392.

D. Robin and L. Babin, "Making Sense of the Research on Gender and Ethics in Business: A Critical Analysis and Extension," *Business Ethics Quarterly,* October 1997, pp. 61-90.

W.E. Stead, D.L. Worrell, J.B. Spalding, and J.G. Stead, "Unethical Decisions: Socially Learned Behaviors," *Journal of Social Behavior and Personality, 2* (1987): 105-115.

R.N. Taylor, "Age and Experience as Determinants of Managerial Information Processing and Decision-Making Performance," *Academy of Management Journal, 18,* 1 (1975): 74-81.

J. Tsalikis and O. Nwachukuru, "Cross-Cultural Business Ethics: Ethical Beliefs Differences Between Blacks and Whites," *Journal of Business Ethics, 7* (1988): 743-754.

T. Tyson, "Believing That Everyone Else Is Less Ethical: Implications for Work Behavior and Ethics Instruction," *Journal of Business Ethics, 9* (1990): 715-721.

C.S. White and R. Dooley, "Ethical or Practical: An Empirical Study of Student Choices in Simulated Business Scenarios," *Journal of Business Ethics, 12* (1993): 643-651.

John Dunkelberg is the Kemper Professor of Finance at Wake Forest University in Winston-Salem, North Carolina, where **Donald P. Robin** is the J. Tylee Wilson Professor of Business Ethics.

BANKING

DIRTY MONEY GOES DIGITAL

Criminals tap into the high-speed world of wire transfers

In the annals of organized crime, money laundering once was hard work. Consider the plight of a typical 1980s Florida drug smuggler looking to move his money offshore. A boatload of marijuana could be sold on the street back then for $20 million. But pot smokers paid in small bills, and the cash would weigh a ton and a half, says David L. McGee, a former federal prosecutor. Talk about heavy lifting. "You can't carry $20 million in street cash in a pickup truck," McGee says.

The solution for drug dealers was called "smurfing." Smugglers would hire people—smurfs—to go to as many banks as possible and buy cashier's checks under $10,000, the threshold for filing a government disclosure report. The smurfs would then fly the checks to an offshore bank and deposit them. From there, the money could be used or invested in ways to make the dealers look like legitimate businessmen.

What a difference a decade makes. Federal authorities are now investigating a case that makes the smurfs look like the cavemen of some criminal Stone Age. Russian racketeers are suspected of laundering up to $10 billion through accounts at the Bank of New York. And all the Russians needed to do was switch on their personal computers.

Money laundering is taking a terrifying high-tech turn. Criminals sitting at keyboards are concealing their gains by mixing them with the trillions of dollars that swirl through the global banking system every day. And slowing down the money launderers will almost certainly impose costs on banks and other legitimate businesses that benefit from rapid movements of money.

"There is no panacea available today," says Jerome Walker, a former federal banking regulator and now an attorney who specializes in money-laundering matters. "There is no silver bullet that will get you where you want to be."

CRUDE SCHEMES. Properly understood, money laundering is the final act of any financial crime—the real getaway, in which criminals hide the origins of their proceeds so they can be used. The key is moving money through as many bank accounts and countries as possible so it takes on the appearance of legitimate income. How this is done involves any number of variations—crude schemes from the past can coexist with the latest ruses. But the idea is to be able to claim that the boss is a legitimate businessman.

The problem facing law enforcement is that big criminals no longer need furtive couriers with fancy briefcases to move money. The staggering amounts allegedly involved in the Bank of New York case suggest that Russian mobsters have advanced beyond street businesses like drugs or prostitution. The suspicion is they are diverting government or corporate funds—that is, money in its electronic form. Nor did the Russians even have to go on the street to transport funds. They could initiate their own wire transfers using bank software—standard stuff for business customers these days, but a potent weapon for a money launderer.

Once plugged in, criminals can take advantage of the Achilles' heel in the global battle against money laundering—the high-speed wire-transfer system. Money put in any bank anywhere in the world can be transferred just about anywhere else in the blink of an eye. And criminal groups can execute so many transfers so quickly that law enforcement authorities can't keep up.

In effect, the wire-transfer regime undercuts U.S. laws that require banks to "know their customer," that is, to know the customer's source of funds. In a transfer, the bank's customer often is an-other bank, acting on behalf of an account holder. If that first bank doesn't know its customer—or doesn't care to—the sky is the limit for the criminal. Wire transfers are "one of the most used techniques" for laundering money, says Patrick Moulette, executive secretary of the Financial Action Task Force on Money Laundering in Paris, which was set up by the leading industrial countries to combat the problem. "It's very easy for the launderer."

Compounding the problem is the staggering volume and velocity of wire transfers. More than $2 trillion moves every day through the U.S., and globally the total is more than that. The Bank of New York says it handles $600 billion in wire transfers every day. All this traffic makes it hard for human beings such as bank examiners and compliance officials to spot unusual action—even on the scale of the Russian case.

You need technology to fight technology. Software filters that enable banks to monitor wires for suspicious patterns of activity are being developed. But these filters are costly and could slow down transfers, punishing legitimate businesses. Banks, in turn, would have to sacrifice earnings to scrutinize wire traffic more thoroughly. And neither senior compliance officers at some big banks nor federal regulators are convinced that the results from more filtering justify the potential losses.

But the Russian episode may be a reason to start thinking more seriously about such responses. Money is pouring out of Russia. And while there's a debate about what kind of money is actually moving—one man's criminal proceeds are another's capital flight—there is a U.S. interest in making sure Russia isn't bled dry. Russia remains a nuclear power, after all. "This is a national security issue more than a banking issue," says House Banking Committee Chairman James A. Leach (R-Iowa), who will be holding hearings on whether International Monetary Fund loan money was diverted through the Bank of New York. "If Russia can't get itself together on the financial side, it could return to communism." To be sure, money laundering hasn't become completely automated. Account officers—who are supposed to know the bank's customers—can make it easier for criminals to launder money through sins of omission or commission.

And so far, the Bank of New York has taken action against three employees. Two were fired, including Lucy Edwards, a Russian-born vice-president. Her husband is Peter Berlin, the director of Benex Worldwide Ltd., who set up the accounts being investigated. Natasha Gurfinkel Kogalovsky, who headed BONY's Eastern European business, is on leave. She, too, is married to a Russian businessman: banker and oil executive Konstanin Kogalovsky, who once represented Russia in talks with the IMF. The Bank of New York is cooperating with the investigation, noting there have been no allegations of wrongdoing on its

part. Attempts to reach the three employees and Berlin were unsuccessful.

DAISY CHAIN. But senior bankers and money laundering experts say the Bank of New York accounts could turn out to be just one stop in a daisy chain of accounts around the world through which suspicious Russian money moved. And that points up the difficulties that authorities are having in policing international money flows.

Currently, money is routed around the world via three major computer superhighways: Fedwire, in the U.S.; the Society for Worldwide Interbank Financial Telecommunication (SWIFT), overseas; and the Clearing House Interbank Payment Systems (CHIPS) in New York, for payments moving into and out of the U.S.

Together, these systems make it possible to conduct global commerce and currency trading on a grand scale. But the underside of this efficiency is a lack of supervision. CHIPS and SWIFT are private, while Fedwire is run by the Federal Reserve. And all three are lightly regulated; you can think of the systems as bank clubs run on an honor system. At CHIPS, for example, a couple dozen

HOW TO WASH A MILLION DOLLARS

Using bank transfers, money-laundering mobsters can easily move cash across borders, swiftly turning dirty money into squeaky-clean greenbacks.

1 A Moscow gangster is sitting on millions of dollars. The cash came from a prostitution ring, legal income from several strip clubs that he controls, and funds that he has diverted from a government account. He wants to move the money overseas.

2 Using wire transfers and deposits, the gangster's underlings direct the money to a Russian bank, mixing legal and illegal funds. They then ask the Russian bank to wire the money to a lawyer representing a Miami realtor who is in cahoots with the Russian mob.

ILLUSTRATIONS BY RAY VELLA/BW

3 The Russian bank sends instructions for a fund transfer to its "correspondent," a New York money-center bank, which only knows that it is helping a licensed Russian bank. The New York bank doesn't know the Russian bank's customer is the Moscow mobster.

4 The New York bank arranges a funds transfer through its CHIPS interface computer. CHIPS debits the New York bank and credits the account in Miami. Like the New York bank, the Miami bank knows nothing about the actual source of the funds.

5 A U.S. associate of the Moscow mobster uses the cash to buy an office building at an inflated price. The realtor collects an outsized fee, which is legitimate income. And the Moscow mobster can say he's earning rental income from overseas.

The Canadian government estimates that up to $1 trillion in criminal proceeds gets laundered every year

leading banks handle the bulk of more than $1 trillion a day in transfers, often serving smaller banks, known as correspondents. Once a big bank decides it can work with a smaller bank—in Russia, say—it processes transfer requests more or less automatically.

However, big banks can have thousands of correspondents—the Bank of New York serves 2,300. And there is pressure to move quickly. If a big bank doesn't process a correspondent's transaction by day's end, it can wind up paying interest costs.

As a result, anonymous money moves easily through the global banking system. A Canadian government report estimates that up to $1 trillion in criminal proceeds gets laundered every year. But given the black hole of wire transfers, no one can know for sure.

Handling these massive money movements, though, has become a key business for banks. In recent years, banks have lost market share in any number of core areas as savers plow more money into stocks and nonbanks extend credit. But only a bank can handle payments—and that leads to other opportunities. By managing a company's cash, for example, a bank positions itself to conduct currency trades, even design derivatives for hedging. Yet those huge cash flows in banks also attract individuals with illicit intentions.

Cash processing has been a particularly important business at the Bank of New York. Fees from that business added up to $256 million in 1998, up 13% from the year before. And in its last annual report, the bank bragged: "In the last five years, we were the only bank to significantly increase our market share" in the global cash processing business.

One way the bank expanded its processing income was by moving quickly into Russia. The bank began operations there in the early 1990s, working first through its Swiss-based private banking joint venture—the Bank of New York-Inter Maritime Bank of Geneva.

The Bank of New York, in turn, became one of the first foreign banks to set up correspondent relationships with Russian banks. One Russian bank, In-kombank, averaged more than 250 wire transfers a day with the Bank of New York. When Inkombank applied to set up a representative office in the U.S., Gurfinkel Kogalovsky, the now-suspended head of BONY's Eastern European business, wrote a letter of recommendation in 1996 to Federal Reserve Chairman Alan Greenspan. "Having worked with all the top banks in Russia, there is no question that Inkombank is one of the most stable, sophisticated, and technologically advanced commercial banks in Russia," she wrote. Inkombank is now insolvent.

Bank of New York officials also helped its Russian business customers obtain the latest tools in computer banking. At least one of the accounts under investigation was equipped with a product that enables the account holder to transfer money, a government source says.

The quandary for banks is that each time they introduce a new service, they may inadvertently be helping money launderers. And it's a dilemma that will only deepen as technology develops. Indeed, the Financial Action Task Force on Money Laundering warned this year that criminals could begin using smart cards, online banking, and electronic cash to launder money.

Just consider the potential threat from smart cards—which electronically store cash. They would enable criminals to move money in bulk without using banks at all. And because they are plastic, the cards might even elude one of man's best friends in the fight against money-laundering—cash-sniffing dogs used at border crossings.

Small wonder, then, that bankers and law enforcement officials differ about the proper response to the latest high-tech money laundering schemes. "There is no doubt we could design a system that would be impenetrable to people who want to launder money, but I doubt the banks would stand for it," says Samuel D. Porteous, director of business intelligence for Kroll Associates Canada, the Canadian arm of the investigative firm. "It's a question of how much people want to spend."

There is precedent for action. Currently, banks use software that screens transfers to make sure they don't go directly to enemies of the U.S. The Treas-

---

A MONEY LAUNDERING PRIMER

Money laundering is easy to define: It's the process of making dirty funds appear to be clean. But the legal definition is narrower and more precise—and may not include the type of asset-stripping occurring in Russia.

mon•ey laun•der•ing (mə-nē län-dər-iŋ) *v*: th ~~dirty funds appear clean. The legal definition~~

The test: There are several federal laws designed to curb money laundering. But under the main statute, prosecutors must prove that a suspect (1) knowingly, (2) took the financial proceeds of a crime, and (3) did hide the illegal origin of the money.

The loopholes: While that test sounds simple, it's often not so easy to meet in practice. For example, criminals frequently hand over their stolen funds to professional money launderers. It's hard for the feds to prove that these outfits "knew" the money was dirty since they played no role in the orignal crime.

Foreign crime: One problem with the money laundering laws is that they only cover the funds received from seven specific foreign crimes: drug trafficking, bank fraud, murder, kidnapping, robbery, extortion, and the detonation of explosives. Any other illegal act that a criminal commits abroad—can't be the basis for a money laundering convictin. Legislation to broaden the scope of the law to cover additional foreign crimes was shelved last year and is expected to be resubmitted to Congress later this year.

By Mike France in New York

Bank of New York officials also helped its Russian business customers obtain the latest tools in computer banking

ury Dept.'s Office of Foreign Assets Control, or OFAC, prints a detailed list of countries, companies, and people that aren't allowed to receive wires. Banks have staffs that do nothing but monitor transfers to make sure money isn't being sent to the likes of Saddam Hussein or Slobodan Milosevic.

But there's a big difference between the OFAC list and a search for money launderers. The OFAC list requires banks to look for particular needles in the haystack of fund transfers. Detecting money laundering would require programs that would notice transfers exceeding amount or frequency parameters. Transfer messages are short and not particularly standardized. Computers could be faked out—and the result could be just reams of paper.

The case of suspected Russian money laundering seems to suggest software filters could help. In August, 1998, a year before the case broke, Republic National Bank of New York filed a government report noting suspicious transfers of money from Russia—through Republic—to BONY. Republic de-

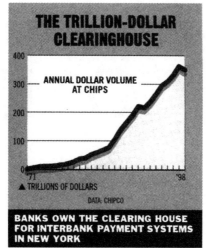

THE TRILLION-DOLLAR CLEARINGHOUSE

ANNUAL DOLLAR VOLUME AT CHIPS

400

300

200

100

0

'71   '98

▲ TRILLIONS OF DOLLARS

DATA: CHIPCO

BANKS OWN THE CLEARING HOUSE FOR INTERBANK PAYMENT SYSTEMS IN NEW YORK

CHART BY ERIC HOFFMAN/BW

tected the activity only a month after installing a filtering system. The Bank of New York declined comment on whether it had such software filters at the time.

But more monitoring would be a tough sell. This year, federal officials dropped proposed rules that would have tightened "know your customer" require-

ments after fierce protests. "We don't need new laws and regulations," says John J. Byrne, senior counsel at the American Bankers Association. "The easiest thing is to overreact."

That raises the question of whether monitoring could be done at the computer highways that carry transfers—at CHIPS, say. But again, that's unlikely. "If we took a role like that, we would have to do things for the IRS, try to hunt down deadbeat dads, things like that," says George F. Thomas, senior vice-president at CHIPS. "It's the bank's responsibility."

It should be someone's.

By Gary Silverman in New York, with Margaret Coker in Moscow, Joseph Weber in Toronto, Laura Cohn in Washington, and Carol Matlack in Paris

For a Q&A with Russian banking kingpin Alexander Smolensky, see the Sept. 20 issue online at www.businessweek.com.

Legal Intelligence

Harassment Grows More COMPLEX

BY CAROLE O'BLENES

THE ISSUE Aside from gender, harassment claims are being asserted based on other protected characteristics, including race, religion, age, disability and national origin.

WHAT'S HAPPENING Sexual harassment complaints filed with the EEOC have more than doubled since 1991, and some recent Supreme Court decisions provide new guidance to employers.

THE IMPLICATIONS In addition to damage awards, harassment complaints carry many intangible costs, such as adverse publicity and reduced morale. Retaliation claims also are a risk.

ACTION PLAN Develop a comprehensive policy that addresses all forms of unlawful harassment, outlines procedures for reporting and investigating complaints and prevents retaliation.

Awareness of sexual harassment in the workplace has reached unprecedented levels as President Clinton's sexual encounters—Monica Lewinsky, Paula Jones and others—have made sexual harassment a common topic in the news. For employers, this heightened awareness often results in additional sexual harassment complaints as employees develop higher expectations about what behavior is appropriate and conclude that their workplaces fall short of those expectations.

In 1998, more than 15,000 sexual harassment charges were filed with the U.S. Equal Employment Opportunity Commission (EEOC), up from about 6,900 in 1991. Amounts paid out by employers charged with sexual harassment in EEOC proceedings and actions alone exploded from $7.1 million in 1990 to $49.5 million in 1997.

But unlawful workplace harassment is not limited to sexual harassment of women by men. Men also can be (and are) sexually harassed.

And harassment claims are being asserted based on protected characteristics other than gender, such as race, age, religion, disability and national origin. Such recent cases include a black Muslim correction officer who claimed he was subjected to racial and religious harassment by coworkers and supervisors; a disabled employee who asserted she was ridiculed about "the disability being in her mind only"; and an Italian-American who claimed he was subjected to racist comments, slurs and jokes based on his national origin. Lifestyle issues also can lead to harassment claims, as in the case of a gay employee offended by a "born-again Christian" coworker's views on homosexuality.

RISK REDUCTION

Every employee falls into at least one of the protected categories, and many belong to several. Therefore, it's essential to prevent incidents that might lead to harassment claims and respond effectively when they do arise. This will reduce your exposure to liability and maximize workplace productivity.

The litigation costs associated with the rise in harassment complaints are enormous and increasing. As a result of the Civil Rights Act of 1991, jury trials are now available in federal harassment cases, and the remedies available to plaintiffs in such cases have expanded to include not just equitable relief, such as reinstatement and back pay, but also compensatory and punitive damages.

Last year, a federal jury awarded nearly $5.7 million to the family of a former U.S. Postal Service engineer who complained of sexual harassment prior to committing suicide. A male dude ranch wrangler was awarded $300,000 by a federal jury based on his claim that he was sexually harassed by his female supervisor. In California, the average jury verdict in employment cases in 1998 was $2.5 million. Equally important are the intangible damages associated with harassment claims, such as absenteeism, employee turnover, low morale and low productivity.

WHAT IS UNLAWFUL HARASSMENT?

The concept of unlawful harassment grew out of sexual harassment claims, but it has been applied in cases involving other protected characteristics as well. The EEOC's "Guidelines on Discrimination Because of Sex" define sexual harassment as "unwelcome sexual advances, requests for sexual favors, and other verbal or physical conduct of a sexual nature." The EEOC, commentators and courts have identified two types of harassment: "quid pro quo" and "hostile environment."

> **Employees who are subjected to harassment tend to assume it's because of a protected characteristic.**

In two cases last summer, *Faragher v. City of Boca Raton* and *Ellerth v. Burlington Indus.,* the Supreme Court clarified the definition

BRIEF CASES

THE ADA AND CORRECTIVE DEVICES

Two cases currently before the Supreme Court will resolve a difference of opinion among the courts as to whether an individual can be considered "disabled," and thus protected by the Americans with Disabilities Act (ADA), if his or her medical condition is corrected with medication or assistive devices. The two cases involve employees who were denied jobs because of medical conditions—twin pilots who are nearsighted in *Sutton v. United Airlines,* and a truck mechanic with high blood pressure in *Murphy v. United Parcel Service.* In both cases, the 10th Circuit ruled that the employees were *not* disabled because their conditions were corrected with lenses and medication, respectively.

NEW GUIDANCE ON 'REASONABLE ACCOMMODATIONS'

The EEOC issued new Guidance in February that addresses some tough questions about the reasonable accommodation requirements of the ADA. Among those questions: When must you provide an accommodation? What type is required? Under what circumstances can you claim that a requested accommodation would impose an undue hardship? According to the EEOC, once an employee indicates that her medical condition is affecting some aspect of her work, the employer is obligated to clarify her needs and identify an appropriate accommodation. Reasonable accommodations may include restructurings of some job functions, leaves of absence, modified or part-time work schedules, modified workplace policies and job reassignments.

EEOC CHALLENGES AN ENGLISH-ONLY POLICY

A federal district court recently denied an employer's motion to dismiss a lawsuit filed by the EEOC that challenges the company's brief use of an English-only policy. The employer, Synchro-Start, had established a policy requiring employees to speak only English during work hours, allegedly in response to complaints that multilingual employees were harassing and insulting coworkers in their native tongues. It rescinded the policy within nine months. The EEOC suit claims the policy discriminates on the basis of national origin because it focuses on employees whose primary language is not English. EEOC Guidelines express a presumption that English-only rules create a discriminatory environment based on national origin.

of sexual harassment. The court explained that quid pro quo harassment occurs when a "tangible employment action," such as termination, demotion or a significant change in assignment or benefits, results from a refusal to submit to a supervisor's sexual demands. If there is no tangible employment action, an employee may still be a victim of sexual harassment if he or she is subjected to unwelcome sexual conduct that is sufficiently severe or pervasive to unreasonably interfere with his or her work performance or create an intimidating, hostile or offensive work environment.

Quid pro quo claims are limited to the sexual harassment context.

Not so for the hostile work environment standard, which the courts have applied to other types of harassment claims. Regardless of the protected characteristic relied on by the plaintiff, in these cases the courts look to the severity and pervasiveness of the alleged harassment. To prevail on a hostile environment claim, the plaintiff must also show that he or she was subjected to severe and offensive conduct *because* of his or her protected characteristic.

When a company can show that the alleged harasser treated all employees in the same negative manner—sometimes referred to as an "equal opportunity harasser"—the harassment would not be unlawful because it is not related to the plaintiff's membership in a protected class. In *Pavone v. Brown,* for example, the court held that a disabled plaintiff could not prove unlawful harassment because other, nondisabled employees complained of the same mistreatment by the plaintiff's supervisor. But companies need to be aware that employees who are subjected to verbal abuse and other harassment tend to assume that it is because of a protected characteristic. Thus, such behavior (particularly by supervisors) presents risks of claims, litigation costs and workplace disruption even if the employer may ultimately prevail on an "equal opportunity abuser" theory.

Proof that harassment was because of a protected characteristic was the pivotal issue in a case decided by the Supreme Court last year. In *Oncale v. Sundowner Offshore Services, Inc.,* the plaintiff, a male employee alleged, among other things, that he was grabbed by his male supervisor and a male coworker who physically abused him while threatening rape. The Supreme Court concluded that a heterosexual can state a viable claim of sexual harassment against another heterosexual of the same gender (i.e., same-sex harassment), but remanded the case to the lower court to determine whether Oncale was in fact harassed *because of his sex.*

EMPLOYER LIABILITY

The Supreme Court's recent decisions in *Ellerth* and *Faragher* also clarified the circumstances under which an employer can be held liable for harassment by a supervisor. When an immediate (or successively higher) supervisor's harassment culminates in a tangible employment action, such as discharge, demotion or undesirable reassignment, the employer will be liable for the supervisor's actions.

When the harassment does not result in a tangible employment action, the employer may raise an "affirmative defense" to liability or

---

▇ POINTS OF POLICY

Here are the hallmarks of an effective nondiscrimination and anti-harassment policy:

▇ Introductory statement that expresses a commitment to a work environment that is free of discrimination and harassment.

▇ Equal employment opportunity statement.

▇ Definitions of harassment, with examples of behaviors that may constitute harassment.

▇ Coverage extending to all applicants, employees and third parties, such as outside vendors, consultants or customers, and to all conduct in a work-related setting—including social occasions such as client lunches and holiday parties.

▇ Prohibition of retaliation, enforced through disciplinary action.

▇ Complaint procedure designating several different "avenues of complaint" and strongly urging the reporting of all incidents.

▇ Assurance of a prompt investigation of complaints.

▇ Confidentiality maintained to the extent consistent with adequate investigation and appropriate corrective action.

▇ Corrective action upon a finding of misconduct, with specific examples of possible actions.

—C.O.

---

damages. This defense is made up of two parts: First, that the employer exercised reasonable care to prevent and correct promptly any harassing behavior. Second, that the plaintiff employee unreasonably failed to take advantage of any preventive or corrective opportunities provided by the employer or to avoid harm otherwise.

The reasonableness of an employer's response also determines liability in hostile environment cases involving harassment by a coworker, nonsupervisory employee or nonemployee (such as a vendor, customer, consultant or client). For example, a local Pizza Hut franchise was held liable for $200,000 in compensatory damages plus nearly $40,000 in attorney's fees and costs because it failed to prevent two of its customers from sexually harassing a waitress. In *Lockard v. Pizza Hut, Inc.,* the waitress claimed that her manager forced her to wait on two customers who pulled her hair and sexually assaulted her. The customers had engaged in other abusive conduct in prior visits and the plaintiff had complained to her manager. A federal appeals court up-

held the verdict, observing that the manager had been given notice of the harassing conduct and had unreasonably failed to remedy or prevent the harassment.

In light of the Supreme Court's recent decisions, it is critical for employers to take affirmative steps to prevent and remedy harassment. At a minimum, they should:

• Develop a written nondiscrimination and anti-harassment policy (see box).

• Ensure that the policy provides employees with effective avenues to bring complaints forward (not just through their supervisor, who may in fact be the harasser).

• Include the policy in a prominent place in an employee handbook (if there is one).

• Widely disseminate the policy (independent of the handbook) throughout the workplace on a periodic basis to make sure all employees know of its existence and understand the complaint procedure.

• Train appropriate segments of the workforce, such as senior management, managers/supervisors and complaint-receivers, to understand and apply the policy.

• Promptly respond to complaints brought under the policy by thoroughly investigating them to determine if policy violations have occurred.

• Take prompt, effective remedial action to respond to violations.

PREVENTING RETALIATION

In addition to distributing an anti-harassment policy, companies need to develop policies and procedures to prevent retaliation against individuals who file complaints of harassment or discrimination or who participate in their investigation. Charges of retaliation are on the rise, with more than 19,000 claims filed with the EEOC in 1998 alone.

Retaliation is an independent basis for employer liability under the federal discrimination laws. All too often, companies are finding that even after a discrimination or harassment claim has been dismissed for lack of evidence, the courts are ordering them to proceed to trial on claims of unlawful retaliation. This is because adverse action taken against an employee who opposes unlawful practices (by filing or threatening to file a complaint) can be considered unlawful retaliation.

For example, a federal appellate court recently reinstated a retaliation claim filed against Wal-Mart, while affirming the dismissal of the plaintiff's claims of racial harassment and discrimination. The plaintiff had alleged that within the two months after she filed a discrimination complaint with the EEOC, she was listed as a "no-show" on a scheduled day off, twice reprimanded by her manager and then given a one-day suspension. In addition, she claimed, her manager began soliciting negative statements about her from coworkers. The court held that this conduct was sufficient to support a claim of retaliation, especially because the plaintiff had not received any reprimands in the 11 months before she filed her EEOC charge.

To minimize the risk of liability for such claims, employers need to incorporate a strong prohibition against retaliation in their anti-harassment policies. They also should advise employees at all levels that retaliation will not be tolerated and will result in disciplinary action up to and including termination. Then make sure the policies are fully enforced.

After filing a charge of harassment or discrimination, employees often perceive any adverse actions as related to their complaint. Therefore, a human resources officer or other appropriate manager should carefully monitor a complainant's work environment and work with his or her supervisor to avoid even the appearance of retaliation. Further, ensure that the complainant is not shunned by his or her coworkers, and counsel managers to make a conscious effort to include complainants in appropriate workplace meetings or events.

If a complainant is a candidate for discipline for performance-related reasons, his or her manager should consult with human resources before any discipline is imposed to verify that it is warranted and consistent with comparable situations. Similarly, decisions involving raises and promotional opportunities in the complainant's department should be discussed with HR to ensure the complainant received appropriate consideration and was treated even-handedly.

Carole O'Blenes, a partner in the New York office of Proskauer Rose LLP, has practiced labor and employment law since 1976. She has represented employers in collective bargaining, arbitration, administrative proceedings and employment litigation. She also provides advice and guidance to clients on a wide range of employment and labor law matters. E-mail: coblenes@proskauer.com. Tracey I. Levy, an associate at Proskauer Rose, also contributed to this article.

Tales From the Front Line of Sexual Harassment

By MARGOT SLADE

Sexual harassment laws have always been notoriously confusing, so there was much cheering when the Supreme Court clarified things by issuing new harassment guidelines last month. The Court made it clear that employers are always legally responsible for the harassing behavior of supervisors. But it made the world a bit safer for employers by offering them a defense: an effective anti-harassment policy and complaint procedures that employees disregard at their own risk. The Court helped both sides understand what harassment is by explaining in a case involving men that it is the conduct that is at issue—not the sex or sexual desires of the people involved.

In clarifying matters, however, the Court invited new kinds of sexual harassment complaints, from people who turned down sexual advances or felt threatened in the workplace but did not suffer professional harm, and from men and women intimidated by the behavior of people of the same sex.

So there's still plenty of uncertainty for employers and employees alike. In the wake of the Court's new rulings, for example, employers must consider how to make policies com-

prehensive and what kinds of policies reflect "reasonable care" in preventing and correcting harassment. And even where ineffective policies exist, employees must now consider the consequences of side-stepping them.

Lawyers for both plaintiffs and employers, and the consultants who help companies devise and update their policies, say it will all come down to the white-knuckle moment when a judge or jury decides what is reasonable or not. Here are case studies drawn from the files of consultants and interpreted in light of the Supreme Court's new rulings.

Sexual Hazing

A manufacturing company has a heavily immigrant multiracial work force. At one of its union plants, the integration of women has been recent and difficult. There is a history here of hazing that takes a sexual form. There is a history, too, of management efforts to discipline men for harassing women—the company has a written anti-harassment policy— and of union support for the men.

An African man, a recent arrival to the United States, is hired. Within

days, he makes clear that he objects on religious grounds to explicit discussions of sexuality, whether in words, jokes or descriptions of someone's sexual activities. But the more he protests, the more his co-workers—joined occasionally by a department manager—indulge in sexual banter.

Soon, the new employee is ostracized. He spends more time alone reading, sometimes religious materials, which prompts more heckling. The shop steward warns the men to tone it down or risk management discipline. They don't.

The new employee disregards the union's grievance procedure—he does not report management's inaction. He also disregards the chain of command spelled out in the company's complaint process and goes to an executive demanding relief.

Resolution: Management transfers the worker to another plant, explaining that the workplace environment was too poisonous to heal. His co-workers are chastised, and for a while the atmosphere during breaks is less sexually charged.

Comments: Management is lucky, said Peggy Garrity, a Santa Monica, Calif., litigator who represents plaintiffs in discrimination cases. Even though the company had a policy and acted appropriately in the end, "the new employee could have sued and the company would have had little defense," she said.

Supervisors knew what was happening. And given the company's history, and a supervisor's participation in the heckling, the employee's action was not unreasonable. Freada Klein of Klein Associates Inc. in Cambridge, Mass., a consultant on issues of workplace bias, said the company needed to retool its policy "to articulate general principles, not situation-specific rules." And it should institute a training program so everyone understands that crude or sexual behavior is no longer tolerated.

Falling Off the Fast Track

At a profitable, publicly held company, rumors of the chief executive's affairs with women on staff are rampant. This executive has even acted inappropriately at social gatherings toward the wives of the company's directors—uninvited touching, for example. The wives have told their husbands.

In recent months, the executive has become smitten with the business acumen and beauty of a female manager, who is perceived by many colleagues as being on a fast track. She is bold in her thinking and actions, which to many male colleagues makes her a threat. She has enjoyed a string of business successes, but a recent deal went badly awry.

At a company cocktail party, the chief executive continually brushes against her as he talks about his sexual conquests. She resorts to the company's complaint process, which is spelled out in a policy distributed to employees.

During the weeks after the party, the manager is denied a bonus and is removed from a high-visibility task force. She cries retaliation. The executive insists the company was responding to her soured deal. "She wants to be judged on her performance," he tells his directors. "So be it."

Resolution: The woman is leaving the company, which is trying to head off a lawsuit with a negotiated settlement.

Comments: The company, Ms. Klein said, would lose a lawsuit, since "reasonable care" means taking preventive measures. "The directors knew there was a problem" and should have been predisposed to interpret the executive's actions as retaliation.

Paul Salvatore, a partner in the labor and employment law department of Proskauer Rose in New York, agreed, saying, "This c.e.o. was a walking liability." This kind of situation is extremely difficult, he added, because few company policies anticipate that the problem supervisor will be a chief executive. "Who are you going to complain to and about?" he said.

The Reluctant Complainer

A high-level manager visits a client in Scandinavia, where he attends an office function. Returning to the United States, he regales his female colleague with stories of late-night dinners and club hopping, where the entertainers were scantily clad women. He even brings photographs, knowing his female colleague is a world traveler who has visited Scandinavia.

An administrative assistant who works for him and several other executives overhears the conversation. She is scandalized. After a time, the manager offers to show her the photographs. She says no thanks, so he removes them from sight.

There is more. The administrative assistant knows through the grapevine that the manager belongs to an in-house group whose members exchange bawdy jokes via E-mail. One day, the manager inadvertently sends her such a message. He realizes his mistake and apologizes. Later, he asks her to retrieve a budget report from his in-box, but the top item is a soft-porn video.

The administrative assistant tells no one, but avoids working for the manager. She explains to her supervisor that she's not comfortable with him. The supervisor inquires further and she recounts the E-mail and video stories. When asked why she didn't speak up earlier, the administrative assistant says she thought she wouldn't be taken seriously.

Resolution: Following the company's sexual harassment policy, an investigator determines that the E-mail message was indeed inadvertent and that the video had been manufactured by the manager's client. But a memo is sent to all employees saying that the use of E-mail for bawdy jokes is inappropriate and must stop. The manager is sent for training to help him develop better judgment. He is also given a new assistant, so that no one need worry about perceived retaliation or the fairness of the woman's job evaluations.

Comments: "Well handled," Mr. Salvatore said. "That's how it should work." Had the woman sued, he added, the company had a defense: a viable complaint process and her decision not to use it. But Ms. Garrity and Ms. Klein said the woman's situation needs monitoring since other employees might blame her for the manager's censure and the shutdown of the E-mail exchange.

One of the Guys

A woman works as a supervisor at a construction company—a traditionally male environment. She prides herself on being able to deflect the sexual bantering common on the job.

There is a problem with one project and the company brings in a new district manager, expressing confidence that he can salvage it.

The manager arranges to meet the woman at different times to observe the crews, review the books and, he says, learn from her expertise. Soon he's calling her at home suggesting they meet for breakfast. She senses that something's amiss, but she figures she can handle it.

Then she starts getting job-related messages on her home answering machine at all hours of the night. She E-mails responses to the office. One evening she answers the phone and it's him, asking questions he could have posed at the office. Suddenly he says: "I always see you in a hard hat and overalls. What are you wearing now?" She changes the subject and hangs up.

She is panicked. After all, he's a star and she's expendable; the company and the industry have long tolerated sexual bantering and worse, and she has a reputation for being unflappable, which she wants to uphold. So although the company has a written sexual harassment policy and process—admittedly minimal and devoid of training—she doesn't use it.

The woman loses sleep and feels ill much of the time. Meanwhile, the man takes her to lunch, casually brushing against her hand during the meal.

One night, while she is working late, he appears and insists they go out. She says no and tries to leave. He blocks the way, kissing her on the mouth. She pushes him aside and rushes home.

Resolution: Her health deteriorates. She goes on disability leave, never to return, and then sues.

Comments: "This is the cutting edge of rock-and-roll," Mr. Salvatore said. "The company policy may be ineffective, but I don't know that she'd win." Forget her pride and the disparity between her power and his, Ms. Garrity said—she was a supervisor who understood complaint procedures. "She'd have to throw herself on the mercy of the court to explain why not using them was reasonable," she said. This company, she added, "has a good shot at a solid defense."

WHAT **Minority Employees** REALLY **Want**

IT'S SIMPLE: INCLUSION, ENCOURAGEMENT, AND OPPORTUNITY. BUT HOW DO YOU KNOW YOU'RE REALLY PROVIDING IT?

BY STEPHANIE N. MEHTA

A group of scientists from Lucent Technologies' vaunted Bell Labs are eating lunch and talking about the most delicate subject in corporate America, or anywhere else in America: race. Over sandwiches and pasta salad, they offer FORTUNE an upbeat view of opportunities for minorities at their company. Larry Seibles, a researcher in Lucent's process and chemical engineering department, proudly notes that everybody up his management chain is either a woman or a minority. Materials scientist Ainissa Ramirez is still amazed that her bosses let her give speeches on company time about diversity. Dora Abreu, a computer programmer, recalls interviewing for a job at Lucent three years ago and watching from the lobby as people of all racial and ethnic backgrounds streamed through the door. "They aren't just saying they're diverse. They *are* diverse," she remembers thinking.

When a reporter asks how Lucent could improve, however, the room goes quiet. Abreu suggests that the company could try to attract more Hispanics, who make up about 5% of Lucent employees. The others stare silently at their half-eaten meals.

So it goes with race relations in the workplace. The good news is, there's plenty of progress for companies and employees to talk about, especially at a place like Lucent, which ranks 25th on our list of the 50 best places for minorities. But what often doesn't get said, especially in mixed-race settings, is how much remains to be done. Executives may have no idea how differently minority colleagues can view the corporate culture that treats whites so well. Just ask Nextel Communications, which is facing complaints of racial and sexual discrimination filed by minority employees in late June. Or talk to Doug Ivester and Doug Daft, Coca-Cola's former and current

CEOs, who both seemed genuinely shocked that anyone could consider Coke a biased place. Some of the company's black employees apparently saw things another way.

That's why it's in everyone's interest to identify and honor the corporations that have done the most to make employees of all races into full participants in their businesses. In our third annual list of the best companies for minorities, assembled for FORTUNE by the nonprofit Council on Economic Priorities, we do just that: Each company on our list has made an exemplary commitment to diversity at every level—from its new hires, to its suppliers, to the charities its supports. In this year's rankings we pay enormous attention to diversity in the upper ranks of each company. In our average top-50 corporation, members of ethnic minorities hold about 16% of the board seats, make up 22% of the officials and managers, and pull down 13% of the 50 largest paychecks. Those are all key signs that a company has gone beyond political correctness. After all, no company would fill its top slots with unqualified people just to look multicultural.

Not that anyone would need to, since the nation is blessed with more executives of color than at any time in recent memory. Consider this: About 65% of the FORTUNE 1,000 have at least one member of an ethnic minority on their board of directors, up from 55% in 1998. Nearly one in five members of the Harvard Business School class of 2000 is a person of color, up from about 13% of the class of 1990. And Fannie Mae, Applied Materials, and Merrill Lynch all have African-American executives as the No. 1 or the heir apparent.

Indeed, it's now considered self-evident that a diverse work force is not just "the right thing to do"; it's a competitive advantage. The more points of view from which you attack a problem, the more creative your solutions will be. That's especially true in marketing: A unicultural management can't sell to multicultural customers. In addition, a reputation for including people of all kinds— and offering them good jobs and good salaries—will give you a leg up in luring new employees and keeping the current staff from exiting.

The question today, then, isn't whether you want minority workers. It's whether you are giving them what they want—and giving it to them consistently enough to get them to stick around. And what they want, of course, is what all your employees want: confidence that their efforts will pay off in money, fulfilling work, and opportunity for advancement.

Before you respond reflexively that of course your company is a level playing field, *consider this:* A staggering 45% of minority executives— these are senior people, mind you—say they've been the target of a racial or cultural joke at work, according to a study by search firm Korn/Ferry International and Columbia Business School. And while you may protest that no such outrage would ever occur in your office, remember that this figure does not count the unwitting acts of insensitivity that probably occur there all the time. Earl G. Graves, founder of *Black Enterprise* magazine, recalls inviting some businessmen to a charity dinner that his magazine was sponsoring. Before accepting, some guests demanded to know whether there would be other white people at the table. Every minority executive has similar stories to tell.You'd have to be non-white to know what it's like to have others assume you must be junior to a colleague because the colleague is white; to lose a sale when a customer finds out you are not Caucasian; to be waiting for your car and be mistaken for the valet. Some 44% of executives in the Korn/Ferry survey say they've had to stifle anger to avoid being seen as having a chip on their shoulder.

How might such experiences color the way minorities *really* perceive opportunity at your company? It's naive to think that unconscious, patronizing attitudes don't find their way into decisions directly affecting minority employees' careers. The minority executives in the Korn/Ferry survey clearly felt they did. Nearly 60% of them say they've observed a double standard in the delegation of assignments. Little wonder, then, that almost half of all minority employees feel their employers aren't doing enough to create opportunities for people of color, according to employee-attitude research by Sirota Consulting. If you want to win the trust of your minority employees, then, there's no way around it. You're going to have to work at it.

Racial stereotyping may be the most pernicious when applied to black employees, but it's hardly limited to them. James Cheng, a director in the mergers and acquisitions department for phone company GTE, tries to be

Black employees are just as upbeat about work as white . . .

How would you rate your overall job satisfaction?
Percent responding favorably

| **Blacks** | Whites |
| **64%** | **62%** |

Are you proud to work for your present employer?
Percent responding favorably

| **Blacks** | **Whites** |
| **74%** | **72%** |

but are far less positive about issues of fairness and pay

The better my performance, the bigger my pay increases
Percent responding favorably

| **Blacks** | Whites |
| **35%** | **51%** |

Are you paid well?
Percent responding favorably

| **Blacks** | Whites |
| **42%** | **51%** |

FORTUNE GRAPHICS / SOURCE: SIROTA CONSULTING

philosophical about it. "I have close friends who will tell me, 'Well, you're Chinese, therefore blah, blah, blah.'" he says. "That's not discrimination, it's just opinions between co-workers." Not everyone would be as good-natured about this as Cheng, but even he acknowledges that co-workers' "opinions" can leach into the culture and affect opportunities. "Have I been viewed positively or negatively because I am a minority? Definitely," he says. Cheng, 47, says "positive" characterizations of Asians as hard-working and deferential can be just as damaging as negative ones: Asian employees can end up relegated to roles as corporate workhorses—not leaders. "You do see at the entry level a lot of Asians in GTE on the technical side," Cheng says. "Why aren't we being pushed toward higher-level positions?"

Hazel Weathers, a no-nonsense senior marketing manager at GTE, describes how an unfavorable stereotype can snowball without any conscious act of discrimination. Weathers spent most of her career at IBM, a company she credits with being fairly forward-thinking on the issue of diversity. Still, she remembers a time at the computer giant when she supervised a group of about a dozen people, and her top employee was an African-American man. As it turns out, he also was the lowest-paid person in her group. "How does that happen?" she asks. "It doesn't happen because one manager decides to cut his pay by 25%, but because one manager looks at raises and gives him 5% less, and the next does the same. By the time five managers have done that, well, he's making 25% less. It is done in little pieces along the way."

Very often minority executives are held back because no white manager will take a chance on handing them that first important management gig. David A. Thomas, a professor at Harvard Business School and the author of a book on successful executives of color, says minority managers spend more time than their peers in the "bull-pen" waiting for their big chance. If they get it, they then have to prove themselves all over again with each new post. "We see people of color incurring a tax, even when they are superior performers," Thomas says.

In this way, discrimination is almost clandestine. Minority employees get left out of high-profile projects, so they can't exhibit skills needed to earn promotions. They start at a lower base salary, and fall a little further behind with each pay raise. A manager looks at that low pay and assumes there must be something wrong with the employee—not with the system.

Thomas' research supports the feeling, widespread among successful minorities, that they've had to put in extra hours and additional effort to achieve the same status as their white contemporaries. Bruce Gordon, president of Bell Atlantic's enterprise group, says he has always felt that he needed to be better than—not equal to—the competition. But he also thinks that these added efforts have made him a better executive, and he counsels other minority employees to pursue the same ethic. "It's not enough to be as good as the next person," says the 54-year-old executive. "We have to be better."

Far and away the best way for companies to level the playing field is to cultivate and promote minority achievers like Gordon. Minority executives in senior posts not only keep the corporate culture honest—they don't have the same blinders as white executives—but also reinforce the essential message that employees of color can succeed there. Dixie Garr, a vice president at Cisco Systems, echoes that thought: "When talented minorities thrive in an organization, it sends a powerful message to up-and-comers in the company."

And to those outside. "Minority executives tend to be more careful in evaluating the quality of the corporate culture of companies they might be joining," says Joanna Miller, a managing director with Korn/Ferry International. Putting high-achieving minority executives in high-profile jobs is the best way to signal that the culture welcomes the sort of manager you'd like to attract.

At Lucent's Bell Labs, chemical engineer Ralph Taylor-Smith says that the presence of role models with his complexion gave him assurance that his ability, not his

---

It's not the same workplace
Percent of minority executives who have . . .

Observed a double standard in delegation of assignments
59%

Personally been a target of racial or cultural jokes
45%

Held back anger for fear of being seen as having a chip on shoulder
44%

FORTUNE GRAPHIC / SOURCES: KORN/FERRY; COLUMBIA BUSINESS SCHOOL

---

race, would decide his professional success. "I interviewed at a lot of top FORTUNE 500 companies," he says. "At Lucent, there were a number of clear-cut, successful people of color." He cites Jim West, a renowned Bell Labs scientist who invented a key microphone technology; Shirley Jackson, who has since left to become president of Rensselaer Polytechnic Institute; and Jim Mitchell, materials research vice president at Bell Labs. "It was an easy decision to come here," he says. Taylor-Smith, 32, is no slouch himself, by the way. He holds three patents, and MIT's *Technology Review* recently named him one of the nation's top young innovators.

Quickly getting minorities into decision-making roles also helps counteract the wrong kind of buzz. And as of the early 1990s, perhaps no company had worse word of mouth among minorities than Shoney's. (In 1992 the company paid $132.8 million to settle a class-action lawsuit brought by 20,000 employees and rejected job applicants.) "Our former leadership had a practice of—I guess this is the best way to put it—promoting from the 'buddy system,' " says Jesse Spaulding, a regional director of operations for Captain D's, a seafood chain owned by Shoney's. "That left people of color by the wayside, because there were no people of color in higher positions who could make decisions on promotions." Spaulding's own career is a case in point. The talkative go-getter started at Captain D's in 1981 as a 21-year-old manager trainee. He quickly became an assistant manager, then a general manager. While he was still in his mid-20s, he was named an area supervisor—at which point his career stagnated for ten years.

Shoney's is a different place now. In the wake of the lawsuit, management has made a decisive effort to broaden opportunity, and the company (this year's No. 36) has ranked in FORTUNE's top 50 for each of the three years we have done the list. And Spaulding has vaulted from being a victim of Shoney's old, all-white "buddy system" to helping to shape its new, multi-ethnic version.

He delights in bringing along qualified people of color. For example, Spaulding says, he recently hired a new area director from a rival. "He was a topnotch performer, but his former bosses were waiting for a spot to open up in an area where they thought he would 'fit in' " (in other words, a nonwhite community). "We hired him right away."

The turnaround at Shoney's—and at that other reformed sinner, Denny's (No. 1 on this year's list under its corporate moniker, Advantica)—demonstrates what Coke is learning only now. You don't gain the trust of minority employees simply by having vague multicultural intentions. You need to give minorities great jobs. You need to set measurable goals and track your progress using the sorts of yardsticks employed by FORTUNE's ranking. You also need to give managers an incentive to reach those goals. It's no accident that 38 of the 50 best companies for minorities, or about 76%, tie managers' bonuses to diversity goals. By comparison, a 1998 sample of human resources executives found that only one in four FORTUNE 500 companies made the same commitment.

There is, after all, no reason that corporations shouldn't lead America in eradicating discrimination. Bruce Gordon, the Bell Atlantic group president, says he chose a business career because he felt the private sector had the greatest power to effect change. "It all comes down to profits," he says. "You get over your discriminatory instincts when you realize that you're getting paid to win, and it doesn't matter what the skin color is of the person who helps you win."

In the meantime, businesses that have been the first to put their money where their hearts are will be the first to reap the rewards. Jennifer Kannar, 44, a Hong Kong-raised product manager at UPS (No. 31 on our list), recently proposed a bilingual support center to win the business of Korean-American entrepreneurs in Southern California. The company took a couple of months to evaluate the proposal, to Kannar's frustration, but it ultimately gave the center the green light. Kannar is now expanding to include Vietnamese, Chinese, and Japanese businesses. Had UPS not consciously striven for a diverse work force, it might well have missed the opportunity Kannar saw.

In fact, who knows how much talent might have been lost to the work force had the companies on our list not made the effort to bring minorities along? Ludyn Campos, a native of Guatemala, rose from houseman—essentially the man who hands out supplies to the maids—to chief engineer at a Marriott Residence Inn in Manhattan Beach, Calif. That might not have been possible had Campos not learned English, with the help of his employer (No. 37 on our list). Then there's Dora Abreu, the Dominican-American programmer at Lucent. Where she grew up, in Queens, New York, girls were urged to be teachers or secretaries, if they were to work at all. Abreu nevertheless poured her energy into math and went on to earn two master's degrees. Who wouldn't want employees like Campos or Abreu? The only question is, are you worthy of them?

REPORTERS: *Christine Y. Chen, Feliciano Garcia, Karen Vella-Zarb*
FEEDBACK: *smehta@fortunemail.com*

STAFF SMARTS

Silver Lining

Hesitant about hiring older workers? Then you're ignoring a talented labor pool.

BY ROBERT MCGARVEY

How MANY OF YOUR employees are older than you? Your current answer doesn't matter—quite soon you'll likely report that many of your workers are older, and, what's more, you'll be singing their praises.

"Initially, it was very awkward for me to hire and manage older people," admits Jay Goltz, 42, owner of three Artists' Frame Service stores, a $10 million business in Chicago, and author of *The Street-Smart Entrepreneur* (Addicus Books). "But that was 20 years ago when I was 22 and *everybody* was older than me. It took time for me to get comfortable with managing older workers, but today, I'd guess one-third of my 120 employees are older. And I have absolutely no complaints about that."

POWER IN NUMBERS

Chew on this: Thirty-five million Americans (13 percent of the population) are over 65 years of age, and this 65-plus group is currently the fastest-growing population group tracked by the U.S. Census Bureau. In fact, the Census Bureau estimates that this group will comprise 20 percent of the total U.S. population by 2020.

But that's just one sign of a nation that, across the board, is rapidly graying. As baby boomers continue to cross the 50-year mark and health care continues to rapidly advance, we're all living longer, higher-quality lives. The most telling statistic: The Census Bureau projects that America's median age will shift from 34 in 1994 to 38.7 by 2035, an immense jump for such a large and diverse country.

According to Gangaram Singh, a professor of human resources policy at Case Western Reserve University's Weatherhead School of Management in Cleveland, if you study the statistics, the simple fact is that with current economic conditions, including low unemployment and worker scarcities, "The pool of young workers is no longer sufficient to meet employment needs."

Is that an unsettling reality? Say "yes," and you're in the majority. Most managers approach the notion of supervising workers older than themselves with sizable anxiety.

"Age is often referred to as 'the subtle bias,'" says Elissa Perry, an assistant professor of psychology and education at Columbia University Teacher's College in New York City and a specialist in age discrimination. "While most companies recognize the need to address gender and race diversity and the tensions that arise [from that], few have done anything but ignore age diversity."

For its part, the federal government has already addressed these tensions. The Age Discrimination in Employment Act of 1967 (ADEA) sets out unmistakable protections for workers 40 years of age or older. The Equal Employment Opportunity Commission (EEOC), which enforces ADEA, spells out the law's impact: "Under the ADEA, it is unlawful to discriminate against a person because of his/her age with respect to any term, condition, or privilege of employment—including but not limited to hiring, firing, promotion, layoff, compensation, benefits, job assignments and training." That's a sweeping law, and, especially as more small businesses see an increasing

number of older job applicants, it's a law you need to digest. Bumping up against ADEA can be every bit as painful (and expensive) as running afoul of the sexual harassment or race discrimination laws the EEOC administers.

The trouble is, many businesses violate ADEA, possibly unintentionally. "Many studies have shown when an older and a younger job candidate apply for an entry-level position, the younger candidate more consistently gets the job," says Perry. "That has to change."

Singh agrees. "There are many stereotypes against hiring older workers," he says, ticking off the three most common:

✓Older workers are absent more frequently.

✓Older workers are short-term employees who only stay on the job briefly.

✓Older workers are less productive than younger workers.

"None of these stereotypes are true," says Singh. "Research has shown them all to be false, but many employers entertain these beliefs, and that makes them reluctant to hire older workers."

Adds Perry: "Businesses hold more myths about older workers, probably subconsciously. For instance, you'll hear that older workers are more accident prone, but there's no basis for believing it. You'll hear older workers will not retrain; there's no evidence that a willingness to retrain has anything to do with age."

OLDER BUT WISER

Obviously, hiring older workers needn't be damaging to your business. In fact, it may add a competitive zing to your work force. "Older workers are a very under-utilized resource," contends Perry. "Most companies don't understand the advantages of hiring them."

Jay Goltz heartily agrees with the endorsements of graying employees. "Older workers are often less trouble than younger workers," he says. "They've already figured out the rules for succeeding on the job.

"So many of the 20-year-olds [I've hired] have never had another job, and from them, I often hear what I call the 'f-word'—'fair.' 'It's *unfair* that I can't park in front of the business, but the customers can.' I don't hear that kind of thing from my older workers, ever."

But, still, aren't older workers resistant to taking orders from younger bosses? That may be the big psychological stumbling block for many managers, but, says Singh, "A lot of older workers have taken instructions from bosses all their lives. They understand the role of the boss, and the boss's age won't matter to them."

Often the hang-up rests with the business owner. "The problem of managing older workers is 75 percent in your own head," says Goltz. "Show them respect, and you'll get the same back. They know who the boss is. Act like one, and you won't have problems."

One tip to defuse possible tensions, says Perry, is to try to shift attention away from the age difference. Age is just one of many things people potentially have in common. There are also hobbies, shared values and common interests. Put plainly, you may be a generation younger than Joe, but you're both San Francisco Giants fans, love hot dogs and can't wait for baseball season to start. As you focus on those shared interests, Joe's birth date will matter less and less in your mind, suggests Perry.

Make no mistake, however: Some older job candidates might grumble at taking orders from "a kid." Regardless of age, that's what interviews are for—to sort out who will mesh with the chemistry of your workplace and who won't.

Keep in mind, too, that older workers know that plenty of businesses discriminate against them throughout the hiring process. Because they want to keep their jobs, odds are, despite moments of occasional irritation that may crop up, their overall attitude just might be gratitude toward a boss who saw their potential despite a few gray hairs. "Research shows that older workers value their jobs more than younger workers. It also shows that they are less likely to quit and are more likely to stay committed to the organization," says Singh.

Can you really afford to ignore all the positive attributes older workers offer? "There are no valid arguments that older workers perform less effectively," says Singh. "They are good workers, and they want to work."

Robert McGarvey writes on business, psychology and management topics for several national publications. To reach him online with your questions or comments, e-mail rjmcgarvey@aol.com.

Sorrow and Guilt: An Ethical Analysis of Layoffs

Joseph T. Gilbert

College of Business, University of Nevada, Las Vegas

Closing the office door, looking straight into an employee's face, and telling him that he no longer has a job is not an easy task. When that employee's performance has been satisfactory or even exemplary, it is even more difficult for a manager to terminate him or her. Yet, this happens hundreds of thousands of times when companies decide to reduce the size of their workforce by layoffs. From the stock market's point of view, such a decision is usually a good thing—a company's stock price often rises on the day that a layoff decision is announced. From top management's point of view, such a decision can seem to be the best, or even the only one, available to solve serious problems that the top manager must address. From the point of view of the managers or supervisors assigned to deliver the news to individuals about to be terminated, the decision often produces sorrow or guilt, or both. From the point of view of the terminated employees, shock, disbelief, and anger are among the typical reactions.

Sorrow and guilt are among the emotions associated with layoffs. Sorrow often arises as a response to suffering, whether the suffering befalls the one feeling sorry or another for whom the sorrowful person sympathizes. Guilt is usually reserved for situations involving moral issues. It typically arises when a person has done something he or she should not have done, and therefore implies some degree or moral wrong. Since layoffs cause suffering, sorrow is an appropriate emotion. Is guilt appropriate, and if so on whose part? In other words, is moral or ethical wrong involved in layoffs?

This article focuses on the decision to conduct layoffs and the subsequent decision about which employees will be laid off. Once these decisions have been reached, the managers or supervisors who conduct the interviews in which those losing their jobs receive the news are executing a strategy or decision that they usually cannot change. A manager or supervisor who

felt strongly enough that the decisions were wrong could resign, but short of that their assigned role is to carry out decisions that have been made. Employees who are laid off have little choice but to leave. They can sue their former employer subsequently, but they cannot reverse the layoff decision. Financial analysts and investors who reward the decision to conduct layoffs by bidding up the price of the company's stock are reacting to the expected financial results of the decision, not to the terminations that result from it.

By concentrating our analysis on these two aspects of the subject, we deal with the key points where senior managers decide among options, and, by their decision, set a course of action with serious consequences for others (Child, 1997; McCann, 1997). We will argue that in some circumstances, laying off some employees is the ethical thing to do, and managers who fail to do so are guilty of unethical conduct. In other circumstances, no ethical defense of layoffs can be found, and managers who decide on layoffs in these circumstances are guilty of unethical acts. In a wide range of circumstances in between, there are ethical arguments for and against layoffs. For these cases, we show how ethical reasoning can be applied to assist managers in determining the morally right thing to do.

One common definition of an act with ethical or moral consequences is that such an act involves decisions freely taken that will have positive or negative consequences for others (Velasquez & Rostankowski, 1982). Layoff decisions clearly fall within this definition. Our analysis will employ the three major approaches often used in writing and teaching about managerial ethics: utilitarianism (the greatest good for the greatest number), rights and duties, and justice and fairness. The first section of this article briefly describes the most common approaches to managerial ethics as described in journal articles and books for practitioners (Arneson, Fleenor & Toh, 1997; De-

George, 1995). The next section reviews various reasons for layoffs, and divides them into three basic categories. The three following sections analyze the layoff decisions from these perspectives, and the final section draws conclusions about the morality of layoffs as a management tool for improving a business.

Ethical Analysis: The Basic Tools

To determine whether a decision, such as downsizing, or an action, such as laying off an employee, is ethical, managers have certain analytical techniques available to them. While these techniques are not as widely known as statistical analysis or flow charting, they are gradually becoming part of a manager's standard tool kit. Business schools are placing more emphasis on ethics, partly because of the large number of clearly unethical business practices exposed during the 1980s (Piper, Gentile & Parks, 1993; Williams, 1992).

Most business school textbooks and courses on ethics take the same basic approach to analyzing the morality or ethics (we use the words interchangeably in this article) of business decisions. The three most commonly accepted approaches draw on the work of moral philosophers dating back more than two thousand years to Plato and Aristotle. While these philosophers were not familiar with corporations or computers, they did think long and deeply about issues of morality. The fact that their writings are still read and discussed indicates that they have something worthwhile to say.

Ethics is the branch of philosophy that deals with the morality of human decisions and actions, and business ethics deals with them in a business setting. These dry-sounding definitions point to the link between the best work of some deep moral thinkers and particular decisions or actions taken by managers in a contemporary business setting.

While many people get their sense of ethics or morality from their religion, philosophy attempts to reach conclusions about right and wrong behavior without reliance on divinely inspired teaching. It asks what we as humans (rather than as Christians or Buddhists or Muslims) can conclude about the moral rightness or wrongness of our decisions and actions. Ethics also does not assume the moral correctness of laws. In other words, it is not a sufficient moral justification of an act to say that it is legal. After all, what is legal in one state or country may be illegal in another. Most people are troubled to think that the morality of their actions depends on political borders.

Utilitarianism. One approach to determining the morality of a decision or action is utilitarianism, which holds that a moral decision or action is one that results in the greatest good for the greatest number of people. The philosophers most commonly identified with this view are two nineteenth century Englishmen,

Jeremy Bentham and John Stuart Mill. The assumption of this approach is that pleasure causes happiness and pain takes it away. Since pleasure and the happiness it causes are the ultimate good for humans, the act that causes the greatest pleasure or happiness for the greatest number of people is the morally good act. This view also assumes that people live in communities and must take this fact into account in deciding on the moral rightness of what they do. While this view may sound simplistic, it is often called upon in business settings to justify or condemn certain actions. We will examine the issue further, but it is common to justify layoff on the basis that terminating 500 people will save the company from bankruptcy and hence preserve the jobs of 2,500 others.

Rights and duties. A second approach to ethical analysis is to examine the issues of rights and duties. The basic position here is that individuals have rights, either as humans, as citizens of a given country or state, or as occupants of a particular position. These rights confer duties on others, and the morality of a given decision or act can be determined by an analysis of these rights and duties. The philosopher most commonly associated with this view is Immanuel Kant. While issues of rights and duties may sound more philosophical and less mathematical than that of determining the greatest good for the greatest number, it is not necessarily so. My right to personal comfort may be outweighed by your right to live. My duty to my family may be outweighed by my duty to serve my country in time of war. Once again, calculation enters into many, but not all, ethical decisions. Few people would question that humans have a basic right to life, and that random killing is morally wrong. A somewhat different question, related to layoffs, is whether workers have a right to their jobs (and, therefore, managers have a duty not to lay them off).

Justice and fairness. The third basic approach involves issues of justice and fairness. While some would treat justice and fairness as issues within the first two approaches, others maintain that they constitute a third approach. Both utilitarianism and rights and duties have been criticized for being unfair in certain cases (Scheffler, 1988). In some situations, you may not have a clear right to your job, and it may not be clear that maintaining your job serves the greatest good of the greatest number, but does not seem fair for you to be terminated when you have been performing well and earning both praises and raises. In the United States, we tend to equate justice with legality, but there are situations where an action that is legal does not seem fair or just. As with the previous two approaches, calculation sometimes enters into considerations of justice and fairness, because it may be impossible in a given situation to be fully fair to everyone involved. The philosopher whose work is most often cited on issues of justice and fairness is John Rawls (1971), a professor at Harvard University.

With this brief summary of the three most common approaches to analyzing issues of managerial ethics, we now turn to the issue of layoffs. Reductions in staff or layoffs are different from termination for cause. An employee who is fired for stealing or fighting on the job is not laid off. Layoffs are also different from reductions in staff that are accomplished by attrition (choosing not to fill vacant positions). There are a variety of reasons why managers may choose to lay-off employees. An ethical or moral analysis of layoffs requires that we identify some of these reasons.

At one extreme is the situation where a company ceases operation, either at the choice of its owners or because of bankruptcy. In this case, obviously, all employees lost their jobs, but this is not usually referred to as a layoff. A similar situation, but not as drastic, occurs when a company is in serious danger of going out of business, and reducing labor costs through layoffs is the only apparent alternative. We will refer to such situations as *layoffs to save the company*. In other situations, layoffs are a preventative measure. In such cases, managers analyze their company's competitive situation, see that it is deteriorating and that labor costs are a significant factor, and move to reduce these costs before the company reaches the life or death stage. We will refer to this category as *layoffs to improve the company*.

In still other situations, layoffs are conducted to improve an already good situation. Here it is the judgment of managers that while the company is not deteriorating, greater profits could be achieved by reducing labor costs. Such layoffs may come about in mergers or acquisitions. Here two companies become one, and frequently plants or offices are closed and their employees laid off to reduce duplication. These layoffs are also conducted to reduce labor costs, but the motivating factor (or at least the precipitating factor) is the merger or acquisition.

Another circumstance in which layoffs are conducted to improve an already good situation involves outsourcing. The theory of core competency, popular in current strategy literature (Prahalad & Hamel, 1990), suggests that a company can perform best by identifying its core competency, concentrating its efforts and its employees on performing core functions, and contracting with other companies to perform other functions. In practice, this can lead to layoffs if a company decides to stop performing certain functions and not to employ those people who formerly carried them out. We will categorize these situations (mergers, acquisitions, and outsourcing) as *layoffs to change the company*. The three categories of layoffs that we have identified (to save, to change, or to improve the company) are not mutually exclusive, but they are sufficiently different to provide a basis for further discussion.

Utilitarianism and Layoffs

On the face of it, deciding the morality of a decision or action by counting may seem strange. Yet it is an approach to decision-making that is frequent in everyday life and in the business world. Businesses in many predominantly Christian countries treat Christmas as a holiday, even though some of their employees and customers are non-Christian. All employees on a certain work shift may be required to start work at the same time even though some might prefer to start a bit earlier or later. The headwaiter who prefers to work in tanktops and cut-off jeans will soon seek other work or a different wardrobe. The greatest good of his fellow employees and the restaurant patrons will outweigh his preference for casual dress.

When a manager terminates an employee who has done nothing wrong, it can scarcely be argued that this is good for the employee. Whether the action is called downsizing, rightsizing, outplacement, or some other term, the terminated employee had a job yesterday and now does not. He or she had a regular salary, health insurance, hopes for promotion, daily social interaction with a group of fellow workers, and an identity as a salesperson or programmer or supervisor. Today these are gone, not because the employee was negligent or lazy or incompetent, but because from management's point of view, the employee was unneeded. The employee was doing a satisfactory or even a superior job in contributing to the company's success, but now has no part in the company's future. It is not surprising that laid-off employees feel that the actions of the manager who terminated them were not right.

The utilitarian argument focuses on obtaining the greatest happiness or good of the greatest number. Happiness is also the goal in other systems of ethics, dating back to Aristotle in the fourth century, B.C. This basis for deciding on moral acts makes some intuitive sense. Most people would probably agree that [it] is morally better, in general, to make people happy than to make them unhappy, to bring them pleasure rather than to bring them grief. What the utilitarian argument maintains is that it is not enough to consider the happiness or unhappiness of a single individual. Attention must be focused on the sum of happiness or grief resulting from a decision or action. Thus, the terminated employee receives pain rather than pleasure from his termination. The manager who conducts the face-to-face interview terminating the employee is likely to suffer grief rather than happiness as a result of the termination interview. If there is any moral justification for this action, it must lie in a greater sum of happiness coming to a larger number of others. An echo of this approach can be heard in the stakeholder analysis approach to issues of business strategy (Freeman, 1984; Freeman & Gilbert, 1988).

This line of reasoning is strengthened if the company, and hence the jobs of employees who are not laid off, can only be saved by reducing the labor force. If this is the case, then the happiness or pleasure of employment for all those who remain justifies the pain of those laid off and those managers who conduct the termination interviews. Further justification can be found in the happiness of stockholders, bondholders, and others who would be hurt by the company's bankruptcy. Given this situation, the utilitarian approach would clearly condone the layoffs as the moral thing to do. But how can we be sure that we are dealing with layoffs to save the company rather than to improve it.

Resolving this issue is not easy. When a company is in serious trouble, there is usually a perceived need to act quickly. Thoughtful consideration of all available alternatives is not likely to occur. Competing by price reductions only worsens a company's financial situation unless there are accompanying cost reductions. Competing by improving the present products or services, or introducing new and better ones, is often not a short-term possibility. Competing by greatly increased marketing efforts is costly, and if the company is already in financial trouble, costly solutions do not appear practical. Reducing staff can be done quickly, and there is ample precedent for such a decision (Cascio, 1993; Mabert & Schmenner, 1997). Accounting rules allow all the costs of staff reduction to be expensed in one quarter, and financial analysts usually see such one-time expenses as good for a company. While not an attractive alternative, a U.S. company in financial trouble can seek protecting by entering Chapter 11 bankruptcy, reorganizing its finances, and continuing as a going concern. As an alternative to layoffs, this solution may postpone the action, but often companies in Chapter 11 bankruptcy reduce staff as part of their reorganization before emerging from bankruptcy. So layoffs are still carried out, and the negative consequences of bankruptcy are added to the mix. In a utilitarian analysis, such a scenario is apt to result in greater unhappiness for more people (suppliers, creditors, shareholders) than would occur with layoffs alone.

In the final analysis, the only way to know for sure whether a company was in a situation of either conducting layoffs or going out of business is to wait and see. Yet it is cold comfort to managers or employees to find out after the fact that layoffs were needed to save the company and that, as a result of inaction, all jobs have been lost. Some uncertainty is inevitable regarding the question of whether the situation involves saving or improving the company. The luxury of waiting for definite answers is simply not available. Hence, we suggest a decision rule which says that if, in the judgment of senior management at the time the layoff decision is made, the situation was one of saving the company, it should be treated as such for purposes of ethical analysis.

Another possibility is that layoffs are not the only step between the present situation and a company's closing, but are seen as a way of dealing with deteriorating performance (layoffs to improve the company). In this case, it is more difficult to conclude that the unhappiness of those laid off and of managers who conduct the terminations is outweighed by a greater good for a greater number of people as a result of the company's improved performance. The unhappiness is clear, the greater good and those who benefit from it is less clear (DeMeuse, Bergmann & Vanderheiden, 1997). In this category of layoffs, the further the situation deviates from a clearcut choice between layoffs and the company's closing, the less compelling the utilitarian argument becomes. However, top managers, by their positions, are charged with the future as well as the present well-being of the company. They are responsible for being proactive as well as reactive. In a situation where layoffs now can prevent a crisis later, choosing layoffs can be the best decision for the greatest number.

In the case of layoffs to improve already adequate performance (layoffs to change the company), the decision might bring happiness to managers whose compensation is tied to company performance through stock options or bonus plans, and to stockholders if the resulting improvements in performance cause the stock price to rise. However, in many cases companies conducting layoffs to improve performance do not attain the hoped-for results (DeMeuse, Vanderheiden & Bergmann, 1977). Even if the results are achieved, unhappiness comes not only to the workers laid off and their managers, but also to many of the workers who remain. They face increased workloads and uncertainty about their own future with the company. Further, the families of those laid off also suffer pain. Workers at competing companies, observing the layoffs earned out by their rival may well suffer pain at the prospect that their own company will lay them off to maintain competitive. Thus, by a utilitarian analysis, it is by no means clear that layoffs to improve a company's position are always moral.

One further point to be noted is that in layoffs to improve the company, management is typically focused on the causal link between reducing the number of employees and improving the company's performance. In layoffs to change the company, managers may focus on the terms of a merger or acquisition agreement, or on the new company structure after a merger, or on the benefits of focusing all management attention on things that make up the company's core competencies. Managers may not give any or enough attention to the issue of layoffs, which might be seen as an administrative detail. The same basic issue needs to be considered in both kinds of layoffs (to improve and to change), but the pressure to complete a change may divert the attention of top managers in situations involving mergers and acquisitions.

The second question concerns how many and which employees are to be laid off. A utilitarian analysis emphasizes the impact of these choices (how many and who) on the results to be obtained. For the choices to be moral, the unhappiness caused must be offset by a greater sum of happiness for others resulting from the company's improved performance.

If labor costs are to be reduced sufficiently to improve competitive performance, the percentage of total employees to be laid off is likely to be impressive. As a starting point, it seems clear that enough employees must remain to produce the company's products or services in a reasonably timely manner and at a reasonably high level of quality. If timeliness or quality slip noticeably, the company's competitive position is likely to deteriorate further and financial performance will continue to worsen. In retailing and some other industries, this issue is often addressed when troubled companies close a number of outlets and lay off all employees who worked in those stores or branches.

If the reason for layoffs is to reduce labor costs, then it seems clear that laying off highly paid employees will reduce cost most. Older employees with greater seniority are normally more highly paid than newer and younger employees. A utilitarian analysis would note that older employees may suffer a greater degree of pain, since they often have a more difficult time finding new jobs than younger employees. Where negotiated contracts between labor and management prevail, unions typically negotiate as part of the contract that any layoffs occurring during the contract period will be based on reverse seniority, with the newest workers being laid off first. Another factor to be considered in a utilitarian analysis is that employees who perform their jobs best provide the most good to the company. Following this approach, the poorest performers should be laid off. However, many companies do not document performance in a way that can serve as a ground for determining layoffs on merit. Others do not choose to follow such an approach, even if they are able to.

A utilitarian approach concludes that layoffs are sometimes ethical, but some circumstances involving the desire to change a company, this approach finds that layoffs are not ethical. This approach emphasizes a consideration of human as well as financial factors and a concern for balancing the unhappiness which such actions bring to some participants with the benefits that result to others. The utilitarian approach does not assume that the company's financial situation is paramount, but does consider that greater good may come to a larger number of people, and that the unhappiness resulting from layoffs, might be morally justified by an analysis of the whole situation. It further

considers that, if layoffs are to occur, the basis for deciding who will be laid off is also open to moral analysis.

Of the three approaches to ethical analysis used in this article, utilitarianism is the least abstract. Because major corporate decisions are so often based on impersonal analysis of financial considerations, the utilitarian approach adds an important perspective to those decisions.

Rights, Duties, and Layoffs

Much of philosophy deals with what it means to be human. There is general agreement that humans have a right to live, and that they have this right not because of their citizenship in one or another country, or because of their membership in a religion, or because of their occupation or position in life (Buckle, 1991). If humans have a right to live, then they have a duty not to randomly take each other's lives. In general, rights imply duties. This is obvious with a little thought. If I have a right to privacy, you have a duty not to invade my privacy. If I have a right to free speech, you have a duty not to silence me.

In addition to rights that people may have simply by reason of being human, other rights are conveyed to all or some citizens of a country. In the United States, citizens who are at least 18 and are not felons have a right to vote. Not all humans have this right, but citizens of some countries have it. Rights can also be granted to citizens of a state or province. Citizens can also have duties by virtue of their status as citizens. In time of war, it is generally agreed in many countries that citizens have a duty to perform military service, subject to considerations of age and physical conditions. This is not a mere theoretical duty; in time of war it may be a duty to die in combat.

A third group of rights consists of those a person may have by virtue of their positions in a company or agency. A supervisor may have the right to sign company checks for up to $5,000, while the chief financial officer may have the right to sign for up to $5 million. A police officer has the right to apprehend and jail a suspect, while ordinary citizens do not. These rights can be very powerful in practice. The central point is that a person has these rights not as a human or as a citizen, but by virtue of occupying a certain position.

It is important in conducting an ethical analysis to distinguish legal rights and duties from moral rights and duties. They often overlap: most people agree that random killing is both legally and morally wrong. However, they are not always identical. In the not-so-distant past, it was illegal to drive over 55 miles per hour in the U.S., but one could argue that it was not morally wrong. If legal and moral rights and duties are always identical, then a change in the legal speed limit results in a change in the moral rightness of driving at a certain speed. A further argument against identity of legal and moral rights and duties lies in the source of laws. In the U.S., federal laws that apply to all citizens are made by Congress. Many people are uneasy with the idea of Congress as their source of moral right and wrong.

The law in the U.S. as to whether an employer can terminate an employee at will (for any reason or no reason) varies from state to state (Halbert & Ingulli, 1997). Federal law prohibits termination for some reasons (age, gender, disability). In cases where a labor-management contract determines wages and conditions of work, grounds for termination are usually specific and limited. Whatever rights to a job an employee has under such agreements come from the employee's membership in a group covered by the negotiated contract. Applying a rights and duties approach to the ethical analysis of layoffs, it appears that the central question is whether an employee has a moral right to his or her job, and whether supervisors then have a corresponding moral duty not to determine that employee until he or she forfeits that right.

Upon reflection, it is clear that an employee does not have an absolute right to retain a job. An employee who shoots his boss or is caught embezzling large amounts of money does not have a right to keep a job. A more limited question involves the right of an employee to keep a job as long as he or she is performing it satisfactorily. It is difficult to see the basis of such a right. As indicated, some rights come from our status as humans. Philosophers have argued for right to life, and to rights to truth-telling and private property, but not for a right to keep a job. With some few exceptions, U.S. employees do not have legal rights (rights as a citizen) to keep their jobs as long as they perform well. Some countries do provide such rights; others provide less legal job protection than the U.S. The third source of rights is from status in an organization, but the general status of employee does not in and of itself seem to confer the right to keep a job. Additional light is shed on this issue by considering it under our third basis of analysis, namely that of fairness and justice, in the next section.

The moral analysis of layoffs in terms of rights and duties requires an emphasis on the individual. What a manager may or may not morally do is determined by examining the rights of the individual employee. If the manager has a duty to retain the employee the duty results from the employee's right. If the manager is free to determine whether the employee keeps or loses a job, and can morally make either decision, in terms of this analysis the manager has that freedom because the employee does not have a right which constrains the manager's freedom. This part of the

analysis, then, concludes that under a rights and duties approach, managers are not morally prohibited from conducting layoffs.

Managers have duties by virtue of their positions as manager. Top managers have a duty to act in the best interests of their company and its stakeholders; a wealth of literature on agency theory analyzes the manager's role as an agent for the owners or stockholders of a company (Eisenhardt, 1989). In the extreme case that characterizes our first category, where layoffs provide the only means to save the company, one could argue that top managers have a duty to do what is best for the company, and that in this case conducting layoffs is best. This approach leads to the conclusion that managers sometimes have a duty to conduct layoffs, and that failure to act on this duty would be unethical.

It is considerably less clear whether managers have a duty to conduct layoffs to improve or to change their company. Because such attempts in the past have often failed to improve performance (DeMeuse, Bergmann & Vanderheiden, 1997), it makes sense to ask whether managers have a duty to take steps that might fail. The discussion of rights and duties leads to the conclusion that managers have a right to conduct layoffs in these situations (since employees do not have an overriding right to keep their jobs); it is much harder to prove that they have a duty to do so. If they have a right to conduct layoffs to improve or change the company, then under this method of analysis, it would not be unethical to do so. Particularly in the case of layoffs to change the company, when performance is already good, it does not appear that a credible arguments can be made for a managerial duty to conduct lay-offs.

A related issue is whether an employee has a right to be treated fairly in terms of keeping a job or losing it, and what comprises such fair treatment. It is difficult to argue that an employee has no right to be treated fairly, but what constitutes fair treatment is where difficulty arises. Analysis of this issue leads to the third basic approach to determining the morality of decision.

Fairness, Justice, and Layoffs

Whether it is children complaining of their parents, baseball players complaining about an umpire's call, or employees complaining about their supervisors, disagreements about fairness and justice are commonplace. In everyday language, most people tend to equate fairness and justice, and conversely, unfairness and injustice. It seems like only a small step to say that a decision that is fair and just is also ethical or moral. As we did with rights and duties, we need to note specifically the relation between justice or fairness and the law. While they are often the same, it is possible to find examples of unjust laws and also to find examples of things not legally required that are still fair and just. In our analysis of the fairness and justice approach to ethics, then, we will not automatically assume that justice means legal justice.

A philosophical approach tries to remove the level of analysis from what an individual perceives to be fair and just, and to prescribe some rules and guidelines that can be applied across many situations. Many philosophers, beginning with Plato discuss justice as involving a sense of proportion. The just reward for a heroic deed is greater than for a minor, inconsequential action. The punishment for murder is greater than for petty theft. An unjust consequence (reward or punishment) is one that is out of proportion to the action that triggers it. Justice, in most philosophical analyses, also involves a sense of consistency. If certain actions are judged worthy of reward or punishment, each person who performs the action should, in justice, receive the same reward or punishment. This idea is sometimes expressed in the statement that those similarly situated should receive similar treatment (White, 1993: 79-129).

Perhaps the most frequently cited modern philosopher to discuss justice is John Rawls. His major work, *A Theory of Justice* (1971), analyzes justice not in terms of individual actions, but in terms of social systems. He suggests that one way to decide whether a social system is just is to ask what we would think of it if we were behind a veil of ignorance and did not know what our position was in that system. In other words, if we did not know whether we would be ruler or ruled, well-to-do or poor, talented or unskilled, would we judge the distribution of benefits and burdens, rewards and punishments, to be fair? Rawls, like philosophers, attempts to state analytic principles that can be used to judge particular cases and determine their fairness or justice.

Applying this analysis to the question of layoffs, it appears that a central question is that of the fairness to the laid-off employee. Since the employee has, by our earlier definition of the situation, performed well and done nothing to trigger termination, it does not appear that there is a proportion between the action (termination) and the preceding behavior (satisfactory performance). It also does not appear that the principle of consistency is followed, since some employees who have performed well lost their jobs, while others who have performed similarly remain employed.

An approach that is sometimes taken in the name of fairness is to lay off a certain percentage of employees "across the board." In practice, this means that each division or department or region must lay off some percentage of its employees. This does not solve the problem of fairness or consistency but merely shifts it to a lower level of decision-maker. Under this approach, the head of each unit must still decide which employees will keep their jobs and which will lose them. A disadvantage of this approach is that it disconnects layoff decisions from improving the company's performance, since it is rare that all units are equally overstaffed or equally important in their contribution to the company's overall performance.

Viewed from the perspective of the social system or the whole company, the discussion of fairness changes. In the extreme case, where failure to reduce labor costs by conducting layoffs results in the company's closing, all employees lose their jobs. If we were behind Rawls' veil of ignorance, we would certainly not choose this as a fair arrangement. Only a twisted kind of logic can defend everyone losing jobs as better than only some.

As the cause for layoffs deviates from the clearcut case where they represent the only way to avoid the company's closing, the argument from fairness when the system is viewed as a whole becomes weaker. Layoffs taken as a proactive step to forestall problems management foresees are less clearcut but still defensible. If layoffs are conducted to increase the profits of an already profitable firm, it is unlikely that a person behind Rawls' veil of ignorance would consider the system allowing this to be just.

Would it be fair and just if the employees laid off were those with the least seniority or those who, while performing adequately, did not perform as well as others who retain their jobs? From the point of view of the system, seniority or merit present arguably consistent bases for deciding who loses their job and who keeps it. We should note, however, that relative seniority is much easier to establish than relative merit in performance. From the point of view of the individual, although these approaches attain some consistency, the problem of lack of proportion remains.

Rawls would argue that we cannot lightly pass over the system point of view in analyzing moral fairness and justice. His argument here is similar to one used in another context by Ackoff (1981), who maintains that many management problems are better understood by thinking about the system of which the particular problem is a part (synthesis) rather than by breaking the problem into its constituent parts (analysis).

Grant for the sake of argument that we live in a less-than-perfect world where layoffs are necessary from time to time to preserve a company as a going concern. In this situation, if we were behind Rawls' veil of ignorance, would we approve of a system of layoffs based on either seniority or merit. In other words, is this a fair and just system?

Of the two approaches, merit would appear to be more defensible, since it ties the goal of layoffs (improved company performance) to the judgment of which individuals should suffer layoffs (those who contribute least to the company's performance). Seniority might be defensible if there is not sufficient evidence to use merit. The defense of seniority would lie in the fact that it is measurable and might be seen as a proxy for individual performance in the sense that employees with more experience will, in general, contribute more to the company's performance than those with less experience. Rawls would then ask whether we could conceive of a more fair system that was practical enough to work in the real world. If not, then by his analysis fairness and justice would be observed, and the layoff actions would be moral.

The fairness and justice approach requires an emphasis on more than just the individual, who is the center of the rights and duties approach. Questions of fairness and justice address issues of proportion and consistency, but within a narrower setting than that addressed by the utilitarian approach. Of the three methods for ethical analysis, then, utilitarianism takes the widest view, considering the greatest good of the greatest number, whoever and wherever they might be. A major criticism of this approach is that it neglects important individual concerns. The rights and duties approach, as we have noted, centers on the individual, and looks out from the individual's rights to those on whom these rights impose duties. The fairness and justice approach considers both the individual and the social system within which he or she operates. The major focus of this approach is limited to a company or agency or possibly a community.

Comments and Conclusion

We have applied the three basic theories commonly used in managerial ethics to analyze the issue of the morality of layoffs. The views of these three basic theories generally coincide. In the extreme case where layoffs are the only way to save a company, the utilitarian approach finds the decision to conduct layoffs to be moral, because the layoffs generate the greatest good for the greatest number. The rights and duties approach sees the action of layoffs in the same situation to be moral because employees do not have absolute rights to their jobs. However, this view also requires that layoffs be conducted in a fair and just manner, because employees do have a right to be treated fairly. Finally, the justice and fairness approach, does not find layoffs to be moral, because they lack proportionality between the individual's behavior (good performance) and the resulting action (termination of employment). However, when the focus is changed from fairness to each individual to fairness in the total system, layoffs are justified—at least when the alternative is that all employees lose their jobs. Since all the individuals involved are part of the system, a reasonable argument can be made that the system view is the more appropriate one to be used

here. Given that layoffs are to be conducted, this approach finds seniority or merit to be moral bases for determining who will lose jobs and who will keep them.

In the opposite extreme case, where layoffs are proposed in an attempt to change a company that is already performing well and does not appear to be in danger, none of the three approaches supports the conclusion that such layoffs are ethical. In this situation, the greatest good for the greatest number is not achieved. While employees do not have rights to their jobs, managers do not have a duty to conduct such layoffs. Finally, justice and fairness are not served.

What is a manager to do in the large middle ground where the three approaches to ethical analysis do not yield clear answers? First, it is useful to note that the three approaches use different bases for deciding what is a moral act. It is clear from the history of ethics and the disputes among thoughtful individuals, that ethics is not like mathematics. It does not yield indisputable conclusions (at least, not all the time). Managers bring to their decisions their own sense of right and wrong and their own set of priorities among the three systems outlined in this article. In the last analysis, ethics is at least as much about how to think as what to think.

Yet, managers must ultimately decide whether to conduct layoffs or not. If the decision is for layoffs, they must then decide how many employees, and which ones, are to lose their jobs. Thinking through the decision in the way outlined in this article shows that ethical implications are involved in the layoff decision. Analyzing the decision and its consequences from three different perspectives brings out considerations that might otherwise have been missed. Understanding the factors involved from different perspectives presents a fuller basis for making judgments. Finally the manager must choose, even when the analysis does not provide a clear right answer.

Decision making often involves ambiguity, and top managers are selected for their ability to make decisions under uncertainty. As the cause for layoffs shifts from saving the company to improving the company (correcting performance which is deteriorating) to changing the company (mergers, acquisitions, outsourcing), each of the three ethical analyses provides less and less support for layoffs. We have outlined basic approaches to determining whether an action or decision is moral. As the moral justification of layoffs becomes less clear, the concern that managers may be acting immorally increases. The strength of the argument for "last-ditch" layoffs (reduce staff or close) carries over to cases where a worsening situation will later lead to the worse-case scenario. The weakness of the argument for layoffs when company performance is excellent and there is no apparent danger on the horizon also carries over to cases that are not quite as positive.

Managers who find themselves faced with decisions in such gray areas can apply the analytic tools outlined here. They can then make their decision knowing that they have identified the right issues and applied well-established methods for analysis. Managers who do not make such decisions, yet must carry them out, can better understand the ethical issues involved. Sorrow because of the suffering caused by layoffs may be unavoidable and appropriate. Guilt because a manager feels he or she did something morally wrong can be addressed and perhaps eliminated by the thoughtful exercise of moral judgment.

REFERENCES

Ackoff, R. (1981). *Creating the Corporate Future,* New York: John Wiley and Sons.

Aristotle, *The Nichomachean Ethics,* J. Harper, translator, Baltimore, MD: Penguin Books, 1953.

Arneson D., Fleenor C., & Toh, R.S. (1997, January–February). The ethical dimensions of airline frequent flier program, *Business Horizons* 40:1, 47–56.

Bentham, J. *An Introduction to the Principles of Morals and Legislation* (London: 1823); J.H. Burns and H.L.A. Hart, Eds. (London: Athlone Press, 1970).

Buckle, S. (1991). Natural Law, in Peter Singer, Ed., *A Companion to Ethics,* Cambridge MA: Blackwell, 161–174.

Cascio, W. (1993). Downsizing: What do we know? What have we learned? *Academy of Management Executive,* 7(1). 95–104.

Childs, J., Jr., (1997, March). Lutheran perspectives on ethical business in an age of downsizing, *Business Ethics Quarterly* 7(2). 123–131.

DeGeorge, R., *Business Ethics,* Fourth Edition, (Englewoods Cliffs, NJ: Prentice-Hall, 1995).

DeMeuse, K., Bergmann, P., & Vanderheiden. (1997, June). Corporate downsizing: Separating myth from fact, *Journal of Management Inquiry* 6(2). 168–176.

Eisenhardt, K. (1989, January). Agency theory: An assessment and review, *Academy of Management Review* 14(1). 57–74.

Freeman, R.E. (1984). *Strategic Management; A Stakeholder Approach,* Marshfield MA: Pittman.

Freeman, R.E., & Gilbert, D.R. (1988). *Corporate strategy and the search for ethics,* Englewood Cliffs, NJ: PrenticeHall.

Halbert, T. & Ingulli, E. (1997). *Law and ethics in the business environment,* Second Edition, Minneapolis/St. Paul: West Publishing.

Kant, I. (1997). *Critique of Practical Reason,* translated by L.W. Beck. Indianapolis: Bobbs-Merrill.

Mabert, V. , & Schmenner, R. (1997, July–August). Assessing the roller coaster of down-sizing, *Business Horizons,* 49(4). 45–53.

McCann, D. (1997, March). Catholic social teaching in an era of downsizing: A resource for business ethics, *Business Ethics Quarterly,* 7(2). 57–70.

Mill, J.S., *Utilitarianism* (London: 1863); in M. Warnock, Ed., Mill: *Utilitarianism and Other Writings* (Glasgow: Collins, 1962).

Piper T., Gentile, M., & Parks, S. (1993). *Can ethics be taught?* Boston MA: Harvard Business School.

Plato, *The Collected Dialogues,* E. Hamilton and H. Cairns, Eds. (New York NY: Pantheon Books, 1961).

Prahalad, C.K., & Hamel, G. (1990, May–June). The core competence of the corporation, *Harvard Business Review.* 79–91.

Rawls, J. (1971). *A theory of justice,* Cambridge, MA: Harvard University Press.

Scheffler, S. (1988). (Ed.), *Consequentialism and its critics,* New York NY: Oxford University Press.

Valesquez, M., & Rostankowski, (1982). *Ethics: Theory and practice,* Englewood Cliffs, NJ: Prentice-Hall.

White, T., (1993). *Business ethics: A philosophical reader,* New York NY: Macmillan.

Williams, G., (1992). *Ethics in modern management,* New York, NY: Quorum Books.

Dr. Gilbert teaches strategy and management ethics in the MBA program and team-teaches law, regulation, and ethics; his research has been published in a number of journals.

ALTERNATIVES
To Downsizing

Trimming your workforce may seem like the only solution during an economic downturn, but creative options can make the difference.

BY MARLENE PITURRO

Is the sole purpose of business the creation of shareholder value, as articulated by Nobel Prize-winning economist Milton Friedman? Or is the intellectual capital created by employees a company's greatest resource? If you believe the latter, then it follows that layoffs separate the company from its most valuable asset.

Although many companies do consider their employees to be an important asset, corporate downsizing continues unabated. Layoffs reached a 10-year high of 677,795 in 1998 and totaled 438,257 for the first seven months of 1999, according to research by Challenger, Gray & Christmas Inc., an executive recruitment firm in Chicago. On the surface, this slimming down seems to make sense: Companies can rid themselves of the cumbersome bureaucracy that often bogs down decision making. Most importantly, staff cuts fall directly to the bottom line.

But does downsizing create value for a company? Some experts say that it destroys a company's intangible assets, such as the organizational memory that resides within its employees. Paul Davis, president of Scanlon Associates in Lansing, Michigan, a nonprofit organization that shares HR best practices among its 23 members, says, "Whoever retains organizational memory has a priceless asset. The people who know what makes an organization perform maximally are assets, not costs to be reduced."

John Challenger, CEO of Challenger, Gray & Christmas, agrees with that notion. "We are cutting the muscle as well as fat. To please Wall Street, shareholders drive companies to cut costs and get high returns," he says. In the financial sector, for example, his firm recorded

an unprecedented 21,660 job cuts across the United States this March alone—2,999 jobs every business day—without an improvement to the bottom line in most institutions.

Recognizing that downsizing doesn't necessarily add value to the business, some companies are starting to explore options that defy the Al "Chainsaw" Dunlap template of cutting the workforce, driving up the stock price and getting out. These strategies include retraining, rightsizing the workforce, temporary work and turning employees into entrepreneurs.

New Skill Sets

Surprisingly, downsizing hasn't significantly increased the national unemployment rate, which hovers at 4.5 percent. Several key factors help explain this paradoxical relationship: layoffs occur over time so the unemployment rate is attenuated; workers often have hefty severance packages and little incentive to look elsewhere immediately; and many laid-off workers are close enough to retirement to leave the workforce.

The decisions of near-retirees to forego new jobs may also be driven by the underlying assumption of many top managers that these downsizees do not have sharp enough skill sets to be reabsorbed into the economy. But some companies and community officials believe that these downsized workers can be "captured" and made employable by helping them upgrade their skills. The Minneapolis-St. Paul area, which had both record downsizings and unemployment in the past few years, established an Adult Training and Dislocated Worker Service

Lincoln Electric redeployed 54 factory workers as salespeople. THE RESULT: $10 million in first-year sales.

to do just that. John Harvanko, the agency's rapid response coordinator, has seen downsizings continue, but they are smaller because laid-off workers are being retrained.

Companies can take the same approach, according to David DeMarco, president of Rochester, New York-based Idea Connections. Through internal retraining, employees can acquire the skills needed in other jobs and areas of the company. "Instead of downsizing, the company should revisit a department's goals and evaluate its challenges. This often leads to effective results," he says.

Looking for alternatives to downsizing has been the policy at Lincoln Electric Holdings [www.lincolnelectric.com] since the Depression. As a result, there have been no layoffs at the Cleveland, Ohio, manufacturer of arc-welding products, even though the company has faced several economic downturns. In 1992, for instance, it suffered severe losses following an expansion into Europe, Asia, Russia and Latin America. The departments involved with the international operation were in trouble. "We redeployed people, turning 54 factory workers into salespeople who made $10 million in sales their first year. We called that our Leopard Program. We also used the slow time to upgrade our facilities," says Roy Morrow, director of corporate relations.

LINCOLN'S LESSONS

In more than 60 years without downsizing, Lincoln Electric has learned how to balance business peaks and valleys with its commitment to employees. Here are some insights for other companies:

- Avoid thinking of downsizing as a viable management strategy.
- By *right*sizing—meaning, don't overhire—you won't have to downsize.
- Set aside funds for growth and productivity.
- Introduce new products and services during a business downturn so that your company remains innovative.
- When customers demand a discount during bad times, partner with them to deliver services or products faster and cheaper. The goal is to deliver 10 percent to 20 percent in added value instead of giving a discount.

—M.P.

Lincoln pulled out of its 1992 tailspin, returning a bonus to all employees and top management that has averaged between 52 percent and 56 percent of salary for 65 straight years. "Our people are too valuable. The loss of one person costs us $100,000 to replace them. We don't do business that way," concludes Morrow.

Rhino Foods, a specialty dessert maker in Burlington, Vermont, also used an economic downturn as a catalyst to teach people new skills. In 1994, President Ted Castle considered cutting employees from the 60-person company when operational inefficiencies and a drop in orders occurred. However, Rhino's small size and high level of trust and camaraderie among employees generated another solution.

Approximately a dozen workers were outplaced to Rhino's biggest customer, Ben & Jerry's Ice Cream [www.benjerry.com] in Waterbury, Vermont. They learned new skills, gained a better understanding of their customer's needs and business practices, earned the same or higher pay, and kept their Rhino benefits and seniority. Rhino recalled these employees during the following two years as business conditions improved. Today, Rhino is going strong. It recently introduced new products and added to its workforce.

Prudent Pruning

Layoffs can send shock waves through a local economy when a company that downsizes is large or when several firms in the area opt to downsize at the same time. For example, Lima, Ohio, with a population of 48,000, was reeling in 1997 and 1998 from defense cutbacks that led to plant closings at Sundstrand and Airfoil Textron, and an 80 percent downsizing at Lima's General Dynamics plant. The final nail in the coffin was British Petroleum's decision to close its plant there and eliminate 470 jobs.

Fearing that its unemployment rate of 8.6 percent would skyrocket, Lima's local politicians turned to Allen County economic development officials for help. With the aid of the county and HR consultants, British Petroleum discerned that the skill sets of its Lima workforce fit with its needs for a BDO plant—which makes chemicals used in the manufacturing of spandex and automotive bumpers—even though the location for the new facility had not yet been set. This successful downsizing alternative led BP to retain all 470 jobs and created 800 new construction jobs in the community as well.

Sometimes the impact of downsizing in just one industry is felt throughout an entire community. Sacramento, California, a city of 375,000 people in 98 square miles, offers an example of how sophisticated people-sizing can work. In Sacramento, bank mergers and consolidations in the '80s and '90s affected hundreds of bankers, but many of them were absorbed by nonbank financial institutions, such as credit unions and mortgage lenders.

When banking rebounded, Sacramento banks found themselves short of experienced talent. As a result, HR departments now proactively avoid excessive downsizings by tying pay more closely to performance so that costs and profitability are aligned. Smaller base salaries, complemented with bonuses and stock options to reward stellar officers, control costs and retain valued employees. Helping to keep the hiring/firing ratio in balance is Mike Bergovich, downsized from banking three times and now prime mover of the Bankers Connection, an employment Web site [www.bankconnect.com] that links local job seekers with positions. Overall, the Sacramento banking community has developed a strategy to right-size its workforce for the long haul.

Looking at the aftermath of the global consolidation binge in banking, Joel Friedman, a worldwide managing partner of banking and financial markets at Andersen Consulting in New York City, thinks there is a better way. According to Friedman, who advises major banks on consolidating their operations, which often involves staff cuts. "One-third to one-half of the players would have seen better performance if they put their money in T-bills rather than into merger or consolidation."

The challenge is to get lean without getting anorexic, which means eliminating unnecessary, redundant, excessive or obsolete business processes that fail to provide sustained value, according to Roger Herman and Joyce Gioia, co-authors of *Lean & Meaningful* (Oakhill Press, 1998). To do so, companies should carefully analyze people and processes separately to make accurate decisions about trimming the workforce, say the authors.

Herman and Gioia cite the federal government's Office of Personnel Management and its elimination of

TRIMMING THE PAYROLL

The following approaches involve micromanagement, but they achieve the goal of cutting payroll costs without wholesale layoffs:

- Find volunteers who are interested in reduced hours, part-time work, job sharing, leaves of absence or sabbaticals to work in the community.
- Network with local employers concerning temporary or permanent redeployment.
- Use attrition effectively by examining whether a job needs to be filled or hiring someone with competitive skill sets.
- Use natural attrition to maximize fit between jobs and incumbents.
- Develop multistep, voluntary early retirement packages.

—*M.P.*

351,000 jobs and $137 billion as sophisticated downsizing. OPM reduced its workforce by 48 percent and its expenses by 33 percent during the mid-90s by brainstorming 30 cost-cutting options, which included job sharing, furloughs, voluntary reassignment, cross-training and an employee stock option plan. The program was so successful that 96 percent of the people who lost their jobs found new government positions.

One company that took steps to ensure the community would not suffer a setback from its relocation is EloTouch Systems [www.elotouch.com]. The manufacturer of computer monitors and other screens, a wholly owned subsidiary of Raychem Corp. since 1986, made an expensive against-the-grain decision to help its 300 employees find new jobs when plans were announced in 1996 to relocate from Oak Ridge, Tennessee to Freemont, California.

The company kept employees informed about the transition, beginning with the relocation announcement. A company newsletter, hotline, e-mail and face-to-face meetings were used to help employees get answers to their questions promptly and candidly. EloTouch also worked with local newspapers and radio and television stations to publicize the availability of its workforce and downplay the negative impact the plant relocation would have on the community.

EloTouch used a variety of venues to help its downsized employees find new jobs, including job fairs, networking with local companies, classes in career development and change management, and outplacement counseling. It also offered generous retention bonuses for those who agreed to relocate and severance pay to those left behind. Once in California, EloTouch bulked up to 500 employees and incurred the costs associated with new hires. Despite the costly move, it posted impressive gains after one year: a 30 percent increase in product volume, a 6.5 percent gain in productivity per employee, a 7.5 percent increase in customer satisfaction, and zero increase in the cost of workers' compensation.

Temps and Entrepreneurship

From a big picture perspective, another downsizing alternative is temporary personnel. Companies can use temps to fill a short-term need created by a specific initiative such as a merger or to test out whether a position needs to be filled permanently. In this way, companies can avoid taking on full-time workers where a need doesn't exist. According to the National Association of Temporary and Staffing Services in Alexandria, Virginia, 300,000 people signed up with temporary staffing firms last year. That brought daily temp employment last year to 2.9 million, a 10 percent increase from 1997.

Temping can even extend to skilled managers such as accountants, COOs, CIOs and the like, which grew eightfold from 1991 to 1998. John Tatum, founder of Tatum CFO Partners in Atlanta, Georgia, has enlisted 140 ex-CFOs in 18 months for interim assignments. "Since the average tenure of a CFO is only between 30 and 36 months anyway, short-term assignments are a logical next step." Tatum's temp CFOs go on a company's payroll as long as the engagement lasts, then they're gone. "Our people, nearly all of whom have been downsized, aren't interested in being traditional employees anymore," he says.

Another way to avoid layoffs is to help your employees become "entrepreneurs." When Bell Labs of Morristown, New Jersey, morphed into Lucent Technologies [www.lucent.com], it had a marketing contingent that was too large, but found an alternative to downsizing—spinning off a new business unit. In 1998, it helped several marketing teams create a new business stemming from the firm's rollout of complex voice messaging systems. The team had become so good at producing internal marketing materials that it started offering them as fee-paid services to clients, according to Lisa Bhattacharya, a Lucent spokesperson. By building on skill sets and the parent company's reputation, Lucent got people off the payroll and increased its visibility in the market.

HR in the Lead

Top managers faced with a possible downsizing should follow two guiding principles, according to Rick Maurer, president of consulting firm Maurer & Associates in Arlington, Virginia: One is to share the pain, which means that no one is exempt from devising money-saving strategies that will avoid layoffs. The second is for HR to be proactive. It must seek out options in retraining, job placement, career assessment and redeployments, revamped pay and benefits packages, and so forth. To ensure that every alternative is considered, Maurer says, "reach out to top managers who care about people, who have an investment in the corporate culture. They will be allies."

In fact, the HR department must play a critical role for any downsizing alternative to succeed. The staff needs to explore options with an eye toward developing personnel budgets based on outcomes rather than head-count. Two hot spots for HR to consider are the compensation system and career assessment programs.

For NOVA Chemicals Corp. [www.novachem.com] in Calgary, Canada, hard times hit its ethylene, chemical and energy products in 1993. In that year, the HR department started a job database, which included available internal and external positions, for a downsizing program available to 6,000 employees. The program continues today, and more than 1,000 employees have used the database to transition to new jobs. There are also

DOES DOWNSIZING WORK?

Downsizing may not improve the bottom line in the long run, according to a seven-year study of 46 "radical downsizers" (which had cut 28% of more of their workforce) and a control group of 45 companies:

	RADICAL DOWNSIZERS	COMPARISON GROUP
Sales growth per year	8.8%	25.9%
Cumulative earnings increase after three years	183.4%	422.5%

Source: U.S. Department of Labor's Office of the American Workforce, 1996

awards of up to $25,000 for employee startup ventures, contingent on the presentation of a business plan. For employees transitioning to careers in nonprofit organizations, the company provides help that includes 50 percent of salary and full medical and pension benefits for a trial period decided by the employee, NOVA and the nonprofit. If the employee chooses the nonprofit career, he or she gets a full severance package.

Similarly, the cornerstone of success at the Office of Personnel Management was a comprehensive federal career assessment center. It provided counseling, training, career resources and job-search help for all the downsized looking for new jobs within the federal system.

During consolidation the cost of failing to maintain a skills database is substantial. According to a 1998 Hay Group study of top executives and senior HR staff at 60 high-tech companies, 74 percent believed they didn't do a good job during the merger of placing the right people in the right jobs. Eighty-five percent admitted to not successfully communicating their company's goals and visions post-deal. The respondents also stated that career assessment tools could have helped during the transition.

HR can respond to changing market conditions and skill mixes by:

- Using strong career assessment tools.
- Building an employee skills database.
- Going to that database first for internal redeployments.
- Looking for cross-training opportunities for employees when some jobs are drying up but new ones are emerging.
- Reengineering career ladders in accordance with the skill database.

Aside from developing a career skills database, the HR department can also search for ways to improve a company's profitability. They include working with employees to develop cost-saving and risk-sharing strategies; creating new revenue centers or spin-offs of

EloTouch minimized the effects of its relocation by helping employees find new jobs.

operations for employees willing to share risk; and considering an employee buyout for an operation slated to close.

What's Next?

Despite the trend toward downsizing, Challenger sees the pendulum swinging back eventually. In the meantime, he advises companies to "make training and development core values and to redeploy downsized employees to other positions whenever possible."

Exploring alternatives to downsizing makes sense to managers who grasp the complex interplay among unemployment, layoffs and profitability. Downsizing has a ripple effect throughout a community, and in buoyant times of low unemployment, salvaging good people even if they have to be retrained is a decent value proposition.

Since all downsizing alternatives are grounded in a knowledge of each employee and his or her skills, a company must start with comprehensive employee assessment tools. A skills database that helps match people with business needs is the basis of effective redeployments. A tuned-in employer community—wider than just the downsizing firm—can retrain and reabsorb workers who have been downsized, thereby keeping downsizing to a minimum and addressing personnel shortages.

Marlene Piturro is a business journalist based in Hastings-on-Hudson, New York. She has traveled and written extensively for publications such as the "New York Times," "Worth," "Omni," "Profiles," "World Trade," "Latin Trade" and "Global." Consulting clients include Pricewaterhouse-Coopers, Deloitte & Touche, MBIA Insurance Corp. and Microsoft.

Blowing whistles, blowing smoke

In the halls of Congress and the columns of newspapers, all whistle-blowers are saints. But the truth is a little more complicated.

BY DAN SELIGMAN

WHISTLE-BLOWERS HAVE BEEN onstage a lot lately. A Nexis search yields 2,700 articles thus far in 1999 mentioning them. In the vast majority of these articles, it is assumed that the whistle-blower in question is a selfless protector of the public good. It is high time we examined this assumption.

One of these articles reported Al Pacino's embrace of a new script in which he plays a *60 Minutes* producer working with a tobacco industry whistle-blower. Nonfictional entries included the Microsoft internal auditor who spoke up and said the company's bookkeeping did not conform to Generally Accepted Accounting Principles. Also Predrag Markovic, said to have been fired for whistle-blowing on alleged corruption in the New York City School Construction Authority. Also assorted witnesses testifying against Columbia/HCA Healthcare for its suspected overbilling of the government in connection with Medicare reimbursements.

Perhaps the biggest media sensation of all was the saga of Jennifer Long, the IRS auditor who had earlier (September 1997) denounced what she characterized as the agency's brutality in Senate Finance Committee testimony and now (April 1999) appeared to be on the verge of getting vengefully fired for this exercise in whistle-blowing.

Whistle-blowers are ordinarily depicted as lone voices of reason, driven by idealism, courageously standing up to lawless bureaucracies, selflessly risking careers to get out the truth. This has long been the only view deemed socially acceptable in Washington. It was unmistakably on display a decade ago, when Congress passed the Whistle-Blowers Protection Act of 1989 without a single recorded nay.

This law encourages federal employees to step forward and point to fraud, waste and abuse in their agencies, and offers them considerable protection against retaliation. But that's only one highly generalized whistle-blower act. An avalanche of other federal laws on air pollution, consumer protection, occupational safety, safe drinking water, energy conservation, solid waste disposal—you name it—redundantly provide similar mixes of encouragement and protection to folks inside the agencies wishing to step up to the plate. And numerous state laws offer whistle-blower protection to both government and private sector idealists who believe their employers are doing something evil.

What's wrong with all these laws? Their failure to acknowledge the possibility that whistle-blowers are mere human beings like you and me, who go through life thinking deeply about what's best for number one. Also, the possibility that when you offer special job protection to whistle-blowers, then any human being needing job protection will suddenly have a huge incentive to blow a whistle if he can get his hands on one.

This is not to deny that some of the high-profile cases of recent months featured truly conscientious employees driven to step forward and point up outrages. The Energy Department employees who blew the whistle on the pillaging of military secrets by Chinese spies really do seem to have been performing a public service.

But some of the other cases are more nuanced. When you look at the facts more closely, you discover that the Microsoft internal auditor had been discharged for poor performance before getting into the whistle-blowing business, and the

School Construction Authority official blew the whistle only after losing his job. It is hard for outsiders to judge the merits of each case, but it seems reasonable—and unsurprising—to note that a high fraction of whistle-blowing is performed by folks with personal reasons to be sore at their bosses. I recently spoke with Jeffery Trinca, a lawyer now in private practice, who in 1997 was chief of staff of the national commission to restructure the IRS, and he observed: "You have to be careful about whistle-blower cases. An awful lot of the time, there's another agenda."

Then there is the case of Jennifer Long, the IRS whistle-blower. The story line pounded home by the media was that (1) she was being fired by the IRS for her prior revelations before the Finance Committee; (2) this action signified the total depravity of the IRS; and (3) Long kept her job only because Finance Committee Chairman William Roth of Delaware came riding to the rescue. My own take is that it is possible to (1) hate the IRS with a vengeance and also (2) admire tax-cutter Bill Roth, while (3) still sensing that there was a huge amount of baloney in the whistle-blower story he sold the press.

From the *New York Times* to Sam Donaldson on *20/20*, the mighty American media played it the same way. The heroine was a noble IRS agent who had received top performance reviews until she blew the whistle. She said the agency fabricated evidence against taxpayers and selectively targeted poor, uneducated folks with little ability to defend themselves. She was a profile in courage—she had appeared on camera during the proceedings,

> ### Take care with whistle-blowers: Even when they're right, they sometimes have an agenda of their own.

while other IRS whistle-blowers testified while seated behind screens and using voice-modification equipment that left them sounding like Bugs Bunny. Intoned the *Times:* "The fact that her employers had no inhibitions about harassing her is clear evidence that the laws protecting whistle-blowers need to be strengthened."

It was very hard this year to find any back talk to this party line on whistle-blowers. (One rare exception: a not-for-profit magazine called *Tax Notes,* published in Arlington, Va.) A more skeptical view might have pointed up some awkward details about the Finance Committee's presentation.

Contrary to endlessly reiterated statements in the press and on *20/20,* Jennifer Long had not received repeated rave reviews before her 1997 testimony. In fact, her work had been severely critiqued for several years, and she had reason to fear for her job. Her problems in 1996 are lengthily particularized in a race- and age-discrimination suit she brought against the IRS shortly after her testimony. Long, who is white, complained in the suit that she was

being victimized by some of her black bosses in the agency—details that have gone broadly unmentioned in this year's media frenzy and were also unmentioned in her 1997 testimony, where any such allegations would, to be sure, have sent the Finance Committee script orbiting in directions uncontrollable.

Her decision to appear on camera was not an act of courage, but of prudence. It was proposed by her attorney precisely because he felt the public identification would make it harder for the agency to fire her—a judgment that turns out to have been quite shrewd.

Would Long have been a whistle-blower if she hadn't received those repeated criticisms before the Finance Committee opportunity came along? Probably not. I asked her, in a recent telephone interview, whether she would have testified if the hearings had been held five years earlier, and she said no, adding: "I believed in the system then."

Big question: Were her allegations supported by the evidence? After her 1997 testimony, the IRS agreed to an examination of her charges, to be made by the Treasury Department's Office of the Inspector General. On a few issues, e.g., the tendency of the Houston office to favor managers over subordinates in disciplinary cases, the inspectors supported her views. But in most instances they found against her. After examining returns audited in Houston, they found no evidence that low-income taxpayers were being targeted, and no evidence of fabricating evidence against taxpayers.

It's a terrible thing to be defending the IRS, of all agencies. But I have to do that here.

Columbia/HCA Whistle-Blowers to Fight for Gold

Lawyers and Clients Maneuver As Settlement Talks Heat Up In Probe of Medicare Fraud

By Lucette Lagnado

Staff Reporter of The Wall Street Journal

Donald McLendon, a former health-care executive, is joining the ranks of the newly rich. He recently purchased a home on the grounds of a Florida country club and hired a decorator to outfit it with Italian marble, antiques and Oriental rugs. His wife has treated herself to a jaunty new convertible. Up next: a housekeeper.

Mr. McLendon is a whistle-blower in the federal government's six-year Medicare fraud probe of Columbia/HCA Healthcare Corp., the giant hospital chain based in Nashville, Tenn. In September, he received a $10 million windfall, his portion of the settlement the U.S. Justice Department reached with Olsten Corp., a Melville, N.Y., home health-care management firm and former Columbia/HCA business partner that the government also investigated for Medicare fraud.

Now, with settlement talks heating up in the government's massive investigation of Columbia, Mr. McLendon and his attorney could rake in millions of dollars more. Mr. McLendon's piece of a Columbia settlement could bring him upwards of $10 million to $20 million, his lawyer says.

According to people familiar with the talks, a resolution of at least some of the outstanding civil issues could come in as little as a few weeks, representing an initial settlement of several hundred million dollars.

Expectations of a settlement have been raised and dashed many times in the course of the investigation. "The feeling among many on Wall Street is they'll believe it when they see it," says A.J. Rice, an analyst who follows the company for Merrill Lynch & Co.

Still, with Columbia's ultimate payout expected to reach as much as $1 billion—the company already has given the Justice Department a letter of credit for that amount—participants are eagerly anticipating an end to the civil case.

"The dialogue has gotten hotter," says Marlan Wilbanks, Mr. McLendon's attorney. "The potential for settlement on key issues is very real."

"There's a quickening of the pace," agrees a high-level Justice Department official. But he cautions there's no deal until the parties "shake hands."

Mr. McLendon and his wife are mulling trips to Paris and the French Riviera, a golf holiday in the Scottish

Highlands, a second home. As a result of the legal fees he has received so far, Wilbanks also has had a lifestyle change: He recently bought land in Georgia with its own waterfall and is spending more time with his daughter and sick father.

Columbia is the target of the largest Medicare-fraud investigation in history. The probe, which surfaced publicly in 1997, has focused on allegedly improper and illegal practices the government alleges took place, including false billing for simple laboratory blood tests, financial rewards to physicians for admitting patients into Columbia hospitals and "upcoding," or charging the government for costlier care than what was provided. The alleged wrongdoing also involved how Columbia and Olsten financed the acquisition and expansion of home-health agencies, Mr. McLendon and his attorney said in interviews.

Columbia declines to comment on Mr. McLendon's allegations, according to Victor Campbell, a senior spokesman. It has steadfastly declined to comment on negotiations.

The government's inquiry has relied heavily on documents and

If you fail, 'you end up with no money, no savings and no career,'
one whistle-blower says.

testimony provided by 26 whistle-blowers including Mr. McLendon, now 47, who was vice president of client development and marketing at Olsten. After years of battling Columbia and cooperating with prosecutors, some of the witnesses and their lawyers are turning on each other and on the Justice Department, which will play a key role in dividing up the spoils.

Attorneys for some of the earliest whistle-blowers are at odds with those who surfaced more recently. Some attorneys are concerned that when the settlement comes down, the government will stiff them. "This could turn out to be like the O.K. Corral—people could start shooting at each other," says Mike Bothwell, an Atlanta attorney who represents two recent whistle-blowers whose suits are currently sealed.

Mr. Bothwell has been conducting an e-mail campaign to organize the attorneys for the Columbia whistle-blowers to form a united front in the postsettlement free-for-all. In one message, he warned of "a bloodbath in this litigation," referring to potential battles among the lawyers, their clients and the Justice Department.

Mr. Bothwell hopes to avoid what has happened in an unrelated case involving SmithKline Beecham PLC and its $325 million civil settlement of Medicare fraud charges. In that situation, roughly $42 million earmarked for whistle-blowers has been held up for the past 2½ years as the government has battled with attorneys over who gets what.

In the case of Columbia, the Justice Department says it will be fair. "We take pride in how well we work together" with the whistle-blowers, says Stuart Schiffer, deputy assistant attorney general in the civil division.

"A lot of money is paid out to relators," the legal term for whistle-blowers, he says. He says that of several hundred cases concluded so far, "in only a handful" were there issues regarding the relators' settlement share that needed to be resolved in the court system.

The wrestling over money is made possible by a 1986 amendment to the federal False Claims Act, which allows whistle-blowers to sue a federal contractor on behalf of the government and collect from 15% to 25% of what the government recoups.

Sometimes, whistle-blowers strike it rich: Earlier this year, in an unrelated Medicare fraud case, Evelyn Knoob, a mailroom supervisor turned whistle-blower, took on Health Care Services Corp. of Chicago, known as Blue Cross Blue Shield of Illinois, and received $29 million. In the Olsten inquiry settled over the summer, Mr. McLendon received 24% of the $41 million civil penalty Olsten agreed to pay in connection with the probe of false Medicare claims. In all, Olsten paid $61 million, including a $10 million criminal fine by a subsidiary.

Olsten declines to comment on Mr. McLendon's allegations. At the time of the settlement, a spokeswoman said the company was hoping to move forward and trying hard to put the past behind it.

Mr. McLendon's fateful relationship with Columbia began in 1996, when the hospital chain acquired many of Olsten's home-care agencies. As part of the deal, Olsten agreed to continue managing the agencies. Mr. McLendon's unit was deeply involved in the day-to-day activities.

Before becoming a government witness, Mr. McLendon says, he tried to alert colleagues about alleged wrongdoing he was witnessing, in which Medicare guidelines involving what could and couldn't be reimbursed were being stretched. According to his attorney, Mr. McLendon sent a memo to his colleagues at Olsten—which is sealed in court—in which he warned that a whistle-blower would emerge if the alleged practices didn't stop.

Mr. McLendon filed his suit in 1997, and the Justice Department joined it in July 1999. His decision to become a whistle-blower wasn't entirely altruistic, his lawyer concedes. "He became scared that he was really exposed," Wilbanks says. "He had clear knowledge of the frauds—and he thought it was so flagrant." If he hadn't turned into a witness, "he would have been caught in the web." Mr. McLendon also was motivated to act from a sense of right and wrong, he says.

The attorney maintains his client didn't personally take part in the fraud, although he did "supervise people" who were being asked to take actions he thought skirted the law. Mr. McLendon maintains the companies overcharged Medicare by submitting claims for services that were ineligible and by inflating the cost of others.

Mr. McLendon says he turned over thousands of pages of internal documents to the government. Wearing a wire, he secretly tape-recorded conversations he had with some key Olsten and Columbia executives, including one discussion among Columbia managers in which one said, "It is an asset problem. . . . You want your asset, (your) ass, to sit in jail or not?" Mr. McLendon says the remark suggested Columbia executives knew they were violating the law. Columbia wouldn't comment on the alleged conversations.

Mr. McLendon says the asset statement came during an exchange about Medicare reimbursement Columbia and Olsten were receiving to pay the salaries of community educators, who were supposed to help seniors understand how to use home-health services, for example, to stay out of nursing homes. Columbia and Olsten, he says, were turning the community educators into full-time salesmen, dispatching them into doctors' offices to urge more referrals and billing Medicare for their services.

Mr. McLendon resigned from Olsten in late 1997 after letting the company know through his lawyer that he had become a whistle-blower. With that declaration, Mr. McLendon was protected by the law and couldn't be fired. The Federal Bureau of Investigation was set to mount raids on Columbia and Olsten, and Mr. McLendon had directed the agents to pick up specific documents, even indicating the file drawers where they could be found.

Mr. McLendon sold his house, quit his job and moved his wife and children to a cheaper, rented home in Orlando. Zachary, a son with Down syndrome who is now seven, had to stop private speech lessons and other therapy, and the couple pulled a daughter out of private preschool. They stopped going out for dinner and movies.

Mr. McLendon spent the next two years cooperating with the government for no pay. "You risk almost everything, and if you fail, you could end up with no money, no savings and no career," he says.

It was an eerie life, says his wife, Elizabeth. By day, she says, her husband was "James Bond"—by night, an unremarkable, and unemployed, family man. Then, over the summer, the government announced a settlement with Olsten, and their life changed.

Mr. McLendon says he tries not to dream about additional bounty that may come his way when and if Columbia settles. "There are a lot of people eyeballing that money." He says.

Leaders as Value Shapers

Leading through vivid, living, personal example is still the best, perhaps the only, way to lead. There is power in personal example.

KEVIN FREIBERG

GREAT LEADERS UNDERSTAND that their capacities to shape values and educate through vivid, living, personal example ultimately directs the course of a firm. The way people think about customers and coworkers, the way they behave, and their impressions of right and wrong are all influenced by watching their leaders live out their values.

Every firm builds its reputation on a set of values. The question is whether the values driving the business have been haphazardly acquired or purposefully instilled, protected, and promoted. This is why leaders must embrace their role as value shapers.

Values are the emotional rules that govern people's attitudes and behaviors. They establish boundaries that influence how an organization fulfills its mission. Values are deep-seated beliefs we have about the world and how it operates. They influence outcomes and ultimately determine quality. Values provide a framework for making choices and decisions. Values are the non-negotiables, the principles for which we stand.

I see two types of values—espoused values and the values people practice. When there is alignment, leaders operate out of personal integrity—doing what they say they're going to do.

Where there is a disconnect between our espoused values and the values we practice, we find hypocrisy. Professing a belief, philosophy, or standard to which you don't hold yourself accountable is an act of pretension and insincerity. Leaders who operate out of hypocrisy breed compliance because they lack influence and must lean on positional power.

Leadership functions on the basis of trust and credibility. That's why leaders must close the gap between their espoused values and the values they practice. Leaders who live their values inspire tremendous commitment and loyalty in others. As a result, they expand their influence and their ability to affect change.

Being Faithful to Our Values

When customers, suppliers, shareholders, and employees evaluate whether or not we are faithful to the values we profess, they use the following criteria.

1. How you spend your time. If you want to know what an executive values watch the way he or she allocates time. We spend time on those things that are most important to us. On the busiest days of the airline industry,

you'll find Herb Kelleher, Southwest Airlines' indefatigable chairman and CEO, loading bags on the tarmac, working the galleys with the flight attendants, or helping mechanics in the maintenance hangar. The way he spends his time says, "We don't hide behind titles and job descriptions; we do whatever it takes to help each other out and serve the customer."

Make a list of the top five values driving your organization. Then look at your calendar and analyze the way you allocate your time. What does your schedule say to others about what you value?

2. How you spend your money. Take out your checkbook and audit your expenditures. Examine the last

 From *Executive Excellence*, November 1998, pp. 7-8. © 1998 by Executive Excellence Publishing. Reprinted by permission.

budget you prepared. Is it consistent with what you value? The way we spend money says a lot about our priorities. If you say people are your most important assets, is that reflected in your compensation structures and your policies?

3. Your reaction to critical incidents. Whether it is a customer complaint or commendation, how you handle the event sends a message. When a customer asks your team to go beyond the call of duty, how do you respond? When your people do something heroic, do you celebrate and publicize their actions?

At Southwest Airlines, they celebrate the courage and competence of individuals who rise to the occasion and protect the lives of the company's valued customers.

Critical incidents do not have to be monumental in nature. When Mike Snyder, CEO of Red Robin International, picks up a candy wrapper outside of one of his restaurants, he sends a message to his people that the details count.

4. What you reward and punish. Do your rewards specifically reinforce the values that are driving your business? Do your incentives promote internal competition or cooperation? When one of your people takes an intelligent risk with the intent to benefit the company and fails, do you reward or punish their effort? When someone who reports to you gives you constructive feedback, how do you respond? At Southwest Airlines, people are given awards for fun and humor, sensational service, telling it like it is, creativity, and risk-taking.

5. Questions you ask. Do the questions you ask demonstrate your concern for your employees? Do your questions encourage people to focus on the customer or on the numbers?

The questions you ask and answer reveal a lot about what you value. When asked about the money spent on reward and recognition Herb Kelleher said, "I could cut our budget substantially by cutting recognition events, but that would be like cutting out our heart."

6. Things you measure. If you believe your people are your major point of differentiation, are you as rigorous about measuring their satisfaction as you are about measuring their productivity or financial results? If you believe that part of leadership is serving your internal customers, do you give those customers a chance to evaluate the quality of the services you provide? Do your team leaders go through a 360-degree feedback process, and are the results tied to their compensation structure?

As leaders we also need to remember that *our walk talks.* Everything we do and everything we choose not to do says something about what we value.

The Power of a Strong Value System

Southwest Airlines, Disney, General Electric, Federal Express, Johnson & Johnson, TDI Industries, HewlettPackard, and Merck all rank among the most admired companies in the world. They find enormous strength in their core values because strong values:

1. Build trust and confidence. In organizations where a strong set of shared values exists, leaders have more confidence to let go of power and authority.

2. Foster accountability. A strong value system creates boundaries. When the boundaries are clear, employees have more freedom and authority to act. People willingly assume responsibility and accountability when you reduce the uncertainty that comes with ill-defined boundaries.

3. Establish a unified front. Strong values concentrate the efforts of a team. When people are drawn together by a common set of beliefs, the values holding them together suddenly become more important than the agenda or special interests of any one individual. The result is a spirit of cohesiveness that captures the diversity of gifts and talents people bring to the team.

4. Provide guidance in times of crisis. In a chaotic world where people feel pressured to compromise ethics and cut corners to get results or cover up mistakes, strong values serve as a moral compass. Where there are no easy answers to difficult challenges, a strong value system can help determine the rightness of your direction.

5. Create competitive advantage. People want to do business with leaders who have similar values. Customers want to do business with organizations they can count on. There is a strong sense of sincerity and authenticity in firms with clearly defined values. These companies are less likely to project a false image and make promises that they can't keep.

People who are not clear about those guiding principles for which they stand can never expect to lay a foundation for trust and credibility, let alone develop the capacity to exercise leadership. Great leaders understand that every moment of every day is a symbolic opportunity to communicate their values. They do not underestimate the power of personal example. Through their daily choices leaders carve out the character and reputation of the organization. And they provide the standard by which others calibrate their own behaviors.

Kevin Freiberg is a professional speaker and co-author of Nuts! Southwest Airlines' Personal Success, *619-624-9691.*

Motivating moral corporate behavior

Geoffrey P. Lantos

Professor of Business Administration and Marketing Area Co-ordinator, Stonehill College, North Easton, Massachusetts, USA

Keywords *Codes of practice, Corporate policy, Ethics, Marketing philosophy, Moral responsibility*

Abstract *Although companies are institutionalizing ethics, ethical infractions continue unceasingly, causing questions as to where ethical emphasis is going awry. Suggests that businesspeople need not only the intellect but also the will to do the right thing in the face of temptations. Proposes several reasons why businesspeople should want to take the moral high road, including the fact that usually ethical behavior proves to be profitable in the long run. However, such a pragmatic consideration is not sufficient to motivate a person of ethical character. The ethical person chooses the moral course of action regardless of personal sacrifice. It is such virtuous people that business leaders should be hiring and cultivating in ethical mentoring and training which instills an absolutist (not relativist) philosophy and reinforces the importance of willpower. Uses an advertising case study to illustrate how common ethical fallacies can be uncovered and dispelled among employees.*

Companies institutionalizing ethics

Introduction to the problem

Historically, few people appreciated the pervasiveness of moral dilemmas in business decisions, and few business people were adequately trained to balance their business interests with the underlying moral issues, to avoid the fallacy of putting profits above principles. Yet, a key idea from the 1980s business bestseller *In Search of Excellence* (Peters and Waterman, 1982) was that organizational excellence must be evaluated not only from an economic perspective but also from a moral viewpoint. Discussions of ethics in business have now been big business for over a dozen years. Today we are having the most lively ethics discussions since ancient Greece more than 2,300 years ago, when philosophers such as Plato and Aristotle tackled questions of right and wrong. Companies are institutionalizing ethics through formal structures such as codes of conduct; reporting mechanisms like ethics compliance officers, hot lines, and whistle blowing; organizational structures like ethics and

social responsibility committees, ethics advisory councils, and judicial boards; and control devices such as social and ethics audits and performance evaluations which contain ethical criteria.

Moreover, ethics training programs are popping up across the corporate landscape. Typically led by either internal ethics directors/officers or outside ethics consultants, they are designed for upper and middle management as well as (less frequently) lower-level employees. Using means to generate discussion such as hypothetical or real case studies, videos, and role playing, their objectives are to instill ethical awareness, uncover and investigate ethical issues, discuss criteria for ethical decision making, and encourage "cognitive moral development". At a minimum, ethics training can help already ethical people to better face the moral dilemmas that arise in the business world, since it assures they have already put some thought into how they would handle these challenging situations in advance rather than on the spot, where it is too easy to give in to temptation, allowing reason to be overridden by passion. It is well-known that many people become involved in white-collar crime not out of greed or malevolence but rather out of weakness; they drift or stumble over the ethical line in the sand rather than crossing over it purposively.

Business pages like crime sheets

The skeptics continue to question whether all this consciousness-raising activity is reducing the rate of ethical infractions in the marketplace. Along with Plato, they ask: "Can virtue be taught?". Business executives continue to be one of the lowest ranked professional categories according to Gallup polls. The empirical evidence is not encouraging as the business pages continue to read like crime sheets. Sensational headlines have been generated by major organizations like Columbia/HCA Healthcare Corporation. Sears, Roebuck & Company, Archer Daniel Midland, and Cendant. There are a lot of people who passed through ethics programs now rotting in prisons.

Cynicism also prevails owing to the "business is war" mentality. This philosophy is held by basically "good guys" who are moral in their personal lives but are convinced that business is a game, sport, or even war, governed by its own rules of fairness, and therefore must be played outside the realm of individual morality and societal mores ("All's fair in love and war!"). Too many businesspeople believe that to be victorious on the business battlefield you must leave your personal morals at the business door

From *Journal of Consumer Marketing*, Vol. 16, No. 3, 1999, pp. 222-233. © 1999 MCB University Press Limited. Reprinted by permission.

when you check in each morning. We hear such pragmatic maxims as: "It's survival of the fittest", "Might makes rich", "It's dog eat dog, and the dog that snaps fastest gets the bone", "Do whatever you have to do to get the job done", and (my personal favorite), "Go ahead and do it, just don't get caught/don't tell me about it".

However, this thinking sets up a false dichotomy between one's business life and personal life. You cannot neatly partition your life into work and personal, or business and pleasure. These two spheres do at times overlap, and what a person does in "company time" often spills over into their private life. The term "business ethics" suggests a different (lower) set of standards should be applied in the business domain as in other realms since we still have human beings causing potential harms to other human beings. Being a businessperson is not a license to do things you are not permitted to do as an everyday person.

Business leaders must impart value of values

The bottom line, so to speak, is that business leaders must impart the value of values, converting the moral agnostics and unbelievers to a conviction of the worth of virtue in the marketplace. This requires more than just the head knowledge—it also necessitates heart knowledge. Aristotle said that virtue consists not merely in knowing what is right but in having the will to do what is right, i.e., the power to carry out the mind's judgment into action. The apostle Paul lamented: "The good that I wish I do not do; but I practice the very evil I do not wish". Former Watergate conspirator and Prison Fellowship founder Chuck Colson has noted that: "Reason alone is no match for passion. The fundamental problem with learning how to reason through ethical solutions is that it doesn't give you a mechanism to override your natural tendency to do what is wrong." Knowledge of the good does not guarantee a commitment to the good. Even though some people know the ethical rules and how to make an ethical decision in theory, when the rubber meets the road they experience emotional highjackings.

Business people need not only the intellect but also the will to do the right thing. Short of religious regeneration, can the solution lie in on-the-job education? I say "yes" if business leaders succeed in creating a felt need for ethics in business. The $64,000 question for us to help our employees and co-workers answer is "Why should individual businesspeople want to be ethical?".

Understanding why business people should want to be ethical

Let us begin with the reasons for ethics in business that are easiest to object to through those which even the hard-nosed pragmatist finds difficult to dispute. First, we can appeal to a sense of altruism, the love of one's fellow humans that leads to de-emphasis on one's self-interest and focuses instead on the interests of others. Altruistic acts lead to that "warm glow" and sense of moral satisfaction that comes from helping (or, at least, not harming) others. Moral philosophers down through the ages have accentuated "constrained self-interest", which is bound by what is perceived as right, proper, moral, or appropriate. The Judeo-Christian tradition sums it up in the maxims "Love they neighbor as thyself" and "It is more blessed to give than to receive". Altruists believe that happiness is a condition of the soul that comes from self-denial by giving oneself to others and by constantly doing what is right. In fact, the marketing concept suggests that to succeed financially in business one must first serve the customers; the economic and ethical *raison d'être* for a business enterprise is to honestly serve others.

Ethical for the sake of society

But what of the misanthropes who are only concerned with self? Ethical mentors can explain to them that we should be ethical for the sake of society. Unethical business practices lead to societal costs which are borne in part by everyone who wishes to survive and thrive in that society. Deceptive practices increase transactions costs, which in turn raise business costs, thereby reducing corporate profits and/or increasing consumer prices (and we are all consumers). For instance, many service providers "forget" to report cash payments to the IRS, thereby increasing everyone's taxes to make up the shortfall. A moral system is mandatory for an orderly society and earning the public's trust. Deceptive marketing practices reduce consumer confidence in the marketing system. When the business system collapses in the absence of morals, we end up in a Hobbesian "war of all against all". Commenting on Americans' ethical standards in the nineteenth century. French historian and politician Alexis de Tocqueville declared that the nation had become great because it was good.

Also, it can be argued that morally upright behavior can help fend off government regulation, something which the sane businessperson seeks to minimize in most instances, preferring the "invisible hand" of the free marketplace to the heavy, visible hand of government intervention in that market. Excessive government regulations increase compliance costs (bureaucratic red tape, increased business taxes, higher prices and consequent lower profits). A heavy-handed, paternalistic government guardian restricts the US ideal of freedom, which can prevail only if most citizens believe that economic and social justice prevail, not to the extent that society is layered with rules and regulations. Ben Franklin said it best: "Only a virtuous people are capable of freedom". Over-zealous government regulatory agencies breathing down our backs, such as the Environmental Protection Agency and OSHA, are monsters of our own making. Our democratic way of life depends on the willingness of individuals to behave according to high ethical and moral standards. Government cannot decree goodness.

However, some might think that one person (themselves) acting unethically alone cannot "make a difference". They might be better convinced by a reminder that we should act ethically for the sake of our conscience, that still, small voice inside our heads that creates a sense of sin leading to shame and following the commission of immoral acts. We should be able to pass the "sleep test"; it is unpleasant to lose sleep at night over abandoning loyalty to one's own principles. We should want to feel good about ourselves, as should our families and friends. As they say, "Virtue is its own reward", and doing right will soothe our conscience.

Fear of God

While this point will appeal to those with decent moral character, unfortunately some people's conscience is seared—for them the only definition of "value" worthy of consideration is the economic worth of commercial products. How do we appeal to the moral eunuchs with *mammon über alles* tattooed on their shriveled hearts? A fourth line of argument is to strike the fear of God into those hearts. Workers need to be reminded of those long-forgotten Sunday school lessons that say we are ultimately personally responsible to a God who will on Judgment Day hold us accountable for how we lived our lives ("payday someday").

A well-known Bible verse poses an important question: "What good is it for a man to gain the whole world (a top career and fat salary) and yet lose or forfeit his very soul?" (That is the *real* bottom line.) The Old Testament *Book of Deuteronomy* proclaims: "For the Lord your God detests anyone who does these things, anyone who deals dishonestly". Ask your co-workers whether worldly wealth and power are worth having God abhor you.

Nonetheless, some will be willing to make that trade-off, either because they do not take

God seriously or because they do not believe in God. For these individuals, the only appeal left that might work is Adam Smith's enlightened self-interest, a pragmatic, temporal reason to take the high road. Contrary to clichés, nice guys finish first in the business race: there is a "return on integrity".

"Good ethics is good business"

Why is this? First, ethical behavior tends to be profitable in the long run. One of King Solomon's biblical proverbs declares that: "Treasures of wickedness disappear but not before they lead you into the jaws of death". Experience, anecdotal evidence, and empirical documentation reveal that "good ethics is good business", "honesty is the best policy", and "you can make money while maintaining your principles". Doing good and doing well are not mutually exclusive but rather are complementary; doing good can be good for you and your business; you can make more money while maintaining your principles. Biblical proverbs say; "Ill-gotten gains do not profit" and "Treasures of wickedness profit nothing". A modern maxim declares that "Crime doesn't pay".

The reason is simply that market forces provide financial incentives for ethical behavior. In the long run, owning to the tendency for the free enterprise system to self-regulate, the businessperson who eyeballs only the bottom line regardless of morals, while perhaps prospering in the short run, harms the firm in the long run by tarnishing the image of the business world, his industry, his profession, and his organization (e.g., negative publicity from consumer boycotts, class action lawsuits, etc.). For instance, it is well-known in marketing circles that satisfaction is a function of fulfilled expectations and desires. Dishonest advertising which exaggerates the product's performance will raise expectations to unrealistically high levels which cannot be fulfilled, resulting in dissatisfaction and the ills which follow (no repeat patronage, negative word of mouth, complaints to government agencies, etc.). Thus, in pursuing today's profits immorally, we might be sacrificing tomorrow's business success. Recall that the marketing concept views customer-sensitivity as a means to the ends of enhanced financial performance.

Long-term gain

While being socially responsible and ethical often entails short-run pain, it usually ultimately results in long-term gain. A promotional mailing from *Business Ethics* magazine points out some examples: 75 percent of customers would switch brands to be associated with a good cause, 80 percent of the time low-polluting companies are better financially performers than high-polluting ones, and the socially screened Domini Index has outperformed the S&P for the past five years. Managerial decisions might not always be optimal, but they should always be ethical. The success of any business rests heavily on its reputation, and the cream usually rises to the top with the truth emerging. As the adages suggest: "The chickens come home to roost", and "What goes around comes around". The idea that the good you do comes back to you is suggested by the marketing concept and is written in the Bible: "As ye sow, so shall ye reap". The same social and spiritual laws apply whether we are in the walls of business or the halls of a house of worship. Simply, moral behavioral builds trust, which attracts customers, employees, suppliers, and distributors, not to mention earning the public's goodwill. Conversely, immoral behavior chases these various groups away.

Second, enlightened managers realize that unethical actions can result in punishment, which can be monetarily costly in the form of fines and litigation, reputationally costly in the form of bad publicity for the organization, and personally costly in the form of imprisonment.

Personal reputation at stake

Third, self-interested businesspeople should understand that their personal reputation is at stake. Shame from being caught in an unethical act leads to a decline in one's human dignity. Nobody wants a reputation as a sleaze. One of King Solomon's biblical proverbs warns: "If you must choose between a good reputation and great wealth, choose a good reputation". Workers must be admonished to take their reputation seriously. It will follow them wherever they go, in both their business and their personal lives, so they must nourish it as their most valuable asset.

Needed: people of good character

However, if the selfish motive of prospering via moral behavior is the only driver of ethical actions, that person is acting wisely and prudentially but not morally since the motives are not pure. What really matters is a person's character. Since President Clinton's capers were publicly exposed the mantra we have repeatedly heard has been "character counts". Character is a person's inner constitution that causes that person to be able to distinguish between right and wrong and then have the will to choose the right thing despite the possibility of personal sacrifice. The ancient Greeks understood the classic virtues of a person of good character to be fortitude (the courage to persevere in the face of adversity), temperance (self-restraint in the face of temptation), prudence (practical wisdom and the ability to make wise choices), and justice (fairness, honesty, and lawfulness in society). Western tradition added to these virtues such as patience, sympathy, benevolence, generosity, self-discipline, selflessness, and others. To these, St Paul, in a letter to the Galatians, added the character traits of faith, hope, love, peace, and kindness.

A *Communications Briefings* newsletter reports that a survey of more than 15,000 people reveals that the top trait found in effective leaders was believed to be honesty (87 percent), followed by forward-looking (71 percent), inspirational (8 percent), and being competent (58 percent). Honest, credible leaders kept promises, followed through on commitments, believed in the inherent self-worth of others, admitted their mistakes, and created a climate for learning by trust and openness. In short, they were people of character.

Managerial recommendations

So what action steps can business leaders take? First, ethical character needs to be, and reportedly is increasingly being, used as a hiring criterion. Executives need to probe candidates for important characteristics like self-discipline, openness, and other virtues by posing hypothetical dilemmas to potential employees. In these, the moral employee will ask: "What is the best for others?" (the company, customers, suppliers, etc.), not "What is best for me?".

Lead by example

Second, executives should mentor peers and subordinates by their own words and (most important) deeds. They should lead by example, not just "talking the talk" but "walking the walk". One of the most important influences on an individual and for creating a moral corporate culture is the behavior of superiors and peers. Business leaders' example serves as a model and a message-sender to all employees. Also, written policy statements on social responsibility and the moral dimensions of the business need to be drafted and enforced. Periodic meetings of management to discuss the implementation of these and to revise them where necessary should be held.

Third, business leaders need to cultivate ethical sensitivity. Ethical sensitivity is a personal characteristic, which enables people to recognize the presence of an ethical issue and its importance. To raise employees' ethical sensitivity, periodic ethics training exercises can be undertaken. These are premised on the idea that some people are unaware that some of their decisions have an ethical content and that they might behave differently if that ethical makeup were made known to them.

Ethical reasoning fallacies

The literature is rich in business ethics case studies, which can be used in ethical training. These need not be long and involved. To illustrate their use and to point out some common ethical reasoning fallacies that by and large stem from a relativist worldview, the following example is a short case I wrote for my advertising management course. By probing employees and potential employees for what they view as the ethical issues (situations that require a person to choose among several actions that must be evaluated as right or wrong) you can discover if they commit some of the most common fallacies in ethical reasoning:

Betty, who has been employed for three years as a copywriter for HK&M, a mid-size advertising agency specializing in consumer packaged goods, has been feverishly working for the past week on a new advertising campaign for Great State's wheat flakes, a regional breakfast cereal. The account has been with the agency for several years. Although Charlie, the brand manager on this cereal, has been pleased with the agency's work over the years, the old positioning, which stressed taste attributes and fun-filled family breakfasts, has become tired and dated. Marketing research shows a high degree of consumer wearout (people are tired of the campaign, even annoyed with it, and are ready for something fresh). Betty's task was to rejuvenate the brand via repositioning it to take advantage of and tie into the health trend, notably the interest in eating "good-for-you" food as well as in physical fitness. The brand was to be pitched as an important part of an active, healthy lifestyle.

Betty thought she had come up with the perfect theme line: "Great State's wheat flakes will give a great start to your active day", and she had developed what she believed were some clever scenarios for TV and print advertisements featuring the product being consumed after workouts in health clubs, following a morning jog, after a snowboarding expedition, and even while rollerblading. However, upon reviewing her proposals, Charlie said that while the vignettes were on target because targeted customers would relate well to them, the slogan was off base. He wanted something

more specific and hard-hitting, and so Charlie developed the theme line, "Great Wheat can't be beat. No other wheat flake offers you more vitamins and minerals and fewer calories". Betty tried to kindly tell Charlie that this was misleading because it implies that Great State's brand is healthier than most, if not all, of the others, whereas actually all wheat flake cereals are parity products—they are virtual photocopies of each other in terms of taste, texture, and, most important here, composition and therefore nutritional value. In fact, blind taste tests have shown that between 70 and 80 percent of consumers cannot identify their favorite brand of wheat flakes and that loyalty levels are low—with price incentives consumers will readily switch brands. Charlie, obviously irritated, explained that his tag line was an honest exaggeration, what the advertising trade termed "puffing", and that consumers are expected to see through it. He felt that it offered the point of difference needed to increase brand loyalty.

Claims for commodity brands

Betty, feeling uneasy, later that day approached her boss Steve, the copy chief at HK&M, asking his counsel. Steve explained that Charlie's suggested slogan is what is called an "implied superiority" claim. Steve explained that such claims are commonly made for commodity brands. They stake out a parity position, which does not claim to be superior to, but only as good as, other brands, while using copy that suggests or implies superiority for the named brand. He cited several current and classical examples, such as "nothing else cleans better", "the maximum fluoride protection in any toothpaste", "you can't beat the savings" and "you can't buy a more effective pain reliever". In effect, these brands are claiming that they are unsurpassed. However, none claims to be truly better. Betty, recalling several other such implied superiority claims she had recently seen, realized that it was, indeed, a popular technique.

Steve reminded Betty that there is a distinction between deceptive advertising, which creates false impressions and misleads a consumer acting reasonably, and "trade puffing", which is exaggerated praise of the product, viewed as acceptable in a society of the superlative. Consumers are assumed to see through the exaggeration or at least engage in a "willing suspension of disbelief". He explained to her that whereas deceptive advertising is illegal, the Federal Trade Commission (FTC), which monitors national advertising for accuracy and fairness in claims, views puffery as legitimate.

"What's more", Steve concluded somewhat sarcastically, "using your line or rea-

soning, Betty, we shouldn't advertise any parity products at all, since all brand advertising is designed to create a brand distinction in the buyer's mind. Advertising is necessary to differentiate yourself from the pack of imitators." Betty thought that, in fact, Steve's taunting comment might, indeed, have some merit, but she still felt uneasy.

Clearly, Betty faces an ethical dilemma regarding whether or not it is ethical for her to go ahead and run the potentially misleading comparison advertising suggested by the client, Charlie, and supported by Steve, the agency copy chief. Current employees and prospective employees can be asked to put themselves in Betty's shoes in order to take their ethical temperature and see if they succumb to some of the most commonly-committed ethical fallacies. Ethical issues (situations where there is possible violation of ethical standards which could lead to potential harms to others) to be raised include those involving the advertising claim as well as organizational issues.

Talking points

Here are some issues and suggested "talking points" to discuss on the morality of the proposed comparative advertising claim:

(1) Are implied superiority claims such as those examples in the case, even though literally true, misleading/deceptive, or are they merely honest exaggeration ("puffery"/"puffing") which consumers will see through?

Deception involves:

- materially false advertising (materially false, i.e. there is a claim-fact discrepancy—not the case here); or
- misleading advertising, whereby false subjective consumer impressions or perceptions are created—possibly the case here.

Consumer research could be used to determine where a significant number of buyers are fooled or whether they merely willingly suspend their disbelief. If consumers are fooled, the comparative claim is unethical since it misleads them; if people are willingly suspending their disbelief then no deception is involved and making a comparative claim does not violate any moral standard. Furthermore, if the claim provides useful information for informed decision making, it is morally justifiable. However, if it is used simply to bash the competitor with the intent to damage their image or reputation via derogatory statements, as seems to be the case here, then the advertising could be viewed as a malicious violation of fair play.

Correctness of action depends on situation

(2) Because implied superiority claims are commonly used (perhaps by Great State's competitors too) does that make them acceptable? A common fallacy is that because everyone (or at least many people) does something, that makes it morally acceptable. Relativists (also known as situation ethicists) would say that morality can be determined by what the majority believes or by what many others are doing. In general, relativists believe that the correctness of a particular action depends on the situation. Morals are relative to:

- the individual ("You must do what's right for you"; "What's right for you might not be right for me");
- the circumstances (e.g. a store can install TV cameras and one-way mirrors in dressing rooms to curtail shoplifting; theft is justified if you cannot earn enough money to support yourself); and
- the society's norms and values (e.g. if most people believe sexual intercourse outside of marriage by consenting adults is allright, then it is; if the majority find it acceptable to tell "little white lies", then so be it).

However, relativism has declined in acceptability among ethicists in recent years owing to the many problems it raises; it often means no consensus if people and societies clash in their ethical beliefs; it leads to uncertainty since right and wrong differ over time, place, and people; it is often morally impotent and corrupt as rationalizations and pragmatic considerations override morality (e.g. "It is all right as long as no one finds out and no one gets hurt", but what if someone does find out or get hurt?); and it is logically inconsistent to make pronouncements such as "All truth is relative" (an absolute statement) and "The only thing that is absolute is that nothing is absolute".

Ethical standards immutable

Absolutists, who hold to fixed standards of right and wrong, would say that ethical standards are immutable regardless of what is currently popular. Absolutists believe in definitive, objective, universal, unchanging standards which hold true over circumstances, time, place, and person. They contend that there are certain behaviors that are inherently right or wrong regardless of the individual or culture.

What is the source of absolute standards? Although we can look to those of world cultures that thrived for long periods of time, society makes its decisions in its own wisdom and for the welfare of its own members. These are still rules made by fallible humans; society might be right about drug abuse but wrong on abortion (or vice versa). The best source is the moral standards decreed by the great world religions. It goes back to the Greeks and Plato's saying that if there were no transcendent ideas, there could be no concord, justice, and harmony in society, which cannot survive without an ultimate source of authority. Cicero believed that there is no justice without God. There is, in 23 centuries of Western civilization, a belief in a transcendental value system. Every society which has abandoned its religious moral base for human reasoning has collapsed violently (e.g. the French Revolution). Absent a religious foundation, morality becomes a matter of personal or societal preference. Whether it was the unknown god of the Greeks, Yahweh of the Old Testament Jews, Jesus Christ of the New Testament, or even the enlightenment natural law (which, while in some cases denying divine will, nevertheless was compatible with it), while they might disagree on the exact nature of God and theological issues such as the requirements for salvation, these religions all agree on the virtuous elements of people of good character outlined above. People of character believe in the unbending adoption of these absolutes. The virtuous pagan, guided by restraints he alone has imposed, is a greater rarity than the yellow-bellied sapsucker. Dostoyevsky, in *The Brothers Karamazoy,* had one of the characters exclaim: "Ah, if there is no God, everything is permissible". George Washington, in his farewell address to Congress in 1796, said: "And let us with caution indulge the supposition that morality can be maintained without religion . . . reason and experience both forbid us to expect that national morality can prevail in the exclusion of religious principle". Even Nietzsche, who believed that morality is not a problem, predicted that it would become a problem when the people discovered that without religion there is no morality.

"Everybody is doing it"

But, I disgress. The main point for the case and ethics is that the "everybody is doing it" argument is morally indefensible. It remains one of mom asking the child who argues that what he is doing is OK because Billy is doing it, "If Billy jumped off the bridge, would you jump off the bridge?".

- Because puffing and implied superiority claims are legal does that make them proper? The legality argument is another common fallacy in ethical reasoning. Legality is not synonymous with ethicality, for civil laws, which are established by fallible humans, simply reflect a consensus of what society believes is morally right. Laws can be immoral (e.g. laws allowing capital punishment and abortion are currently controversial, and slavery as well as "separate but equal" facilities were once legal in the USA). Also, because they are limited to a particular time and place, laws can be inconsistent over time (e.g. legality of advertising various "sin products" on TV) and place (e.g. state laws often conflict, as do laws in the international arena). St. Thomas Aquinas said: "An evil law is no law". Montesquieu believed that: "We should never create by law what we can accomplish by morality". Generally, the law provides a moral minimum and is reactive, telling us what ought to not be done, rather than proactive, explaining what should be done in terms of virtuous behavior. Aquinas declared, "Human laws do not forbid all vices from which the virtuous abstain but only the most grievous vices from which it is possible for the majority to abstain and chiefly those which are to the hurt of others, without the prohibition of which human society could not be maintained". The low standard of the law was perhaps best recently illustrated by President Clinton's claim in his deposition about his relationship with Monica Lewinsky, that his answers were "legally accurate", although most people agree that his actions were morally wrong. Thus, although the FTC does allow puffery and implied superiority claims, this is not sufficient justification for their use by Great State.

Relativistic justification

- Does the fact that Wonderwipes is a small brand just starting out against a large, entrenched competitor justify making the suggested comparison? This too is a relativistic justification, in effect a rationalization. To make such ethical distinctions among players is discriminatory, and where do you draw the line on doling out ethical handicaps? Wrong behavior is wrong regardless of who or what you are.

- Does the possibility that competitors will respond to Wonderwipe's comparison advertising by improving their graphics, thereby benefiting consumers, justify making the suggested comparison? This is the worst kind of utilitarian thinking (a moral act results in the greatest good for the greatest number of people), in effect asserting that the ends justify the means. If society (consumers in this case) ends up with a net gain in satisfaction, then supposedly the act is justifiable. However, ends do not necessarily justify means; in effect, this says: "Let us do evil, that good may come". Using this logic, it would be OK to have prostitutes work out of church basements if the money was to be donated to the poor or for a student to cheat on an examination so as to get a good grade and hence land a decent job. Yet, some studies suggest that basically honest people under pressure to achieve bottom-line results, which are believed to be what is most important, commit most unethical acts in business.

There are also several organizational issues to be discussed:

- Does a client have the right to overrule the copywriter's ideas? Certainly—the client can even fire the advertising agency if dissatisfied. But exercising this right might not be the morally right thing to do.
- Is the copywriter obligated to accept the client's ideas, even when she/he disagrees or they are in conflict with her/his own values? While they might not have the power to override the ideas, they have the moral obligation to speak out if they feel the client is wrong. Every honorable individual has the obligation to speak out against wrongdoing, to say that such and such is wrong and should not be done. However, in practice, when the rubber meets the road, this is not always easy. Yet, one of the cardinal virtues is fortitude, having the courage of one's convictions, even at personal cost. In fact, it has been said: "A principle isn't a principle until it costs you something". Although it is much easier to "go along to get along", having integrity, while entailing sacrifice and struggle, makes life ultimately more joyful and peaceful.
- Is a copywriter obligated to abide by his/her superior's judgment? Organizationally, perhaps, but morally not if he/she feels that the judgment is not morally correct. Blind loyalty and going along just because the boss says so is to succumb to the plea of the Nuremberg war crimes trials defendants that "we were just following orders". As we have learned from the rule of despotic leaders such as Hitler and Stalin, when the authorities are wrong we should not obey them. If this is true at the government level, how much more so at the organizational level!

Psychological torment

People of character look for the creative way out when there is an ethical dilemma. They know that economic security is not worth the psychological torment that normally follows a wrong choice. Ask your employees or potential employees what they would do if they were Betty and genuinely felt that going along with the client's wishes would be wrong. Although quitting might be ethical, it might not be feasible, especially if Betty were helping to support a family. Better solutions for Betty could include:

- arguing more persuasively against using an implied superiority claim;
- explaining that it would be ineffective (a pragmatic argument) and/or immoral (which could be a hard sell but does demonstrate integrity);
- developing copy which focuses solely on the positive virtues of Wonderwipes and hoping this will please Charlie:
- ignoring Charlie and Steve and proceeding with her original slogan;
- developing a new slogan which is straightforward yet which might please both Charlie and Steve;
- suggesting that Charlie improve the quality of his product and then advertise this, benefiting him in the long run;
- suggesting running the proposed campaign but not directly naming the competitor (e.g. the "leading brand" approach); and
- asking to be allowed to resign working on the account since to continue to do so would conflict with her personal values.

Rule of thumb

Conclusion

Knowing what is ethical is not all that difficult. Simple rules of thumb can suffice in most situations: "Would I do it to my friends and family?", "Would I feel comfortable explaining my action to my friends and family?" and "When in doubt, don't". Doing what is ethical is another matter. One must have not only the knowledge but also the commitment to doing the right thing. Plato and Aristotle understood reason to be the master of passion. Unfortunately, there is a wide gap between knowing and doing in the moral realm. It is in our nature to flirt with compromising our principles. For instance, although people know that smoking and excessive drinking are harmful, some persist in this behavior; while we realize that consumption of junk food is unhealthy, we continue to indulge. A goal of philosophy was (and is) for reason to control passion so people can make right choices. When passion gets control, reason becomes its slave, and we rationalize our known wrongdoing, deluding ourselves in the process. An employee's ethical instruction has to focus on changing behavior. Knowing that a given action is wrong does not do any good if we lack the motivation to take an alternative course of action.

Where does such motivation come from? Personally, I would say that the greatest motivator is belief in and a personal relationship with God. Although Paul at times found himself practicing the evil he wished to shun, in his letter to the Romans he concluded that by calling on the Lord for strength, God could rescue him from his "body of death". A lot of ethical motivation is, I believe, an internal phenomenon, which is why it is important to consider ethical criteria when hiring people. But, nurture can supplement nature. I believe that instilling an understanding and fomenting an internalization of the above arguments for ethical behavior along with a resolve to set a good example by words and deeds, along with commitment to an absolutist philosophy of ethics, can be helpful. Such ethical tutelage will help in training not just the mind but also the will. Willpower is won't power.

Perhaps I am a bit idealistic, but if we work on this motivation in ourselves and in the employees that we carefully hire, perhaps tomorrow's business headlines will read less like a police blotter.

Reference

Peters, T. J. and Waterman, R. H. Jr (1982). *In Search of Excellence: Lessons from America's Best-run Companies*. Harper & Row, New York, NY.

CHEMICALS

3M'S BIG CLEANUP

Why it decided to pull the plug on its best-selling stain repellant

At first, Dr. Larry R. Zobel and other researchers at 3M Co. figured the findings had to be a mistake. Investigators from Cornell University, using a powerful new technique to scan the blood of 3M's factory workers, were testing some serum they bought from commercial blood banks to establish base lines for the machines. The highly sensitive devices kept turning up the same odd results: Tiny amounts of a chemical 3M had made for nearly 40 years were showing up in blood drawn from people living all across the country, even in places far from 3M factories. "It took months before all the chemists were convinced that it was there," recalls Zobel, 3M's medical director. "There was disbelief."

For 3M, the late 1997 test results were troubling. If they held up, it meant that virtually all Americans—and folks far beyond the U. S.—may be carrying some minuscule amount of a 3M chemical, called perfluorooctane sulfonate (PFOS), in their systems. How PFOS got there, whether it could pose a health risk and, more important, what should be done about it, were questions that 3M executives felt driven to ask. Although they have yet to come up with definitive answers—and they insist that there's no evidence of danger to humans—the Minnesota company's research led it to a drastic decision. On May 16, 3M decided to phase out PFOS and products containing related chemicals, first and foremost among them its ubiquitous Scotchgard fabric protector. Since there is no replacement chemical as yet, that means a potential loss of $500 million in annual sales,

---

THE PROBLEM WITH SCOTCHGARD

It contains POSF, an organic fluorine that repels water and oil. It can turn into a second fluorine, PFOS, when it gets into mammalian cells.

DANGER The chemicals persist in the environment for decades, and PFOS shows up in trace amounts in human blood.

EFFECT At very high daily doses, PFOS has killed monkeys and new born rats in lab tests.

---

out of total corporate revenues of $16 billion, and one-time restructuring charges of up to $200 million.

The news caused a rush to stockpile Scotchgard by the clean and the careless. Heloise, author of the syndicated "Hints from Heloise" housekeeping column, says everyone from clothes-conscious TV hosts to flight attendants have fretted to her about the loss of Scotchgard. Even she, an expert at stain-removal, admits: "When my husband gets a new tie I spray it on right away."

"**GUTS.**" Scotchgard's popularity makes its removal particularly noteworthy, given that 3M was under no mandate to act. "3M deserves great credit for identifying this problem and coming forward voluntarily," says Environmental Protection Agency Administrator Carol M. Browner. Even environmental activists like Linda E. Greer, senior scientist at the Washington-based Natural Resources Defense Council, gives plaudits to the company. "It took guts," she says,

even if they did it out of fear of governmental action. "The fact is that most companies, when faced with government nudging, go into anger, denial, and the rest of that stuff. What we are accustomed to seeing is decades-long arguments about whether a chemical is really toxic."

The long and tortuous trail that led 3M to its decision highlights the growing concern within the chemical industry over persistent chemicals, a relatively recent environmental worry. There are scores of these chemicals, woven into the very fabric of modern life, that resist natural processes of decay and can linger in the environment for decades. Some have already been banned—most prominently DDT, PCBS, and CFCS—but no one is quite certain what damage, if any, the rest might be causing. The EPA is pressing the chemical industry to reduce the manufacture of these substances, however, and is currently negotiating international conventions with Canada aimed at reducing their presence in the Great Lakes.

PFOS is not on environmentalists' list of the most worrisome persistent chemicals. But 3M, which is responsible for most of the world's supply of the substance, decided not to wait until all the scientific cards fell into place. It took its costly step based on scientific detective work that has built up incrementally over the past 30 years—and far more damningly in the past two years. Its choice threatens the jobs of some 1,500 3M workers in Alabama, Minnesota, even Belgium. It also discomfits scores of industrial customers, chiefly papermakers and textile mills, who apply the 3M chemicals to goods as far-ranging as pet-food bags, candy wrappers, and carpeting.

BLOOD TESTS. The first big twist in the tale took place in 1968, with a physician at the University of Rochester. Dr. Donald R. Taves was studying the effects of water fluoridation when he found tiny quantities of an unusual form of fluorine—a kind that didn't come from fluoridated water—in human blood. Just how it got there and what its presence meant were unclear. But scientists familiar with the organic fluorines, known as POSF, took note. The finding drew still more attention when Taves, working with colleagues at the University of Florida, confirmed the results in a 1976 study. Chillingly, Taves even found the fluorine in his own blood, though he lived far from any potential factory source.

Researchers at 3M, which says it is vigilant about chemical exposure of its workers, were paying particular attention. They quickly launched programs to test employees at plants in Cottage Grove (Minn.), Decatur (Ala.), and later Antwerp (Belgium), to see if fluorine exposures were high. While they found that fluorines were registering at higher levels in workers' blood than in the general population, the medical evidence suggested that they posed no problem. Researchers found no unusual ailments in the living workers and, after scanning death records, nothing unusual in the deaths of former workers. "Physicians who were seeing the employees generally found no significant health problems, no health problems that would be unexpected in a typical population like this," says Zobel.

For 3M veterans, the cheerful medical results were not surprising. Although unusually hardy, organic fluorines for decades were thought to be inert. PFOS, a 3M product used in fire-fighting foams and industrial acid-suppression products, is also produced in animals and humans when certain precursor chemicals get into the cells. These precursors are part of the chemical makeup of

Scotchgard fabric protector and are valued precisely for their hardiness. They repel water and oil like nothing else, making them potent stain-resisters. Instead, 3M has long revered the in-house scientists who developed the manmade chemicals, after a lab staffer in the early 1950s had spilled one of the chemicals on her sneaker, found it impossible to wash out with either water or solvents, and started investigating its repelling powers.

While routine employee monitoring continued throughout the 1980s, the company had little reason to worry. Even when blood tests grew more sophisticated in the early 1990s—and 3M could screen for specific fluorines such as PFOS or related chemicals—the lack of any damning health effects kept concerns to a minimum. Repeated medical reviews seemed to clear the chemicals of any problems.

Then, in 1997, powerful new detection techniques changed everything. The new tests turned up evidence of the chemicals in levels as low as 0.5 parts per million in human blood. "That is not much," says Zobel drily. "It's like 50 seconds in 32 years." It was by using the new techniques that the Cornell University lab, working for 3M, found the PFOS in blood from the scattered blood banks. 3M promptly launched an international testing program, screening blood from 18 U. S. blood banks along with samples from Europe and Asia. It even scanned old, stored blood samples from Korean War veterans. The result: tiny amounts of contamination in the U. S. and Europe, except in the veterans' blood, which predated the Scotchgard chemical.

3M regularly updated the EPA on all of its research. For their part, EPA officials were particularly concerned by the persistence of PFOS. It is so hardy that no one knows when, if ever, it will break down. Worse, it accumulates in human and animal tissues. "With things that are persistent, the only way for the concentrations to go is up—in our bod-

ies and in wildlife," says the Natural Resources Defense Council's Greer. "And pretty much every chemical in the world is toxic at some dose."

Because PFOS is both enduring and widespread, 3M made some crucial choices in mid-1998. Company executives decided they would—eventually—abandon such formulations and find replacements for the troublesome fluorines. "We began to realize then, and came to realize more later, that this would be a chemical that would constantly be involved in environmental debate," says Charles Reich, a chemist in charge of Scotchgard as the company's executive vice-president for specialty-material markets.

NO SURE THING. Still, 3M's top executives argued over just how long they could continue. Could they wait until replacements for the chemicals were found? That might take seven years or more, and was not a sure thing. And what about the effect on corporate customers, who valued the 3M products for their ability to repel water or oil? Shouldn't 3M keep the supplies coming, since there was no hint of human danger. "All the data we had on health . . . pointed toward no health effect," says William E. Coyne, senior vice-president for research and development.

But then 3M took a couple of crucial steps that sped up its decision to chuck the product: It ordered up studies on rats, monkeys, and other animals to see what heavy doses of PFOS might do. And it commissioned more research, forking over $800,000 for an investigator at Michigan State University to test wildlife samples to see just how pervasive the chemicals were. The results of both sets of tests, though preliminary, proved fatal for the chemicals.

The wildlife tests confirmed the initial fears of the 3M executives. Michigan State University researcher John P. Giesy, a zoologist and a faculty member of the school's National Food Safety & Toxicology Center, found PFOS in some very odd places. Scanning samples of animal

THE PATH TO A PAINFUL CHOICE

1968 A researcher at the University of Rochester finds organic fluorine in human blood samples from the general population. Publishes finding in *Nature*.

1976 Academic researchers refine the earlier find, and the Rochester investigator, D. R. Taves, discovers the chemical in his own blood.

1978 3M reviews 30 years of death records among factory workers exposed to organic fluorine on the job but finds nothing unusual.

EARLY 1990s 3M uses enhanced mass spectrometry to scan workers' blood. Reliably detects contamination down to the level of 0.5 parts per million.

1993 Researchers at University of Minnesota report finding no increased mortality in workers exposed to an organic fluorine. Elsewhere, it is linked to cancer in rodents and changes in reproductive hormones in humans.

1996 University of Minnesota researchers publish study finding no toxicity to the liver in 115 3M workers from PFOS exposures.

1997 Researchers at Michigan State University and 3M report that organic fluorine chemicals are appearing in water, air, and soil.

MAY, 1998 3M advises EPA that it found organic fluorine in blood-bank samples in tiny amounts. Company decides to move away from this chemistry.

SEPTEMBER, 1998 Company tells EPA of disturbing animal-test findings. The offspring of rats heavily dosed with organic fluorine die within days.

SEPTEMBER, 1999 3M researchers find no adverse health effects from on-the-job exposure to PFOS.

FEBRUARY, 2000 Researchers alert 3M that PFOS is found in tissue of birds from the Pacific Ocean to the Baltic.

MARCH, 2000 3M and EPA discuss latest findings, including the deaths of heavily dosed monkeys.

MAY 16, 2000 3M and EPA announce that the company will voluntarily phase out the organic fluorines.

DATA: 3M, EPA, BUSINESS WEEK

"3M deserves great credit for identifying this problem and coming forward voluntarily," says the EPA's Browner

tissue from all across the globe, which he keeps on hand in lab freezers, Giesy found the chemical in "various animals from various places." While he won't list the animals or locations—for fear of preempting scientific publication—3M executives say PFOS turned up in flesh-eating birds in the Pacific Ocean and the Baltic regions. Giesy is now halfway through tests on 2,000 tissue samples drawn from as far away as the Arctic and Antarctic.

When Giesy started presenting his initial results to 3M officials in February, the concern level at the company rose sharply. He was summoned back to repeat his presentation for Chief Executive Officer Livio D. DeSimone and his most senior executives. "This was very important to 3M," recalls the researcher.

Since neither Giesy nor in-house scientists could say just how PFOS got into the far-flung animal tissues, the 3M scientists now plan a global research effort aimed at tracking the chemical's sources and destinations. Says Katherine E. Reed, a chemist who is 3M's executive director of environmental technology: "We believe that our responsibility for materials continues . . . into disposal. It's a concept we call life-cycle management."

The most damning evidence against PFOS began emerging in September, 1998. That's when 3M got the results of animal tests in which heavy doses of PFOS were administered to rats—10,000 to 100,000 times what humans would ever likely be exposed to. The investigators found that the rats' offspring were dying within days of birth. Then, this past March, they reported that two monkeys that were also dosed heavily died, after suffering severe gastrointestinal problems and convulsions. The company promptly notified the EPA of the results.

Those animals tests got the agency's attention. Although 3M had kept the EPA informed of all its PFOS studies, the animal mortality data—and especially the rat fatalities—sparked a steady series of "no lunch, no refreshments . . . roll-up-your-sleeves" meetings in March at EPA headquarters in Washington, one top EPA official recalls. Says the official: "The seriousness of the issues grew over time."

When the 3M executives finally decided to pull the plug on PFOS and related products, they didn't need the heavy hammer of an EPA ruling—but that possibility hung heavily in the background. "They could see the writing on the wall," argues the senior EPA official. "They could see we were going to continue our assessment of this and it would get more detailed and at the end of the day we would make some kind of decision . . . 3M decided that the better course of action was to get out of it early." For their part, 3M officials say they would have made the same decision whether the EPA pushed them or not.

Just how quickly 3M can adapt to its far-reaching decision isn't clear. It intends to be out of production on most, if not all, PFOS-related products by yearend. With a few products, such as fire-fighting foams, it may take longer to adjust. With over $1 billion pouring in each year from all sorts of new products that don't use the chemicals, the company feels sure it can come up with substitutes—ideally, nonpersistent ones. And it expects it will find jobs elsewhere or will pay separation benefits to affected workers. Meanwhile, the worries about PFOS are not yet over. For years to come, 3M will be keeping track of the stuff it has already put out there.

By Joseph Weber in St. Paul, Minn.

After encountering a dying pilgrim on a climbing trip in the Himalayas, a businessman ponders the differences between individual and corporate ethics.

The Parable of the Sadhu

by Bowen H. McCoy

Last year, as the first participant in the new six-month sabbatical program that Morgan Stanley has adopted, I enjoyed a rare opportunity to collect my thoughts as well as do some traveling. I spent the first three months in Nepal, walking 600 miles through 200 villages in the Himalayas and climbing some 120,000 vertical feet. My sole Western companion on the trip was an anthropologist who shed light on the cultural patterns of the villages that we passed through.

During the Nepal hike, something occurred that has had a powerful impact on my thinking about corporate ethics. Although some might argue that the experience has no relevance to business, it was a situation in which a basic ethical dilemma suddenly intruded into the lives of a group of individuals. How the group responded holds a lesson for all organizations, no matter how defined.

The Sadhu

The Nepal experience was more rugged than I had anticipated. Most commercial treks last two or three weeks and cover a quarter of the distance we traveled.

My friend Stephen, the anthropologist, and I were halfway through the 60-day Himalayan part of the trip when we reached the high point, an 18,000-foot pass over a crest that we'd have to trav-

Bowen H. McCoy retired from Morgan Stanley in 1990 after 28 years of service. He is now a real estate and business counselor, a teacher, and a philanthropist.

erse to reach the village of Muklinath, an ancient holy place for pilgrims.

Six years earlier, I had suffered pulmonary edema, an acute form of altitude sickness, at 16,500 feet in the vicinity of Everest base camp—so we were understandably concerned about what would happen at 18,000 feet. Moreover, the Himalayas were having their wettest spring in 20 years; hip-deep powder and ice had already driven us off one ridge. If we failed to cross the pass, I feared that the last half of our once-in-a-lifetime trip would be ruined.

The night before we would try the pass, we camped in a hut at 14,500 feet. In the photos taken at that camp, my face appears wan. The last village we'd passed through was a sturdy two-day walk below us, and I was tired.

During the late afternoon, four backpackers from New Zealand joined us, and we spent most of the night awake, anticipating the climb. Below, we could see the fires of two other parties, which turned out to be two Swiss couples and a Japanese hiking club.

To get over the steep part of the climb before the sun melted the steps cut in the ice, we departed at 3:30 A.M. The New Zealanders left first, followed by Stephen and myself, our porters and Sherpas, and then the Swiss. The Japanese lingered in their camp. The sky was clear, and we were confident that no spring storm would erupt that day to close the pass.

At 15,500 feet, it looked to me as if Stephen were shuffling and staggering a bit, which are symptoms of altitude sickness. (The initial stage of altitude sickness brings a headache and nausea. As the condition worsens, a climber may

encounter difficult breathing, disorientation, aphasia, and paralysis.) I felt strong—my adrenaline was flowing—but I was very concerned about my ultimate ability to get across. A couple of our porters were also suffering from the height, and Pasang, our Sherpa sirdar (leader), was worried.

Just after daybreak, while we rested at 15,500 feet, one of the New Zealanders, who had gone ahead, came staggering down toward us with a body slung across his shoulders. He dumped the almost naked, barefoot body of an Indian holy man—a sadhu—at my feet. He had found the pilgrim lying on the ice, shivering and suffering from hypothermia. I cradled the sadhu's head and laid him out on the rocks. The New Zealander was angry. He wanted to get across the pass before the bright sun melted the snow. He said, "Look, I've done what I can. You have porters and Sherpa guides. You care for him. We're going on!" He turned and went back up the mountain to join his friends.

I took a carotid pulse and found that the sadhu was still alive. We figured he had probably visited the holy shrines at Muklinath and was on his way home. It was fruitless to question why he had chosen this desperately high route instead of the safe, heavily traveled caravan route through the Kali Gandaki gorge. Or why he was shoeless and almost naked, or how long he had been lying in the pass. The answers weren't going to solve our problem.

This article was originally published in the September–October 1983 issue of HBR. For its republication as an HBR Classic, Bowen H. McCoy has written the commentary "When Do We Take a Stand?" to update his observations.

Stephen and the four Swiss began stripping off their outer clothing and opening their packs. The sadhu was soon clothed from head to foot. He was not able to walk, but he was very much alive. I looked down the mountain and spotted the Japanese climbers, marching up with a horse.

Without a great deal of thought, I told Stephen and Pasang that I was concerned about withstanding the heights to come and wanted to get over the pass. I took off after several of our porters who had gone ahead.

On the steep part of the ascent where, if the ice steps had given way, I would have slid down about 3,000 feet, I felt vertigo. I stopped for a breather, allowing the Swiss to catch up with me. I inquired about the sadhu and Stephen. They said that the sadhu was fine and that Stephen was just behind them. I set off again for the summit.

When I reached them, Stephen glared at me and said, "How do you feel about contributing to the death of a fellow man?"

Stephen arrived at the summit an hour after I did. Still exhilarated by victory, I ran down the slope to congratulate him. He was suffering from altitude sickness—walking 15 steps, then stopping, walking 15 steps, then stopping. Pasang accompanied him all the way up. When I reached them, Stephen glared at me and said: "How do you feel about contributing to the death of a fellow man?"

I did not completely comprehend what he meant. "Is the sadhu dead?" I inquired.

"No," replied Stephen, "but he surely will be!"

After I had gone, followed not long after by the Swiss, Stephen had remained with the sadhu. When the Japanese had arrived, Stephen had asked to use their horse to transport the sadhu down to the hut. They had refused. He had then asked Pasang to have a group of our porters carry the sadhu. Pasang had resisted the idea, saying that the

porters would have to exert all their energy to get themselves over the pass. He believed they could not carry a man down 1,000 feet to the hut, reclimb the slope, and get across safely before the snow melted. Pasang had pressed Stephen not to delay any longer.

The Sherpas had carried the sadhu down to a rock in the sun at about 15,000 feet and pointed out the hut another 500 feet below. The Japanese had given him food and drink. When they had last seen him, he was listlessly throwing rocks at the Japanese party's dog, which had frightened him.

We do not know if the sadhu lived or died.

For many of the following days and evenings, Stephen and I discussed and debated our behavior toward the sadhu. Stephen is a committed Quaker with deep moral vision. He said, "I feel that what happened with the sadhu is a good example of the breakdown between the individual ethic and the corporate ethic. No one person was willing to assume ultimate responsibility for the sadhu. Each was willing to do his bit just so long as it was not too inconvenient. When it got to be a bother, everyone just passed the buck to someone else and took off. Jesus was relevant to a more individualistic stage of society, but how do we interpret his teaching today in a world filled with large, impersonal organizations and groups?"

I defended the larger group, saying, "Look, we all cared. We all gave aid and comfort. Everyone did his bit. The New Zealander carried him down below the snow line. I took his pulse and suggested we treat him for hypothermia. You and the Swiss gave him clothing and got him warmed up. The Japanese gave him food and water. The Sherpas carried him down to the sun and pointed out the easy trail toward the hut. He was well enough to throw rocks at a dog. What more could we do?"

"You have just described the typical affluent Westerner's response to a problem. Throwing money—in this case, food and sweaters—at it, but not solving the fundamentals!" Stephen retorted.

"What would satisfy you?" I said. "Here we are, a group of New Zealanders, Swiss, Americans, and Japanese who have never met before and who are

I asked, "Where is the limit of our responsibility in a situation like this?"

at the apex of one of the most powerful experiences of our lives. Some years the pass is so bad no one gets over it. What right does an almost naked pilgrim who chooses the wrong trail have to disrupt our lives? Even the Sherpas had no interest in risking the trip to help him beyond a certain point."

Stephen calmly rebutted, "I wonder what the Sherpas would have done if the sadhu had been a well-dressed Nepali, or what the Japanese would have done if the sadhu had been a well-dressed Asian, or what you would have done, Buzz, if the sadhu had been a well-dressed Western woman?"

"Where, in your opinion," I asked, "is the limit of our responsibility in a situation like this? We had our own well-being to worry about. Our Sherpa guides were unwilling to jeopardize us or the porters for the sadhu. No one else on the mountain was willing to commit himself beyond certain self-imposed limits."

Stephen said, "As individual Christians or people with a Western ethical tradition, we can fulfill our obligations in such a situation only if one, the sadhu dies in our care; two, the sadhu demonstrates to us that he can undertake the two-day walk down to the village; or three, we carry the sadhu for two days down to the village and persuade someone there to care for him."

"Leaving the sadhu in the sun with food and clothing—where he demonstrated hand-eye coordination by throwing a rock at a dog—comes close to fulfilling items one and two," I answered. "And it wouldn't have made sense to take him to the village where the people appeared to be far less caring than the

Sherpas, so the third condition is impractical. Are you really saying that, no matter what the implications, we should, at the drop of a hat, have changed our entire plan?"

The Individual Versus the Group Ethic

Despite my arguments, I felt and continue to feel guilt about the sadhu. I had literally walked through a classic moral dilemma without fully thinking through the consequences. My excuses for my actions include a high adrenaline flow, a superordinate goal, and a once-in-a-lifetime opportunity—common factors in corporate situations, especially stressful ones.

Real moral dilemmas are ambiguous, and many of us hike right through them, unaware that they exist. When, usually after the fact, someone makes an issue of one, we tend to resent his or her bringing it up. Often, when the full import of what we have done (or not done) hits us, we dig into a defensive position from which it is very difficult to emerge. In rare circumstances, we may contemplate what we have done from inside a prison.

Had we mountaineers been free of stress caused by the effort and the high altitude, we might have treated the sadhu differently. Yet isn't stress the real test of personal and corporate values? The instant decisions that executives make under pressure reveal the most about personal and corporate character.

Among the many questions that occur to me when I ponder my experience with the sadhu are: What are the practical limits of moral imagination and vision? Is there a collective or institutional ethic that differs from the ethics of the individual? At what level of effort or commitment can one discharge one's ethical responsibilities?

Not every ethical dilemma has a right solution. Reasonable people often disagree; otherwise there would be no dilemma. In a business context, however, it is essential that managers agree on a process for dealing with dilemmas.

Our experience with the sadhu offers an interesting parallel to business situations. An immediate response was mandatory. Failure to act was a decision in itself. Up on the mountain we could not resign and submit our résumés to a headhunter. In contrast to philosophy, business involves action and implementation—getting things done. Managers must come up with answers based on what they see and what they allow to influence their decision-making processes. On the mountain, none of us but Stephen realized the true dimensions of the situation we were facing.

One of our problems was that as a group we had no process for developing a consensus. We had no sense of purpose or plan. The difficulties of dealing with the sadhu were so complex that no one person could handle them. Because the group did not have a set of preconditions that could guide its action to an acceptable resolution, we reacted instinctively as individuals. The cross-cultural nature of the group added a further layer of complexity. We had no leader with whom we could all identify and in whose purpose we believed. Only Stephen was willing to take charge, but he could not gain adequate support from the group to care for the sadhu.

Some organizations do have values that transcend the personal values of their managers. Such values, which go beyond profitability, are usually revealed when the organization is under stress. People throughout the organization generally accept its values, which, because they are not presented as a rigid list of commandments, may be somewhat ambiguous. The stories people tell, rather than printed materials, transmit the organization's conceptions of what is proper behavior.

For 20 years, I have been exposed at senior levels to a variety of corporations and organizations. It is amazing how quickly an outsider can sense the tone and style of an organization and, with that, the degree of tolerated openness and freedom to challenge management.

Organizations that do not have a heritage of mutually accepted, shared values tend to become unhinged during stress, with each individual bailing out for himself or herself. In the great takeover battles we have witnessed during past years, companies that had strong cultures drew the wagons around them and fought it out, while other companies saw executives—supported by golden parachutes—bail out of the struggles.

Because corporations and their members are interdependent, for the corporation to be strong the members need to share a preconceived notion of correct behavior, a "business ethic," and think of it as a positive force, not a constraint.

As an investment banker, I am continually warned by well-meaning law-

> **As a group, we had no process for developing a consensus. We had no sense of purpose or plan.**

yers, clients, and associates to be wary of conflicts of interest. Yet if I were to run away from every difficult situation, I wouldn't be an effective investment banker. I have to feel my way through conflicts. An effective manager can't run from risk either; he or she has to confront risk. To feel "safe" in doing that, managers need the guidelines of an agreed-upon process and set of values within the organization.

After my three months in Nepal, I spent three months as an executive-in-residence at both the Stanford Business School and the University of California at Berkeley's Center for Ethics and Social Policy of the Graduate Theological Union. Those six months away from my job gave me time to assimilate 20 years of business experience. My thoughts turned often to the meaning of the leadership role in any large organization. Students at the seminary thought of themselves as antibusiness. But when I questioned them, they agreed that they distrusted all large organizations, including the church. They perceived all large organizations as impersonal and opposed to individual values and needs. Yet we all know of organizations in which people's values and beliefs are respected and their expressions encouraged. What makes the difference? Can we identify the difference and, as a result, manage more effectively?

The word *ethics* turns off many and confuses more. Yet the notions of shared values and an agreed-upon process for dealing with adversity and change— what many people mean when they talk about corporate culture—seem to be at

I wrote about my experiences purposely to present an ambiguous situation. I never found out if the sadhu lived or died. I can attest, though, that the sadhu lives on in his story. He lives in the ethics classes I teach each year at business schools and churches. He lives in the classrooms of numerous business schools, where professors have taught the case to tens of thousands of students. He lives in several casebooks on ethics and on an educational video. And he lives in organizations such as the American Red Cross and AT&T, which use his story in their ethics training.

As I reflect on the sadhu now, 15 years after the fact, I first have to wonder, What actually happened on that Himalayan slope? When I first wrote about the event, I reported the experience in as much detail as I could remember, but I shaped it to the needs of a good classroom discussion. After years of reading my story, viewing it on video, and hearing others discuss it, I'm not sure I myself know what actually occurred on the mountainside that day!

I've also heard a wide variety of responses to the story. The sadhu, for example, may not have wanted our help at all—he may have been intentionally bringing on his own death as a way to holiness. Why had he taken the dangerous way over the pass instead of the caravan route through the gorge? Hindu businesspeople have told me that in trying to assist the sadhu, we were being typically arrogant Westerners imposing our cultural values on the world.

I've learned that each year along the pass, a few Nepali porters are left to freeze to death outside the tents of the unthinking tourists who hired them. A few years ago, a French group even left one of their own, a young French woman, to die there. The difficult pass seems to demonstrate a perverse version of Gresham's law of currency: The bad practices of previous travelers have driven out the values that new travelers might have followed if they were at home. Perhaps that helps to explain why our porters behaved as they did and why it was so difficult for Stephen or anyone else to establish a different approach on the spot.

Our Sherpa sirdar, Pasang, was focused on his responsibility for bringing us up the mountain safe and sound. (His livelihood and status in the Sherpa ethnic group depended on our safe return.) We were weak, our party was split, the porters were well on their way to the top with all our gear and food, and a storm would have separated us irrevocably from our logistical base.

The fact was, we had no plan for dealing with the contingency of the sadhu. There was nothing we could do to unite our multicultural group in the little time we had. An ethical dilemma had come upon us unexpectedly, an element of drama that may explain why the sadhu's story has continued to attract students.

I am often asked for help in teaching the story. I usually advise keeping the details as ambiguous as possible. A true ethical dilemma requires a decision between two hard choices. In the case of the sadhu, we had to decide how much to sacrifice ourselves to take care of a stranger. And given the constraints of our trek, we had to make a group decision, not an individual one. If a large majority of students in a class ends up thinking I'm a bad person because of my decision on the mountain, the instructor may not have given the case its due. The same is true if the majority sees no problem with the choices we made.

Any class's response depends on its setting, whether it's a business school, a church, or a corporation. I've found that younger students are more likely to see the issue as black-and-white, whereas older ones tend to see shades of gray. Some have seen a conflict between the different ethical approaches that we followed at the time. Stephen felt he had to do everything he could to save the sadhu's life, in accordance with his Christian ethic of compassion. I had a utilitarian response: do the greatest good for the greatest number. Give a burst of aid to minimize the sadhu's exposure, then continue on our way.

WHEN DO WE TAKE A STAND?

by Bowen H. McCoy

The basic question of the case remains, When do we take a stand? When do we allow a "sadhu" to intrude into our daily lives? Few of us can afford the time or effort to take care of every needy person we encounter. How much must we give of ourselves? And how do we prepare our organizations and institutions so they will respond appropriately in a crisis? How do we influence them if we do not agree with their points of view?

We cannot quit our jobs over every ethical dilemma, but if we continually ignore our sense of values, who do we become? As a journalist asked at a recent conference on ethics, "Which ditch are we willing to die in?" For each of us, the answer is a bit different. How we act in response to that question defines better than anything else who we are, just as, in a collective sense, our acts define our institutions. In effect, the sadhu is always there, ready to remind us of the tensions between our own goals and the claims of strangers.

---

the heart of the ethical issue. People who are in touch with their own core beliefs and the beliefs of others and who are sustained by them can be more comfortable living on the cutting edge. At times, taking a tough line or a decisive stand in a muddle of ambiguity is the only ethical thing to do. If a manager is indecisive about a problem and spends time trying to figure out the "good" thing to do, the enterprise may be lost.

Business ethics, then, has to do with the authenticity and integrity of the enterprise. To be ethical is to follow the business as well as the cultural

goals of the corporation, its owners, its employees, and its customers. Those who cannot serve the corporate vision are not authentic businesspeople and, therefore, are not ethical in the business sense.

At this stage of my own business experience, I have a strong interest in organizational behavior. Sociologists are keenly studying what they call corporate stories, legends, and heroes as a way organizations have of transmitting value systems. Corporations such as Arco have even hired consultants to perform an audit of their corporate culture. In a company, a leader is a

person who understands, interprets, and manages the corporate value system. Effective managers, therefore, are action-oriented people who resolve conflict, are tolerant of ambiguity, stress, and change, and have a strong sense of purpose for themselves and their organizations.

If all this is true, I wonder about the role of the professional manager who moves from company to company. How can he or she quickly absorb the values and culture of different organizations? Or is there, indeed, an art of management that is totally transportable? Assuming that such fungible managers do exist, is it proper for them to manipulate the values of others?

What would have happened had Stephen and I carried the sadhu for two days back to the village and become involved with the villagers in his care? In four trips to Nepal, my most interesting experience occurred in 1975 when I lived in a Sherpa home in the Khumbu for five days while recovering from altitude sickness. The high point of Stephen's trip was an invitation to participate in a family funeral ceremony in Manang. Neither experience had to do with climbing the high passes of the Himalayas. Why were we so reluctant to try the lower path, the ambiguous trail? Perhaps because we did not have a leader who could reveal the greater purpose of the trip to us.

Why didn't Stephen, with his moral vision, opt to take the sadhu under his personal care? The answer is partly because Stephen was hard-stressed physically himself and partly because, without some support system that encompassed our involuntary and episodic community on the mountain, it was beyond his individual capacity to do so.

I see the current interest in corporate culture and corporate value systems as a positive response to pessimism such as Stephen's about the decline of the role of the individual in large organizations. Individuals who operate from a thoughtful set of personal values provide the foundation for a corporate culture. A corporate tradition that encourages freedom of inquiry, supports personal values, and reinforces a focused sense of direction can fulfill the need to combine individuality with the prosperity and success of the group. Without such corporate support, the individual is lost.

That is the lesson of the sadhu. In a complex corporate situation, the individual requires and deserves the support of the group. When people cannot find such support in their organizations, they don't know how to act. If such support is forthcoming, a person has a stake in the success of the group and can add much to the process of establishing and maintaining a corporate culture. Management's challenge is to be sensitive to individual needs, to shape them, and to direct and focus them for the benefit of the group as a whole.

For each of us the sadhu lives. Should we stop what we are doing and comfort him; or should we keep trudging up toward the high pass? Should I pause to help the derelict I pass on the street each night as I walk by the Yale Club en route to Grand Central Station? Am I his brother? What is the nature of our responsibility if we consider ourselves to be ethical persons? Perhaps it is to change the values of the group so that it can, with all its resources, take the other road.

Unit Selections

Key Points to Consider

❖ How well are organizations responding to issues of work and family—for example, flexible schedules, day care, job sharing, and telecommuting? Defend your answer.

❖ What do you believe will be the hottest issue (such as sexism, racism, ageism) in the next decade? Why?

❖ Is it fair to bring criminal charges against corporations and executives for unsafe products, dangerous working conditions, or industrial pollution? Why or why not?

❖ What online activities and issues do you believe will be the primary focus of ethical concern in the next decade? Explain.

❖ What ethical dilemmas is management likely to face when conducting business in foreign environments? How can management best deal with these dilemmas?

 **Links** www.dushkin.com/online/

19. **CIBERWeb**
    http://ciber.centers.purdue.edu

20. **Communications for a Sustainable Future**
    http://csf.colorado.edu

21. **National Immigrant Forum**
    http://www.immigrationforum.org

22. **Sympatico: Workplace**
    http://www.ntl.sympatico.ca/Contents/Careers/

23. **Stockholm University**
    http://www.psychology.su.se/units/ao/ao.html

24. **United Nations Environment Programme (UNEP)**
    http://www.unep.ch

25. **United States Trade Representative (USTR)**
    http://www.ustr.gov

These sites are annotated on pages 4 and 5.

Both at home and abroad, there are social and environmental issues that have potential ethical consequences for management. Incidents of insider trading, deaths resulting from unsafe products or work environments, AIDS in the workplace, and the adoption of policies for involvement in the global market are a few of the issues that need to be seriously addressed by management.

This unit investigates the nature and ramifications of prominent ethical, social, and environmental issues facing management today. The unit articles are grouped into three sections. The first subsection article, "Work & Family: Family-Friendly CEOs Are Changing Cultures at More Workplaces," suggests a possible positive change in management's attitude toward balancing work and family. The next two selections point to the importance of companies' taking environmental responsibility more seriously. The next subsection scrutinizes the importance of companies' gaining and maintaining trust in the marketplace.

The subsection *Global Ethics* concludes this unit with five readings that provide helpful insight on ethical issues and dilemmas inherent in multinational operations. They describe adapting ethical decisions to a global marketplace and offer guidelines for helping management deal with ethical issues in international markets.

WORK & FAMILY

By Sue Shellenbarger

Family-Friendly CEOs Are Changing Cultures At More Workplaces

ADVOCATES of a more family-friendly workplace have long blamed glacial progress on resistance from the nation's CEOs, almost universally older men without much experience with work-family conflict.

Now that's changing. A new generation of younger leaders is taking the helm of upstart and fast-growing companies. These baby-boom CEOs have suffered work-family conflict, talk openly about it and often integrate job and family in a visible way.

That doesn't mean these New Age CEOs are paragons of balance, nor do the workplaces they run make life easy for jugglers. Like most employees, these CEOs' workers are dogged by long hours, bitter competition and inadequate child- and elder-care choices. Charter Communications, St. Louis, headed by family-friendly CEO Jerald Kent, has grown sixfold in the past year, driven partly by employees' hard, long hours at work.

What's new is that the attitudes of these CEOs toward balancing work and family differ so sharply from those of the post-World War II generation of executives, yielding subtle but profound changes in workplace cultures. These executives accept their employees' struggle to achieve balance as a part of corporate life. They're also convinced that a rich, rewarding family life tends to increase a worker's long-term productivity. Often, they take steps to make the workplace more flexible and supportive.

Examples aren't hard to find. My own unscientific survey of 13 of the nation's fastest-growing companies, drawn at random from published lists, turned up five CEOs in their 40s who met my criteria: They talk openly about work-family conflict, conscientiously juggle their own work and family duties and take steps to help employees to the same.

DRIVEN by his desire to be an involved father, as well as his belief that a happy family life makes a happy employee, Charter's Mr. Kent, 43, blocks out time on his calendar to coach his two children's soccer, hockey and baseball teams and to make nearly all their games. He and his secretary talk openly about family commitments that take him away from work. His juggling act sends a message to the cable giant's 12,000 employees. "The biggest way to illustrate the importance [of balancing work and family] is to believe in it and do it yourself," he says. Indeed, the corporate culture statement he helped draft in 1993, as a Charter co-founder, actually says, "Families come first."

While negotiating the final terms of software billionaire Paul Allen's purchase last year of a controlling stake in Charter, Mr. Kent left the talks at 7:30 p.m. one evening, telling Mr. Allen's lawyer that he'd promised his kids to see "The Parent Trap" with them. He returned to the session after the movie.

At Seattle retailer Cutter & Buck, Harvey Jones, the 48-year-old founder and CEO, knows firsthand the trials of the dual-earner family. For four years, he and his wife, then a computer programmer, juggled two jobs and two preschoolers. "Our life became very frantic," he recalls, before his wife quit to stay home. Watching his employees start families, "I know how hard it is."

Mr. Jones remains involved with his children, now 11 and 13, eating breakfast with them and driving them to the school-bus stop every morning.

Like many of these family-friendly CEOs, Mr. Jones is honest about the workplace obstacles to balance. "We don't do enough to keep much of a family feeling as we should," he says. "I need to implement more" changes to support the company's 400 employees. "I'm trying to work on that." He has made a good start. Unlike other retailers, Cutter & Buck doesn't expect headquarters employees to work weekends. The company is also exploring child-care options as it plans to a move to larger headquarters.

JONATHAN SPILLER, 48, of Armor Holdings, has to travel a lot as CEO of the Jacksonville, Fla., maker of law-enforcement gear. But the father of two also made a commitment to his daughter last year that he'd attend her weekly Indian Princess meetings, and "by hook or crook, I managed to find a way to be there," he says. He also tries to ensure that at his 4,000-

employee company, "nobody has to make excuses for wanting to be involved with their families. Life's too short." Armor is teaming up with nine other employers to help build a new near-site child-care center.

These emerging-company executives join a short but growing list of relatively young, family-friendly CEOs at older, bigger firms. Pitney Bowes's Michael Critelli, 50 and a father of three, recently conducted a dozen focus groups on life-balance issues among the company's 30,000 employees. "I know that work-life balance is an issue," he wrote in an employee newsletter. As a father, "I feel it directly."

Another example is Baxter Healthcare's CEO, Harry Jansen Kraemer, 44, a father of four. Before his wife quit her

job as a bank vice president, the couple balanced two careers and child-rearing. Catalyst, a nonprofit New York research and advisory concern, took the unusual step recently of citing Mr. Kraemer as a good work-family role model.

In the past, pioneering older CEOs, such as Walter Shipley, 63, now chairman of Chase Manhattan, and J. Michael Cook, 56, retired from Deloitte & Touche, have transformed their companies' cultures with family-friendly leadership. If these young CEOs follow suit, the winners will be kids and companies alike.

Send your work-family experiences and comments to sue.shellenbarger@ wsj.com, or fax me at 503-636-6951.

ENVIRONMENT

THE GREENING OF
CORPORATE
AMERICA

Corporate America is jumping on the green bandwagon, and many companies have found the payoff is much more than enhanced good will.

Harvey Meyer

"WE'RE FROM THE ENVIRONMENTAL PROTECTION AGENCY, AND WE'RE here to help you" sounds like one of the punch lines for that old joke we all know. But there can be positive payoffs—in money as well as goodwill—for companies that take environmental protection seriously.

Natural yogurt producer Stonyfield Farm of Londonderry, N.H., for example, is convinced its environment-friendly reputation has enhanced its image and helped it attract new customers. Interface, Inc., an Atlanta supplier of commercial interior products, claims to have reaped not only millions of dollars in energy savings and waste reductions but also a palpable increase in employee motivation and pride. And at Xerox Corporation, environmental awareness has inspired innovative remanufacturing, parts reuse and recycling, and new products, and it also reduced raw materials and energy use.

"Everybody, even our customers and suppliers, is energized by our environmental efforts," says Ray Anderson, Interface CEO, who speaks with evangelical zeal since experiencing a tearful "epiphany" several years ago over his company's lackluster environmental performance. "There's no doubt the initiatives are giving us a competitive edge."

"Green" firms such as Interface, Xerox, and Stonyfield are fast wading into the corporate mainstream. Just a decade ago, perhaps a handful of companies produced stand-alone environmental reports—documents testifying to their environmental accomplishments. Now more than 1,000 firms produce such reports, and "virtually every" firm acknowledges its environmental commitment, says Bob Massie, executive director for the Coalition of Environmentally Responsible Economics (CERES), a Boston group of environmental organizations and institutional investors.

Harvey Meyer is a Minnesota-based business journalist who frequently writes for the **Journal of Business Strategy.**

From the *Journal of Business Strategy,* January/February 2000, pp. 38-43. © 2000 by Faulkner & Gray. Reprinted by permission.

Even at small firms, energy conservation and waste and pollution reductions can produce substantial savings.

And these efforts are not all in the service of good public relations. Evidence suggests that superior environmental performance can enhance worker productivity and product quality, and, in many cases, environmentally responsible firms also boast superior financial performance.

"We've done a lot of research that shows that companies that do better environmentally achieve better financial performances in the stock market," says Frank Dixon, managing director of research and development at New York-based Innovest Strategic Value Advisors. "The main reason for that is environmental performance is a good proxy for overall management quality, which is the No. 1 determinant for stock price."

While greening your company appears to offer multiple advantages, firms would be foolish to embrace all things environmental blindly. For one thing, many environment-related actions are costly, time-consuming, and complex; there are often numerous trade-offs; and few things are either black or white—or green.

"If you want to do the right thing environmentally, you could literally spend every capital dollar you have," says Brad Whitehead, a principal with McKinsey & Co., a New York City management consulting firm. "If you did that, pretty soon your company would be paralyzed."

From Regulatory Burden to Strategic Necessity

Environmental management first captured most U.S. corporations attention in the early 1970s, when the federal government passed a slew of new environmental laws. The new regulations weren't exactly lauded in Corporate America. In fact, many companies dragged their feet on environmental issues, often viewing the new regulations as expensive new "taxes" on business.

Environmental advocacy groups—among them, the Environmental Defense Fund and the National Resources Defense Council—vociferously denounced this recalcitrance, at first with only mediocre success. But after catastrophes such as the 1984 chemical explosion in Bhopal, India, and the Exxon Valdez oil spill in 1989, the activists gained credibility and were able to ratchet up their demands. Thus organizations like CERES proposed that corporations publicly report on their environmental management schemes and results, and the Council on Economic

Priorities began grading companies on their environmental performance.

Corporate environmental consciousness was further raised when the International Organization of Standards (ISO) became involved. In 1996, the organization, known for its ISO 9000 quality-control standards, developed a new series of guidelines—ISO 14000—aiming to create uniform environmental standards among products, companies, industries and nations.

Today, environmental awareness isn't the exclusive domain of activists and rule-makers. Increasing numbers of consumers are getting into the act, diligently monitoring companies' environmental actions. Many now simply expect corporations to be environmentally responsible and express that expectation by voting with their pocketbooks.

Companies are paying attention. Environmental awareness has become so pervasive at many larger U.S. corporations that it is emerging as a strategic business issue on par with, and integrated into, operations and marketing.

"The transition is largely complete, from looking at environmental issues as regulatory issues to looking at them as strategic business issues," says Whitehead. "That's a fundamental and important change that's occurred."

The Low-Hanging Fruit

Of course, the types of environmental activities companies engage in varies according to industry, need, outside pressures, and other factors. But many firms that started out picking the low-hanging fruit—reducing energy consumption, waste, and pollution, and increasing recycling—have reaped huge rewards:

- 3M estimates that its Pollution Prevention Pays initiative, launched in 1975, has eliminated about 1.6 billion pounds of air, water, and land pollution for a total savings of $810 million.
- General Motors has pledged to cut 20% of energy use from 1995 levels by 2002.
- DuPont has reportedly more than halved its landfill waste, decreased its waste-treatment costs by hundreds of millions of dollars, and drastically reduced toxic releases.
- The U.S. Postal Service estimates that a $300,000 lighting upgrade at its sorting facility in Reno, Nev., which was supposed to pay for itself in energy savings

over 10 years, actually paid for itself in less than a year in whopping productivity gains.
- Boeing's reports that its "healthier" building design strategy paid off in documented productivity gains of between one and 15%.

Even at small firms, energy conservation and waste and pollution reductions can produce substantial savings. At $60 million Stonyfield Farm, the natural yogurt producer is garnering revenues from wastes it formerly dumped and is generating sizeable benefits from a comprehensive energy conservation retrofit conducted on its facilities three years ago, says Gary Hirshberg, CEO and president.

"One of the great things about energy retrofit is that it's kind of the gift that keeps on giving," says Hirshberg, adding that Stonyfield required payback on its investment within two years. "We've grown about four-fold since the retrofit, and our energy requirements have grown at least four-fold, but we've found our energy savings have ballooned over the years."

Adds Steve Lippman, program manager for Business and Social Responsibility (BSR), a San Francisco organization assisting environmentally-minded member companies with innovative products and services: "Starting out, it's a good idea to pick an easy win, something that will generate both environmental and business benefits. Things like energy efficiencies and lighting upgrades often pay for themselves quite quickly and help generate enthusiasm and support for the next project."

After initial successes, many companies have had to become more enterprising to chart continuing gains. But it can be worth the effort. Firms embracing sustainable development claim that the out-of-box thinking required sparks fresh technology and management innovations.

"There's no question our environmental efforts have been a galvanizing force, giving us fresh perspectives," says Interface's Anderson, who wants to redeem his company's past "plundering" so he can leave a lasting legacy for his six grandchildren. "One of our persons described it as like entering a room from a different door, one never used before. It's opened up all kinds of vistas for creativity." One new door Interface recently opened as its "One World Learning," a for-profit subsidiary that offers courses to other corporations on sustainable development.

AN IDEA WORTH COPYING

Perhaps no larger U.S. firm does a better job at remanufacturing, reuse, and recycling than Xerox, which is committed to becoming a "waste-free" company. Environmental groups commend the Webster, N.Y., copier giant for the hierarchy of ways in which it treats product take-backs, and Xerox credits those efforts with helping to produce $250 million in annual savings.

The $19.5 billion company monthly takes back from buyers or lessees thousands of used machines. Workers install parts that can be reused or refurbished in remanufactured machines, which carry the same total satisfaction guarantee as new machines, says Jim Cleveland, a Xerox quality, technology, and engineering manager.

Xerox's move toward green manufacturing started simply enough in 1990, when the company began recycling melted-down materials. But members of the firm's Environmental Leadership Program quickly determined recycling wasn't having demonstrable environmental—or economic—impact.

Initially, Xerox's Design for the Environment (DfE) approach concentrated on toner cartridge redesign, but then the effort expanded to examine producing entire machines that are recyclable and remanufacturable. Influencing the company's examination were customers, many of whom claimed it was immaterial whether machines were new or refurbished as long as they functioned properly.

Now, when Xerox designs a machine, processes are developed for both "new-build" and remanufactured equipment; 90% of Xerox-de-signed equipment is remanufacturable, and some remanufactured parts are used in several product life cycles.

Among the keys to Xerox's efforts: choosing more durable materials for components; installing a system for quickly determining the amount of time and money needed to fix a part instead of discarding it; designing parts that can be quickly disassembled; and minimizing the number of parts and designing them for a variety of machines. One popular—and profitable—machine contains 200 replicable parts, compared to the 2,000 previously needed for a machine of similar complexity.

"We might take a good copier back from a customer and we'll convert it to a printer," because the "xerographic engine," the core of most Xerox copiers and printers, is multifunctional, says Cleveland. "The machine gets a brand new serial number and the same satisfaction guarantee as a new machine, but it may contain a percentage of older components."

Xerox has gained at least two substantial financial benefits from remanufacturing: The cost of remanufacturing parts is considerably cheaper than making new ones, and remanufacturing extends the productivity of Xerox's assets.

"Overall, if you look at our total remanufacturing operations, it's paying off and is good business," Cleveland says. "It's good business if it's not costing us any more to remanufacture than to build new machines."

A number of companies are working with their suppliers on innovations and environmental initiatives. Some are screening suppliers' environmental performance, collaborating with them on green design initiatives, and offering training and information to build their management skills.

"We've been a force in waking suppliers up to the urgency of the matter," says Anderson. "And since we have a lot of purchasing power, they can't ignore us. We've conducted green supply chain conferences and told suppliers where we're going and invited them to come along. If they don't, they suffer the consequences."

And there can be a payoff in getting suppliers on board. Cosmair, Inc., a hair-care products manufacturer, has worked with suppliers to recycle or reuse its shipping containers. The initiative reportedly saves Cosmair several hundred thousand dollars annually in components, and waste handling and disposal costs, and helps attain a 90% reuse/recycle ratio at Cosmair's Clark, N.J., plant.

Another area where companies have reaped sizeable dividends: innovations in product design. Many new products can be more easily upgraded, disassembled, recycled, and reused than their predecessors, all while using fewer materials. And because diverse functional groups usually take a hand in these designs, process innovation can be a welcome byproduct of redesign.

"Companies have found, by integrating environmental considerations into the design of their products, there can be a range of benefits," says Lippman. "You'll learn more about the productive use of resources and come across innovative processes. And you may enhance your margins because with assembly and reuse, you're often reducing the number of product components, which can reduce assembly time, waste, time to market, and energy costs."

Designing with the environment in mind is paying off for Electrolux Corporation. The company reported that its most environmentally sound product lines accounted for 10% of sales but 15% of profits in 1997.

Interface has even found a way to improve customer service through an innovative environmental initiative. The firm offers an "Evergreen Lease"—renting a carpet instead of selling it. Interface will replace worn-out carpet tiles as needed; lessees save by not having to replace an entire carpet every time a section is ripped or stained. Interface also recently introduced "Solenium," which requires 30% less raw material to manufacture. "We describe Solenium as the first product of the next industrial revolution in that it's the first product truly designed with sustainability as the foundation," Anderson says.

"Environmental management," says BSR's Lippman, "provides another lens through which you can look to enhance quality and value to customers."

Interface and other environment-friendly firms say their efforts have helped them assuage skittish investors and a large, influential network of ever-vigilant environmental groups, many of which aren't afraid to use the Internet and audacious publicity to embarrass firms for environment slip-ups.

"Improving your environmental record is sort of like making sure you've covered all the bases in preparation for Y2K," says CERES' Bob Massie.

The Unexpected Benefits

Environmental friendliness impresses a broad range of stakeholders, from customers and employees to investors. Jim Cleveland, a Xerox quality, technology, and engineering manager, says customers are impressed with the raft of awards the company has won for its environmental performance (see the sidebar). And Compaq Computer Corporation reports its environmental efforts have been

> **Compaq Computer Corporation reports its environmental efforts have been deciding factors in winning key corporate and governmental customers.**

deciding factors in winning key corporate and governmental customers.

At Stonyfield Farm, both qualitative and quantitative consumer research shows customer purchases are heavily influenced by the company's environmental actions. While a natural yogurt product might be expected to attract eco-conscious consumers, the company constantly reinforces its pro-environment image, which it considers a distinct competitive advantage. It includes messages about its environmental actions—it gives 10% of net profits annually to environmental causes—on yogurt lids, newsletters, its Web site, and in guerrilla marketing efforts. The good will it is building should help Stonyfield, whose sales are increasing 35% annually, if the company encounters growing pains, Hirshberg says. "One hopes our efforts will help us," he says. "Those hiccups are inevitable, especially as we grow larger."

The benefits of environmental friendliness can go beyond good PR. In a tight labor market, where employee recruitment and retention are serious concerns, environmental friendliness can help.

- At Interface, a number of employees say they were attracted to the company because of its environmental policies and, once aboard, felt empowered by the initiatives they're encouraged to pursue.
- Xerox employees are "very proud of the fact we're so environmentally conscious and doing the right thing," Cleveland says.
- A Nortel Networks survey showed more than nine in 10 employees considered the company's environmental actions "personally" valuable to them.

Meanwhile, Stonyfield has found a way to directly link environmental performance to employee retention. If, for example, energy use and solid waste generation can be sub-

stantially reduced, a percentage of the money saved goes toward employee bonuses. "I think our environmental effort has a positive effect on morale because employees have an opportunity to make more money and they're proud to work for a company that values these things," Hirshberg says.

Another very significant benefit: Companies with superior environmental records tend to chart better financial performance.

The Alliance for Environmental Innovations, a Boston nonprofit, recently evaluated 70 research studies, concluding that companies out-performing their peers environmentally will also outperform them in the stock market. They found no studies recording a negative association between financial and environmental performances. Frank Dixon of Innovest says his investment firm has calculated similar benefits.

"Environment issues in certain industries are some of the most complex challenges facing management because of all the stakeholders, different regulations, many things to measure, and a high degree of uncertainty," says Dixon. "Doing a good job of managing that high degree of complexity should be transferable to other areas of business, and that's why you see good environmental companies consistently outperforming bad ones."

It's Not Easy Being Green

As much as most companies want to do the right thing environmentally, there are trade-offs. Environmental initiatives can consume a lot of time, money, and effort. And at a time when companies' resources are already squeezed, environmental actions sometimes take a lower priority.

"There are a lot of examples of environmental innovations that could have a positive economic return," says Jonathon Adler, sen-

ior fellow in environmental policy at Competitive Enterprise Institute, a Washington, D.C., research and advocacy organization with a free-market orientation. "The question is, do they compare favorably with investment alternatives facing the company. If the answer is no, then they aren't competitive investments."

Additionally, many companies have already taken advantage of the easy-to-identify energy and waste savings. Further easy-win environmental initiatives are more complex, difficult to pinpoint and prioritize.

"We can do a million things, but the challenge is determining which is the most important from a financial and environmental perspective. Those are tough decisions," says Nancy Hirshberg, director of natural resources at Stonyfield Farm.

Even when a company has a grasp on environmental issues, the complexity can be mind boggling. Xerox has to develop a sophisticated returns system to track the myriad machines and components in its remanufacturing effort. Moreover, as Xerox's Cleveland points out, rapidly changing technology and rising customer demands shorten product life cycles, thus increasing pressure to quickly determine machines' reconfigurability and acceptable margins.

Unfortunately, many environmental actions offering more dramatic impact may require lots of time and money. Management consultant Brad Whitehead says it's prohibitively expensive for a company to, for example, install a closed-loop system for all waste, always use alternative energy, and replace all products with recyclable materials.

Sometimes what appears to be a sound environmental action actually conflicts with another environmental benefit. Adler cites the case of companies seeking alternative energy from wind farms. On the one hand, fossil fuel isn't being used, but the turbines are

> **An analysis of 70 research studies concluded that companies outperforming their peers environmentally will also outperform them in the stock market.**

reportedly causing avian mortalities, including those of endangered birds.

And Adler, who several years ago wrote a book assessing the environmental movement, isn't convinced environmental actions are generating the good will and burnished public image companies often expect.

"An individual corporation might improve the public perception of that company, but its efforts won't improve the overall image of an industry," says Adler. "Thus, for example, if the company is trying to avoid regulatory burdens, its environmental actions won't make much difference because Congress and regulatory agencies are looking at the entire industry."

Companies operating internationally also confront the challenge of meeting varied—and often tougher—environmental regulations in different countries. Of course, there are also continuing concerns about meeting ever-mounting U.S. environmental regulations. Furthermore, many well-intentioned companies, particularly those aiming for sustainable development, come up against road-blocks when they try to quantify the impact of their environmental actions on society. While organizations like CERES are working on developing a common framework to more easily benchmark companies' environmental performance, at this time myriad formats and measurements thwart meaningful comparison.

Mountain Climbing

Despite the trade-offs, the future for greening corporate America looks promising. External pressures, including from government, consumers, and environmental watchdogs, and internal encouragement from eco-conscious employees will spur companies to step up their strategic environmental initiatives.

More companies are expected to file stand-alone annual reports outlining their environmental and even social achievements. Addressing consumer skepticism over these reports' reliability, firms are expected to continue a trend of hiring accounting firms to audit these documents.

And expect continued progress on developing standards for environmental reporting that offers meaningful measurements and comparisons. The hope is global standards will eventually achieve the credibility now accorded financial reporting.

Perhaps Interface represents many American companies as they ponder their environmental future. Interface came charging out of the gate several years ago, making substantial progress on a host of environmental initiatives. The giddy enthusiasm of that early period has been tempered by knowledge that scoring further environmental gains will likely require hundreds of small steps and sustained hard work.

"We're more than 25% there," CEO Anderson says of the company's long-term environmental goal. "But we're still on a lower slope of a mountain that's higher than Mount Everest. I'm holding out hope I'll live to see us accomplish our goal."

The Elephant at the Environmental Cocktail Party

There's an elephant-sized issue corporate environmentalists are pretending not to see: the element of ethics, or soul. Grasping this means moving to a whole new level—a fourth era of corporate environmentalism.

BY CARL FRANKEL

BUSINESS DISCUSSIONS OF SUSTAINABLE DEVELOPMENT often leave me vaguely disquieted—as though there's something missing, some core element we're talking around rather than about. We might call it the ethical dimension. We might call it soulfulness. With rare exceptions, business people leave such topics off the table. One exception was a presentation by AT&T's chief environmental officer, Brad Allenby, at the 1997 DeLange/Woodlands conference on sustainable development, where he interwove ethical and technical issues. When I complimented him on this afterward, he said: "You have no idea how many arrows in the back I've taken for precisely that reason."

Why does soulfulness make business so squirmy? More crucially: How can we move to a sustainable world without it? This ethical dimension is like an elephant at a cocktail party which everyone pretends not to see. It's the big issue specialists don't want to talk about. And pretending it's not there is the reason we got ourselves into our environmental mess in the first place.

Reprinted with permission from *Business Ethics,* September/October 1998, pp. 12-14. Adapted from *In Earth's Company* by Carl Frankel, New Society Publishers. © 1998.

Corporate commitment to the environment has fallen consistently short of what needs to be achieved. For—and this is a crucially important point—the global challenge is centrally but not solely environmental. It is a system problem, with poverty, population growth, and environmental degradation feeding each other in a self-perpetuating downward spiral.

To adopt the world's problems as our own—that is one of the great leaps forward of fourth-era corporate environmentalism.

Some companies do grasp this, and they are making a path into the emerging fourth era of corporate environmentalism. It will be an era marked by zero waste, whole-system thinking, and other principles of truly sustainable development. But most companies aren't that far along, and are instead fixated on questionable third-era principles like "win-win" solutions: the idea that serving the environment and enriching profits can always go hand-in-hand. They can't. I'll return to these ideas in a moment. But before we can see where we need to go, it's helpful to see where we've been.

Broadly speaking, corporate environmentalism has passed through three eras, and the stage has been set for a fourth. The first was launched in 1962 with the publication of Rachel Carson's *Silent Spring,* which depicted in chilling detail the environmental damage wrought by chemicals. The resulting furor produced a geyser of environmental laws that flowed for the next twenty years. The National Environmental Policy Act, the Superfund law, the Toxic Substances Control Act, the Resource Conservation and Recovery Act, and the Clean Water Act all belong to the legacy of Carson's work.

Collectively these laws ushered in what might be called the **Era of Compliance.** During this period, good corporate citizenship consisted of obeying the law. Corporations routinely proclaimed a policy of meeting all regulatory requirements—rather an odd pronouncement, considering that the alternative was to declare themselves outlaws.

The second era of corporate environmentalism came into being on the night of December 2, 1984 with the accidental release of 15,000 gallons of methyl isocyanate from a Union Carbide plant into the air over Bhopal, India. Over the next three days,

1,500 people died and many thousands more were blinded or otherwise harmed. Literally overnight, it became clear that corporate environmental practices had to change.

The chemical industry responded aggressively. The U.S. Chemical Manufacturers Association implemented a program called Responsible Care to improve environmental, health, and safety performance. Compliance was made a condition of membership. Union Carbide and other chemical companies overhauled environmental management procedures—with a new slant on external communications. Chemical companies introduced Community Action Panels (CAPs), which increased communication between factory managers and concerned citizens. CAPs had no say in corporate decisions, but they were more than window dressing. By encouraging dialogue in a non-confrontational setting, they made corporate managers more sensitive to community concerns.

In 1986 the U.S. Congress enacted SARA (Superfund Amendments and Reauthorization Act) Title III, which requires companies to publish annual emission levels of hundreds of chemicals. Corporate America abruptly found itself cast into an entirely new relationship with the public. Not all the corporate books were open, but important pages were. A new **Era of Public Accountability** had arrived.

Because of the heightened scrutiny, companies began placing more priority on reducing emissions. In 1988 Monsanto announced its intention to voluntarily reduce air emissions by 90 percent, a goal it met five years later. Other major corporations, including Polaroid and AT&T, followed suit. Thus was launched the third era of corporate environmentalism: the **Era of Beyond Compliance.**

That same year, *Time* magazine declared the environment the media event of the year. The following year, 1989, the supertanker Exxon Valdez ruptured, spilling 11 million gallons of crude oil into Alaska's Prince William Sound, upping the environmental ante once again. This event, coupled with the extraordinary ballyhoo surrounding the twentieth anniversary of Earth Day in 1990, lifted corporate environmentalism to yet a new level. The Era of Beyond Compliance was now in full swing: To qualify as forward-thinking, companies had to commit not to meeting but to exceeding emissions requirements. It was no longer enough to obey the law and disclose some information: Companies had to set off on their own, into the trackless wilds of "continuous improvement."

Today, Beyond Compliance corporate environmentalism is by no means universal, but it is well on the way to becoming *de rigeur* among the transnational powerhouses that act as role models for the broader corporate community.

Third-era corporate environmentalism has brought into the management lexicon a new term—"eco-efficiency." Eco-efficiency aims to streamline the full range of corporate metabolic processes: less stuff in, less waste out. Strategies run the gamut from energy-efficiency retrofits and the use of recovered materials, to what has become known as "de-materialization" (reducing the amount of materials used, by making packaging lighter, for instance).

The logic behind eco-efficiency is "win-win"—embracing the belief that business can improve the bottom line by helping the environment. In its 1993 environmental report, Baxter International captured the essence of win-win in a single sentence. After detailing reductions in waste and packaging, the company declared: "The total savings generated from Baxter's environmental program were $48 million in 1993. This added eight cents per share to Baxter's profitability." In other word, eco-efficiency is worthwhile because it creates shareholder value.

Does eco-efficiency always work? Some consultants contended as much, but this was a bubble that deserved to be burst. In 1994, the popping sound was heard when McKinsey consultants Brad Whitehead and Noah Walley published a *Harvard Business Review* article, arguing that win-win situations are very rare. "We must question the current euphoric environmental rhetoric by asking if win-win solutions should be the foundation of a company's environmental strategy," they wrote. "We must answer no."

As useful as it is, eco-efficiency is a local solution addressing local problems. To meet the challenge of sustainable development, more—much more—than third-era corporate environmentalism is required. And so we come to the matter of guiding vision: In what ways much the dominant vision be amended? How can corporations target sustainable development in its fullness, rather than in a watered-down version?

Answering these questions moves us toward the fourth era of corporate environmentalism—the **Era of Sustainable Development**—which will be characterized by four interrelated principles.

Principle #1: Toward Zero Waste. The more we keep fouling our air and water, the less able they are to sustain life in a maximally diverse and vital form—and our industrial processes are doing most of the fouling. Sustainability calls for a radical transformation in how corporations manage their metabolic inputs and outputs. Rather than reducing waste, companies need to come as close as possible to eliminating it completely.

Major corporations that have committed to reaching zero emissions include Du Pont in the U.S., and EBARA, Chichibu Onoda Cement, and Ogihara in Japan—where the Environment Agency concluded in a white paper sanctioned by the powerful Ministry on Trade and Industry that zero emissions was an appropriate standard for industry.

Principle #2: Whole-system thinking. The transition to a zero-waste industrial economy cannot be achieved via linear strategies working within the status quo. A broader approach, one that allows strategists to re-conceptualize their industrial processes *ab novo,* is required. This design approach is intrinsically radical: It looks to "re-invest" rather than "fix" or "improve."

Many companies have incorporated whole-system thinking into the product-design process in the form of "design for environment," or DFE. This strategy considers the entire product life-cycle, up to and including product takeback, during the upfront design process.

Whole system thinking considers the entire product life-cycle, including product takeback, in the design process.

IBM's PS/2 E personal computer (the "E" stands for "environment"), introduced in 1993, used the DFE process to create competitive advantage. The computer utilize PCMCIA cards—the same cards used in laptops—for add-on applications such as fax/modems. In addition to reducing energy usage, this design shrank the computer's "footprint" by reducing the need for bulky internal pieces like add-ons and—significantly—a fan. The elimination of a fan also made operation more silent, another selling point to consumers.

Principle #3: Looking outward. So far, corporations have focused largely on cleaning their own houses. But the world's house also needs cleaning, and business, as the sector with the most resources, must help. To adopt the world's problems as their own—that is one of the great leaps forward of fourth-era corporate environmentalism.

Companies can do this in three basic ways. The first is *technology transfer*—providing smaller companies and developing countries with the equipment and expertise to help address environmental problems. The second is *industrial ecology*—which means multiple corporations working in concert, such that one company's wastes become another's raw materials. The best-known example of industrial ecology comes from Kalundborg, Sweden, where a group of local companies—a refinery, a power plant, a pharmaceutical company, and a fish farm, among others—found they could use each others' wastes as resource inputs. Stonyfield Farms, a New Hampshire-based yogurt manufacturer, has similar plans. It is working with the town to develop a 95-acre site adjacent to its main factory and hopes to attract a cluster of eco-compatible enterprises to it.

The third external strategy calls for corporations to *see sustainable development as a business opportunity*—instead of seeing it as "somebody else's problem." Monsanto, for example, is betting that "restorative" products can bring a marketing edge. As Kate Fish, a sustainability specialist and the company's director of public policy, described it: "We are betting that as global pressures continue to build, the market will increasingly 'select' products and services that are dramatically more efficient, provide much more value with much less throughput, and, in the future, that have a net restorative impact at all levels—social, ecological and economic."

Monsanto's initiative is not without controversy, largely because biotechnology is at the heart of the company's vision. For Monsanto, biotech is perhaps the only way to boost agricultural productivity while dramatically reducing material throughput. "I would like to replace the stuff of pesticides with the information of biotechnology," Monsanto CEO Robert Shapiro told *Tomorrow* magazine in 1997. "When we put a gene, which is essentially coded information, into cotton and reduce insecticide use by 30 percent, that's a major step towards sustainability." Opponents of biotech, however, are less sanguine about tampering with the planet's gene pool.

Another example of a strategic commitment to sustainability—one that dates back decades—comes from Aracruz Cellulose, a $2 billion Brazilian producer of eucalyptus pulp. Starting in the late 1960s, Aracruz Cellulose took advantage of a tax incentive to acquire and reforest badly degraded land. By the early 1990s, the company had planted 130,000 hectares with managed eucalyptus, while restoring an additional 70,000-plus hectares as conservation. The company also directly addressed local social issues by annually distributing millions of seedings to farmers (reducing their need to harvest wood from local forests), and by investing heavily in the creation of schools, housing, hospitals, and a training center for employees. As business professor Stuart Hart noted in an award-winning *Harvard Business Review* article, "until recently, Aracruz spent more on its social investments than it did on wages [about $1.20 for every $1 in wages]." As a result, "the standard of living has improved dramatically, as has productivity. The company no longer needs to invest so heavily in social infrastructure."

Principle #4: Remembering sustainable development. This means that corporate strategists must expand their vision from "the environment" to "sustainable development." And not just its objective, technical aspect, but its subjective, ethical aspect as well. This might mean daring to "conjure the spirits of frugality and the devils of production restraints," as Claude Fussler, Dow Europe's former v.p. for environment, health and safety, put it. He wrote those words in the introduction to a provocative 1995 report that Dow Europe helped to fund, by the U.K. consultancy SustainAbility, which projected drastically reduced consumption in the years ahead.

Or it might mean truly bringing the community in on corporate strategy—not only in an advisory capacity, but in a genuinely democratic decision-making role. Weyerhaeuser did this in its early-1990s analysis of the Tolt watershed in Washington state, when the company worked with the Tulalip Tribes, the Seattle Water Department, the Washington Environmental Council, and various state departments to develop a collectively acceptable forest-management strategy. The company ended up setting aside two to three times more forest area as free from logging than it had planned.

Companies are starting to tiptoe into this area. Several years ago, the consultancy Roy F. Weston identified some 43 companies—including major transnationals like Mitsubishi, Honeywell, Ford, General Motors and Procter & Gamble—that had publicly embraced sustainable development, as distinguished from environmental protection. Whether these companies have meaningfully expanded their vision along with their terminology is, of course, another question.

So how far are we into the fourth era? Certainly, recent years have shown a positive trajectory in corporate behavior, especially—ironically—at the Fortune 500 level. Three years ago the term "sustainable development" was nowhere to be found in corporate communications, but that has changed lately, especially among more forward-thinking companies.

At the same time, however, there are other imperatives at work, such as globalization—which allows companies to leave environmental restraints at home as they leap national boundaries. So there are steps backward, even as there are steps forward. There's no doubt that progress is happening. The question is whether it's happening fast enough.

Adapted from In Earth's Company, *by Carl Frankel, New Society Publishers, P.O. Box 189, Gabriola Island, BC V0R 1X0 Canada (paperback, $16.95 U.S.). Phone 800–567–6772. Web site www.newsociety.com. Frankel is North American editor for* Tomorrow *magazine. He can be reached directly at CFrankel@aol.com.*

TRUST
IN THE
MARKETPLACE

John E. Richardson and
Linnea Bernard McCord

Traditionally, ethics is defined as a set of moral values or principles or a code of conduct.

> ... Ethics, as an expression of reality, is predicated upon the assumption that there are right and wrong motives, attitudes, traits of character, and actions that are exhibited in interpersonal relationships. Respectful social interaction is considered a norm by almost everyone.
>
> .... the overwhelming majority of people perceive others to be ethical when they observe what is considered to be their genuine kindness, consideration, politeness, empathy, and fairness in their interpersonal relationships.

When these are absent, and unkindness, inconsideration, rudeness, hardness, and injustice are present, the people exhibiting such conduct are considered unethical. A genuine consideration of others is essential to an ethical life. (Chewning, pp. 175–176).

An essential concomitant of ethics is of trust. Webster's Dictionary defines trust as "assured reliance on the character, ability, strength or truth of someone or something." Businesses are built on a foundation of trust in our free-enterprise system. When there are violations of this trust between competitors, between employer and employees, or between businesses and consumers, our economic system ceases to run smoothly. From a moral viewpoint, ethical behavior should not exist because of economic pragmatism, governmental edict, or contemporary fashionability—it should exist because it is morally appropriate and right. From an economic point of view, ethical behavior should exist because it just makes good business sense to be ethical and operate in a manner that demonstrates trustworthiness.

Robert Bruce Shaw, in *Trust in the Balance,* makes some thoughtful observations about trust within an organization. Paraphrasing his observations and applying his ideas to the marketplace as a whole:

1. Trust requires consumers have confidence in organizational promises or claims made to them. This means that a consumer should be able to believe that a commitment made will be met.
2. Trust requires integrity and consistency in following a known set of values, beliefs, and practices.
3. Trust requires concern for the well-being of others. This does not mean that organizational needs are not given appropriate emphasis—but it suggests the importance of understanding the impact of decisions and actions on others—i.e. consumers. (Shaw, pp. 39–40)

Companies can lose the trust of their customers by portraying their products in a deceptive or inaccurate manner. In one recent example, a Nike advertisement exhorted golfers to buy the same golf balls used by Tiger Woods. However, since Tiger Woods was using custom-made Nike golf balls not yet available to the general golfing public, the ad was, in fact, deceptive. In one of its ads, Volvo represented that Volvo cars could withstand a physical impact that, in fact, was not possible. Once a company is "caught" giving inaccurate information, even if done innocently, trust in that company is eroded.

Companies can also lose the trust of their customers when they fail to act promptly and notify their customers of problems that the company has discovered, especially where deaths may be involved. This occurred when Chrysler dragged its feet in replacing a safety latch on its Minivan (Geyelin, pp. A1, A10). More recently, Firestone and Ford had been publicly brought to task for failing to expeditiously notify American consumers of tire defects in SUVs even though the problem had occurred years earlier in other

countries. In cases like these, trust might not just be eroded, it might be destroyed. It could take years of painstaking effort to rebuild trust under these circumstances, and some companies might not have the economic ability to withstand such a rebuilding process with their consumers.

A 20/20 and New York Times investigation on a recent ABC 20/20 program, entitled "The Car Dealer's Secret" revealed a sad example of the violation of trust in the marketplace. The investigation divulged that many unsuspecting consumers have had hidden charges tacked on by some car dealers when purchasing a new car. According to consumer attorney Gary Klein, "It's a dirty little secret that the auto lending industry has not owned up to." (ABC News 20/20)

The scheme worked in the following manner. Car dealers would send a prospective buyer's application to a number of lenders, who would report to the car dealer what interest rate the lender would give to the buyer for his or her car loan. This interest rate is referred to as the "buy rate." Legally a car dealer is not required to tell the buyer what the "buy rate" is or how much the dealer is marking up the loan. If dealers did most of the loans at the buy rate, they only get a small fee. However, if they were able to convince the buyer to pay a higher rate, they made considerably more money. Lenders encouraged car dealers to charge the buyer a higher rate than the "buy rate" by agreeing to split the extra income with the dealer.

David Robertson, head of the Association of Finance and Insurance Professionals—a trade group representing finance managers—defended the practice, reflecting that it was akin to a retail markup on loans. "The dealership provides a valuable service on behalf of the customer in negotiating these loans," he said. "Because of that, the dealership should be compensated for that work." (ABC News 20/20)

Careful examination of the entire report, however, makes one seriously question this apologetic. Even if this practice is deemed to be legal, the critical issue is what happens to trust when the buyers discover that they have been charged an additional 1–3% of the loan without their knowledge? In some cases, consumers were led to believe that they were getting the dealer's bank rate, and in other cases, they were told that the dealer had shopped around at several banks to secure the best loan rate they could get for the buyer. While this practice may be questionable from a legal standpoint, it is clearly in ethical breach of trust with the consumer. Once discovered, the companies doing this will have the same credibility and trustworthiness problems as the other examples mentioned above.

The untrustworthiness problems of the car companies was compounded by the fact that the investigation appeared to reveal statistics showing that black customers were twice as likely as whites to have their rate marked up—and at a higher level. That evidence—included in thousands of pages of confidential documents which 20/20 and The New York Times obtained from a Tennessee court—revealed that some Nissan and GM dealers in Tennessee routinely marked up rates for blacks, forcing them to pay between $300 and $400 more than whites. (ABC News 20/20)

This is a tragic example for everyone who was affected by this markup and was the victim of this secret policy. Not only is trust destroyed, there is a huge economic cost to the general public. It is estimated that in the last four years or so, Texas car dealers have received approximately $9 billion of kickbacks from lenders, affecting 5.2 million consumers. (ABC News 20/20)

Let's compare these unfortunate examples of untrustworthy corporate behavior with the landmark example of Johnson & Johnson which ultimately increased its trustworthiness with consumers by the way it handled the Tylenol incident. After seven individuals, who had consumed Tylenol capsules contaminated by a third party died, Johnson & Johnson instituted a total product recall within a week costing an estimated $50 million after taxes. The company did this, not because it was responsible for causing the problem, but because it was the right thing to do. In addition, Johnson & Johnson spearheaded the development of more effective tamper-proof containers for their industry. Because of the company's swift response, consumers once again were able to trust in the Johnson & Johnson name. Although Johnson & Johnson suffered a decrease in market share at the time because of the scare, over the long term it has maintained its profitability in a highly competitive market. Certainly part of this profit success is attributable to consumers believing that Johnson & Johnson is a trustworthy company. (Robin and Reidenbach)

The e-commerce arena presents another example of the importance of marketers building a mutually valuable relationship with customers through a trust-based collaboration process. Recent research with 50 e-businesses reflects that companies which create and nurture trust find customers return to their sites repeatedly. (Dayal. . . . p. 64)

In the e-commerce world, six components of trust were found to be critical in developing trusting, satisfied customers:

- State-of-art reliable security measures on one's site
- Merchant legitimacy (e.g., ally one's product or service with an established brand)
- Order fulfillment (i.e. placing orders and getting merchandise efficiently and with minimal hassles)
- Tone and ambiance—handling consumers' personal information with sensitivity and iron-clad confidentiality

- Customers feeling that they are in control of the buying process
- Consumer collaboration—e.g., having chat groups to let consumers query each other about their purchases and experiences (Dayal . . . , pp. 64–67)

Additionally, one author noted recently that in the e-commerce world we've moved beyond brands and trademarks to "trustmarks." This author defined a trustmark as a

. . . (D)istinctive name or symbol that emotionally binds a company with the desires and aspirations of its customers. It's an emotional connection—and it's much bigger and more powerful than the uses that we traditionally associate with a trademark. . . . (Webber, p. 214)

Certainly if this is the case, trust—being an emotional link—is of supreme importance for a company that wants to succeed in doing business on the Internet.

It's unfortunate that while a plethora of examples of violation of trust easily come to mind, a paucity of examples "pop up" as noteworthy paradigms of organizational courage and trust in their relationship with consumers.

In conclusion, some key areas for companies to scrutinize and practice with regard to decisions that may affect trustworthiness in the marketplace might include:

- Does a company practice the Golden Rule with its customers? As a company insider, knowing what you know about the product, how willing would you be to purchase it for yourself or for a family member?
- How proud would you be if your marketing practices were made public. . . . shared with your friends. . . . or family? (Blanchard and Peale, p. 27)
- Are bottom-line concerns the sole component of your organizational decision-making process? What about human rights, the

ecological/environmental impact, and other areas of social responsibility?
- Can a firm which engages in unethical business practices with customers be trusted to deal with its employees any differently? Unfortunately, frequently a willingness to violate standards of ethics is not an isolated phenomenon but permeates the culture. The result is erosion of integrity throughout a company. In such cases, trust is elusive at best. (Shaw, p. 75).
- Is your organization not only market driven, but also value-oriented? (Peters and Levering, Moskowitz, and Katz).
- Is there a strong commitment to a positive corporate culture and a clearly defined mission which is frequently and unambiguously voiced by upper-management?
- Does your organization exemplify trust by practicing a genuine relationship partnership with your customers—*before, during, and after* the initial purchase. (Strout, p. 69).

Companies which exemplify treating customers ethically are founded on a covenant of trust. There is a shared belief, confidence, and faith that the company and its people will be fair, reliable, and ethical in all its dealings. *Total trust is the belief that a company and its people will never take opportunistic advantage of customer vulnerabilities.* (Hart and Johnson, pp. 11–13)

References

ABC News 20/20, "The Car Dealer's Secret," October 27, 2000.
Blanchard, Kenneth, and Norman Vincent Peale, *The Power of Ethical Management*, New York: William Morrow and Company, Inc., 1988.
Chewning, Richard C., *Business Ethics in a Changing Culture* (Reston, Virginia: Reston Publishing, 1984).

Dayal, Sandeep, Landesberg, Helen, and Michael Zeissner, "How to Build Trust Online," *Marketing Management,* Fall 1999, pp. 64–69.

Geyelin, Milo, "Why One Jury Dealt a Big Blow to Chrysler in Minivan-Latch Case," *Wall Street Journal,* November 19, 1997, pp. A1, A10.

Hart, Christopher W. and Michael D. Johnson, "Growing the Trust Relationship," *Marketing Management,* Spring 1999, pp. 9–19.

Hosmer, La Rue Tone, *The Ethics of Management,* second edition (Homewood, Illinois: Irwin, 1991).

Kaydo, Chad, "A Position of Power," *Sales & Marketing Management,* June 2000, pp. 104–106, 108ff.

Levering, Robert; Moskowitz, Milton; and Michael Katz, *The 100 Best Companies to Work for in America* (Reading, Mass.: Addison-Wesley, 1984).

Magnet, Myron, "Meet the New Revolutionaries," *Fortune,* February 24, 1992, pp. 94–101.

Muoio, Anna, "The Experienced Customer," *Net Company,* Fall 1999, pp. 025–027.

Peters, Thomas J. and Robert H. Waterman Jr., *In Search of Excellence* (New York: Harper & Row, 1982).

Richardson, John (ed.), *Annual Editions: Business Ethics 00/01* (Guilford, CT: McGraw-Hill/Dushkin, 2000).

_____, *Annual Editions: Marketing 00/01* (Guilford, CT: McGraw-Hill/Dushkin, 2000).

Robin, Donald P., and Erich Reidenbach, "Social Responsibility, Ethics, and Marketing Strategy: Closing the Gap Between Concept and Application," *Journal of Marketing,* Vol. 51 (January 1987), pp. 44–58.

Shaw, Robert Bruce, *Trust in the Balance,* (San Francisco: Jossey-Bass Publishers, 1997).

Strout, Erin, "Tough Customers," *Sales Marketing Management,* January 2000, pp. 63–69.

Webber, Alan M., "Trust in the Future," *Fast Company,* September 2000, pp. 209–212ff.

Dr. John E. Richardson *is Professor of Marketing in the Graziadio School of Business and Management at Pepperdine University, Malibu, California*

Dr. Linnea Bernard McCord *is Associate Professor of Business Law in the Graziadio School of Business and Management at Pepperdine University, Malibu, California*

Virtual Morality:
A New Workplace Quandary

By Michael J. McCarthy
Staff reporter of The Wall Street Journal

WHERE DO YOU DRAW THE LINE.COM? The explosion of the Internet into the workplace has empowered millions of employees, in a matter of keystrokes, to quietly commandeer company property for personal use. And ethical questions are mushrooming well beyond the propriety of workers frittering away a morning shopping online or secretly viewing pornographic Web sites.

Cautionary tales are piling up—from United Parcel Service of America Inc., which caught one employee using a UPS computer to run a personal business, to Lockheed Martin Corp., where a single e-mail heralding a religious holiday that was sent to 60,000 employees disabled company networks for more than six hours. The flood of e-mail traffic cost Lockheed Martin hundreds of thousands of dollars in lost productivity, and the employee lost his job.

Every day, companies face unexpected twists in the world of virtual morality. With the surge in day trading, is it OK for employees to log on to make a quick stock deal? How about sending out e-mails from work supporting a politician? Or using office computers to hunt for a new job? And if any of this is permissible occasionally, just when does it cross into excess?

This is a new spin on the old nuisance of employees making personal phone calls at work, but with

---

The Wall Street Journal Workplace-Ethics Quiz

The spread of technology into the workplace has raised a variety of new ethical questions, and many old ones still linger. Compare your answers with those of other Americans. See answers at end of article.

Office Technology

1. Is it wrong to use company e-mail for personal reasons?
   ☐ Yes   ☐ No

2. Is it wrong to use office equipment to help your children or spouse do schoolwork?
   ☐ Yes   ☐ No

3. Is it wrong to play computer games on office equipment during the workday?
   ☐ Yes   ☐ No

4. Is it wrong to use office equipment to do Internet shopping?
   ☐ Yes   ☐ No

5. Is it unethical to blame an error you made on a technological glitch?
   ☐ Yes   ☐ No

6. Is it unethical to visit pornographic Web sites using office equipment?
   ☐ Yes   ☐ No

Gifts and Entertainment

7. What's the value at which a gift from a supplier or client becomes troubling?
   ☐ $25   ☐ $50   ☐ $100

8. Is a $50 gift to a boss unacceptable?
   ☐ Yes   ☐ No

9. Is a $50 gift FROM the boss unacceptable?
   ☐ Yes   ☐ No

10. Of gifts from suppliers: Is it OK to take a $200 pair of football tickets?
    ☐ Yes   ☐ No

11. Is it OK to take a $120 pair of theater tickets?
    ☐ Yes   ☐ No

12. Is it OK to take a $100 holiday food basket?
    ☐ Yes   ☐ No

13. Is it OK to take a $25 gift certificate?
    ☐ Yes   ☐ No

14. Can you accept a $75 prize won at a raffle at a supplier's conference?
    ☐ Yes   ☐ No

Truth and Lies

15. Due to on-the-job pressure, have you ever abused or lied about sick days?
    ☐ Yes   ☐ No

16. Due to on-the-job pressure, have you ever taken credit for someone else's work or idea?
    ☐ Yes   ☐ No

Sources: Ethics Officer Association, Belmont, Mass.; Ethical Leadership Group, Wilmette, Ill.; surveys sampled a cross-section of workers at large companies and nationwide

---

greatly magnified possibilities. For one thing, the Web can be extremely seductive, lulling users to click screen after screen for hours at a time. Productivity can indeed suffer when dozens or hundreds of workers succumb to the temptation. What's more, unlike phone calls, electronic messages are often retrievable months or years later, and can be used as evidence in litigation against companies or individual employees.

In addition, though many workers don't realize it, when they surf the Web from work they are literally dragging their company's name along with them. Most Web sites can, and often do, trace the Internet hookups their visitors are using and identify the companies behind them. That leaves a serious potential for embarrassment if employees are visiting any number of places, from job-search sites to racist chat rooms. Caught off guard by the geometric growth of such issues, many companies have lost all hope of handling matters case by case. Some are using sophisticated software that monitors when, how and why workers are using the Internet (See "Now the Boss Knows Where You're Clicking"). Others are taking first stabs at setting boundaries.

Boeing Co., for one, seems to accept the inevitable with a policy specifically allowing employees to use faxes, e-mail and the Internet for personal reasons. But the aerospace and aircraft company also sets guidelines. Use has to be of "reasonable duration and frequency" and can't cause "embarrassment to the company." And chain letters, obscenity and political and religious solicitation are strictly barred.

Other companies are more permissive, but make it abundantly clear that employees can't expect privacy. Saying it recognizes that employees may occasionally need to use the Web or e-mail for personal reasons, Columbia/HCA Healthcare Corp. issues this warning in its "electronic communication" policy: "It is sometimes necessary for authorized personnel to access and monitor their contents." And, it adds, "in some situations, the company may be required to publicly disclose e-mail messages, even those marked private."

Attorneys have been advising companies to write such policies and alert employees that online activities will be monitored and that they can be disciplined. Such warnings make it difficult for employees to win any suit asserting that they expected their communications to be private—already an uphill claim given that the equipment belongs to the company in the first place.

Some 27% of large U.S. firms have begun checking employee e-mail, a huge jump from 15% in 1997, the American Management Association recently found. Some routinely do this to search for obscene language or images. Passed along employee to employee, those could constitute grounds for a sexual-harassment suit.

But the practice has generated controversy, particularly when workers are not forewarned. Earlier this month, California Gov. Gray Davis vetoed a measure that would have barred employers from secretly monitoring e-mail and computer files. Under the bill, companies would be allowed to do so only after they established monitoring policies and notified employees of them. Asserting that employers have a legitimate need to monitor company property, Gov. Davis said, "Every employee also understands that expense reports submitted for reimbursement are subject to employer verification as to their legitimacy and accuracy."

But even if a manager is within legal rights to peek at employee e-mail, does that make any kind of digital fishing expedition ethical? What's an employer to do, for example, if such a search of an employee's e-mail reveals that he has an undisclosed drug problem or is looking for another job?

To balance employee rights and a company's legal interests, some privacy advocates say, employers should check e-mail only after a worker is suspected of misconduct. "Just because companies own bathrooms doesn't mean they have the right to install cameras and monitor whatever goes on in there," says Marc Rotenberg, executive director of the Electronic Privacy Information Center, an advocacy group in Washington.

Against the tide, some companies and government agencies are trying to cling to "zero tolerance" policies, prohibiting any personal use of company equipment. One is Ameritech Corp., whose business code of conduct specifically states that computers and other company equipment "are to be used only to provide service to customers and for other business purposes," says a spokeswoman for the telecommunications company. The "policy ensures our employees are focused on serving customers," she adds. Reminders about the policy are sent periodically.

BellSouth was a similar hard-liner until the summer of 1998, when it caved. "We got a lot of questions from people saying they were afraid to give someone their company e-mail address for things like weekend soccer clubs," says Jerry Guthrie, the company's ethics officer. "We work long hours—we wanted to offer it as a benefit to employees."

Before BellSouth employees can log on to their computers, however, they now must click "OK" to a message warning them against misuse of e-mail and the Internet, and alerting them that their actions can be monitored. Since the company changed the policy to allow for personal use, its security department has conducted more than 60 investigations of abuse. Some employees were suspended or fired for violations including accessing pornographic sites and spending too much time on non-business Web pages, including sports sites.

BellSouth, like many other companies, uses filtering technology to block certain sites, but even that is a chore. Since each division currently filters different sites, the company is in the process of standardizing which sites will be blocked company-wide. "Some [other] companies block sports and financial sites," says Mr. Guthrie, though BellSouth doesn't intend to. But, he says, BellSouth will probably block access to "sex sites, hate sites and gambling sites."

In May, Zona Research Inc., an Internet market researcher in Redwood City, Calif., found that fully one-third of companies screen out any sites not on an approved list. In its survey of more than 300 companies, Zona also found that 20% of companies filter sites based on the user's job and another 13% based on the time of day.

But companies trying to construct such dams are discovering leaks all the time. Gambling, adult and other controversial sites are sanitizing or disguising their address names to operate under the radar of firms monitoring and blocking Internet content. One site remained undetected to cyber-smut police until it made headlines recently. Not to be confused with 1600 Pennsylvania Avenue, www.whitehouse.com offers X-rated content.

Now the Boss Knows Where You're Clicking

By Michael J. McCarthy
Staff Reporter of The Wall Street Journal

When labor laws changed recently in England, Turner Broadcasting System Inc. worried about a pileup of overtime claims from employees in its CNN London bureau. Then the Turner computer-security group sprang into action.

The department decided to order software that could monitor every Web page every worker visits—and help pinpoint anyone wasting company time online. "If we see people were surfing the Web all day, then they don't have to be paid for that overtime," says Darren Valiance, a Turner network-security specialist, referring to the British operation. "In a perfect world, people would realize they're at work to work."

Get ready for a combustible new office issue. Advancing technology is rapidly extending electronic-eavesdropping capability to every office that uses the Internet. There is a new set of Internet-surveillance systems, with names like WEBsweeper, Disk Tracy and SecureVIEW. Some can conduct desktop-to-laptop sweeps, monitoring Web use from the mailroom to the executive suite.

Turner, a unit of Time Warner Inc., says it is planning to install software called Telemate.Net, which plumbs a company's network and churns out reports identifying and ranking its heaviest individual Internet users. It details the top sites visited across the whole company, and can do the same for particular departments, like sales or accounting.

Telemate.Net can also report Web site visits by individual employees and rank them by roughly two dozen categories, including some that most employers wouldn't be to happy about—from games, humor and pornography to cults, shopping and job-hunting. And it can instantly generate logs naming precisely who went to what sites at what times.

Telemate.Net Software Inc., an Atlanta company that went public last month, lists some blue-chip corporate clients: Arthur Andersen & Co., Maytag Corp., Philip Morris Cos. and Sears, Roebuck & Co.

Right after installing Telemate.Net in February, says Douglas Dahlberg, the information-technology manager for Wolverton & Associates Inc., he unearthed some disturbing results. Something called broadcast.com was the company's third-most-visited site. People were downloading music from the site, it turns out, using up 4% of the company's bandwidth, or Internet capacity. "When I saw that, I yanked it," says Mr. Dahlberg, who removed the so-called RealAudio capability from Wolverton's system.

Before starting Telemate.Net up, Wolverton, a civil-engineering company in Norcross, Ga., notified its three dozen employees that it would be monitoring their computer usage. "It just mustn't sink in," says Mr. Dahlberg. "I can see every little Web page you read—and still there were problems."

Indeed in April, E*Trade Group Inc., the online investment service, showed up as Wolverton's eighth-most-visited site, using up nearly 3% of overall bandwidth. That transmission capacity is a precious resource, since Wolverton's engineers routinely have to send data-heavy computer-aided-design files to clients through e-mail during the workday. In June, Mr. Dahlberg was irritated to find cnnsi.com pop up as Wolverton's No. 8 site. "Our clients should be in [the top 10], not CNN Sports," he says.

This type of electronic-file analysis hasn't been available until very recently, computer-network specialists say. The raw data have always been there, but in a form that was virtually impenetrable. From his cramped cubicle at CNN Center in Atlanta, network security specialist Mr. Vallance, a 27-year-old in black Converse high-tops, taps away at his keyboard to demonstrate one recent afternoon.

Pulling up data logs, he reveals screen after screen of enigmatic coding, individuals identified by numbers like 123.43.87.99 and other gobbledygook. A former Air Force information-security expert, Mr. Vallance knows how hard it is to scan these logs to separate routine Web site visits and e-mails from suspicious transactions. There are some easy tip-offs, though: late-night log-ons, and any lines marked "rejected" by Turner's firewalls, or devices that protect computer networks from hackers and other outsiders.

It's only 1 p.m. and Mr. Valiance guesses that these logs, just since that morning, would fill about 2,000 screens. "Trying to look through all this is impossible," he says, but scrolling through them manually is the only way he can do surveillance on employee Web usage right now.

At many companies, information technicians are called upon only after a supervisor suspects an employee is burning up hours online or visiting pornographic or other offensive pages. The computer department can quickly generate a report on an individual's transactions, and the suspicion can be rapidly borne out or disproved.

New software like Telemate.Net completely reverses that process, allowing the computer department to tip off the manager. The software systematically sorts through all employee Web site visits every day, and sorts them into categories. Any visits to amazon.com, for instance, would show up on a company report under "shopping." Visits to jobhunt.com go under "employment." By clicking on a category, a company manager can pull up "drill down" reports revealing the name of each visitor to each site, as well as what times he or she logged on to it.

Certainly there are privacy issues here. Though the company says it isn't aware of any legal challenges to its system, some overseas laws restrict what it can do. In Germany, for instance, laws forbid Telemate.Net to generate reports on Internet usage by individual employees. Mindful of privacy issues in the U.S., Telemate.Net has designed a special "VIP" function that will automatically erase the specific Web pages of any-

one the computer department programs it to—the CEO, for example.

Telemate.Net's founding business 13 years ago was selling systems to help companies monitor phone usage, checking for such things as excessive personal calls. Two years ago, the company developed a sister system for the Internet. It sells Telemate.Net for $995 to $4,995 for each system a company requires. The price depends on the number of reports generated and other factors.

Several companies listed as clients in a Telemate.Net filing with the Securities and Exchange Commission had little to say on the subject. "I don't have time to run this down," said a spokesman for Maytag, the appliance maker. A Sears spokeswoman said the retailer couldn't confirm if it was a client and "didn't want to participate" in a story about monitoring employee Web use.

By policy, Philip Morris said, it won't discuss anything that might jeopardize its computer-network security. An Arthur Andersen spokeswoman said, "Our IT [information technology] folks say we don't use it much."

While marketing itself as "network intelligence for the Internet economy, Telemate.Net says it hopes its software will also be used as a tool to use the Web more productively. "Lots of companies gave employees Internet access as a perk, and now they're realizing it's an asset that has to be managed," says Vijay Balakrishnan, senior vice president, marketing.

When asked, Telemate.Net said it does indeed turn the system on itself, conducting surveillance on its 170 employees. And it has turned up some surprises. "We have a guy here—one of our top salespeople—who surfs a lot, spends an hour to an hour and a half a day working on his stock portfolio—but he's a top performer," says Morten Jensen, Telemate.Net's director, product management. "Does Jim, our VP for sales, care?" asks Mr. Jensen. "No."

How One Firm Tracks Ethics Electronically

By MICHAEL J. MCCARTHY
Staff Reporter of THE WALL STREET JOURNAL

BETHESDA, Md.—Lockheed Martin Corp. is turning business ethics into rocket science.

While some companies worry about workers wasting time on the Web, the aerospace giant is aggressively steering them into cyberspace as part of a broad program—born of a bribery scandal—to audit, record and perfect the measurement of employee morals.

Using internal computer programs with names like Merlin and Qwizard, many of Lockheed Martin's

160,000 employees go online these days for step-by-step training on ethics and legal compliance. The system records each time an employee completes one of the sessions, which range from sexual harassment and insider trading to kickbacks and gratuities. Last month, it began alerting managers to employees who haven't yet taken required sessions.

Lockheed Martin's electronic ethics program also closely tracks alleged wrongdoing inside the company.

Rocket Science

Lockheed keeps close tabs on how employees are disciplined for ethics violations.

	1995	1999*
Discharge	56	25
Suspension	47	14
Written reprimand	59	51
Oral reprimand	164	146
Other	60	66
Total sanctions	386	302

*Figures to June 30.
Source: Lockheed Martin

It knows, for example, that it takes 30.4 days on average to complete an internal investigation of ethics violations, and that the company has fired 217 people for them since 1995. In the first six months of this year, 4.8% of its ethics allegations involved conflicts of interest, while 8.9% involved security and misuse of assets.

In short, Lockheed Martin is tackling ethical matters with a scientific precision usually associated with its F-16 fighter jets.

One big reason for these complex ethics metrics: legal defense in case the company faces charges again.

Lockheed Corp. did not have such a sophisticated program in place in 1995, when, on the eve of its merger with Martin Marietta Corp., it agreed to pay a $24.8 million fine and plead guilty to conspiring to violate U.S. antibribery laws. Lockheed admitted that it illegally paid $1 million to an Egyptian lawmaker in 1990 for helping sell its C-130 aircraft in that country.

To keep from losing government contracts, Lockheed Martin submitted to a 60-page administrative agreement that amounted to a three-year probationary period. Like clockwork, it was required to turn over to the U.S. Air Force periodic ethics reports, including details of ethical complaints made to its employee hotline and other misconduct allegations.

In its leafy, suburban office park here in the shadow of the federal government, Lockheed Martin hardly wants to jeopardize its contractor status. Fully 70% of its $26.3 billion in sales comes solely from the U.S. government. "If they debar the corporation, that's death

for this company," says David T. Clous, vice president for ethics and business conduct.

What's more, the electronic ethics program could win the company lenient treatment should it be indicted in a future case. The decade-old Federal Sentencing Guidelines, which codified fines and penalties for corporate wrongdoing, also established that fines for criminal conduct could be reduced by as much as 95% if a company had concrete internal programs to detect and prevent illegal acts. But if a company couldn't produce a paper trail of proof that it had tried to prevent wrongdoing, fines and penalties could be ratcheted up by 400%.

As part of its drive to stay on the straight and narrow, Lockheed Martin also developed an ethics game, which every single employee, up to Chairman Vance D. Coffman, must play once a year. With cards and tokens, workers spend one-hour sessions packed around tables, considering how to handle ethical quandaries drawn from actual Lockheed Martin cases—from harassment to padded work schedules.

The Ethics Challenge, as it is called, has been a hit— except for one year, when the ethics department revised the game so that it no longer indicated which answers were right or wrong. The idea was to let players debate. But the indecision drove the company's exacting engineers nuts. "They had a hard time with it," says Brian Sears, an ethics officer for the aeronautics division. The game was revised again, to offer "preferred answers."

Meanwhile, the ethics department went to work developing numerous "interactive" training sessions, on security, software-license compliance and labor charging. The courses, with actors playing out hypothetical cases, were originally produced for CD-ROMs, at a cost of about $150,000 apiece.

Clicking along at a workstation, an employee usually takes about 45 minutes to complete a session. A sample question from the kickback-and-gratuity clinic:

A kickback may be in the form of:
  A. Cash
  B. Gift to a family member
  C. Donation to a charity at your request
  D. All of these
(The correct answer is D.)

From the sexual-harassment segment:

Which is the best means of addressing harassment when it first occurs?
  A. Ignore the harasser
  B. Be direct and tell the harasser his or her behavior is unwelcome and offensive
  C. Report the harasser to your manager or Human Resources
(The correct answer is B.)

Ethics-Quiz Answers

1. 34% said personal e-mail on company computers is wrong
2. 37% said using office equipment for schoolwork is wrong
3. 49% said playing computer games at work is wrong
4. 54% said Internet shopping at work is wrong
5. 61% said it's unethical to blame your error on technology
6. 87% said it's unethical to visit pornographic sites at work
7. 33% said $25 is the amount at which a gift from a supplier or client becomes troubling, while 33% said $50, and 33% said $100

8. 35% said a $50 gift to the boss is unacceptable
9. 12% said a $50 gift *from* the boss is unacceptable
10. 70% said it's unacceptable to take the $200 football tickets
11. 70% said it's unacceptable to take the $120 theater tickets
12. 35% said it's unacceptable to take the $100 food basket
13. 45% said it's unacceptable to take the $25 gift certificate
14. 40% said it's unacceptable to take the $75 raffle prize
15. 11% reported they lie about sick days
16. 4% reported they take credit for the work or ideas of others

To provide proof that it has been systematically teaching employees the laws appropriate to their divisions and positions, Lockheed Martin also wanted an up-to-the-minute auditing system, which would track who had taken what training session and when. Last year, turning to the power of the Web, it began using its automated Merlin system to instantly track the number of courses taken and by whom.

The company says employees have warmed up to the program, particularly since it went online and workers no longer have to check out CD-ROMs or visit special workstations to meet their training requirements. But Lockheed is realistic. "We never envision people lining up and saying, 'Rah-rah, it's time for compliance training,'" says Tracy Carter Dougherty, director of ethics communication and training.

"Computer-based training can't completely replace personalized training," says Joseph E. Murphy, an ethics and compliance specialist with Compliance Systems Legal Group in Warwick, R.I. But having a system with mandatory clinics and quizzes will help "convince a prosecutor or regulator that the company is trying to prevent and detect problems," he adds

Indeed, Steven Shaw, the U.S. Air Force deputy general counsel who held a debarment ax over Lockheed Martin until the probationary period ended last year, says he is pleased the company is still keeping close statistical tabs on ethical conduct and compliance training. And noting that the company hasn't been indicted since the Egypt case, he adds, "To me, that says a lot about a company that large. You'll always have people who will make mistakes."

ONLINE PRIVACY:

IT'S TIME *for* RULES *in* WONDERLAND

Here's BUSINESS WEEK's four-point plan to solve the Internet privacy mess

IF LEWIS CARROLL HAD WRITTEN ABOUT ALICE'S ADVENtures today, she would find herself passing through the looking glass and into cyberspace. She would meet up with dodos, duchesses, and eggheads, some of whom would spout the rough equivalent of "'Twas brillig, and the slithy toves...." The journey also would be full of rude surprises. As in Carroll's books, she would eventually discover who she really was. But many others she had never met would learn about her, too. Indeed, with every click of the mouse, a bit more of her privacy would vanish down the rabbit hole.

These days, a lot of people are stumbling on similar unpleasant surprises. Thanks to a string of privacy gaffes involving DoubleClick, RealNetworks, Amazon.com, and other major Web sites, consumers are learning that e-commerce companies have an intense interest in their private information. For about 9¢, some medical data sites will sell you your neighbor's history of urinary tract infections. Your speeding tickets, bounced checks, and delayed child-support payments are an open book. In the background, advertising services are building profiles of where people browse, what they buy, how they think, and who they are. Hundreds of sites already are stockpiling this type of information—some to use in targeted advertising, others to sell or trade with other sites.
GOLD RUSH. It will get worse. The tricks being played today are child's play compared with what's coming. Web sites that want to know you better will soon be able to track your movements on Web phones, palm devices, and video games, and parse the data with more subtle software. Online services can be layered with mounds of data about each person. Interactive TVs, for instance, have the potential to correlate the Web sites you visit at work with the ads you see at home in the evening.

Web surfers don't need extra proof that this gold rush for personal data is alarming. In a new BUSINESS WEEK/

Soon cybersnoops will be able to track your use of Web phones, palm devices, and video games

Harris Poll, 92% of Net users expressed discomfort about Web sites sharing personal information with other sites. The public outcry has grown so loud that in February, search engine AltaVista Co. promised to ask explicit permission before sharing visitors' personal information with other companies. On Mar. 2, DoubleClick bowed to public pressure on a similar point: The company, which serves up ads on many Web sites, has created anonymous digital snapshots, or "profiles," of millions of cybersurfers, based on where they browse and what they do online. DoubleClick had planned to link profiles with much more specific information, including names and addresses culled from real-world databases that cover 90% of American households. The company dropped that controversial plan, and within days, smaller rival 24/7 Media Inc. abandoned a similar strategy.

Anonymous tracking and profiling by DoubleClick and 24/7 can be very subtle. But sometimes privacy violations hit you in the face. We have all heard the examples of sociopaths who stalk their victims online. We have seen the statistics on "identity theft," in which criminals suck enough personal data off the Net to impersonate other people. Perhaps these are extreme examples. Even without them, many cybersurfers are starting to feel that they have spent quite enough time at this particular Mad Tea Party. They are ready for privacy rules that set some plain and simple boundaries. In the March BUSINESS WEEK/Harris Poll, 57% of respondents said government should pass laws on how personal in-

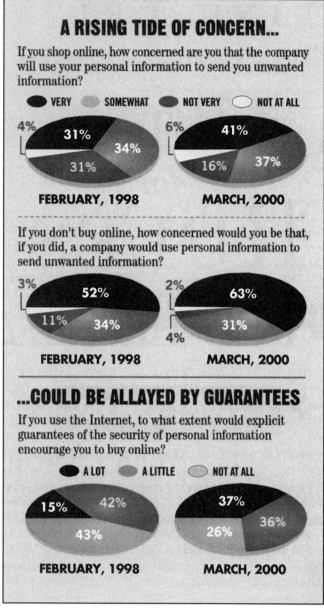

A RISING TIDE OF CONCERN...

If you shop online, how concerned are you that the company will use your personal information to send you unwanted information?

● VERY   ● SOMEWHAT   ● NOT VERY   ○ NOT AT ALL

FEBRUARY, 1998
4%
31%
34%
31%

MARCH, 2000
6%
41%
16%
37%

If you don't buy online, how concerned would you be that, if you did, a company would use personal information to send unwanted information?

FEBRUARY, 1998
3%
52%
11%
34%

MARCH, 2000
2%
63%
4%
31%

...COULD BE ALLAYED BY GUARANTEES

If you use the Internet, to what extent would explicit guarantees of the security of personal information encourage you to buy online?

● A LOT   ● A LITTLE   ○ NOT AT ALL

FEBRUARY, 1998
15%
42%
43%

MARCH, 2000
37%
26%
36%

CHARTS BY LAUREL ALLEN/BW

NOTE: "DON'T KNOW" AND "REFUSED" NOT INCLUDED.
FULL RESULTS, END OF ARTICLE
DATA: BUSINESS WEEK/HARRIS INTERACTIVE POLL OF 1,014 PEOPLE

BUSINESS WEEK believes there is a better way. Instead of a conflicting patchwork of state rules, the federal government should adopt clear privacy standards in the spirit of the Fair Information Practices—a philosophical framework for privacy protection that has been adopted worldwide over the past 25 years. The broad principles are essential:

- Companies conducting business online should be required by law to disclose clearly how they collect and use information.
- Consumers must be given control of how their data are used.
- Web surfers should also have the ability to inspect that data and to correct any errors they discover.
- And when companies break the rules, the government must have the power to impose penalties. "All of these bits you are sending out are your digital DNA," says Tara Lemmey, president of the Electronic Frontier Foundation. "You should have control of that."

Regulation flies in the face of the approach industry has been championing. For the past four years, Net companies have insisted that they can police themselves on privacy. "Industry initiatives and market forces are already doing a good job," says Daniel J. Jaye, co-founder of Engage Technologies Inc., which dishes up ads on the Web.

In other words, the market will punish companies that fall afoul of consumers. Bringing in the government, execs say, will pile bureaucratic layers on top of the Net. This could undercut the very promise of efficiency that many online businesses are counting on. The Internet, they say, is supposed to draw companies closer to their customers, allowing them to anticipate their desires. With profile data, they can target their ads, slash wasteful and random marketing costs, design products faster, and build higher profit margins. Profiling provides the underpinnings of a new way of doing business upon which the Net Economy is built.

Laws that require businesses to seek users' permission before they collect or use data about Web-surfing habits could kill this goose, they say. And why do that, industry execs ask, when they are making such fine strides in protecting consumer privacy? As a positive sign, Net businesses trumpet a May, 1999, Federal Trade Commission survey in which 66% of companies queried had privacy policies.

SELF-REGULATORY SHAM. We are not persuaded by these arguments. Few Web sites give consumers real choices over the data that get collected online. There is no proof that if given a choice—especially bolstered with financial incentives proffered by Web merchants—consumers won't willingly hand over some personal data. As for privacy policies, the same FTC survey showed that while more than 90% of companies polled collected personal

formation is collected. "What's going on today is exponentially more threatening to those who want to protect privacy," says Eliot Spitzer, New York's state attorney general who has proposed privacy legislation. People can't make informed decisions on the Net because they lack the necessary information. "What we're confronting is a market failure," says Spitzer.

Responding to a growing chorus of privacy-related complaints, some states have drafted legislation ranging from curtailing the sale of personal information to the creation of a privacy ombudsman. But this piecemeal, state-by-state approach is a muddle. Scattershot laws will only create more confusion. Over time, they will choke budding e-business in complex litigation and red tape.

Because privacy breaches are so corrosive to consumer trust, some Web executives welcome broad national standards

information, fewer than 10% actually followed all of the established Fair Information Practices.

In short, self-regulation is a sham. The policies that companies have posted under pressure from the government are as vague and confusing as anything Lewis Carroll could have dreamed up. One simple example: When people register at Yahoo! Inc. for one of its services, such as My Yahoo, they are asked to provide their birth date and e-mail address—ostensibly as a safeguard if they forget their user name and need prompting. But Yahoo also uses that information for a service called the Birthday Club, sending product offers from three to five merchants to users via e-mail on their birthday.

Don't look for transparency here. Most sites don't limit how they or their partners use consumer information. And Web sites can transfer information to partners without telling their own customers. Many sites also change their practices at will and without warning.

Because privacy breaches are so corrosive to consumer trust, some Web execs actually welcome broad national standards. IBM and Walt Disney Co. have decided not to advertise on Web sites that don't have privacy policies. Privacy codes must be clearer, says Chris Larsen, CEO and founder of E-Loan Inc., an online loan service that has its privacy policies audited. "I think the industry has squandered the opportunity to take care of this on its own." IBM Chairman Louis Gerstner doesn't go that far. But he has warned Net executives that they must get serious. "I am troubled, very troubled, by leaders who have failed to recognize our responsibility in the transformation of the new economy," he says.

We hope other Web execs are listening closely. The policies we propose are in the best interests of Web businesses. If more consumers can be assured that their personal information is safe, more of them will flock to the Net—and click, not exit. There are other explicit benefits for the industry. Privacy standards create a level playing field, so companies don't fall into an arms war, each trying to collect the most data—at any cost. "Business will benefit from the right level of government involvement," says Nick Grouf, founder of PeoplePC, which offers cheap PCs and Net connections. "Standards are good, but they need some teeth, and this is where government becomes a good partner."

FEDERAL STANDARD. In the long term, the privacy protection that BUSINESS WEEK espouses will make life simpler for businesses on the Net. More than 20 states already are moving to enact some kind of guarantees. A minimum federal standard of online privacy would decrease

THE LANGUAGE *of* ONLINE PRIVACY

COOKIES These tiny software programs keep a log of where people click, allowing sites to track customers' habits. Cookies are placed on consumers' computers when they first visit sites or use things like online calendars, personalized news services, or shopping carts.

ONLINE PROFILING By using cookies, sometimes combined with personal information, sites build profiles about what customers do or don't buy, what they look at, how much time they spend in different areas, and what ads they click on.

REFERERS Information that your Web browser passes along when you move from one site to another or use a search engine or even just send an e-mail. Referers can be collected and used to target advertising.

ADVERTISING NETWORKS The Net equivalent of ad agencies, the most famous being DoubleClick, Engage, and 24/7. They amass millions of profiles of Web surfers based on their online habits. Ads are then aimed at those most likely to buy what is being pitched.

REGISTRATIONS Anywhere you fill out personal information in order to download software, sign up for a free service, or buy something online. The data can be sold or shared with other Web sites or advertisers.

IP ADDRESS A number automatically assigned to your computer whenever you connect to the Net. The numbers are used by network computers to identify your PC so that data can be sent to you. But addresses can be used in profiling and ad targeting.

PRIVACY POLICIES Notices posted on a Web site that disclose how a company collects, uses, and shares data with partners or advertisers. These sometimes include opt-in and opt-out buttons.

OPT-IN AND OPT-OUT Privacy choices that some Web sites offer to their visitors. In opt-out situations, the site is free to gather and sell information on you unless you specifically tell it not to by clicking on a button. With opt-in, gathering or selling your data is forbidden unless you click to give permission.

PERSONALLY IDENTIFIABLE INFORMATION Your name, address, or credit card number and other details linked to your real-world identity.

THIRD-PARTY DATABASES Companies like Acxiom and Experian stockpile information such as name, address, phone number, and income on most U.S. households. Increasingly, these companies are working with Web sites and software makers.

Some 20 states are moving to protect Net privacy. A federal effort would cut costs and complexity

the cost and complexity for companies. It also would increase trust. If businesses really want to be close to their customers, trust is paramount. This approach also will shrink the gap that has arisen between the U.S. and Europe, where privacy already is recognized as a right. The Europeans have stood firm, putting American companies in the peculiar position of extending greater privacy protection in Germany or France than at home.

It's time to iron out the inconsistencies. Here are our prescriptions for protecting personal privacy without jeopardizing the promise of e-commerce:

OUR FOUR-POINT PLAN

E-privacy and e-commerce can coexist. Here's how to safeguard both

1. DISPLAY YOUR PRACTICES

Privacy policies seem like very simple things. Companies put up a notice online about how they gather and use information, and it's win-win from there. Consumers get the lay of the land, and Net companies pass on to consumers the responsibility for their online privacy.

If only it were that simple. These little postings have actually been the focus of rancorous debates for years. The tricky thing is that once policies are up there for all to see, companies are legally obligated to uphold them. That's one reason sites have dragged their feet in putting them up. Or should we say down? The statements are usually buried at the bottom of the page, and seem to be drafted by life-forms on a distant planet.

It's time that policies be written for mere mortals. Not many sites do a great job of explaining how information is tracked, used, and disclosed to partners. Consider the privacy policy of search engine Ask Jeeves. The company first says it always asks permission before providing information to partners. Yet on a registration form, the choice given to consumers is that information is shared unless you say otherwise. To confuse matters further, the policy later states that: "Ask Jeeves sometimes co-sponsors [sweepstakes and contests] with other companies, in which case the user's individual contact and demo-

graphic information is likely to be shared with participating sponsors. [The] information will not be released . . . without the user's consent." So which is it: Is your information automatically shared unless you go the extra step to object? Or is it kept private unless you pipe up and give the green light? When asked directly, Ask Jeeves says it depends. Depends on what? It's fine for companies to have different options, but too vague possibilities baffle consumers, rendering privacy notices useless.

One solution might be simple icons that help to navigate the policies. Like the "Information" sign that is recognized around the world, these symbols could be standardized: a large "p" signifying "privacy policy" could be placed on the top right-hand side of the page, on a registration form, in an electronic shopping cart, or anywhere that information is collected on a site. Often it's not clear, upon registration, whether you need to locate an "opt-out" button and click on it to stop the site from sharing your information with others, or whether the site intends to ask your permission each time it wants to pass information to another site. Icons could help clarify this (see box, "Danger! Danger!").

SECOND OPINION. Simple road signs on the Info Highway may seem trivial, but understanding the full measure of privacy policies is no joke. They resemble contracts. Indeed, they are generally the only privacy-related feature on sites that can actually trip a lawsuit. In January, New York District Attorney Spitzer used privacy policy violations by Chase Manhattan Bank and Sony Music Entertainment Inc.'s InfoBeat to curtail their sharing of data. "We have an obligation to define reasonable boundaries," he says. "We have to articulate what privacy rules should be and then how to enforce them."

It isn't enough to have just any old policy, though. The statements need to follow the Fair Information Practices, clearly laying out how each site addresses choice, access, and security. Policies should outline how a person's information is shared and how to limit its use. Contact numbers or e-mail addresses should be available. And the date on when the policy was last changed should be clearly stated. Web execs make a good argument when they say that it's hard to know how they will use data in the future. But they should alert consumers when the policy changes. Amazon.com, for example, says it doesn't sell or trade information now, but adds: "We may choose to do so in the future." The only notice the company says it will give is a change in its policy online.

The sharing of information is a white-hot button in the privacy debates. And for good reason. A Georgetown University survey of the privacy policies on health-care sites showed how common this is. Of 21 sites sampled, six offered assessments on health conditions that were actually run by other companies. Some companies shared names, ages, and e-mail addresses, which makes it hard for users to know who has their personal data or which privacy policy to rely on.

In the best of all worlds, companies should bind partners with whom they share data to their privacy policies. At the very least, they should inform consumers that they plan to transfer personal information to a partner. That way, consumers can check out the partner's privacy policy and make an informed decision about whether they want to participate.

DEFINING TERMS. It's all too vague on Yahoo's Web site. That's partly because the No. 1 site on the Net has what's known as a "universal registration," where people sign up once and are entitled to a host of different services—from e-mail to auctions to private personal calendars. But the universal registration information also ties in with other services offered through partners, such as the reservation service Travelocity provides. While details about data-sharing practices are explained on Yahoo, they are buried many clicks deep in so-called terms of service agreements, which aren't marked as privacy policies.

Some companies, such as PeoplePC and eBay, have very clear policies that give descriptions of how information could be passed to partners and naming some partners as examples. They also try to provide some level of surety. For instance, eBay Inc. says that before it provides personal information to partners, it lets users see the data it has collected. That's a step forward, but still limiting. To prevent eBay from sharing your data, you must choose not to use the service. And for those who give the O.K.? Once the information is transferred in these co-branded services, eBay says it has no control over how partners use the data.

It's crucial that these partnerships, data-gathering techniques, and customer options are spelled out, especially for Net newbies. Companies must be clear about how they define "personally identifiable information," because that description can change from site to site. Just as vital, they need to spell out the technology used to track and profile consumers. RealNetworks, which overhauled its privacy policies this fall after being accused of compiling information about the musical tastes of users, has a straightforward approach. It breaks out every tracking technique it uses and explains them simply and effectively. In contrast, CBS SportsLine explains that it uses IP addresses to identify users and their shopping carts but doesn't bother to explain what an IP address is. For the record: This is a trackable number assigned to your PC every time you connect to the Web.

DISCLOSURE
"This doesn't make any sense," she said. "You are obliged under law to spell this out more clearly"

Clearly, privacy policies are backbreakers to write. But it seems the hardest part about them for any company is coming up with a privacy philosophy that they will stick to. Once this hurdle is crossed, however, the positive impact might resonate into the brick-and-mortar world as well. Privacy policies governing credit reports, drug prescriptions, and more could follow the new model for the Internet.

2. GIVE PEOPLE A CHOICE

Right now, there's only one way you can be sure that the sensitive details of your life won't spill out over the Internet: Don't log on in the first place.

Short of doing that, consumers who surf the Web do so at their own peril. There are practically no laws to stop sites from ferreting out as much personal information about you as they can get their hands on—and then

---

HOW TO DRAW *the* LINE

DISPLAY YOUR PRACTICES Privacy policies should be mandatory, easy to find, and written in plain English. Companies should clearly state why they are collecting information and collect no more data than they need for that purpose. Data collected for one purpose shouldn't be used for another without consent. A simple set of icons should be developed to warn people about privacy threats.

GIVE PEOPLE A CHOICE If a business wants to collect information about a consumer's health, finances, or sexual orientation, it should ask them for permission first. This allows a Web surfer to opt-in. The same rule applies if the company wants to resell personal data or share it with advertising networks. In all other situations, users should be given the option to withhold their information by checking a prominently displayed, easy-to-understand box. This is called opt-out.

SHOW ME THE DATA Consumers must have the ability to look at and correct sensitive information, such as financial and medical data. There should also be a mechanism for double-checking a profile that combines personal information with online habits or is shared with another company. This is especially urgent when a profile triggers offensive or unwanted marketing solicitations. Web sites and marketers should share the responsibility for this.

PLAY FAIR OR PAY These rules won't enforce themselves. A broad law ensuring privacy online must be passed at a federal level. An agency, such as the FTC, would enforce and interpret the law according to the Fair Information Practices. Companies should also periodically disclose their practices in some kind of public record, such as SEC filings or trusted third-party audits.

DANGER! DANGER!
Nothing gets people's attention like a good, loud warning sign. For those who don't have the patience to burrow through privacy policies, here's a set of icons that could flag potential perils.

This site collects financial information

This site collects health information

This site transfers data to other companies

Privacy policy located here

Opt-In

Opt-Out

ICONS BY ALBERTO MENNA/BW

turning around and selling it to the highest bidder. If an AIDS patient visits a health site to investigate the side effects of the drug AZT, that site is free to market the information to drug companies, insurers, or anyone else.

Things don't have to be this open. What is needed is a way to give consumers more control over what is collected about them and more say over how it can be used. Proposed new federal and state laws would require Web sites to allow consumers to "opt out" of a company's data-collecting and resale operations. How? The new laws would force sites to display a box, which, for example, could be checked off by AIDS patients if they didn't want health-care sites to track the screens they read, store their credit card numbers, or resell any of that information.

OPTING OPTIONS. Of course, many Web sites already let visitors opt out. But most of those opt-out boxes are buried. Some of the proposed new privacy laws, such as a Senate bill being sponsored by Ron Wyden (D-Ore.) and Conrad Burns (R-Mont.), would require every Web site to offer a clearly written, prominently displayed opt-out box. Under such bills, consumers who arrive at the home page of Yahoo, Amazon, or eToys would be able to find the opt-out box right under their nose, perhaps on the upper righthand corner of their screen.

But even such prominently placed boxes might not be protection enough. Studies indicate that people who may otherwise be worried about online privacy are not going to stop their surfing long enough to read a few sentences of dense boilerplate, and then click on a box. That's why some politicians and privacy advocates are pushing even tougher protections. Rather than put the burden on consumers to opt out, they want to put the burden on companies to get Web surfers to opt in. Before a site could start collecting and selling most data, it would have to get people to check a box giving it permission to do so. A controversial Senate bill to do this has been proposed by Robert Torricelli (D-N.J.).

Industry reaction to giving consumers more choice ranges from genuine enthusiasm to hyperventilating hostility. Among critics, opt-out legislation is generally regarded as the lesser evil. But because information technology is evolving rapidly and the Internet soon will be widely available on tiny cell phones and other devices, some online executives worry that a bulky, federally required opt-out notice might not fit. "Having laws get down to pixel counts and screen layouts won't work," says Max Metral, chief technology officer for PeoplePC.

Nonetheless, most Web executives can live with opt-out. But they are terrified of opt-in. Execs worry that many people simply won't be willing to make the extra effort that opting in requires. As proof, some cite the Children's Online Privacy Protection Act, a 1998 law that limits the collection of information about kids under 13. Among other things, COPPA requires parents to opt in, by written letter or fax to the site, before their children can use online chat rooms and message boards. Just ask Julie Richer, president of San Francisco-based cyberkids.com, a site that targets 7- to 12-year-olds. Richard says COPPA has caused message board and chat room

INFORMED DECISION
"Do you wish to reveal personal medical information at this site?" he asked. "If so, this is how we'll share the data with others"

traffic to plummet by more than 40%.

But the objections to the opt-in rule go beyond the issue of reduced traffic. Advertising revenues might also suffer under Torricelli's opt-in proposal. There would be less free information available, making it harder for companies to put together the kinds of demographic profiles that allow them to target customers more precisely. Says DoubleClick President Kevin Ryan: "The Torricelli legislation would have a very negative impact on the Internet."

There's no doubt that opt-in would hike the cost of doing business online. But it's not as bad as its detractors claim. For one thing, companies would be able to lure people to opt-in by offering Web surfers cash and other incentives. It also would earn the goodwill of privacy-conscious Web surfers. One convert is Gregory Miller, chief Internet strategist for MedicaLogic, a Hillsboro (Ore.) site offering online health information, and a member of the Federal Trade Commission's new advisory committee for online access and security. His com-

ACCESS

"I don't think you have understood me properly," she said. "Please show me the online profile that you have compiled about me"

pany supports opt-in on the theory that customers will be attracted to a site that takes privacy concerns seriously. "If you ask someone for permission to market to them, you build a loyal customer," says Miller. "It's our job to convince the consumer that it's a good idea to opt in by being truthful and showing what the benefit is." One way MedicaLogic would do this: It could persuade diabetes sufferers to surrender their personal information by offering timely updates on advances in treatment. "There are so many users out there, and the Net is growing so rapidly, that you can still get a reasonable return on your investment. People can be persuaded to opt in,"says Miller.

Ideally, the best way to protect privacy on the Net is to combine the best elements of both opt-out and opt-in—as the European Union does. Opt-in methods are relatively extreme, so they should be used only for the most sensitive information—your chronic heart problems, for example, or the details of your financial holdings and your sexual preferences. And rules should be strict. No pre-checking of the opt-in box allowed. Instead, companies should be forced to describe what type of information they will be collecting and what they will be doing with it. Finally, opt-in also should be required before a company can resell any information about a Web surfer to a third party or share it with an ad network, since this offers few benefits to the surfer.

Apart from these extreme situations, the rule should be opt-out. Yes, it will be a pain in the neck to offer consumers this much control over how their information is used. But the bigger hurt could come from doing nothing and watching Web surfers opt out of the Internet.

3. SHOW ME THE DATA

Americans gained a precious thing from the Fair Credit Reporting Act of 1970: the right to inspect their credit records and find out why the bank turned them down on a car loan or a mortgage. No such privileges exist when it comes to online profiles, and it won't be easy to invent them. But some experts say the same kinds of tools Web sites use to track visitors could be used to provide at least a partial window into the data banks that store online profiles.

First, the downsides of doing that: The information a Web site collects is often strewn among multiple databases. Companies may not have the resources to query each one every time a surfer gets curious. What's more, the profile of your browsing habits may be based on cookie files—the bits of identifying code that Web sites deposit on your hard drive so they can monitor your comings and goings. If that's the case, those profiles may be linked only to the computer you browse from, not to your identity in the outside world. Do you really want to request access to that profile? The site would have to authenticate you. And in the process, it would acquire even more information about you than it started with. "It's clear that many systems on the Web were designed without much thought to privacy," says David M. Kristol, a member of the technical staff at Lucent Technologies Inc.'s Bell Labs. "These systems may be quite difficult to retrofit."

Hard, but not impossible. Some of these challenges seem tailor-made for smart software solutions. "If there's data in a database, it's there so that you can access it," says Lorrie Cranor, an AT&T Labs researcher who chairs a privacy working group at the World Wide Web Consortium.

Second point: If your profile—warts and all—is pegged to a string of numbers in cookie files, then, in theory, a Web site could manage your request for access by matching it to that same string. Authentication would be far from perfect, but perfection is rare in cyberspace. "We need a button we can push that says 'show me the profile you have on me,'" says personal privacy detective Richard Smith in Boston. "That should be relatively straightforward, because they already have an account mechanism, the sign-in." And if companies refuse? People could take it to the Fair Trade Commission.

The FTC, by the way, is on the case. It established an advisory committee on online access and security that began meeting on Feb. 4. It's made up of 40 people, including lawyers, professors, industry representatives and privacy advocates. And it plans to provide recommendations to the FTC on a range of options by May 15.

Not all the modes of online behavior that come before this committee will be so terribly controversial. Few argue against letting consumers see—and correct if necessary—sensitive data such as financial records and medical data. But many execs say providing access to routine info would be a costly nuisance of dubious benefit to consumers. "Do you really need to see that Banana Republic says you bought five shirts when you bought four, and do you really need to correct that?" says a lobbyist for one Web company.

But even where it's a nuisance to business, consumers should see more of what goes on behind the curtain. If you're being hounded by a direct marketer who is convinced you are interested in sex toys, you should be able to see whose data generated this profile. The marketer will probably argue that the data are culled from too

A GROWING THREAT

Concern is rising over privacy on the Net, with a clear majority—57%—now favoring some sort of laws regulating how personal information is collected and used. Regulation may become essential to continued growth in e-commerce, since 41% of online shoppers say they are very concerned over the use of personal information, up from 31% two years ago. Perhaps more telling, among people who go online but have not shopped there, 63% are very concerned.

MORE AND MORE NET SHOPPERS

If you go online from home, work, or another location, have you ever used the Internet, World Wide Web, or online service to purchase anything?

	MARCH, 2000	FEBRUARY, 1999	FEBRUARY, 1998	SEPTEMBER, 1997
Have purchased	45%	31%	23%	19%
Have not purchased	55%	69%	77%	81%

ONLINE BUYERS DREAD JUNK MAIL

If you have made online purchases, how concerned are you about each of these possibilities?

	VERY CONCERNED	SOME-WHAT	NOT VERY	NOT AT ALL
The company you buy from uses personal information you provide to send you unwanted information				
March, 2000	41%	37%	16%	6%
February, 1998	31%	34%	31%	4%
The company or one of its employees uses your credit-card information to make purchases without your consent				
March, 2000	39%	31%	22%	7%
February, 1998	56%	25%	12%	7%
In the course of the transaction, your credit-card information is made accessible to others who might use it without consent				
March, 2000	42%	34%	17%	6%
February, 1998	56%	28%	11%	3%

NONBUYERS WORRY ABOUT PRIVACY AND FRAUD

If you go online but have not purchased anything, how concerned would you be about each of these possibilities if you were to buy anything?

	VERY CONCERNED	SOME-WHAT	NOT VERY	NOT AT ALL
The company you buy from uses personal information you provide to send you unwanted information				
March, 2000	63%	31%	4%	2%
February, 1998	52%	34%	11%	3%
The company or one of its employees uses your credit-card information to make purchases without your consent				
March, 2000	71%	18%	7%	4%
February, 1998	80%	12%	6%	2%
In the course of the transaction, your credit-card information is made accessible to others who might use it without consent				
March, 2000	76%	20%	3%	*
February, 1998	86%	10%	2%	1%

AN ONLINE PROFILE IS DISCOMFORTING

Some Web sites track users' personal information to match users with products and services that meet the users' needs. Other Web sites profit by sharing or selling user information to other organizations. If you use the Internet, how comfortable would you be if a Web site did the following?

	VERY COMFORTABLE	SOMEWHAT COMFORTABLE	NOT VERY COMFORTABLE	NOT AT ALL COMFORTABLE	DON'T KNOW
Tracked your movements when you browsed the site, but didn't tie that information to your name or real-world identity					
	9%	28%	28%	35%	*
Merged your browsing habits and shopping patterns into a profile that was linked to your real name and identity					
	3%	7%	21%	68%	1%
Created a profile of you that included your real name and identity as well as additional personal information such as your income, driver's license, credit data, and medical status					
	3%	2%	13%	82%	0%

A PRIVACY GUARANTEE WOULD HELP

If you go online, to what extent would a policy that explicitly guarantees the security of your personal information encourage you to do the following?

	A LOT	A LITTLE	NOT AT ALL	DON'T KNOW
Use the Internet more in general				
March, 2000	40%	40%	19%	1%
February, 1998	18%	44%	38%	*
Register on that Web site, providing personal information				
March, 2000	30%	39%	31%	1%
February, 1998	12%	44%	44%	*
Purchase products or service from that company				
March, 2000	37%	36%	26%	1%
February, 1998	15%	42%	43%	0%

If privacy notices let you "opt out"—in other words, you could choose not to have your personal information collected by a particular Web site—how often would you "opt out?"

Always	56%
Sometimes	34%
Rarely	4%
Never	6%

A MAJORITY OF ALL PEOPLE POLLED FAVOR NEW LAWS

Here are three ways that the government could approach Internet privacy issues. Which one of these three do you think would be best at this stage of Internet development?

	MARCH, 2000	FEBRUARY, 1998
The government should let groups develop voluntary privacy standards, but not take action now unless real problems arise	15%	19%
The government should recommend privacy standards for the Internet, but not pass laws at this time	21%	23%
The government should pass laws now for how personal information can be collected and used on the Internet	57%	53%
None of the above	1%	2%
More than one of the above	*	0%
Don't know	5%	3%
Refused	1%	*

Telephone survey of 1,014 adults between Mar. 2 and Mar. 6 by Harris Interactive. Except where noted, don't know and refused not included. Some categories do not total 100% due to rounding.
*Less than 0.5%.

ENFORCEMENT
"Breaching privacy? I didn't know I was doing anything illegal," he said. "And anyway, everybody's doing it"

many places. But there's an easy answer to that, too: Make the marketers keep a source list. Computers excel at keeping track of such things. If they were bad at it, this privacy morass never would have happened.

4. PLAY FAIR OR PAY

Better warnings. More choice. Access to your personal records. These things will go a long way toward protecting your privacy. But they won't be enough. After passing the broad laws that we are proposing, Congress will have to take extra steps to insure that companies honor them.

The reason: Privacy laws are unusually hard to enforce. Say, for example, that you plug information about your stock portfolio into a financial Web site but deny permission for this information to be shared. Say that the site ignores your request and sells the data to a charity anyway. Most likely, you'll never find out about the privacy breach. And even if you do, the infraction didn't cause you any economic harm. That means you wouldn't have much financial incentive to sue the offender—and you'd no doubt have a hard time getting a lawyer to take your case. "Only people with a real privacy vendetta are going to sue," says Jonathan Zittrain, executive director of Harvard University's Berkman Center for the Internet & Society.

Because enforcement is chancy, unethical Web sites will be tempted to cheat on the rules. So, to ensure that crime does not pay, Congress will have to shell out a lot of money for privacy cops. Which agency should handle the job? Some experts have suggested creating a brand-new federal privacy commission—but that would be a political nightmare. Others have suggested a government-authorized, industry-run group such as the Internet Corporation for Assigned Names & Numbers (ICANN). This type of quasigovernmental organization would probably move faster than a typical agency, but it also would be vulnerable to becoming the pawn of the very people they're supposed to regulate.

We favor giving the job to the Federal Trade Commission, which has begun moving aggressively on the issue of Internet privacy and which already enforces the Children's Online Privacy Protection Act, the Truth in Lending Act, and the Fair Credit Reporting Act. The agency should be empowered to impose stiff penalties for violations.

PRIVATE PROTECTION. Of course, any privacy laws will need to evolve. As the Internet makes its way onto cell phones, watches, and other devices, some of the privacy rules that make sense in a world of deskbound PCs may become irrelevant. And the long-term prospect of biometric authentication—where fingerprints and retinal scans may be used as New Age passwords to Web sites—will certainly raise serious new privacy issues. Such a scheme would require nothing less than a national database of identifying biological data, raising the spectre of abuse by both outlaw hackers and Big Brother prosecutors.

Meanwhile, new technologies will certainly emerge to help consumers safeguard their own privacy. This summer may see the launch of the long-awaited P3P software standard, which will provide the means for consumers to set privacy preferences in their browsers and allow them to be automatically alerted when the Web sites they click on have privacy policies that differ from their choices. But this technology won't be a panacea. Privacy isn't just about fancy software. It's also about making sure that information is being used in the ways companies had promised. Technology won't protect people from privacy invasions. Only people can do that.

By Heather Green, Mike France, and Marcia Stepanek in New York, and Amy Borrus in Washington, D.C.

When is different just different, and when is different wrong?

Values in Tension: Ethics Away from Home

by Thomas Donaldson

When we leave home and cross our nation's boundaries, moral clarity often blurs. Without a backdrop of shared attitudes, and without familiar laws and judicial procedures that define standards of ethical conduct, certainty is elusive. Should a company invest in a foreign country where civil and political rights are violated? Should a company go along with a host country's discriminatory employment practices? If companies in developed countries shift facilities to developing nations that lack strict environmental and health regulations, or if those companies choose to fill management and other top-level positions in a host nation with people from the home country, whose standards should prevail?

Even the best-informed, best-intentioned executives must rethink their assumptions about business practice in foreign settings. What works in a company's home country can fail in a country with different standards of ethical conduct. Such difficulties are unavoidable for businesspeople who live and work abroad.

But how can managers resolve the problems? What are the principles that can help them work through the maze of cultural differences and establish codes of conduct for globally ethical business practice? How can companies answer the toughest question in global business ethics: What happens when a host country's ethical standards seem lower than the home country's?

Competing Answers

One answer is as old as philosophical discourse. According to cultural relativism, no culture's ethics are better than any other's; therefore there are no international rights and wrongs. If the people of Indonesia tolerate the bribery of their public officials, so what? Their attitude is no better or worse than that of people in Denmark or Singapore who refuse to offer or accept bribes. Likewise, if Belgians fail to find insider trading morally repugnant, who cares?

Not enforcing insider-trading laws is no more or less ethical than enforcing such laws.

The cultural relativist's creed—When in Rome, do as the Romans do—is tempting, especially when failing to do as the locals do means forfeiting business opportunities. The inadequacy of cultural relativism, however, becomes apparent when the practices in question are more damaging than petty bribery or insider trading.

In the late 1980s, some European tanneries and pharmaceutical companies were looking for cheap waste-dumping sites. They approached virtually every country on Africa's west coast from Morocco to the Congo. Nigeria agreed to take highly toxic polychlorinated biphenyls. Unprotected local workers, wearing thongs and shorts, unloaded barrels of PCBs and placed them near a residential area. Neither the residents nor the workers knew that the barrels contained toxic waste.

We may denounce governments that permit such abuses, but many countries are unable to police transnational corporations adequately even if they want to. And in many countries, the combination of ineffective enforcement and inadequate regulations leads to behavior by unscrupulous companies that is clearly wrong. A few years ago, for example, a group of investors became interested in restoring the SS *United States,* once a luxurious ocean liner. Before the actual restoration could begin, the ship had to be stripped of its asbestos lining. A bid from a U.S. company, based on U.S. standards for asbestos removal, priced the job at more than $100 million. A company in the Ukranian city of Sevastopol offered to do the work for less than $2 million. In October 1993, the ship was towed to Sevastopol.

A cultural relativist would have no problem with that outcome, but I do. A country has the right to establish its own health and safety regulations, but in the case described above, the standards and the terms of the contract could not possibly have protected workers in Sevastopol from known health risks. Even if the contract met Ukranian

The Culture and Ethics of Software Piracy

Before jumping on the cultural relativism bandwagon, stop and consider the potential economic consequences of a when-in-Rome attitude toward business ethics. Take a look at the current statistics on software piracy: In the United States, pirated software is estimated to be 35% of the total software market, and industry losses are estimated at $2.3 billion per year. The piracy rate is 57% in Germany and 80% in Italy and Japan; the rates in most Asian countries are estimated to be nearly 100%.

There are similar laws against software piracy in those countries. What, then, accounts for the differences? Although a country's level of economic development plays a large part, culture, including ethical attitudes, may be a more crucial factor. The 1995 annual report of the Software Publishers Association connects software piracy directly to culture and attitude. It describes Italy and Hong Kong as having "'first world' per capita incomes, along with 'third world' rates of piracy." When asked whether one should use software without paying for it, most people, including people in Italy and Hong Kong, say no. But people in some countries regard the practice as *less* unethical than people in other countries do. Confucian culture, for example, stresses that individuals should share what they create with society. That may be, in part, what prompts the Chinese and other Asians to view the concept of intellectual property as a means for the West to monopolize its technological superiority.

What happens if ethical attitudes around the world permit large-scale software piracy? Software companies won't want to invest as much in developing new products, because they cannot expect any return on their investment in certain parts of the world. When ethics fail to support technological creativity, there are consequences that go beyond statistics—jobs are lost and livelihoods jeopardized.

Companies must do more than lobby foreign governments for tougher enforcement of piracy laws. They must cooperate with other companies and with local organizations to help citizens understand the consequences of piracy and to encourage the evolution of a different ethic toward the practice.

standards, ethical businesspeople must object. Cultural relativism is morally blind. There are fundamental values that cross cultures, and companies must uphold them. (For an economic argument against cultural relativism, see the insert "The Culture and Ethics of Software Piracy.")

At the other end of the spectrum from cultural relativism is ethical imperialism, which directs people to do everywhere exactly as they do at home. Again, an understandably appealing approach but one that is clearly inadequate. Consider the large U.S. computer-products company that in 1993 introduced a course on sexual harassment in its Saudi Arabian facility. Under the banner of global consistency, instructors used the same approach to train Saudi Arabian managers that they had used with U.S. managers: the participants were asked to discuss a case in which a manager makes sexually explicit remarks to a new female employee over drinks in a bar. The instructors failed to consider how the exercise would work in a culture with strict conventions governing relationships between men and women. As a result, the training sessions were ludicrous. They baffled and offended the Saudi participants, and the message to avoid coercion and sexual discrimination was lost.

The theory behind ethical imperialism is absolutism, which is based on three problematic principles. Absolutists believe that there is a single list of truths, that they can be expressed only with one set of concepts, and that they call for exactly the same behavior around the world.

The first claim clashes with many people's belief that different cultural traditions must be respected. In some cultures, loyalty to a community—family, organization, or society—is the foundation of all ethical behavior. The Japanese, for example, define business ethics in terms of loyalty to their companies, their business networks, and their nation. Americans place a higher value on liberty than on loyalty; the U.S. tradition of rights emphasizes equality, fairness, and individual freedom. It is hard to conclude that truth lies on one side or the other, but an absolutist would have us select just one.

The second problem with absolutism is the presumption that people must express moral truth using only one set of concepts. For instance, some absolutists insist that the language of basic rights provide the framework for any discussion of ethics. That means, though, that entire cultural traditions must be ignored. The notion of a right evolved with the rise of democracy in post-Renaissance Europe and the United States, but the term is not found in either Confucian or Buddhist traditions. We all learn ethics in the context of our particular cultures, and the power in the principles is deeply tied to the way in which they are expressed. Internationally accepted lists of moral principles, such as the United Nations' Universal Declaration of Human Rights, draw on many cultural and religious traditions. As philosopher Michael Walzer has noted, "There is no Esperanto of global ethics."

The third problem with absolutism is the belief in a global standard of ethical behavior. Context must shape ethical practice. Very low wages, for example, may be considered unethical in rich, advanced countries, but developing nations may be acting ethically if they encourage investment and improve living standards by accepting low wages. Likewise, when people are malnourished or starving, a government may be wise to use more fertilizer in order to improve crop yields, even though that means settling for relatively high levels of thermal water pollution.

When cultures have different standards of ethical behavior—and different ways of handling unethical behavior—a company that takes an absolutist approach may find itself making a disastrous mistake. When a manager at a large U.S. specialty-products company in China caught an employee stealing, she followed the company's practice and turned the employee over to the provincial authorities, who executed him. Managers cannot operate in another culture without being aware of that culture's attitudes toward ethics.

If companies can neither adopt a host country's ethics nor extend the home country's standards, what is the answer? Even the traditional litmus test—What would people think of your actions if they were written up on the front page of the newspaper?—is an unreliable guide, for there is no international consensus on standards of business conduct.

Balancing the Extremes: Three Guiding Principles

Companies must help managers distinguish between practices that are merely different and those that are wrong. For relativists, nothing is sacred and nothing is wrong. For absolutists, many things that are different are wrong. Neither extreme illuminates the real world of business decision making. The answer lies somewhere in between.

When it comes to shaping ethical behavior, companies must be guided by three principles.

☐ Respect for core human values, which determine the absolute moral threshold for all business activities.

☐ Respect for local traditions.

☐ The belief that context matters when deciding what is right and what is wrong.

Consider those principles in action. In Japan, people doing business together often exchange gifts—sometimes expensive ones—in keeping with long-standing Japanese

---

What Do These Values Have in Common?

Non-Western	Western
Kyosei (Japanese): Living and working together for the common good.	Individual liberty
Dharma (Hindu): The fulfillment of inherited duty.	Egalitarianism
Santutthi (Buddhist): The importance of limited desires.	Political participation
Zakat (Muslim): The duty to give alms to the Muslim poor.	Human rights

---

tradition. When U.S. and European companies started doing a lot of business in Japan, many Western businesspeople thought that the practice of gift giving might be wrong rather than simply different. To them, accepting a gift felt like accepting a bribe. As Western companies have become more familiar with Japanese traditions, however, most have come to tolerate the practice and to set different limits on gift giving in Japan than they do elsewhere.

Respecting differences is a crucial ethical practice. Research shows that management ethics differ among cultures; respecting those differences means recognizing that some cultures have obvious weaknesses—as well as hidden strengths. Managers in Hong Kong, for example, have a higher tolerance for some forms of bribery than their Western counterparts, but they have a much lower tolerance for the failure to acknowledge a subordinate's work. In some parts of the Far East, stealing credit from a subordinate is nearly an unpardonable sin.

People often equate respect for local traditions with cultural relativism. That is incorrect. Some practices are clearly wrong. Union Carbide's tragic experience in Bhopal, India, provides one example. The company's executives seriously underestimated how much on-site management involvement was needed at the Bhopal plant to compensate for the country's poor infrastructure and regulatory capabilities. In the aftermath of the disastrous gas leak, the lesson is clear: companies using sophisticated technology in a developing country must evaluate that country's ability to oversee its safe use. Since the incident at Bhopal, Union Carbide has become a leader in advising companies on using hazardous technologies safely in developing countries.

Some activities are wrong no matter where they take place. But some practices that are unethical in one setting may be acceptable in another. For instance, the chemical EDB, a soil fungicide, is banned for use in the United States. In hot climates, however, it quickly becomes harmless through exposure to intense solar radiation and high soil temperatures. As long as the chemical is monitored, companies may be able to use EDB ethically in certain parts of the world.

Defining the Ethical Threshold: Core Values

Few ethical questions are easy for managers to answer. But there are some hard truths that must guide managers' actions, a set of what I call core human values, which define minimum ethical standards for all companies.[1] The right to good health and the right to economic advancement and an improved standard of living are two core human values. Another is what Westerners call the Golden Rule, which is recognizable in every major religious and ethical tradition around the world. In Book 15 of his Analects, for instance, Confucius counsels people to maintain reciprocity, or not to do to others what they do not want done to themselves.

Many companies don't do anything with their codes of conduct; they simply paste them on the wall.

Although no single list would satisfy every scholar, I believe it is possible to articulate three core values that incorporate the work of scores of theologians and philosophers around the world. To be broadly relevant, these values must include elements found in both Western and non-Western cultural and religious traditions. Consider the examples of values in the insert "What Do These Values Have in Common?"

At first glance, the values expressed in the two lists seem quite different. Nonetheless, in the spirit of what philosopher John Rawls calls *overlapping consensus,* one can see that the seemingly divergent values converge at key points. Despite important differences between Western and non-Western cultural and religious traditions, both express shared attitudes about what it means to be human. First, individuals must not treat others simply as tools; in other words, they must recognize a person's value as a human being. Next, individuals and communities must treat people in ways that respect people's basic rights. Finally, members of a community must work together to support and improve the institutions on which the community depends. I call those three values *respect for human dignity, respect for basic rights,* and *good citizenship.*

Those values must be the starting point for all companies as they formulate and evaluate standards of ethical conduct at home and abroad. But they are only a starting point. Companies need much more specific guidelines, and the first step to developing those is to translate the core human values into core values for business. What does it mean, for example, for a company to respect human dignity? How can a company be a good citizen?

I believe that companies can respect human dignity by creating and sustaining a corporate culture in which employees, customers, and suppliers are treated not as means to an end but as people whose intrinsic value must be acknowledged, and by producing safe products and services in a safe workplace. Companies can respect basic rights by acting in ways that support and protect the individual rights of employees, customers, and surrounding communities, and by avoiding relationships that violate human beings' rights to health, education, safety, and an adequate standard of living. And companies can be good citizens by supporting essential social institutions, such as the economic system and the education system, and by working with host governments and other organizations to protect the environment.

The core values establish a moral compass for business practice. They can help companies identify practices that are acceptable and those that are intolerable—even if the practices are compatible with a host country's norms and laws. Dumping pollutants near people's homes and ac-

cepting inadequate standards for handling hazardous materials are two examples of actions that violate core values.

Similarly, if employing children prevents them from receiving a basic education, the practice is intolerable. Lying about product specifications in the act of selling may not affect human lives directly, but it too is intolerable because it violates the trust that is needed to sustain a corporate culture in which customers are respected.

Sometimes it is not a company's actions but those of a supplier or customer that pose problems. Take the case of the Tan family, a large supplier for Levi Strauss. The Tans were allegedly forcing 1,200 Chinese and Filipino women to work 74 hours per week in guarded compounds on the Mariana Islands. In 1992, after repeated warnings to the Tans, Levi Strauss broke off business relations with them.

Creating an Ethical Corporate Culture

The core values for business that I have enumerated can help companies begin to exercise ethical judgment and think about how to operate ethically in foreign cultures, but they are not specific enough to guide managers through actual ethical dilemmas. Levi Strauss relied on a written code of conduct when figuring out how to deal with the Tan family. The company's Global Sourcing and Operating Guidelines, formerly called the Business Partner Terms of Engagement, state that Levi Strauss will "seek to identify and utilize business partners who aspire as individuals and in the conduct of all their businesses to a set of ethical standards not incompatible with our own." Whenever intolerable business situations arise, managers should be guided by precise statements that spell out the behavior and operating practices that the company demands.

Ninety percent of all *Fortune* 500 companies have codes of conduct, and 70% have statements of vision and values. In Europe and the Far East, the percentages are lower but are increasing rapidly. Does that mean that most companies have what they need? Hardly. Even though most large U.S. companies have both statements of values and codes of conduct, many might be better off if they didn't. Too many companies don't do anything with the documents; they simply paste them on the wall to impress employees, customers, suppliers, and the public. As a result, the senior managers who drafted the statements lose credibility by proclaiming values and not living up to them. Companies such as Johnson & Johnson, Levi Strauss, Motorola, Texas Instruments, and Lockheed Martin, however, do a great deal to make the words meaningful. Johnson & Johnson, for example, has become well known for its Credo Challenge sessions, in which managers dis-

Many activities are neither good nor bad but exist in *moral free space.*

cuss ethics in the context of their current business problems and are invited to criticize the company's credo and make suggestions for changes. The participants' ideas are passed on to the company's senior managers. Lockheed Martin has created an innovative site on the World Wide Web and on its local network that gives employees, customers, and suppliers access to the company's ethical code and the chance to voice complaints.

Codes of conduct must provide clear direction about ethical behavior when the temptation to behave unethically is strongest. The pronouncement in a code of conduct that bribery is unacceptable is useless unless accompanied by guidelines for gift giving, payments to get goods through customs, and "requests" from intermediaries who are hired to ask for bribes.

Motorola's values are stated very simply as "How we will always act: [with] constant respect for people [and] uncompromising integrity." The company's code of conduct, however, is explicit about actual business practice. With respect to bribery, for example, the code states that the "funds and assets of Motorola shall not be used, directly or indirectly, for illegal payments of any kind." It is unambiguous about what sort of payment is illegal: "the payment of a bribe to a public official or the kickback of funds to an employee of a customer. . . ." The code goes on to prescribe specific procedures for handling commissions to intermediaries, issuing sales invoices, and disclosing confidential information in a sales transaction—all situations in which employees might have an opportunity to accept or offer bribes.

Codes of conduct must be explicit to be useful, but they must also leave room for a manager to use his or her judgment in situations requiring cultural sensitivity. Host-country employees shouldn't be forced to adopt all home-country values and renounce their own. Again, Motorola's code is exemplary. First, it gives clear direction: "Employees of Motorola will respect the laws, customs, and traditions of each country in which they operate, but will, at the same time, engage in no course of conduct which, even if legal, customary, and accepted in any such country, could be deemed to be in violation of the accepted business ethics of Motorola or the laws of the United States relating to business ethics." After laying down such absolutes, Motorola's code then makes clear when individual judgment will be necessary. For example, employees may sometimes accept certain kinds of small gifts "in rare circumstances, where the refusal to accept a gift" would injure Motorola's "legitimate business interests." Under certain circumstances, such gifts "may be accepted so long as the gift inures to the benefit of Motorola" and not "to the benefit of the Motorola employee."

Striking the appropriate balance between providing clear direction and leaving room for individual judgment makes crafting corporate values statements and ethics codes one of the hardest tasks that executives confront. The words are only a start. A company's leaders need to refer often to their organization's credo and code and must themselves be credible, committed, and consistent. If senior managers act as though ethics don't matter, the rest of the company's employees won't think they do, either.

Conflicts of Development and Conflicts of Tradition

Managers living and working abroad who are not prepared to grapple with moral ambiguity and tension should pack their bags and come home. The view that all business practices can be categorized as either ethical or unethical is too simple. As Einstein is reported to have said, "Things should be as simple as possible—but no simpler." Many business practices that are considered unethical in one setting may be ethical in another. Such activities are neither black nor white but exist in what Thomas Dunfee and I have called *moral free space.*[2] In this gray zone, there are no tight prescriptions for a company's behavior. Managers must chart their own courses—as long as they do not violate core human values.

Consider the following example. Some successful Indian companies offer employees the opportunity for one of their children to gain a job with the company once the child has completed a certain level in school. The companies honor this commitment even when other applicants are more qualified than an employee's child. The perk is extremely valuable in a country where jobs are hard to find, and it reflects the Indian culture's belief that the West has gone too far in allowing economic opportunities to break up families. Not surprisingly, the perk is among the most cherished by employees, but in most Western countries, it would be branded unacceptable nepotism. In the United States, for example, the ethical principle of equal opportunity holds that jobs should go to the applicants with the best qualifications. If a U.S. company made such promises to its employees, it would violate regulations established by the Equal Employment Opportunity Commission. Given this difference in ethical attitudes, how should U.S. managers react to Indian nepotism? Should they condemn the Indian companies, refusing to accept them as partners or suppliers until they agree to clean up their act?

Despite the obvious tension between nepotism and principles of equal opportunity, I cannot condemn the practice for Indians. In a country, such as India, that emphasizes clan and family relationships and has catastrophic levels of unemployment, the practice must be viewed in moral free space. The decision to allow a special perk for employees and their children is not necessarily wrong—at least for members of that country.

How can managers discover the limits of moral free space? That is, how can they learn to distinguish a value in tension with their own from one that is intolerable? Helping managers develop good ethical judgment requires companies to be clear about their core values and codes of conduct. But even the most explicit set of guidelines cannot always provide answers. That is especially true in the thorniest ethical dilemmas, in which the host country's ethical standards not only are different but also seem lower than the home country's. Managers must recognize that when countries have different ethical standards, there are two types of conflict that commonly arise. Each type requires its own line of reasoning.

In the first type of conflict, which I call a *conflict of relative development,* ethical standards conflict because of the countries' different levels of economic development. As mentioned before, developing countries may accept wage rates that seem inhumane to more advanced countries in order to attract investment. As economic conditions in a developing country improve, the incidence of that sort of conflict usually decreases. The second type of conflict is a *conflict of cultural tradition.* For example, Saudi Arabia, unlike most other countries, does not allow women to serve as corporate managers. Instead, women may work in only a few professions, such as education and health care. The prohibition stems from strongly held religious and cultural beliefs; any increase in the country's level of economic development, which is already quite high, is not likely to change the rules.

To resolve a conflict of relative development, a manager must ask the following question: Would the practice be acceptable at home if my country were in a similar stage of economic development? Consider the difference between wage and safety standards in the United States and in Angola, where citizens accept lower standards on both counts. If a U.S. oil company is hiring Angolans to work on an offshore Angolan oil rig, can the company pay them lower wages than it pays U.S. workers in the Gulf of Mexico? Reasonable people have to answer yes if the alternative for Angola is the loss of both the foreign investment and the jobs.

Consider, too, differences in regulatory environments. In the 1980s, the government of India fought hard to be able to import Ciba-Geigy's Entero Vioform, a drug known to be enormously effective in fighting dysentery but one that had been banned in the United States because some users experienced side effects. Although dysentery was not a big problem in the United States, in India, poor public sanitation was contributing to epidemic levels of the disease. Was it unethical to make the drug available in India after it had been banned in the United States? On the contrary, rational people should consider it unethical not to do so. Apply our test: Would the United States, at an earlier stage of development, have used this drug despite its side effects? The answer is clearly yes.

But there are many instances when the answer to similar questions is no. Sometimes a host country's standards are inadequate at any level of economic development. If a country's pollution standards are so low that working on an oil rig would considerably increase a person's risk of developing cancer, foreign oil companies must refuse to do business there. Likewise, if the dangerous side effects

The Problem with Bribery

Bribery is widespread and insidious. Managers in transnational companies routinely confront bribery even though most countries have laws against it. The fact is that officials in many developing countries wink at the practice, and the salaries of local bureaucrats are so low that many consider bribes a form of remuneration. The U.S. Foreign Corrupt Practices Act defines allowable limits on petty bribery in the form of routine payments required to move goods through customs. But demands for bribes often exceed those limits, and there is seldom a good solution.

Bribery disrupts distribution channels when goods languish on docks until local handlers are paid off, and it destroys incentives to compete on quality and cost when purchasing decisions are based on who pays what under the table. Refusing to acquiesce is often tantamount to giving business to unscrupulous companies.

I believe that even routine bribery is intolerable. Bribery undermines market efficiency and predictability, thus ultimately denying people their right to a minimal standard of living. Some degree of ethical commitment—some sense that everyone will play by the rules—is necessary for a sound economy. Without an ability to predict outcomes, who would be willing to invest?

There was a U.S. company whose shipping crates were regularly pilfered by handlers on the docks of Rio de Janeiro. The handlers would take about 10% of the contents of the crates, but the company was never sure which 10% it would be. In a partial solution, the company began sending two crates—the first with 90% of the merchandise, the second with 10%. The handlers learned to take the second crate and leave the first untouched. From the company's perspective, at least knowing which goods it would lose was an improvement.

Bribery does more than destroy predictability; it undermines essential social and economic systems. That truth is not lost on businesspeople in countries where the practice is woven into the social fabric. CEOs in India admit that their companies engage constantly in bribery, and they say that they have considerable disgust for the practice. They blame government policies in part, but Indian executives also know that their country's business practices perpetuate corrupt behavior. Anyone walking the streets of Calcutta, where it is clear that even a dramatic redistribution of wealth would still leave most of India's inhabitants in dire poverty, comes face-to-face with the devastating effects of corruption.

If a company declared all gift giving unethical, it wouldn't be able to do business in Japan.

of a drug treatment outweigh its benefits, managers should not accept health standards that ignore the risks.

When relative economic conditions do not drive tensions, there is a more objective test for resolving ethical problems. Managers should deem a practice permissible only if they can answer no to both of the following questions: Is it possible to conduct business successfully in the host country without undertaking the practice? And Is the practice a violation of a core human value? Japanese gift giving is a perfect example of a conflict of cultural tradition. Most experienced businesspeople, Japanese and non-Japanese alike, would agree that doing business in Japan would be virtually impossible without adopting the practice. Does gift giving violate a core human value? I cannot identify one that it violates. As a result, gift giving may be permissible for foreign companies in Japan even if it conflicts with ethical attitudes at home. In fact, that conclusion is widely accepted, even by companies such as Texas Instruments and IBM, which are outspoken against bribery.

Does it follow that all nonmonetary gifts are acceptable or that bribes are generally acceptable in countries where they are common? Not at all. (See the insert "The Problem with Bribery.") What makes the routine practice of gift giving acceptable in Japan are the limits in its scope and intention. When gift giving moves outside those limits, it soon collides with core human values. For example, when Carl Kotchian, president of Lockheed in the 1970s, carried suitcases full of cash to Japanese politicians, he went beyond the norms established by Japanese tradition. That incident galvanized opinion in the United States Congress and helped lead to passage of the Foreign Corrupt Practices Act. Likewise, Roh Tae Woo went beyond the norms established by Korean cultural tradition when he accepted $635.4 million in bribes as president of the Republic of Korea between 1988 and 1993.

Guidelines for Ethical Leadership

Learning to spot intolerable practices and to exercise good judgment when ethical conflicts arise requires practice. Creating a company culture that rewards ethical behavior is essential. The following guidelines for developing a global ethical perspective among managers can help.

Treat corporate values and formal standards of conduct as absolutes. Whatever ethical standards a company chooses, it cannot waver on its principles either at home or abroad. Consider what has become part of company lore at Motorola. Around 1950, a senior executive was negotiating with officials of a South American government on a $10 million sale that would have increased the com-

pany's annual net profits by nearly 25%. As the negotiations neared completion, however, the executive walked away from the deal because the officials were asking for $1 million for "fees." CEO Robert Galvin not only supported the executive's decision but also made it clear that Motorola would neither accept the sale on any terms nor do business with those government officials again. Retold over the decades, this story demonstrating Galvin's resolve has helped cement a culture of ethics for thousands of employees at Motorola.

Design and implement conditions of engagement for suppliers and customers. Will your company do business with any customer or supplier? What if a customer or supplier uses child labor? What if it has strong links with organized crime? What if it pressures your company to break a host country's laws? Such issues are best not left for spur-of-the-moment decisions. Some companies have realized that. Sears, for instance, has developed a policy of not contracting production to companies that use prison labor or infringe on workers' rights to health and safety. And BankAmerica has specified as a condition for many of its loans to developing countries that environmental standards and human rights must be observed.

Allow foreign business units to help formulate ethical standards and interpret ethical issues. The French pharmaceutical company Rhône-Poulenc Rorer has allowed foreign subsidiaries to augment lists of corporate ethical principles with their own suggestions. Texas Instruments has paid special attention to issues of international business ethics by creating the Global Business Practices Council, which is made up of managers from countries in which the company operates. With the overarching intent to create a "global ethics strategy, locally deployed," the council's mandate is to provide ethics education and create local processes that will help managers in the company's foreign business units resolve ethical conflicts.

In host countries, support efforts to decrease institutional corruption. Individual managers will not be able to wipe out corruption in a host country, no matter how many bribes they turn down. When a host country's tax system, import and export procedures, and procurement practices favor unethical players, companies must take action.

Many companies have begun to participate in reforming host-country institutions. General Electric, for example, has taken a strong stand in India, using the media to make repeated condemnations of bribery in business and government. General Electric and others have found, however, that a single company usually cannot drive out entrenched corruption. Transparency International, an organization based in Germany, has been effective in helping coalitions of companies, government officials, and others work to reform bribery-ridden bureaucracies in Russia, Bangladesh, and elsewhere.

Exercise moral imagination. Using moral imagination means resolving tensions responsibly and creatively. Coca-Cola, for instance, has consistently turned down requests for bribes from Egyptian officials but has managed to gain political support and public trust by sponsoring a project to plant fruit trees. And take the example of Levi Strauss, which discovered in the early 1990s that two of its suppliers in Bangladesh were employing children under the age of 14—a practice that violated the company's principles but was tolerated in Bangladesh. Forcing the suppliers to fire the children would not have ensured that the children received an education, and it would have caused serious hardship for the families depending on the children's wages. In a creative arrangement, the suppliers agreed to pay the children's regular wages while they attended school and to offer each child a job at age 14. Levi Strauss, in turn, agreed to pay the children's tuition and provide books and uniforms. That arrangement allowed Levi Strauss to uphold its principles and provide long-term benefits to its host country.

Many people think of values as soft; to some they are usually unspoken. A South Seas island society uses the word *mokita*, which means, "the truth that everybody knows but nobody speaks." However difficult they are to articulate, values affect how we all behave. In a global business environment, values in tension are the rule rather than the exception. Without a company's commitment, statements of values and codes of ethics end up as empty platitudes that provide managers with no foundation for behaving ethically. Employees need and deserve more, and responsible members of the global business community can set examples for others to follow. The dark consequences of incidents such as Union Carbide's disaster in Bhopal remind us how high the stakes can be.

1. In other writings, Thomas W. Dunfee and I have used the term *hypernorm* instead of *core human value.*
2. Thomas Donaldson and Thomas W. Dunfee, "Toward a Unified Conception of Business Ethics: Integrative Social Contracts Theory," *Academy of Management Review,* April 1994; and "Integrative Social Contracts Theory: A Communitarian Conception of Economic Ethics," *Economics and Philosophy,* spring 1995.

GLOBAL STANDARDS, LOCAL PROBLEMS

"When in Rome" doesn't work anymore. More and more global firms are finding a correlation between ethical standards and economic success.

Meryl Davids

AH, THE GOOD OLD DAYS. BACK 30, 20, EVEN 10, years ago, companies could run their overseas business pretty much however they wanted. What happened in a land far away bore little consequence to the main operations. If a factory employed underage workers in Third World countries, well, that's just the way things were done over there. Giving and accepting elaborate gifts? Part of the culture. And if your subsidiary didn't adhere to the same pollution control standards as its American counterparts, it was easily justified on the grounds that environmental laws overseas weren't as strict.

But if the world shrinking to a marble has been good for American companies profiting from international operations and trade, it has also added brutal new pressures for principled behavior on a global scale. Global business ethics has now become "the ultimate dilemma for many U.S. businesses," as one business publication stated.

"The world is highly interconnected now, so American consumers increasingly know and care if a company is, say, dumping chemical waste in a river in China," says Robert MacGregor, a leader of the Caux Round Table, a group of international business leaders aiming to focus attention on global corporate responsibility. "Companies that are concerned with their reputations, and that's nearly all companies, recognize they have to focus on their global principles."

Ignoring global ethical issues can even cost you customers at home. "We have evidence that if consumers know that a company is unethical anywhere in the world, they will exercise their disapproval at the cash register," MacGregor says, not to mention the impact it has on employees and investors.

Brother, Can You Spare a Thousand?

While the heightened focus on international ethics—led by a growing charge by nonprofit organizations including Caux, the U.N., the World Bank, and others—does make it riskier to operate overseas, in many ways it is also a welcome relief to many U.S. firms. Companies here have long decried the uneven playing field created by our Foreign Corrupt Practices Act. Passed in 1977, among other things it prohibits American countries from paying bribes for expedited services. Companies from other countries, including several in Europe, however, can not only legally make those payments, but they can also deduct the money from their taxes.

With this disparity, trying to open factories or get products unloaded in countries where such payoffs are the norm has proven difficult, if not impossible, for American companies in many locales. Which areas are the most rife with problems? According to a Corruption Perception Index developed by nonprofit group Transparency International, Cameroon, Paraguay, Honduras, Tanzania, and Nigeria are seen as most corrupt (see table). While Frank Vogl, vice president of the group and a former World Bank official, says the survey measures only perceptions (of ordinary citizens, business leaders, and experts), "countries that are seen to have high levels of corruption almost certainly do

From *Journal of Business Strategy*, January/February 1999, pp. 38-43. © 1999 by Faulkner & Gray. Reprinted by permission.

The Transparency International 1998 Corruption Perceptions Index

Country Rank	Country	1998 CPI Score	Standard Deviation	Surveys Used	Country Rank	Country	1998 CPI Score	Standard Deviation	Surveys Used
1	Denmark	10.0	0.7	9	44	Zimbabwe	4.2	2.2	6
2	Finland	9.6	0.5	9	45	Malawi	4.1	0.6	4
3	Sweden	9.5	0.5	9	46	Brazil	4.0	0.4	9
4	New Zealand	9.4	0.7	8	47	Belarus	3.9	1.9	3
5	Iceland	9.3	0.9	6	48	Slovak Republic	3.9	1.6	5
6	Canada	9.2	0.5	9	49	Jamaica	3.8	0.4	3
7	Singapore	9.1	1.0	10	50	Morocco	3.7	1.8	3
8	Netherlands	9.0	0.7	9	51	El Salvador	3.6	2.3	3
9	Norway	9.0	0.7	9	52	China	3.5	0.7	10
10	Switzerland	8.9	0.6	10	53	Zambia	3.5	1.6	4
11	Australia	8.7	0.7	8	54	Turkey	3.4	1.0	10
12	Luxembourg	8.7	0.9	7	55	Ghana	3.3	1.0	4
13	United Kingdom	8.7	0.5	10	56	Mexico	3.3	0.6	9
14	Ireland	8.2	1.4	10	57	Philippines	3.3	1.1	10
15	Germany	7.9	0.4	10	58	Senegal	3.3	0.8	3
16	Hong Kong	7.8	1.1	12	59	Ivory Coast	3.1	1.7	4
17	Austria	7.5	0.8	9	60	Guatemala	3.1	2.5	3
18	United States	7.5	0.9	8	61	Argentina	3.0	0.6	9
19	Israel	7.1	1.4	9	62	Nicaragua	3.0	2.5	3
20	Chile	6.8	0.9	9	63	Romania	3.0	1.5	3
21	France	6.7	0.6	9	64	Thailand	3.0	0.7	11
22	Portugal	6.5	1.0	10	65	Yugoslavia	3.0	1.5	3
23	Botswana	6.1	2.2	3	66	Bulgaria	2.9	2.3	4
24	Spain	6.1	1.3	10	67	Egypt	2.9	0.6	3
25	Japan	5.8	1.6	11	68	India	2.9	0.6	12
26	Estonia	5.7	0.5	3	69	Bolivia	2.8	1.2	4
27	Costa Rica	5.6	1.6	5	70	Ukraine	2.8	1.6	6
28	Belgium	5.4	1.4	9	71	Latvia	2.7	1.9	3
29	Malaysia	5.3	0.4	11	72	Pakistan	2.7	1.4	3
30	Namibia	5.3	1.0	3	73	Uganda	2.6	0.8	4
31	Taiwan	5.3	0.7	11	74	Kenya	2.5	0.6	4
32	South Africa	5.2	0.8	10	75	Vietnam	2.5	0.5	6
33	Hungary	5.0	1.2	9	76	Russia	2.4	0.9	10
34	Mauritius	5.0	0.8	3	77	Ecuador	2.3	1.5	3
35	Tunisia	5.0	2.1	3	78	Venezuela	2.3	0.8	9
36	Greece	4.9	1.7	9	79	Colombia	2.2	0.8	9
37	Czech Republic	4.8	0.8	9	80	Indonesia	2.0	0.9	10
38	Jordan	4.7	1.1	6	81	Nigeria	1.9	0.5	5
39	Italy	4.6	0.8	10	82	Tanzania	1.9	1.1	4
40	Poland	4.6	1.6	8	83	Honduras	1.7	0.5	3
41	Peru	4.5	0.8	6	84	Paraguay	1.5	0.5	3
42	Uruguay	4.3	0.9	3	85	Cameroon	1.4	0.5	4
43	South Korea	4.2	1.2	12					

The column 1998 CPI Score relates perceptions of the degree of which corruption is seen by business people—a perfect 10.00 would be a totally corruption-free country. Standard Deviation indicates differences in the values of the sources for the 1998 index: the greater the variance, the greater the differences of perceptions of a country among the sources. The number of surveys used had to be at least 3 for a country to be included in the CPI.

have them." Russia, too, falls near the bottom of the scale, as does China, a situation many believe has contributed to these countries' current economic woes.

"The rogue capitalism in Russia, and the cronyism and lack of transparency in Asia, aren't good for business there—or here," MacGregor says. "Principled business is not just a theoretical notion; it has prag-

matic implications." The belief that moral values such as openness and trust are such an integral part of successful capitalism was even held by capitalism's proud papa, Adam Smith, MacGregor says. Before writing his *Wealth of Nations,* Smith penned a treatise arguing that for capitalism to work it must be based on shared rules and common values. "When you violate those rules, the system doesn't work the way it should," MacGregor warns.

Larry Smeltzer, an ethics professor at the College of Business at Arizona State University, also sees a correlation between ethical standards and economic success. "If you look at the more progressive industrialized countries in the world—Canada, Western Europe, parts of Asia—you find a higher sense of ethics there. It goes hand in hand," Smeltzer says. By contrast, countries with low ethical gauges, such as Mexico and many African countries, have equally scant business norms. "The lack of openness and predictable business standards drives companies away," Smeltzer says. "Why would you want to do business in, say Libya, where you don't know the rules?"

Smeltzer uses the analogy of a pickup football game by some guys in a park. If you just start playing without discussing guidelines, he says, conflict is likely to result. If rules are clearly established beforehand, however, the game will run smoothly. "The need for grease payments in China tells me I'm not clear what the rules there are, so someone has to help me navigate," he says. And, Smeltzer recently wrote in an ethics paper, bribes in China given to establish connections in the government add an estimated 3% to 5% to companies' operating costs.

It was China's troubling ethics climate, in fact, that persuaded Levi Strauss & Co. to exit the market there in 1993, despite the lure of a billion potential denim-clad pairs of legs. Levi's elaborate "principled reasoning approach" demanded a thorough ethical analysis and, says, spokesperson Gavin Power, ethical issues, especially regarding workers rights, were too troubling to permit continued operations. (Having closely followed the situation there since, Levi now says it has identified several trustworthy contractors and it may soon reenter the market.) While the 1993 decision might seem financially irrational, Smeltzer believes that a close analysis shows it made good economic sense. "If the rules for business play are uncertain with respect to its citizens, how can the Chinese government provide assurances of fairness to its potential business citizens?" he reasoned in the ethics paper.

People and Pollution Woes

In addition to the issue of bribes, two other areas are increasingly coming under the hot glare of ethics-watchers: human rights and the environment. American consumers may not get too worked up over "gifts" to foreign partners or government officials, but they will quickly show their displeasure at the thought of mistreated—especially underage—workers, and toxic waste polluting pristine waters and wildernesses around the world.

Treating the Earth responsibly has become the third leg of the tripod on which a solid international ethics reputation now rests.

Even an ethically sensitive company like Levi Strauss can find that navigating international human rights offers tough sailing. The company won great praise for its 1993 China decision, and for its handling of an incident at its Bangladesh plants in 1992. (In the latter incident, the company discovered soon after it had stepped up its campaign to monitor foreign plants that two sewing subcontractors employed young children—a norm in a country where kids without jobs frequently beg or prostitute themselves for money. Levi's cleverly solved the problem by having the contractors remove the children from the factory but continue to pay their wages on condition that they attend school full time. When they reached the local maturity age of 14, they were guaranteed back their jobs.) But even this company's ethics record has rough spots. "They treat most of their workers decently, but go to the Philippines and you will see people working 90 hours a week making Dockers," charges Charles Kernaghan, director of the nonprofit watchdog group the National Labor Committee.

Kernaghan and his group are determined to ensure that American consumers know what companies are doing overseas. His group was behind the Kathie Lee Gifford/Wal-Mart incident of 1996, when Gifford cried on air over accusations that her line was produced in sweatshops around the world employing underaged kids.

Gifford may have thought the issue would disappear when she announced that she had hired independent monitors to check conditions in factories where her line is produced, but the National Labor Committee is bent on assuring that it doesn't. The New York-based group claims some of Gifford's items are still made in sweatshops in China, where women work 84-hour weeks in unsafe factories and live 12 to a room in dirty, watched dorms. "There is a Kathie Lee and Wal-Mart Corporate Code of Conduct, but these workers have never heard of them," Kernaghan says. He also claims that Wal-Mart's campaign to assure Americans that many of its garments are made right here "is very much misleading." The NLC physically counted 105,000 private-label items in 14 stores last year and found that 83% of the items were made offshore, compared to an industry norm of 50% to 60%—a disparity Kernaghan continually points out in his numerous speeches, media contacts, and Web site.

Businesses that employ factory workers around the globe are turning to independent monitors to watch out for employee rights overseas.

Meanwhile, treating the Earth responsibly has become the third leg of the tripod on which a solid international ethics reputation now rests. "The environment is an area of concern for companies involved with global ethics plans," says Bob Echols, manager of international compliance at Raytheon Company, in Lexington, Mass., which is currently rolling out an ambitious worldwide plan in the 80 countries in which it does business.

Caux's MacGregor cites three reasons for the increased interest. First, American and international reporters are now likely to write about the chemical waste a company dumps far away in a river in China. Second, he says, the increasing recognition that environmental actions in one part of the world affect all others is leading business people to consider their own children and neighbors, though they live thousands of miles away from the pollution. And third, MacGregor says, there is cost. "If you are dumping waste out the back door [even in an undeveloped country], eventually you will have to spend the money cleaning it up," he says.

What To Do—And Not Do

How does a company doing business internationally navigate these ethical storm waters? According to the experts, by implementing a true ethics program with teeth, not by merely trotting out a piece of paper. And by recognizing that, despite cultural differences, certain core ethical values are held by all people around the globe.

Writing a code of ethics that clearly states what's expected of employees is a typical first step. Then you need to get input on the proposed code from foreign nationals, perhaps via committees made up of people from the various affected cultures. "Often, this is where companies begin to do it wrong," says W. Michael Hoffman, executive director of the Center for Business Ethics at Bentley College in Waltham, Massachusetts. "They take their code of ethics and translate it into foreign languages, and Joe sends it over to Juan and Hans overseas with instructions to roll it out to their divisions. But because it doesn't mesh with their culture and they don't understand why they should care, these guys don't support it." For example, Hoffman says, without a firm rationale, Japanese

will not readily follow a rule that says they should not accept expensive gifts, because presents are an integral part of that society and to refuse such a gift often humiliates the giver.

How to report ethical violations is also sometimes culture-specific. "In France, Germany, and other European countries, it has been my experience that employees are very reluctant to raise an issue regarding a fellow employee," Raytheon's Echols says. Raytheon's solution is to provide numerous reporting mechanisms—ranging from phoning or faxing the corporate headquarters to speaking face-to-face with a local ethics contact, to mailing in an anonymous, postage-paid card—so the staffer can choose the one most comfortable to him. Echols is also investigating incorporating an ethics section in his company's Web site, and allowing staffers to send confidential information that way.

Once signed off on by all the affected cultures, the ethical code must then become a living document for employees. Each worker must be clear how to apply that code to everyday actions. At Minneapolis-based Honeywell Inc., which has nearly half its employees outside the U.S., senior management regularly emphasizes ethics in its regional newsletters. One such publication for the Asia-Pacific, for example, carried a message from the president that the company would prefer to lose business rather than succumb to paying a bribe. An ethics advice line encourages employees to discuss ethical decisions they are unclear about. The company, which recently rewrote its code to be less focused on the U.S. and more applicable globally, also conducts training around the world. The codes various aspects, from child labor issues to gifts and gratuities, are enumerated specifically in its code of ethics handbook.

More and more businesses that employ factory workers around the globe are also turning to independent monitors to watch out for employees rights overseas. The National Labor Committee favors using local religious and human-rights groups to do that job, but companies largely seem to be favoring monitoring by such auditing groups as Pricewaterhouse Coopers and Ernst & Young. Once abuses are discovered, they must be swiftly resolved. "We either work with our subcontractor to correct the problems, or if that can't be done we will and have terminated our relationship with them," Levi's Power says.

Honeywell has put teeth into its ethical principles by making adherence to the company's code a condition of employment. "Sometimes the situation is clear enough that termination is the appropriate response, and we have fired people for violating the code," says Lisa Dercks, vice president and ethics officer at Honeywell. Such consequences are important for telling employees that top management takes this topic seriously, Bentley's Hoffman says. Other companies

CAUX ROUND TABLE GENERAL PRINCIPLES

1. The Responsibilities of Businesses: Beyond Shareholders Toward Stakeholders. Businesses have a role to play in improving the lives of all their customers, employees, and shareholders by sharing with them the wealth they have created. Suppliers and competitors as well should expect businesses to honor their obligations in a spirit of honesty and fairness.

2. The Economic and Social Impact of Business: Toward Innovation, Justice, and World Community. Businesses established in foreign countries to develop, produce, or sell should also contribute to the social advancement of those countries by creating productive employment and helping to raise the purchasing power of their citizens. Businesses also should contribute to human rights, education, welfare, and vitalization of the countries in which they operate.

Businesses should contribute to economic and social development not only in the countries in which they operate, but also in the world community at large, through effective and prudent use of resources, free and fair competition, and emphasis upon innovation in technology, production methods, marketing, and communications.

3. Business Behavior: Beyond the Letter of Law Toward a Spirit of Trust
While accepting the legitimacy of trade secrets, businesses should recognize that sincerity, candor, truthfulness, the keeping of promises, and transparency contribute not only to their own credibility and stability but also to the smoothness and efficiency of business transactions, particularly on the international level.

4. Respect for Rules. To avoid trade frictions and to promote freer trade, equal conditions for competition, and fair and equitable treatment for all participants, businesses should respect international and domestic rules. In addition, they should recognize that some behavior, although legal, may still have adverse consequences.

5. Support for Multilateral Trade. Businesses should support the multilateral trade systems of the GATT/World Trade Organization and similar international agreements. They should cooperate in efforts to promote the progressive and judicious liberalization of trade and to relax those domestic measures that unreasonably hinder global commerce, while giving due respect to national policy objectives.

6. Respect for the Environment. A business should protect and, where possible, improve, the environment, promote sustainable development, and prevent the wasteful use of natural resources.

7. Avoidance of Illicit Operations. A business should not participate in or condone bribery, money laundering, or other corrupt practices: Indeed, it should seek cooperation with others to eliminate them. It should not trade in arms or other materials used for terrorist activities, drug traffic, or other organized crime.

take the opposite approach, basing employee compensation in part on adherence to ethical codes.

When drafting its code of ethics, companies must strike a balance between being sensitive to foreign cultures and their own internal sense of right and wrong. "The two extremes are ethical fanaticism, which says my way is always right, and ethical relativism, which says there are no absolutes," Hoffman says. However, there are several absolute ethical standards that everyone in the world agrees with, "and these become your core values," he says, pointing to the Caux General Principles as a good starting point for corporate discussion (see box, "Caux Round Table General Principles").

"The process that you set up to ensure that you're making solid ethical decisions is key," Hoffman says. "If you follow the process, you can be comfortable with your decision, even if other ethical companies might come to a different conclusion."

Meryl Davids, a business journalist based in Coral Springs, Fla., frequently writes for JBS.

The Environment of Ethics in Global Business

by William J. Kehoe
O'Dell Professor of Commerce
McIntire School of Commerce
University of Virginia
Charlottesville, VA 22903–2493

Over the past several decades there has been an ever-increasing movement toward the globalization of business. This movement has been a constant and, more recently, an imperative for business organizations. An imperative expressed in the statement, "go global or perish."

As businesses of all sizes and types go global, questions of ethics are soon encountered. This manuscript addresses the environment of ethics in global business. First, the diversity in the conduct of global business is discussed. Second, the diversity in the understanding of ethics is examined, and the implications of that diversity for ethics in business are considered. Third, various unethical practices in global business are summarized. Fourth, future directions for the incorporation of ethics in global business are suggested.

Diversity in Conduct of Global Business

Business in the global arena may be characterized as a brilliantly structured mosaic of complexity and diversity composed of various and different places, peoples, cultures, customs, laws, mores, processes, procedures, and ethical systems. A mosaic that challenges, excites, and, at times, frustrates a global business manager.

Within the mosaic of diversity, four broad approaches to the conduct of global business may be generalized. First, a firm may expand from being a domestic firm to being an exporter. Second, a firm may evolve to being a multinational firm, with some type of presence in other countries. Third, a firm may develop into a multilocal firm, in which each market in the world is approached with separate strategies and products. Fourth, a firm may mature to being a global firm. Each of these approaches is discussed below.

Exporter

A firm that is an exporter operates by shipping its product(s) from its home country to host countries around the world. To facilitate the export process, an exporter may contract with a home-country agent to facilitate the export process and/or a host-country agent to receive, finance, market, and distribute the company's products in a host country. The management focus of an exporter is primarily domestic in that the firm considers its home market as a first area of opportunity, but with exports made to various host-country markets where other opportunities have been identified.

Multinational Firm

In time, an exporter may elect to have some type of presence in a host country beyond that provided by a host-country agent. The presence may involve the establishment of a sales office; the leasing, purchase, or construction of an assembly or production facility; and/or making some other type of direct investment in a host country. This means that the firm has changed its focus from the home market being its primary area of opportunity to an emphasis in other areas of the world by establishing, for example, an investment-based presence in a host country and/or placing home-country personnel in a host country. As an exporter becomes a multinational firm, its product strategy tends primarily to be extension, in that the home country's product is extended to world markets. In time, as a multinational firm evolves toward being a multilocal firm, its product strategy may evolve from extension to adaptation, with products being changed to better match the perceived needs of a host-country market. The financial strategy of a multinational firm is to source financing initially in the home country,

Published in the *Journal of Business and Behavioral Science,* Volume 4, Number 2, Fall 1998, pp. 47–56. Presented at the Fifth Annual Meeting of the American Society of Business and Behavioral Sciences.

with host-country financial sourcing used when home-country personnel gain experience in the host-country.

Multilocal Firm

A multilocal firm is a multinational whose global-business strategy has evolved to approach each host country differently and separately based upon the unique characteristics of the country. That is, a multilocal firm uses a market-segmentation approach to each host country, differentiating its products to meet the unique needs of each national market. Its product strategy is one of both extension and adaptation. Depending upon the needs that exist in a foreign market, the firm's product will either be extended without changes to a host-country market, or be redesigned to meet individual market needs in a host country. In addition to having an investment and home-country personnel presence in a host country, a multilocal firm will increasingly employ host-country nationals so as to better differentiate itself in a host country, and will likely source financing in the host country. The focus of a multilocal firm is on customization to meet the requirements of the local market. This may result in separate and distinct operating procedures in each country, and in greater autonomy for country managers.

Global Firm

A global firm has as its focus a world-view of markets. It operates, according to Levitt (1983), "with resolute consistency—at low relative cost—as if the entire world (or major regions of it) were a single entity. . . ." If the firm's output is a product, its operating philosophy as a global firm might be expressed as: one world, one product, one brand, and one marketing approach—that is, it seeks to develop world products, such as an automobile manufacturer attempting to develop a world car. If the firm provides a service instead of a product, its operating philosophy as a global firm might be expressed as: one world, one service-delivery approach, and one marketing approach. A global firm seeks to serve markets as they exist anywhere in the world. As part of its focus, a global firm seeks the best persons for positions anywhere in the world regardless of nationality. Similarly, it places production facilities in low-cost countries around the world and sources financing at least-cost centers wherever they may be located in the world.

Diversity in Understanding of Ethics

Just as there is a great diversity of approaches to global business in the world, so, too, is diversity in the understanding of systems of ethics in the conduct of global business. This diversity of understanding is a function of a host of economic, political, religious, and social variables that define the differences between peoples, nations, and cultures. For example, Donaldson and Dunfee (1994), postulate that "Muslim managers may wish to participate in systems of economic ethics compatible with the teachings of Mohammed, European and American managers may wish to participate in systems of economic ethics giving due respect to individual liberty, and Japa-

nese managers may prefer systems showing respect for the value of the collective." In each of these situations and in similar situations within the many countries of the world, a given system of ethics, particularly a system of ethics that is home-country specific, may not be accepted, respected, understood, or practiced by host-country nationals.

While the ethics of individuals differ around the world and while a system of ethics from a home country may not be embraced by host-country nationals, managers of global firms nevertheless must raise ethics in the consciousness [of] their employees regardless of where employees are assigned in the world or whatever their national origins.

In raising ethical consciousness, it is insufficient to do so simply by establishing a code of ethics in an organization. Rather, O'Mally (1995) suggests that management must develop an ethical culture across an organization. By advocating an ethical culture, Paine (1994) argues that the reputation of a firm is enhanced and its relationships with its constituencies are strengthened. Sonnenberg and Goldberg (1992) have found that employees feel better about a firm and perform at higher levels when they sense ethics as part of its culture. As a result, a firm realizes higher-level results when a concern for ethics pervades the organization and is a part of its culture.

A concern for ethics is a part of the shared values of a global firm. These values must be developed for a global firm to be holistic, to be greater than the sum of its many parts, whether they are located in the home country and/or in host countries. Global holism is a necessity for success in global business and, according to Daniels and Daniels (1994) means that "the organization has shared beliefs, attitudes, and values," including a system of ethics, which, when taken together, "creates a consistency in the way the firm treats customers, vendors, other business partners, and each other, wherever business is being done." In summary, a concern for ethics in global business is a major responsibility of management, is an integral aspect (Roddick, 1994) of international trade, contributes to global holism, and is an imperative for success in global business (Trevino, Butterfield and McCabe, 1998).

Unethical Practices in Global Business

Whether an exporter, a multinational, a multilocal, or a global firm, there are many ways in which a firm may engage in unethical business practices in the global business arena. Some of the ways of acting unethically may be intentional on the part of a firm, while other may have a genesis in a lack of understanding of, or an appreciation for, the culture of a host country in which a firm is operating. Many examples of unethical practices are reported in the literature. Twelve of the most egregious examples are presented in the following paragraphs, in no particular order of significance.

• The first egregious practice presented in this article as an unethical practice is the making of payments, often unrecorded, to officials in a host country in the form of bribes, kickbacks, gifts, and/or other forms of inducement (Kimelman, 1994, and Landauer, 1979). These payments often are made in spite of prohibitions of the U.S. Foreign Corrupt Practices Act against such practices.

- The second example is the marketing of products abroad that have been removed from a home-country market due to health or environmental concerns. Examples given by Hinds (1982) include chemical, pharmaceutical, and pesticide products, as well as contraceptive devices, which were removed from the U.S. market allegedly for being unsafe to the environment and/or to health, but for which marketing in other countries was continued, and, in some cases, was accelerated.

- Marketing products in host countries that are questionable need or which may be detrimental to the health, welfare, and/or economic well-being of consumers is the third egregious unethical practice. An often-cited example (Post, 1985; Willatt, 1970) is the Nestle Company's marketing of infant formula in developing countries. Parents in developing countries are alleged to have been unable to afford the formula, unable to read directions to use the formula appropriately, unable to find sanitary sources of water for preparing the formula, and not to have needed the formula until Nestle convinced them that its use was necessary. Another example (White, 1997) is marketing of cigarettes in developing countries by advertising that implies that most people in the United States smoke and that smoking is "an American thing to do."

- The fourth example is a firm operating in countries that are known to violate human rights and/or failing to be an advocate for human rights in such countries. During the apartheid era in South Africa, Deresky (1994) reported that U.S. firms were criticized for doing business in the country and for failing to advocate human rights by publicly opposing the discrimination, oppression, and segregation of apartheid.

- The fifth example is a firm moving jobs from a home country to low-wage host countries. When this occurs, workers in the home country are hurt because of loss of jobs (Kehoe, 1995), while workers in a host country are exploited by low wages. For example, Ballinger (1992) argues that Nike's profits have increased due, in part, to the lower wages paid to workers in Nike-contracted plants outside the United States. Employees in these plants reportedly work in excess of ten hours per day, six days a week, for a weekly salary of less than U.S.$50 for their efforts. The Associated Press (1997) reports that employees in Nike-contracted plants in Vietnam are paid U.S. 20 cents per hour for working a 12-hour day. Encouragingly, a report in The New York Times (Staff, 1997) suggests that Nike is correcting alleged abuses of employees in contracted plants in Vietnam.

- Utilizing child labor (Nichols, et.al., 1993) in host countries when the law in a firm's home country prohibits such use is the sixth example of an unethical practice. While the use of child labor in a host country may be a necessity to support a child and her/his family, be preferable to unemployment, and not be of a concern to the host government, is it ethical to use children as laborers? Recently, a group of firms (Headden, 1997), including Nike, Reebok, L.L. Bean, and Liz Claiborne, have committed to a policy of prohibiting the employment of children younger than 15 years of age in factories in host countries.

- Seventh is the practice of operating in countries whose environmental standards are lax, or, the converse, being lax in respect for a host country's environment. In the Amazon, global corporations are reported (Thomson and Dudley, 1989) to have ignored their own and the host country's environmental guidelines in extracting oil. In Ireland, global firms are suspected (Keohane, 1989) of ignoring environmental regulations and to be illegally dumping hazardous waste throughout the country.

- Eighth is operating in a host country with a lower regard for workers' health and well-being than in the home country. Japanese companies are alleged (Itoh, 1991) to have overworked their employees both in Japan and in host countries and to have been indifferent to their health. Union Carbide is alleged (Daniels and Radebaugh, 1993) to have operated a plant in Bhopal, India, with lower safety standards than its plants in more developed countries.

- Conducting business in a developing nation in such a manner as to dominate the nation's economy is the ninth example of an unethical practice. Several rubber companies have been accused of dominating the economies of the developing nations in which they operated rubber plantations. Such domination has been called *dependencia* (Turner, 1984), and has been shown to be damaging to a host country's economy, demoralizing to its people, and of questionable ethics.

- The tenth example is intervening in the affairs of a host country through such activities as influence peddling or other efforts to affect local political activity. In Italy, for example (Anonymous, March 20, 1993), an investigation was undertaken into the alleged illegal financing of political parties by Italian business firms, as well as by foreign business entities operating in the country.

- Taking actions abroad that would be unpopular, controversial, unethical, or illegal in the home country is the eleventh example. For instance, MacKenzie (1992) raised the controversial issue of whether, given advances in DNA research, a business firm should have the right to patent a life form? Officials at the European Parliament in Brussels have debated the legal and moral issues of this question. Given the conclusion of that debate is in the affirmative, may a non-European firm, operating in an European market, patent life forms in Europe if such patenting activity is unethical or illegal in the firm's home country?

- The twelfth and final example is an egregious practice of a firm reinvesting little of the profit realized in a host country back in that country due to a restrictive covenant in corporate policy requiring that a majority of profit earned in a host country be repatriated back to the home country. This means that a global firm may reinvest very little back in a host country, and the citizens of the country may be exploited as a result.

Future Directions

The unethical practices identified above have befallen many firms on their journeys in the global business arena. The journeys can be dangerous and difficult, and may, if not carefully charted, change the integrity of a firm in calamitous ways.

Should there be a framework for global business ethics to point a firm safely onward down the global road? A code for the road, as in the lyrics of Crosby, Stills and Nash (1970), "you, who are on the road, must have a code that you can live by. . . ." Is it possible to design such a framework, and to de - velop a code by which global businesses might live? Where do managers begin the process?

What is needed is a framework for ethics that may be used by firms engaged in global business across the many cultures that are encountered. The framework should be anchored in a concept of shared moral values and developed by using moral languages to give meaning to ethics across cultures. The frame- work should allow for a firm to remain loyal to its core values in situations involving questions of ethics, but allow different peripheral-value statements in host countries.

When developing a code of global business ethics, contri- butions must be sought from throughout the world. This means that individuals from throughout a firm's global expanse must be involved in writing the code. Such a code will contribute to a concept of ethics being embraced throughout a firm, and to ethics being a word often spoken by employees throughout a firm, rather than a word seldom spoken, or never spoken.

Conclusion

Of all the ways to imbue holism in a global firm, the prac- tice of ethics may be the most beneficial. When a system of ethics is in place in a firm, the unethical practices that were identified above may be avoided. The practice of ethics en- hances an individual, a global firm, and global business. As global business is enhanced, the world, as the arena of global business, is made better.

References

Anonymous. (1993, March 20). "The Purging of Italy, Inc.," *Economist*, March, pp. 69–70.

Associated Press. (1997). "Conditions Deplorable at Nike's Vietnamese Plants," *The Daily Progress*, March 28, 1997, p. A2.

Ballinger, Jeffrey. (1992). "The New Free-Trade Hall," *Harper's*, August, pp. 45–47.

Crosby, Stills and Nash. (1970).

Daniels, John D. and L. H. Radebaugh. (1993). *International Dimensions of Contemporary Business*. Boston, MA: PWS-Kent Publishing Company, pp.79–80.

Daniels, John L. and N. Caroline Daniels. (1994). *Global Vision: Building New Models for the Corporation of the Future*. New York: McGraw-Hill, Inc., p. 12.

Deresky, Helen. (1994). *International Management*. New York: Harper Collins College Publishers, pp. 516–519.

Donaldson, Thomas and T. W. Dunfee. (1994). "Toward a Unified Conception of Business Ethics: Integrative Social Contracts Theory," *Academy of Man- agement Review*, April, p. 261.

Headden, Susan. (1997, April 28). "A Modest Attack on Sweatshops," *U.S. News & World Report*, p. 39.

Hinds, M. (1982, August 22). "Products Unsafe at Home Are Still Unloaded Abroad," *The New York Times*, p. 56.

Itoh, Yoshiaki. (1991). "Worked to Death in Japan," *World Press Review*, March, p. 50.

Kehoe, William J. (1995). "NAFTA: Concept, Problems, Promise," in B .T. Engelland and D. T. Smart, eds., *Marketing: Foundations for a Changing World*. Evansville, IN: Southern Marketing Association, pp. 363–367.

Kimelman, John. (1994, August 16). "The Lonely Boy Scout," *Financial World*, pp. 50–51.

Laczniak, Gene R. and Patrick E. Murphy. (1993). *Ethical Marketing Deci- sions: The Higher Road*. Boston, MA: Allyn and Bacon, p. 218.

Landauer, J. (1979, September 21). "Agency Will Define Corrupt Acts Abroad by U.S. Businesses," *Wall Street Journal*, p. 23.

Levitt, Theodore. (1983). "The Globalization of Markets," *Harvard Business Review*, May–June, pp. 92–93.

MacKenzie, Debora. (1992, January 4). "Europe Debates the Ownership of Life," *New Scientist*, pp. 9–10.

Nichols, Martha, P. A. Jacobi, J. T. Dunlop, and D. L. Lindauer. (1993). "Third World Families at Work: Child Labor or Child Care?" *Harvard Business Review*, January–February, pp. 12–23.

O'Mally, Shaun F. (1995). "Ethical Cultures—Corporate and Personal," *Ethics Journal*, Winter, p. 9.

Paine, Lynn 5. (1994). "Managing for Organizational Integrity," *Harvard Busi- ness Review*, March–April, pp. 106–117.

Perlmutter, Howard W. (1969). "The Tortuous Evolution of the Multinational Cor- poration," *Columbia Journal of World Business*, January–February, pp. 11–14.

Post, James M. (1985). "Assessing the Nestle Boycott," *California Manage- ment Review*, Winter, pp. 113–131.

Roddick, Anita. (1994, January 15). "Corporate Responsibility," *Vital Speeches of the Day*, pp. 196–199.

Sonnenberg, Frank K. and Beverly Goldberg. (1992, April 6). "Business In- tegrity: An Oxymoron?" *Industry Week*, pp. 53–56.

Staff. (1997). "Nike Suspends A Vietnam Boss," *The New York Times*, p. C3.

Thomson, Roy and Nigel Dudley. (1989). "Transnationals and Oil in Ama- zonia," *The Ecologist*, November, pp. 219–224.

Trevino, Linda K., K. D. Butterfield and D. L. McCabe. (1998). "The Ethical Context of Organizations: Influences on Employee Attitudes and Behav- iors," *Business Ethics Quarterly*, July, pp. 447–476.

Turner, Louis. (1984). "There's No love Lost between Multinational Compa- nies and the Third World," in W. M. Hoffman and J. M. Moore, eds., *Business Ethics*. New York: McGraw-Hill, pp. 394–400.

White, Anna. (1997, April 23). "Joe Camel's World Tour," *The New York Times*, p. A31.

Willatt, Norris. (1970). "How Nestle Adapts Products to Its Markets," *Business Abroad*, June, pp. 31–33.

ACKNOWLEDGMENT—The author wishes to acknow- ledge and to thank the McIntire School of Commerce, Univer- sity of Virginia, for providing a grant to support this research.

THE CAUX ROUND TABLE

Principles for Business

The Rise of International Ethics

JOE SKELLY

EUROPE, the land of Shakespeare and Mozart, was also the birthplace of the Industrial Revolution. So it is fitting that Europe should play host to a new kind of capitalist revolution: an international movement to establish a world standard for ethical business behavior.

This standard is the Caux Round Table Principles for Business. It is believed to be the first international ethics code created from a collaboration of business leaders in Europe, Japan, and the U.S. The Principles are unique because of this collaborative origin, and because they are founded on ideals from East Asia and the West: Japan's concept of *kyosei* (living and working together for the common good), and the Western concept of *human dignity*.

The Principles had their genesis at the Caux Round Table (CRT), a group established in 1986 to bring together global corporate leaders to reduce trade tensions. Held in Caux-sur-Montreux, Switzerland, the meeting was convened by Frederik Philips, former President of Philips Electronics, and Olivier Giscard d'Estaing, vice-chairman of France's leading business school, INSEAD.

Since the CRT launched the Principles in 1994, they have been trans-

---

"What we attempted to do is identify the transcultural values that we can all salute."
Kenneth Goodpaster

---

lated into seven languages and introduced around the world. The Japanese version came out in December 1994 and within two months had already been presented to Japan's five leading business organizations, including the powerful Federation of Economic Organizations (Keidanren).

According to the Japan Coordinator of the CRT in Tokyo, Yukihisa Fujita, a group of 250 business executives of the Keizai Doyukai, will hear a speech this spring about the Principles from Ryuzaburo Kaku, chairman of Canon, Inc. and a key member of the CRT. Fujita also said that the president of Sumitomo Electric Industries was impressed with the Principles and wants the twenty presidents from the Sumitomo Group, one of Japan's oldest and largest conglom-

erates, to hear a presentation on the guidelines.

The CRT Principles are also being presented in Copenhagen, Denmark, to the United Nations World Summit on Social Development in March 1995. The summit marks the 50th anniversary of the U.N., and the Principles are scheduled for discussion.

WIDE DISSEMINATION OF THE Principles is the immediate goal of the CRT, and it seems to be proceeding well. U.S. Coordinator Mike Olson of Minneapolis says, "There's been a continuing steady request for the document."

In addition to Philips and Giscard d'Estaing, other signatories include:

- Ryuzaburo Kaku, chairman of Canon, in Japan.
- Alfredo Ambrosetti, chairman of the Ambrosetti Group of Italy.
- Neville Cooper, chairman of the U.K.'s Top Management Partnership and formerly vice president of ITT.
- Garnett Keith Jr., vice chairman, Prudential Insurance Co. of America.
- Winston Wallin, chairman of Minnesota-based Medtronic, Inc.

The Principles for Business were formed from the experiences and wisdom of numerous senior executives from international companies, such as Philips Electronics, Ciba-Geigy, Cummins, Matsushita, 3M, and Honeywell. These companies have had mission statements and ethics codes in place for years, and pooled their knowledge to craft this credo for worldwide use.

The goal of the CRT Principles is to set "a world standard against which business behavior can be measured," a yardstick which individual companies can use to write their own codes. "Members of the Caux Round Table place their first emphasis on putting one's own house in order, and on seeking to establish what is right rather than who is right," says the document's introduction.

The Round Table format has been helpful in establishing this tone of avoiding blame. At one meeting in Caux, when Europeans expressed frustration at Japan's relentless economic expansion, a senior Japanese executive spoke from the heart about how his generation scavenged for food after World War II and was driven by the horrors of war and poverty—not to conquer world markets, but to build a brighter future for their children.

THE CRT AT FIRST SERVED AS A forum for dialogue like this, and in 1992 members were moved to draft a document of "aspirations." A group of Minnesota executives presented the Minnesota Principles, which they had crafted from the practices of corporations such as Dayton Hudson, Cargill, H. B. Fuller, and Medtronic. At the urging of the Minnesota presenters and Kaku of Canon, the CRT decided to write a document that would incorporate the value systems of each region.

> In the Principles, the Japanese communitarian concept of kyosei is paired with the Western European notion of human dignity.

"We didn't really know if the Japanese, American, and European perceptions and values would coincide," said Neville Cooper. It was left for each region's delegation to work out a code to recommend to the CRT. In January of 1994, the Minnesota Center for Corporate Responsibility in Minneapolis hosted a session to hammer out the final Principles.

"The question was whether we could come up with a coherent and homogeneous work," said discussion leader and contributing writer Professor Kenneth Goodpaster, who is Koch Chair in Business Ethics at the Graduate School of Business, University of St. Thomas in Minneapolis.

"There were some tender moments when a few members felt the work they had done wasn't being recognized," said Goodpaster. "A breakthrough came when Jean-Loup Dherse of France argued forcefully for the Japanese communitarian concept of kyosei being supplemented by the Western European notion of the dignity of the human person. The healthy dynamic tension between kyosei and human dignity would underpin the whole document. And then we brought in The Minnesota Princi-

The Principles at Work

Friedrich Schock, president of Schock & Co., of Schorndorf, Germany, knows what it is like to face difficult ethical decisions. "Recently we sold a license to an Italian company," said Schock, "and they gave me a check from a Swiss bank to avoid the 60 percent German tax. I told their boss that it was wrong and I would follow the German law."

Founded in 1924 by three Schock brothers, the $165 million private manufacturer of "home living" goods, employing 1,000 people, has always tried to live up to high standards. "Just the other day, a company from Nigeria wanted me to send a phony invoice and take a kickback. And there is a permanent temptation to avoid the European Union's 15 percent T.V.A. tax. Almost

every day there are decisions like this that require absolute honesty. Business is like marriage because it requires daily practice," said Schock. One of the few participants in the Caux Round Table from a medium-sized company, Schock gives speeches about the CRT Principles for Business and says that many people are showing interest. The Principles have energized his labor force and reinforced the long-standing mission statement of his company, and he points to reduced employee turnover as one tangible result.

It is early to accurately measure the effects of the CRT Principles, but like Schock & Co., many firms report that the Principles reinforce their corporate mission and ethics programs, And it's hoped others will likewise embrace the

Principles—and help disseminate them. Companies and business organizations worldwide are encouraged to use the Principles for Business as the basis for their own ethics work.

As the Principles' authors wrote, "We seek to begin a process that identifies shared values, reconciles differing values, and thereby develops a shared perspective on business behavior acceptable to and honored by all."

In these times of global interconnectedness, with the growing importance of cross-cultural trade, it's critical that the business community develop shared values. Through the Caux Round Table Principles for Business, this process is now under way on five continents and in diverse cultural settings. **It's a process you are invited to join.**

ples as the body of the CRT Principles document."

The Principles, for example, support the "judicious liberalization of trade" through GATT, and also emphasize human rights.

Overall, the process took two years, and the Principles were formally introduced at the Caux meeting in July 1994, under the chairmanship of Walter Hoadley, past executive vice president and chief economist at Bank of America.

"What the Principles are offering is a template of sorts, which companies can then internalize and particularize to their culture and industry," Goodpaster said. "What we attempted to do is identify the transcultural values that we can all salute."

But Goodpaster and others have stressed that there is much work to be done. "What we have accomplished is essentially an intellectual goal, which is the precursor to the more difficult task of implementation and measurement of behaviors," Goodpaster said. "It's a long growth process that will take many years, and it's going to become more controversial."

CAUX ROUND TABLE

Principles for Business

These principles are rooted in two basic ethical ideals: *kyosei* and human dignity. The Japanese concept of *kyosei* means living and working together for the common good—enabling cooperation and mutual prosperity to coexist with healthy and fair competition. "Human dignity" refers to the sacredness or value of each person as an end, not simply as a means to the fulfillment of other's purposes or even majority prescription.

The General Principles in Section 2 seek to clarify the spirit of *kyosei* and "human dignity," while the specific Stakeholder Principles in Section 3 are concerned with their practical application.

SECTION 1. PREAMBLE

The mobility of employment, capital, products, and technology is making business increasingly global in its transactions and its effects.

Laws and market forces are necessary but insufficient guides for conduct.

Responsibility for the policies and actions of business and respect for the dignity and interests of its stakeholders are fundamental.

Shared values, including a commitment to shared prosperity, are as important for a global community as for communities of smaller scale.

For these reasons, and because business can be a powerful agent of positive social change, we offer the following principles as a foundation for dialogue and action by business leaders in search of business responsibility. In so doing, we affirm the necessity for moral values in business decision making. Without them, stable business relationships and a sustainable world community are impossible.

SECTION 2. GENERAL PRINCIPLES

PRINCIPLE 1. *The Responsibilities of Businesses: Beyond Shareholders Toward Stakeholders*

The value of a business to society is the wealth and employment it creates and the marketable products and services it provides to consumers at a reasonable price commensurate with quality. To create such value, a business must maintain its own economic health and viability, but survival is not a sufficient goal.

Businesses have a role to play in improving the lives of all their customers, employees, and shareholders by sharing with them the wealth they have created. Suppliers and competitors as well should expect businesses to honor their obligations in a spirit of honesty and fairness. As responsible citizens of the local, national, re-

gional, and global communities in which they operate, businesses share a part in shaping the future of those communities.

PRINCIPLE 2: *The Economic and Social Impact of Business: Toward Innovation, Justice, and World Community*

Businesses established in foreign countries to develop, produce, or sell should also contribute to the social advancement of those countries by creating productive employment and helping to raise the purchasing power of their citizens. Businesses also should contribute to human rights, education, welfare, and vitalization of the countries in which they operate.

Businesses should contribute to economic and social development not only in the countries in which they operate, but also in the world community at large, through effective and prudent use of resources, free and fair competition, and emphasis upon innovation in technology, production methods, marketing, and communications.

PRINCIPLE 3: *Business Behavior: Beyond the Letter of Law Toward a Spirit of Trust*

While accepting the legitimacy of trade secrets, businesses should recognize that sincerity, candor, truthfulness, the keeping of promises, and transparency contribute not only to their own credibility and stability but also to the smoothness and efficiency of business transactions, particularly on the international level.

PRINCIPLE 4. *Respect for Rules*

To avoid trade frictions and to promote freer trade, equal conditions for competition, and fair and equitable treatment for all participants, businesses should respect international and domestic rules. In addition, they should recognize that some behavior, although legal, may still have adverse consequences.

PRINCIPLE 5. *Support for Multilateral Trade*

Businesses should support the multilateral trade systems of the GATT/World Trade Organization and similar international agreements. They should cooperate in efforts to promote the progressive and judicious liberalization of trade, and to relax those domestic measures that unreasonably hinder global commerce, while giving due respect to national policy objectives.

PRINCIPLE 6. *Respect for the Environment*

A business should protect and, where possible, improve the environment, promote sustainable development, and prevent the wasteful use of natural resources.

PRINCIPLE 7. *Avoidance of Illicit Operations*

A business should not participate in or condone bribery, money laundering, or other corrupt practices: indeed, it should seek cooperation with others to eliminate them. It should not trade in arms or other materials used for terrorist activities, drug traffic, or other organized crime.

SECTION 3. STAKEHOLDER PRINCIPLES

Customers

We believe in treating all customers with dignity, irrespective of whether they purchase our products and services directly from us or otherwise acquire them in the market. We therefore have a responsibility to:

- provide our customers with the highest quality products and services consistent with their requirements;
- treat our customers fairly in all aspects of our business transactions, including a high level of service and remedies for their dissatisfaction;
- make every effort to ensure that the health and safety of our customers, as well as the quality of their environment, will be sustained or enhanced by our products and services;
- assure respect for human dignity in products offered, marketing, and advertising; and
- respect the integrity of the culture of our customers.

Employees

We believe in the dignity of every employee and in taking employee interests seriously. We therefore have a responsibility to:

- provide jobs and compensation that improve workers' living conditions;
- provide working conditions that respect each employee's health and dignity;
- be honest in communications with employees and open in sharing information, limited only by legal and competitive restraints;
- listen to and, where possible, act on employee suggestions, ideas, requests, and complaints;
- engage in good faith negotiations when conflict arises;
- avoid discriminatory practices and guarantee equal treatment and opportunity in areas such as gender, age, race, and religion;
- promote in the business itself the employment of differently abled people in places of work where they can be genuinely useful;

- protect employees from avoidable injury and illness in the workplace;
- encourage and assist employees in developing relevant and transferable skills and knowledge; and
- be sensitive to serious unemployment problems frequently associated with business decisions, and work with governments, employee groups, other agencies and each other in addressing these dislocations.

Owners/Investors

We believe in honoring the trust our investors place in us. We therefore have a responsibility to:

- apply professional and diligent management in order to secure a fair and competitive return on our owners' investment;
- disclose relevant information to owners/investors subject only to legal requirements and competitive constraints;
- conserve, protect, and increase the owners/investors' assets; and
- respect owners/investors' requests, suggestions, complaints, and formal resolutions.

Suppliers

Our relationship with suppliers and subcontractors must be based on mutual respect. We therefore have a responsibility to:

- seek fairness and truthfulness in all of our activities, including pricing, licensing, and rights to sell;
- ensure that our business activities are free from coercion and unnecessary litigation;
- foster long-term stability in the supplier relationship in return for value, quality, competitiveness, and reliability;
- share information with suppliers and integrate them into our planning processes;
- pay suppliers on time and in accordance with agreed terms of trade;

- seek, encourage, and prefer suppliers and subcontractors whose employment practices respect human dignity.

Competitors

We believe that fair economic competition is one of the basic requirements for increasing the wealth of nations and, ultimately, for making possible the just distribution of goods and services. We therefore have a responsibility to:

- foster open markets for trade and investment;
- promote competitive behavior that is socially and environmentally beneficial and demonstrates mutual respect among competitors;
- refrain from either seeking or participating in questionable payments or favors to secure competitive advantages;
- respect both tangible and intellectual property rights; and
- refuse to acquire commercial information by dishonest or unethical means, such as industrial espionage.

Communities

We believe that as global corporate citizens, we can contribute to such forces of reform and human rights as are at work in the communities in which we operate. We therefore have a responsibility in those communities to:

- respect human rights and democratic institutions, and promote them wherever practicable;
- recognize government's legitimate obligation to the society at large and support public policies and practices that promote human development through harmonious relations between business and other segments of society;
- collaborate with those forces in the community dedicated to raising standards of health, education, workplace safety, and economic well-being;
- promote and stimulate sustainable development and play a leading role in preserving and enhancing the physical environment and conserving the earth's resources;
- support peace, security, diversity, and social integration;
- respect the integrity of local cultures; and
- be a good corporate citizen through charitable donations, educational and cultural contributions, and employee participation in community and civic affairs.

SWEATSHOPS: NO MORE EXCUSES

By Aaron Bernstein

The anti-sweatshop movement has advanced by fits and starts in recent years: Protesters demanded action, and apparel makers responded with a few steps forward—and a wealth of arguments about why they couldn't do more. Now, in just the past month or so, the adversaries are starting to find some common ground, and key elements of a credible sweatshop monitoring system are falling into place.

On Oct. 7, Nike Inc. sought to appease student protesters by releasing the locations of 42 of its 365 factories—reversing its long-standing insistence that doing so would put it at a competitive disadvantage.

Then, on Oct. 18, Reebok International Ltd. released the first independent factory audit undertaken by a human-rights group, involving two Indonesian plants. Liz Claiborne Inc. did the same a few days later, with a remarkably candid outside report on a Guatemalan factory. And Mattel Inc. will soon publish an even more comprehensive review of eight plants in four countries, using hundreds of specific labor standards.

"CRITICAL MASS" All three companies should be applauded for the breakthrough: The audits mark the first time companies have allowed truly independent outsiders with expertise in labor issues to rake over their factories—and then make the unpleasant findings public. Now that the leaders have set a new prece-

dent, other companies will have a more difficult time dragging their heels. "We have raised the ante with external monitoring, which we initiated because we had gone as far as we could by ourselves," says Reebok CEO Paul B. Fireman.

Meanwhile, efforts to construct industrywide inspection systems are finally beginning to jell. Furthest along is the Fair Labor Assn. (FLA), a monitoring group made up of industry and human-rights representatives that was created last fall by a Presidential task force. In September, former White House Counsel Charles Ruff signed on as the FLA's first chairman, giving the group some badly needed leadership. And in recent months, Adidas-Salomon AG and Levi Strauss & Co. joined the eight founding companies, which include Nike, Reebok, Liz Claiborne, and Phillips-Van Heusen, adding to the momentum. "Now, we have a critical mass, enough to start the ball rolling," says Liz Claiborne General Counsel Roberta S. Karp, co-chair of the task force that formed the FLA.

Keeping the heat on the FLA and others have been human-rights and student groups. On Oct. 18, United Students Against Sweatshops announced an even stricter monitoring scheme, which will pressure companies to do even more. And a new study shows that even after companies had pledged to clean up their factories, chronic abuses continued. A New Jersey group, Press for Change,

just completed a survey of 2,300 workers at five Nike factories outside Jakarta employing 45,000 people. More than half, interviewed by an Indonesian human-rights group, said they had seen colleagues yelled at or mistreated, and a third said they had been compelled to work overtime. Nike spokesman Vada Manager says the company, which hasn't yet seen the survey, would look into the matter.

Nonetheless, the new level of scrutiny by Reebok, Liz Claiborne, and Mattel marks a turning point in the anti-sweatshop movement. Since the early 1990s, many major apparel companies have adopted labor codes of conduct for their factories and set up internal monitoring efforts. But these efforts have gained scant credibility. Companies refused to let outside groups see what inspectors found, so critics had no way to judge whether anyone knows what really took place. Until now, that is.

HARSH DETAIL Then, about a year ago, Reebok agreed to outside monitoring. It allowed a respected nonprofit social-research group in Jakarta called Insan Hitawasana Sejahtera (IHS) to conduct inspections of two nearby shoe factories that employ more than 10,000 of the company's 75,000 workers worldwide. An IHS team surveyed workers, performed tests of health and safety, and worked with managers of the Korean-owned factory to remedy the problems they uncovered. The IHS found a wide range of violations, in-

REVERSAL From Nike to Mattel, companies are open to more outside scrutiny—and that's raising the bar for others

cluding poor ventilation, harmful chemicals, inadequate toilets, and sex bias. The report explains how managers agreed to remedy some problems—and candidly lays out those management has failed to address.

Liz Claiborne went even further. In 1997, Guatemalan religious and human-rights activists formed the Commission for the Verification of Corporate Codes of Conduct (Coverco), which last year began inspecting a 900-worker plant outside Guatemala City that belongs to a Liz Claiborne supplier. Liz Claiborne has given BUSINESS WEEK the first report, completed on Oct. 15. In often harsh detail, Coverco lays out the problems it found, from 16-year-olds pressured to work overtime to complaints about inaccurate wage payments. It tells how a line supervisor refused to allow a pregnant worker to leave for the hospital when she went into labor—implying that the delay may have led to her baby's being stillborn the next day.

Coverco also outlines its dialogue with plant managers, who have worked to fix some problems and stonewalled on others, the report says. It says that cooperation improved last summer after the factory's owner, unnamed in the report, replaced the managers. Says Liz Claiborne's Karp: "This is exactly what we wanted: to learn what the problems were and figure out how to make them better."

Mattel has taken an even more rigorous approach. Rather than set up one-time pilot projects like Reebok and Liz Claiborne, the Los Angeles toymaker has appointed an outside group to create a monitoring system, requiring factories to meet hundreds of detailed standards. The group, Mattel Independent Monitoring Council for Global Manufacturing Principles, is headed by S. Prakash Sethi, a management professor at Baruch College in New York with experience in enforcing codes of conduct. Another council member is Murray L. Weidenbaum,

head of Ronald Reagan's Council of Economic Advisers.

In the past year, a team of 50 Mattel managers and outside experts has drawn up standards for five countries where Mattel makes toys. They lay out everything from how many toilets are required per worker to how many calories company cafeterias should serve workers daily. The team audited eight plants in China, Indonesia, Malaysia, and Thailand employing 30,000 workers, and results have been sent to Mattel's CEO for release in November, the company says. Notes Sethi: "We tried to build criteria to measure objective outcomes, like square feet in a worker dorm, which hasn't been done before." The pioneers have shown that outside monitoring by human-rights groups can work, even if the results are painful or embarrassing. Other manufacturers and retailers, largely on the sidelines, should set aside their qualms and join their colleagues as they begin, little by little, to lift global labor standards.

Bernstein watches global labor trends from Washington.

Unit 4

Unit Selections

Key Points to Consider

❖ What responsibility does an organization have to reveal product defects to consumers?

❖ Given the competitiveness of the business arena, is it possible for marketing personnel to behave ethically and both survive and prosper? Explain. Give suggestions that could be incorporated into the marketing strategy for firms that want to be both ethical and successful.

❖ Name some organizations where you feel genuinely valued as a customer. What are the characteristics of these organizations that distinguishes them from their competitors? Explain.

❖ Which area of marketing strategy is most subject to public scrutiny in regard to ethics—product, pricing, place, or promotion? Why? Give some examples of unethical techniques or strategies involving each of these four areas.

 **Links**   **www.dushkin.com/online/**

These sites are annotated on pages 4 and 5.

From a consumer viewpoint, the marketplace is the "proof of the pudding" or the place where the "rubber meets the road" for business ethics. In other words, what the company has promulgated about the virtues of its product or service has little meaning if the company's actual marketing practices and its treatment of the consumer contradict its claims.

At its core, marketing has a very noble and moral purpose: to satisfy human needs and wants and to help people through the exchange process. Marketing involves the coordination of the variables of product, price, place, and promotion to effectively and efficiently address the needs of consumers. Unfortunately, at times the unethical marketing practices of some firms have cast a shadow of suspicion over marketing in general. Since marketing is the aspect of business that is most visible to the public, it has perhaps taken a disproportionate share of the criticism directed toward the free-enterprise system.

This unit takes a careful look at the strategic process and practice of incorporating ethics into the marketplace. The first subsection, *Marketing Strategy and Ethics*, contains three articles describing how

marketing strategy and ethics can be integrated in the marketplace. The first article provides a perspective on ways companies are discovering the value of ethics. Then, "Ethics in the Public Eye" gives a perspective of why the nonprofit sector feels that developing clear ethical guidelines is imperative. The last article in this subsection gives a case in which a company refused to pay a bonus it had promised.

In the second subsection, *Ethical Practices in the Marketplace*, the first article delineates the importance of having an organizational culture that encourages and supports sound ethical behavior and socially responsible business practices. The next selection discloses how many unethical acts in business are the result of foibles and failings rather than selfishness and greed. The next article describes the importance of a mission-driven and values-centered organization. The six characteristics of excellence in stakeholder service that are found in some exemplary organizations are presented in "The 100 Best Corporate Citizens." Finally, "Winery With a Mission" reveals how a vintner endeavors to practice an environmentally and socially responsible business.

Ethics and Social Responsibility in the Marketplace

Companies Are Discovering the
VALUE OF ETHICS

*Employees "motivated by strong moral and religious values
are less likely to behave opportunistically and,
as a result, are more productive and thus more profitable."*

by Norman E. Bowie

Most discussion of business ethics focuses on ethics as a constraint on profit. From this view, ethics and profit are related inversely: the more ethical a business is, the less profitable it is; the more profitable, the less ethical. Certainly, there are times when doing the morally correct thing will reduce profits. Not using an "agent" to provide bribes when doing business abroad is one example. Nonetheless, the traditional characterization of an inverse relationship between ethics and profits is only part of the story at best. A more balanced view points out that there frequently is a positive relation between ethics and profits; normally, ethics enhances the bottom line, rather than diminishing it.

The best news is that the conventional cynical view about business ethics provides a money-making opportunity and can be the source of a competitive advantage. Other things being equal, a firm known for its high ethical standards can have an above-average profit. An auto repair shop known for its honesty is a busy and prosperous one.

Ethical behavior contributes to the bottom line by reducing the cost of business transactions, establishing trust among stakeholders, increasing the likelihood of successful teamwork, and preserving the social capital necessary for doing business.

First, an ethical firm reduces the cost of business transactions. For instance, most economic exchanges have a period of time between the payment for a good or service and delivery, or, conversely, a period of time between the delivery of a good or service and payment for it. This time gap can stand in the way of a profitable transaction. Perhaps the supplier will not deliver or the vendor will fail to pay. A small supplier is offered a large contract by a major manufacturer. Although one might think that the small supplier would be overjoyed by such an arrangement, it should be cautious. It can be held hostage by the much larger manufacturer, which can delay payment for the product or demand other concessions.

Recently, a number of large firms in the U.S. unilaterally announced an increase in the time that they would settle their accounts. Obviously, this fact makes future suppliers more reluctant to do business with these firms. The major manufacturer with a reputation for prompt payment will get the small supplier to provide the quality product. The major manufacturer that lacks a reputation for prompt payment will not.

Yet another illustration concerns the acceptability of checks as a means of payment. A seafood shop in Ocean City, Md., had the following notice posted on the wall: "We will not accept checks and here is why." Below the notice was a row of checks stamped "Insufficient funds." That seafood shop no longer would do business with those who wanted to pay by check.

There are vast regional differences in the acceptability of checks as a means of payment. In the Upper Midwest, they are accepted routinely. In most grocery stores and in some other businesses, the customer even may make the check out for an amount larger than the purchase and thus get both the purchase and some cash. On the East Coast, checks are not accepted routinely as a means of payment. Instead, credit cards are. Since most credit card sales represent additional costs, merchants in the Upper Midwest have lower costs of doing business than those merchants in other parts of the country.

Employee and customer theft is a major problem for business, as are shirking on the job and a declining work ethic. A culture of drug abuse exacerbates the problem. Business incurs great costs in dealing with these issues. Elaborate security systems are put into place. Employees are asked to submit to "honesty tests" and expensive drug screening.

Yet, businesspeople, along with most everyone else, recognize differences in the propensity of individuals to steal, take drugs, or shirk their responsibilities on the job. Again on a statistical basis, there are regional differences. During the 1980s, firms moved to the Upper Midwest despite the harsh climate and high taxes to take advantage of a workforce that had a high work ethic. Recently, the shift has been to Utah, a state with a large percentage of Mormons—a highly religious group that has a strong work ethic. Such examples are not limited to the U.S. In Budapest, Hungary, a large number of managers prefer to

From *USA Today Magazine*, January 1998, pp. 22–24 © 1998 by the Society for the Advancement of Education. Reprinted by permission.

hire only those under the age of 30 because these younger employees are less likely to be infected by the bad work habits that existed under communism.

What these examples show is that those motivated by strong moral and religious values are less likely to behave opportunistically and, thus, will be more productive and more profitable. Employees and customers with the right values need less monitoring and fewer honesty and drug tests. Consequently, employers will try to hire people who statistically are more likely to be honest.

Ethical behavior builds trust, which increases the likelihood of profit. As a company builds trust, customers, employees, and suppliers are less likely to behave opportunistically. A reputation for trust will attract like-minded customers, employees, and suppliers. Thus, trust is reinforcing in a kind of virtuous circle.

Moreover, a firm characterized by high trust stakeholder relationships is likely to have competitive advantages. If trust is defined as keeping one's word and not taking undue advantage (behaving opportunistically) when one has the capability of doing so, the competitive advantage gained by a trusting organization will be clear.

Human resource management will be very different in a trusting organization. The essential point is that trusting relationships change the nature of monitoring. In nontrusting relationships, the supervisor functions as a policeman; in trusting relationships, as a mentor, the way a professor functions with a doctoral student or a coach develops a young pitcher. The kind of monitoring a mentor does is very different from that which a policeman does. A mentoring relationship allows qualitative criteria and uses fewer quantitative measures, is less frequent, and requires less in the way of detail.

Lately, there has been much discussion about teamwork and about eliminating layers of management. Workers are to be "empowered"—i.e., given more responsibility and discretion as the layers of management control wither away. If teamwork and empowerment are not to be empty rhetoric, the nature of supervision must be more of a mentoring than a policing type. Greater trust will be a key element in any cost savings that result from eliminating layers of management and the empowerment of employee teams.

Trust also reduces the amount of bias in forecasts and overstatement of need in budgetary requests. Nearly every person in a business organization has experience with the budget game: A number of budgetary units report to a higher authority that sets the budget for each unit. The authority asks what each of the units need. Each unit knows that there are not sufficient funds to meet all the needs; therefore, the re-

quests of each unit will not be granted fully. Each unit then overstates its need so that the failure to meet the requests will not cause as much pain. As a result, the central authority engages in long costly negotiations with each unit to arrive at a figure that is fairly close to what each unit would have expected to receive. Transaction costs could have been reduced greatly if the information to the central budget authority had reflected true need more accurately. If the various units could agree to make accurate requests and trust one another to keep their promises, these traditional transaction costs could be slashed.

A more trusting organization could help American manufacturing enterprises overcome two disadvantages. Traditionally, the engineering team that designs a product does its work separately. Those who manufacture the product have little, if anything, to say about its design. As a result, some problems with a prototype do not appear until the manufacturing stage. Much time is lost as the prototype is redesigned to meet the requirements of mass production.

The sales unit of a firm and the manufacturing unit often work at cross-purposes. The sales force has incentives to sell as much of a product as it can. Indeed, the commission system is what provides the incentive. However, if quality is to be maintained and backlogged orders are to be kept to a minimum, sales must not exceed the ability of the manufacturing process to produce the goods in question. Given the commission system, there is no incentive for the sales staff to take these limitations into account and to cooperate with manufacturing to secure the optimal amount of sales at any given time.

As the result of Japanese competition, these defects have been recognized, and American companies have realized that there must be greater cooperation among units within the firm. Trust among the units and a supportive compensation scheme are required for greater cooperation. To build that trust, managers need to speak differently about other units in the firm than they do about its competitors. The unit that manufactures the product is not the enemy of the salesperson. Failure to understand that distinction undermines the trust needed to achieve a competitive advantage.

What holds true within a firm will continue to do so as various companies enter into joint ventures. With such cooperation among firms from different countries becoming increasingly common and successful, one would expect to see more joint ventures between corporations that have higher levels of trust. The rationale for this is fairly clear. if one member of the joint venture fails to keep its contract, behaves opportunistically, or provides a shoddy product or service, all parties will suffer. The

unhappy customer will blame all alike. Thus, a trustworthy partner is the best partner in a business sense. Picking a moral partner may be the most important decision to be made when setting up a joint venture.

Finally, trust is needed for successful research and development. The rationale for this contention is based on the knowledge of the environment needed for creative thought, particularly scientific research. Some corporations have adopted a competitive strategy of introducing new products at such a rate that goods created in the last few years account for a certain percentage of the firm's sales. Such companies refuse to rest on their laurels.

How can such a strategy be achieved? There is considerable evidence that creative people are most productive in an environment with minimal monitoring and control? It is counterproductive to have laboratory scientists filling out weekly reports asking them what they discovered that week. Providing research scientists with the freedom and independence necessary to stimulate creative thinking requires a great deal of trust on the part of management. Firms with a culture of trust are likely to be more adaptive and innovative.

Yet another benefit of ethical behavior is that it provides a solution to what theorists call collective action problems. A collective action problem occurs when an obvious public good can not be achieved because it is not in the self-interest of any individual who is a part of the problem to take steps to resolve it. Thus, large cities throughout the world suffer from traffic congestion. All would benefit if many more people used public transportation. For any individual, though, the reduction in congestion resulting from his or her taking the bus is very small, while the inconvenience, especially given its imperceptible effect on congestion, is large. Therefore, this individual, and every other automobile owner, will tend to drive and traffic congestion will remain horrible.

There are many ways of tackling a collective action problem. One traditional means is to provide incentive so that the cost-benefit ratio is reversed. For instance, instituting tolls for cars that greatly increase the cost of driving to work would force drivers onto the bus or train.

Collective action problems exist in business as well. Assume that, in certain situations, the production of a good or service requires a team effort and that the individual contribution of each team member can not be isolated and measured. Any team member who acts in a purely self-interested manner would free ride off the others. This free-riding phenomenon explains why many hard-working students complain bitterly about group projects that are graded on the productivity of the group.

Indeed, if enough members free ride, the gain in potential productivity from teamwork would be lost. In such situations, the benefits of group activity are optimized only when there is no free riding. For that to occur, each member of the group must make a commitment not to free ride. This commitment is most likely in a moral community where the members are bound together by common values and mutual respect.

Social capital

A final benefit of ethical corporate behavior is that it preserves the social capital that makes a free market possible. A market system does not operate in a vacuum, but coexists with many other institutions in society, including the family, the church, and the political, criminal justice, and educational systems. Each of these institutions contributes toward making capitalism possible: The court system enforces contracts; the political system provides monetary stability; and the educational system trains future employees and prepares them for the workforce.

Corporate misconduct raises the cost and reduces the amount of social capital. The more businesspeople try to avoid the terms of their agreement, the greater the number of disputes that end up in court. More and more umpires are needed. When the environment is despoiled or misleading advertising occurs, the public demands more regulation. Increased governmental activity adds to the cost of government.

A market system needs moral capital as well. If capitalism is to be successful, there must be both within society and within capitalism a widespread acceptance of certain moral norms, such as truth-telling, bill-paying, and fair play. When these norms are perceived as being violated, a vicious circle begins. If other people will not play by the rules, then each person reasons there is no longer gain from following the

rules. As more and more people abandon these moral forms, the social capital that makes market activity possible is depleted.

A major concern about Russia is whether the criminal element has gotten such a hold on business activity that capitalism becomes impossible. What some commentators refer to as "wild capitalism" is doomed to failure. Once again, ethical behavior contributes to the bottom line, but in this case to the bottom line of capitalism itself, rather than to the bottom line of an individual firm.

Some may object to this analysis. They might say that businesspeople should do the right thing because it is right, rather than because such actions contribute to the bottom line.

Philosophers are familiar with the hedonic paradox: "The more you consciously seek happiness, the less likely you are to find it." If you do not believe this, just get up some morning and resolve that every act will be done in order to achieve happiness. You soon will be miserable. Happiness is the result of successful achievement, but is not itself something you try to achieve. According to Aristotle, self-realization is what you try to achieve, and happiness is the result of achieving it.

Perhaps, to some extent, profits are like that. If your focus on them is excessive, you are less likely to achieve them. The conventional wisdom is that managers should focus on the bottom line. There is an obsession in America with quarterly reports—one that forces managers to focus on the short run, rather than the long run. If corporations took the moral point of view, they would focus on meeting the needs of their stakeholders. For instance, they might focus on providing secure work for employees and quality products for customers. If they did that, profits likely would follow.

Second, employees are very suspicious of management's motives when new concepts like empowerment or quality circles

are introduced. If the employees think that these ideas are being implemented to increase profits, they often will attempt to sabotage them, even if the workers would be better off. Thus, quality circles and empowerment only can succeed if all those affected believe such practices are being introduced for the right reasons.

Third, media reports of corporate good works frequently are greeted with public scorn because the public is suspicious of the corporation's motives. "They are just trying to buy good will" is a phrase that is heard often. Corporate executives who really do act from ethical motives are frustrated when their motives are questioned. Yet, it is hard for the public to determine motives, which is why reputation, corporate character, and a record of altruistic acts are important. If Johnson & Johnson proclaims moral motives for what the pharmaceutical company does, it tends to be believed. The public remembers how Johnson & Johnson handled the Tylenol poisonings. Not only did the firm do the right thing—pulling the product from the market and repackaging it in a more secure manner—it did so for the right reason. Moreover, Johnson & Johnson profited as a result.

What of the future? All capitalist systems are not alike. Japanese capitalism differs from German capitalism and both differ from the American version. Which will be most successful in the next century? The answer depends on many factors. One is ethics because, as has been shown, ethical behavior can lower costs, increase productivity, and preserve the social capital that makes capitalism possible. It is in our national interest to ensure that American capitalism is a leader in ethics as well as in product development and cheap capital.

Dr. Bowie is Elmer L. Andersen Chair in Corporate Responsibility, University of Minnesota, Minneapolis.

Ethics

in the Public Eye

The nonprofit sector has often operated under the assumption that its underlying mission—to serve the public good—ensures that it will operate ethically. This has, in some cases, led to behavior driven by an "ends justifies the means" mentality and in other cases to a naïve assumption that good impulses immunize nonprofit board members and staff against temptation—with disastrous consequences.

    For-profits have long understood that a top-down focus on ethics can yield such tangible benefits as improved public perception or decreased liability. As corporate ethics programs mature, for-profits cite enhanced employee morale and improved productivity as less-anticipated benefits of bringing ethics to the forefront. Nonprofits are now realizing that bringing ethical issues to the surface and creating clear guidelines for behavior may be the only way to ensure that even the most charitable of institutions are doing the right thing.

Scrutiny of the operations of nonprofit organizations continues to heighten. In fact, open any major metropolitan newspaper and you're likely to find a story about abuses in the nonprofit sector or government. The media has played an important role in feeding the public's cynicism about nonprofit organizations, as Peter Swords of the Nonprofit Coordinating Committee of New York observed in a paper presented at the 1997 Conference on Governance of Nonprofit Organizations at the New York University School of Law:

"Folks proceeding under the banner of being 'charitable' of being altruistic, of working for the good of the community as a whole and not for their own private advancement (in a word, do-gooders) turn out to be as acquisitive as the rest of us," Swords writes. "How exquisitely delicious for hard-news reporters to stumble on this stuff. How many people really like do-gooders? How often are do-gooders perceived as preaching virtue to us and urging us to do more for the community, when we just want to be left alone? Thus, to expose do-gooders as abusing their trust, indeed, as being hypocrites, is an almost gleeful exercise for hard-news reporters."

Michael Josephson, president and founder of the Josephson Institute for the Advancement of Ethics, agrees with Swords. "People are generous, but most will look for excuses not to be." An example is the aftermath of the scandal revolving around executive compensation and financial abuses at the United Way of America in the early 1990s. "Nothing about the national organization's situation would justify less support to local

United Ways," says Josephson. "But donations dropped just the same."

Knowledge that the world is watching has magnified the focus on ethics in the executive offices and boardrooms of nonprofits—a trend that an increasingly cynical public might view with suspicion as a way of improving appearances without addressing systematic problems. In fact, few organizations that begin the process of developing a comprehensive, meaningful ethics program truly understand the complexity of the issues involved, or how deeply the organization may be affected by the inquiry.

It's What Pays That Counts

As a professor of business ethics at the University of Pennsylvania, Robbin Derry spends a good deal of time as an ethics consultant in the for-profit sector. "I find that the people I work with have good intentions. They believe they care a lot about having an ethical organization. But they may not want to go so far as to really integrate ethical standards into performance evaluations, reward systems—the stuff that is so typically tied to profit or salaries or some version of the bottom line."

In her work with nonprofits, Derry is discovering how similar a large nonprofit organization is to its for-profit counterparts, not in structure or purpose, but in "bureaucracy and fear, who gets to talk and who gets listened to."

"Issues of power, reward, and job security are all relevant in any organization, and when they come up they threaten conversations about ethics," Derry explains. "If the organization says it values ethical behavior,

but is going to pay employees for meeting sales quotas, then ethics isn't going to be a top priority for employees because what people get paid for is what they believe is valued by their employer."

For Derry, dealing with ethical issues requires people at the top who are willing to listen to people at all levels in the organization. "Sometimes people want ethical organizations for the managers and the customers, but they don't believe they need to fairly compensate lower-level employees or they don't care about being ethical with competitors. Organizations need to take a broader stakeholder approach and say being ethical requires that we ask ourselves, what does being ethical mean in regard to customers, employees, competitors, our community?"

Integrating ethics into an organization is consistent with management theory on quality and organizational behavior, says Derry— "aligning your goals, communicating effectively, getting people to work together as a team, and making sure what you ask for and pay for aren't totally different."

Can Nonprofits Learn from Corporate America?

A large nonprofit undergoes re-engineering, downsizing, a merger, and organization-wide strategic planning, much like a for-profit company would. Nonprofit executives believe passionately that what they're doing is for the public good, but so do the executives of major corporations—after all, they're providing employment, making useful products, contributing to the economy. For Frank Navran, director of training and senior consultant for the Ethics Resource Center, the distinction between nonprofit and for-profit is becoming less concrete and easy to define.

He believes that nonprofits can learn a lot from their corporate counterparts when it comes to ethics. "One of the most important ways that the corporate world is ahead of nonprofits is in legitimizing the conversation," says Navran. He cites the example of the construction companies where safety is truly valued. "People die and are injured every year on the job. Because people's lives are at stake, safety has to be a primary concern, so any employee who spots a safety problem can stop the job at anytime. This is a legitimate conversation, and the effective manager won't scold the employee for stopping the job but will thank the employee for paying attention to safety."

> "If I want to see the financial statement of XYZ Big Nonprofit, it should be as accessible to me as the financial statement of a comparably sized publicly traded corporation."

In part because the 1991 Federal Sentencing Guidelines (which allow judges to fine companies if their employees or board members commit crimes) require it, corporations have for nearly a decade invested in validating the discussion of ethics. "When workload was stable, change was slow, and people had plenty of time to learn their jobs, they learned to answer tough questions over time;' explains Navran. "Now the pressures are so high and change in the workplace is so rapid that without [ethics] policies, people will resort to using what they interpret as the core values of the institution and their own personal values in their ethical decision-making. It's the responsibility of the organization to clarify expectations about what's right and wrong. Ultimately that rests with leadership, which has to articulate and model the behavior it values."

Measuring Organizational Ethics

It is difficult when talking about ethics to get beyond the subject of scandals and how to avoid them. But as Bennett Weiner, vice president of the Council of Better Business Bureau's Philanthropic Advisory Service, notes, there are practices an organization can engage in that may not be scandalous, but nevertheless may be unethical or create accountability concerns. On the other hand, some of what can attract enough media at-

Putting Teeth in the *New York Times* Test

In the corporate sector, before the end of the Depression, the level of disclosure for publicly traded corporations was comparable to the disclosure provided by nonprofits today, says Harvard Business School professor Regina Herzlinger. For a decade, Westinghouse didn't have an annual meeting of stockholders or give results of its operations. The Depression eroded confidence in business enough to encourage the formation of the Securities and Exchange Commission (SEC).

"Today, if businesses don't meet the SEC's disclosure requirements," Herzlinger explains, "they're out of the market, can't trade their stock, can't raise money. I believe people are basically ethical. But I'm also realistic, and I know that before the SEC existed, voluntary disclosure among for-profits was laughable. And I know that after the SEC came on board, the benefits of mandatory disclosure far exceeded the costs. The market became more efficient, public confidence rose, so it cost less for businesses to raise money." Greater accountability for nonprofits would "put teeth in the *New York Times* test," Herzlinger notes, "by making it real, making information about your organization easier to obtain."

In a 1996 article in the *Harvard Business Review,* Herzlinger proposed that nonprofits be held to a level of accountability similar to that imposed on for-profit businesses by the SEC. Such external oversight is essential, she observed, in part because nonprofits lack the three basic accountability mechanisms of business: self-interest, competition, and the profit measure, all of which help to ensure that businesses operate efficiently and effectively.

To lift what she calls "the veil of secrecy" under which many nonprofits operate, Herzlinger suggested that large nonprofits "increase the disclosure, analysis, and dissemination of information on the performance of nonprofit and governmental organizations, and apply sanctions against those that do not comply with these requirements." Herzlinger explains that such sanctions, written by an organization such as the Financial Accounting Standards Board with input from nonprofits, would be imposed by a yet-to-be-created agency similar to the SEC. Herzlinger outlines her suggestions:

• **Disclosure**—Improve financial disclosure, including the accuracy of Form 990 (the IRS' equivalent of the tax return for nonprofits, which includes executive salaries and other information), by utilizing generally accepted accounting principles and third-party auditing; provide performance information; and make it easier for the public to find data comparable to that available for publicly traded organizations—executive salaries and perks, for example.

• **Analysis**—Improve the quality and meaningfulness of information provided by more widely applying performance standards such as those by the National Charities Information Bureau and the Council of Better Business Bureaus' Phhilanthropic Advisory Service.

• **Dissemination**—Create a clearinghouse for disseminating information about nonprofits; make Form 990 as easy to access as it is for investors to find a publicly traded company's financial statements—on the Internet and elsewhere.

• **Sanctions**—Administered by an agency similar to the SEC, sanctions could range from periodic reviews of organizations' tax-exempt status to "increased civil or criminal penalties for managers and board members who fail to comply with reporting and disclosure requirements."

Adapted from "Can Public Trust in Nonprofits and Governments Be Restored?" by Regina Herzlinger. Harvard Business Review, March-April 1996 (Reprint #96207).

tention to generate a scandal—market-value executive compensation in a large nonprofit, for example—may be perfectly ethical, reasonable, and actually essential to helping the organization fulfill its mission.

Jim Bausch, president and CEO of the National Charities Information Bureau (NCIB), adds that ethics and accountability, while inextricably linked, are not the same

thing. "If an organization isn't fully accountable," he explains, "the opportunity for ethical misdeeds increases." Executive compensation, again, presents both ethical and accountability issues. "Is all the compensation clearly stated and fully disclosed? Is a person paid under more than one entity so you can't find the total compensation? Is there an undisclosed deferred compensation policy? Those kinds of things can come about when an organization isn't fully accountable."

Regina Herzlinger, a professor of business administration at the Harvard Business School, believes the most effective ethics test is both simple and subjective. She calls it the *New York Times* test. "When you're making a decision," she says, "ask yourself, if this were on the front page of the *New York Times,* how would I feel about it? Is this a decision I would be comfortable explaining to a reporter?"

Herzlinger notes that if the board members of the United Way of America had taken the *New York Times* test about William Aramony's compensation, they may have still made the same decisions, "but those decisions would have been debated, thought about, and finally, the board would have had a terrific rationale for what they were doing."

For Herzlinger, one way to "put teeth into the *New York Times* test" is to engage in proactive accountability—ensure the accuracy and completeness of financial statements, and make them readily available to the public. (See "Putting Teeth in the New York Times Test" for more on Herzlinger's proposal to ensure nonprofit accountability.)

"If I want to see the financial statement of XYZ Big Nonprofit," says Herzlinger, "it should be as accessible to me as the financial statement of a comparably sized publicly traded corporation. I just go to the Internet. I'll find everything from the salary and bonus paid to the CEO and top four officers to the arrangements with their board members to their products' market status to their financial results."

Herzlinger acknowledges that such activities—audited financial statements, meaningful annual reports with clear performance measures, and broad dissemination of information—are probably out of reach of many small nonprofit organizations. But. she believes that the largest nonprofits should set the pace for the sector, in part because they are the most visible. Their activities help shape public attitudes toward the sector as a whole.

Both the Council of Better Business Bureaus and NCIB provide reports that assess nonprofits according to clearly defined standards of accountability, efficiency, and effectiveness. Yet Bausch admits that although he believes that most charities tell the truth to his organization and to government reporting agencies, "when they don't want to tell the truth, it's hard to ferret out. Our standards can make things more difficult to hide." Ultimately, much of the responsibility for ensuring that an organization operates in an ethical manner lies with the board.

Defining Ethical Behavior

Ethics can be defined in three different ways, according to Frank Navran:

■ *Legal definitions* are aimed at ensuring that the behavior of individuals and organizations complies with applicable laws.

■ *Structured definitions* often grow out of a particular perspective and may be colored by religion or politics, and ethical behavior by these standards is judged in very concrete terms based on external reference rather than on the general tenor of society.

■ *Moral or character definitions* concern broad, fundamental concepts of rightness, goodness, and fairness as defined by society in general—core human values.

It's the second definition of ethical behavior that Navran believes is most important when thinking about organizational ethics, as seen in organizational codes of conduct. "As a friend of mine's mother used to say, 'There's no right way to do the wrong thing.' The ends don't justify the means. A lot of us will do what's expedient and rationalize that everybody else is doing it so it's okay, or we're accomplishing an important goal, so it's okay to do it in a bad way."

Navran distinguishes between ethical dilemmas—a situation where one must choose between competing values—and ethical differences—where people disagree about whether specific behavior meets an agreed-upon ethical standard.

■ *An ethical dilemma*—A loving aunt gives a child an ugly dress as a birthday gift. This is her first opportunity to learn from her parents that sometimes the value of compassion outweighs the value of honesty in human relationships.

■ *An ethical difference*—In a Congressional debate, all parties agree that fairness is the goal. One representative believes it's fair to continue a housing subsidy to the poor to ensure that every family can live in a safe, affordable home. Another believes that subsidy encourages dependence on the government, putting poor families at a disadvantage in the long term.

Because the questions raised by both ethical dilemmas and differences are so complex, and because there is rarely one right answer to every question, Navran and others believe it's important to create an organizational environment that encourages regular discussion of ethical issues. Developing an effective ethics program cannot be accomplished in a single effort. It is a process that continues throughout the life of the organization, and must be fully integrated at every level of operations—from the boardroom to frontline service sites to the donor cultivation process.

What Would You Do?
The Company Simply Refused to Pay

The sales goals were ambitious, but Jean had hit them.
Now the company was refusing to give her the bonus it had promised.

BY DOUG WALLACE

The Case

After work, Jean Sampson sat with a friend, sipping Chardonnay in a quiet corner at Charlie's Grill. "You won't believe the conversation I just had," she said. With uncharacteristic anger, she went on to describe what had happened.

Jean worked in sales for Salient, Inc., a medium-sized manufacturing company in Milwaukee, which produced a specialized line of high-tech peripherals sold to computer hardware companies. Until recently, nearly all its sales were in the U.S. But that changed a year ago when Salient decided to market worldwide. In the process, it hired Jean and a few others to put together a fast-track sales program, offering substantial bonuses for reaching stretch goals.

Jean, fluent in French, was assigned sales in Canada. She saw this as a professional challenge to demonstrate what she could really achieve. Two weeks ago she had marked her first year anniversary, and her sales were well over the top of annual goals.

This morning she had met with the head of human resources for a performance review. "That's when the wheels fell off the wagon," she muttered between bites of smoked salmon. Her

friend Sara, wide-eyed, just listened. "Instead of congratulating me and handing me a bonus check, the guy told me that I should be happy that I was still working, since the company's financial picture was rocky." When I reminded him that I had a signed contract about the bonus, he repeated that under the difficult company circumstances, I could keep my job. Although the job market for someone like herself was fairly good, Jean thought she would likely be denied a good recommendation. Putting down her wine glass, she sighed, "God, this is so unfair. What should I do?"

Sue Lach, Attorney, Messerli & Kramer, Minneapolis

If she wants to stay with the company, she has to work within the system. This means detective work: is the company really in financial difficulty? Is there a way to go over the head of human resources? Does the v.p. have a hidden agenda? (He may just not like Jean.)

I'd also want to see her contract, to see whether a bonus was guaran-

teed, or contingent on certain things. She needs this for negotiating. On the other hand, if she's really worried about getting another job, she can go to this guy and say, "Look, I'm sorry, apparently I didn't work up to your expectations, but I'm disappointed the company didn't follow through on its commitment," turning the tables to see what they'd say.

If she leaves, she shouldn't make waves, but simply find another job and quit. But she should find out, did everyone get their bonus except her? Did men get bonuses and not women? Then she can go to an employment law attorney and determine whether she has legal recourse.

Peter L. Lafferty, Financial Consultant, Salomon Smith Barney, Minneapolis

First of all, sales people are emotional people. They're highly motivated. You want sales people to succeed, and if they do, you've got to pay them. That's the deal. Part of it is recognition, but the bottom line is money in most cases. If I was counseling Jean, I'd suggest she find another job. I think she's overreacting by worrying about a recommendation. She can just show her numbers, "Here is what I've actually done, they just decided they didn't want to pay me." Any good company would be glad to have a person who can perform as she has.

The whole game of sales is hitting goals and getting paid for it. How can you give 100 percent if you've got a 50–50 chance of getting paid? You've got to pay salespeople, because they drive the company. If this situation reflects the ethics of the company, I wouldn't want to work there. The people who set up these programs must have honor, which is the opposite of the intimidation number the v.p. is playing.

Doug Wallace's Comments

Senior managers generally reflect the company's values. But not al-ways. Over the years this column has had many stories of managers who were cowboys servicing their own interests, or conversely, who thought they were being good soldiers, but tragically cut ethical corners to help the bottom line.

In Jean's case, she doesn't know whether the v.p. is acting on his own, or being directed by someone senior. In other words, is this a problem with a bad apple, or the whole barrel? But once Jean finds the answer, she confronts a set of choices.

Attorney Sue Lach advises that Jean gather information, regardless of whether she decides to stay or leave; she'll need it to make intelligent choices. Peter Lafferty focuses on the psychology of sales, and how the v.p. is crippling Jean's motivation and breaking a promise, thus crossing two ethical lines: respect for persons and promise-keeping.

Many of us find ourselves paralyzed when facing the uncertainty of whether to stay in a bad (but secure) work situation, or leave without knowing what job we'll find. Jean's dilemma is not just ethical, it's spiritual as well. How open are we to the uncertainty of the future? Do we approach it as hospitable or as something to fear?

What Actually Happened?

At this writing, Jean has been stewing about the problem for two months. She indicated her intention to seek legal counsel, but hasn't taken any initiative. My guess is she won't deal directly with the problem, and it will remain unresolved.

Contact Doug Wallace at dwethics@uswest.net.

Managing for Organizational Integrity

By supporting ethically sound behavior, managers can strengthen the relationships and reputations their companies depend on.

Lynn Sharp Paine

Lynn Sharp Paine is associate professor at the Harvard Business School, specializing in management ethics. Her current research focuses on leadership and organizational integrity in a global environment.

Many managers think of ethics as a question of personal scruples, a confidential matter between individuals and their consciences. These executives are quick to describe any wrongdoing as an isolated incident, the work of a rogue employee. The thought that the company could bear any responsibility for an individual's misdeeds never enters their minds. Ethics, after all, has nothing to do with management.

In fact, ethics has *everything* to do with management. Rarely do the character flaws of a lone actor fully explain corporate misconduct. More typically, unethical business practice involves the tacit, if not explicit, cooperation of others and reflects the values, attitudes, beliefs, language, and behavioral patterns that define an organization's operating culture. Ethics, then, is as much an organizational as a personal issue. Managers who fail to provide proper leadership and to institute systems that facilitate ethical conduct share responsibility with those who conceive, execute, and knowingly benefit from corporate misdeeds.

Managers must acknowledge their role in shaping organizational ethics and seize this opportunity to create a climate that can strengthen the relationships and reputations on which their companies' success depends. Executives who ignore ethics run the risk of personal and corporate liability in today's increasingly tough legal environment. In addition, they deprive their organizations of the benefits available under new federal guidelines for sentencing organizations convicted of wrongdoing. These sentencing guidelines recognize for the first time the organizational and managerial roots of unlawful conduct and base fines partly on the extent to which companies have taken steps to prevent that misconduct.

Prompted by the prospect of leniency, many companies are rushing to implement compliance-based ethics programs. Designed by corporate counsel, the goal of these programs is to prevent, detect, and punish legal violations. But organizational ethics means more than avoiding illegal practice; and providing employees with a rule book will do little to address the problems underlying unlawful conduct. To foster a climate that encourages exemplary behavior, corporations need a comprehensive approach that goes beyond the often punitive legal compliance stance.

An integrity-based approach to ethics management combines a concern for the law with an emphasis on managerial responsibility for ethical behavior. Though integrity strategies may vary in design and scope, all strive to define companies' guiding values, aspirations, and patterns of thought and conduct. When integrated into the day-to-day operations of an organization, such strategies can help prevent damaging ethical lapses while tapping into powerful human impulses for moral thought and action. Then an ethical framework becomes no longer a burdensome constraint within which companies must operate, but the governing ethos of an organization.

How Organizations Shape Individuals' Behavior

The once familiar picture of ethics as individualistic, unchanging, and impervious to organizational influences has not stood up to scrutiny in recent years. Sears Auto Centers' and Beech-Nut Nutrition Corporation's experiences illustrate the role organizations play in shaping individuals' behavior—and how even sound moral fiber can fray when stretched too thin.

In 1992, Sears, Roebuck & Company was inundated with complaints about its automotive service business. Consumers and attorneys general in more than 40 states had accused the company of misleading customers and selling them unnecessary parts and services, from brake jobs to front-end alignments. It would be a mistake, however, to see this situation exclusively in terms of any one individual's moral failings. Nor did management set out to defraud Sears customers. Instead, a number of organizational factors contributed to the problematic sales practices.

In the face of declining revenues, shrinking market share, and an increasingly competitive market for undercar services, Sears management attempted to spur the performance of its auto centers by introducing new goals and incentives for employees. The company increased minimum work quotas and introduced productivity incentives for mechanics. The automotive service advisers were given product-specific sales quotas—sell so many springs, shock absorbers, alignments, or brake jobs per shift—and paid a commission based on sales. According to advisers, failure to meet quotas could lead to a transfer or a reduction in work hours. Some employees spoke of the "pressure, pressure, pressure" to bring in sales.

Under this new set of organizational pressures and incentives, with few options for meeting their sales goals legitimately, some employees' judgment understandably suffered. Management's failure to clarify the line between unnecessary service and legitimate preventive maintenance, coupled with consumer ignorance, left employees to chart their own courses through a vast gray area, subject to a wide range of interpretations. Without active management support for ethical practice and mechanisms to detect and check questionable sales methods and poor work, it is not surprising that some employees may have reacted to contextual forces by resorting to exaggeration, carelessness, or even misrepresentation.

Shortly after the allegations against Sears became public, CEO Edward Brennan acknowledged management's responsibility for putting in place compensation and goal-setting systems that "created an environment in which mistakes did occur." Although the company denied any intent to deceive consumers, senior executives eliminated commissions for service advisers and discontinued sales quotas for specific parts. They also instituted a system of unannounced shopping audits and made plans to expand the internal monitoring of service. In settling the pending lawsuits, Sears offered coupons to customers who had bought certain auto services between 1990 and 1992. The total cost of the settlement, including potential customer refunds, was an estimated $60 million.

Contextual forces can also influence the behavior of top management, as a former CEO of Beech-Nut Nutrition Corporation discovered. In the early 1980s, only two years after joining the company, the CEO found evidence suggesting that the apple juice concentrate, supplied by the company's vendors for use in Beech-Nut's "100% pure" apple juice, contained nothing more than sugar water and chemicals. The CEO could have destroyed the bogus inventory and withdrawn the juice from grocers' shelves, but he was under extraordinary pressure to turn the ailing company around. Eliminating the inventory would have killed any hope of turning even the meager $700,000 profit promised to Beech-Nut's then parent, Nestlé.

A number of people in the corporation, it turned out, had doubted the purity of the juice for several years before the CEO arrived. But the 25% price advantage offered by the supplier of the bogus concentrate allowed the operations head to meet cost-control goals. Furthermore, the company lacked an effective quality control system, and a conclusive lab test for juice purity did not yet exist. When a member of the research department voiced concerns about the juice to operating management, he was accused of not being a team player and of acting like "Chicken Little." His judgment, his supervisor wrote in an annual performance review, was "colored by naïveté and impractical ideals." No one else seemed to have considered the company's obligations to its customers or to have thought about the potential harm of disclosure. No one considered the fact that the sale of adulterated or misbranded juice is a legal offense, putting the company and its top management at risk of criminal liability.

An FDA investigation taught Beech-Nut the hard way. In 1987, the company pleaded guilty to selling adulterated and misbranded juice. Two years and two criminal trials later, the CEO pleaded guilty to ten counts of mislabeling. The total cost to the company—including fines, legal expenses, and lost sales—was an estimated $25 million.

Acknowledging the importance of organizational context in ethics does not imply forgiving individual wrongdoers.

Such errors of judgment rarely reflect an organizational culture and management philosophy that sets out to harm or deceive. More often, they reveal a culture that is insensitive or indifferent to ethical considerations or one that lacks effective organizational systems. By the same token, exemplary conduct usually reflects an organizational culture and philosophy that is infused with a sense of responsibility.

For example, Johnson & Johnson's handling of the Tylenol crisis is sometimes attributed to the singular personality of then-CEO James Burke. However the decision to do a nationwide recall of Tylenol capsules in order to avoid further loss of life from product tampering was in reality not one decision but thousands of decisions made by individuals at all levels of the organization. The "Ty-

Corporate Fines Under the Federal Sentencing Guidelines

What size fine is a corporation likely to pay if convicted of a crime? It depends on a number of factors, some of which are beyond a CEO's control, such as the existence of a prior record of similar misconduct. But it also depends on more controllable factors. The most important of these are reporting and accepting responsibility for the crime, cooperating with authorities, and having an effective program in place to prevent and detect unlawful behavior.

The following example, based on a case studied by the United States Sentencing Commission, shows how the 1991 Federal Sentencing Guidelines have affected overall fine levels and how managers' actions influence organizational fines.

Acme Corporation was charged and convicted of mail fraud. The company systematically charged customers who damaged rented automobiles more than the actual cost of repairs. Acme also billed some customers for the cost of repairs to vehicles for which they were not responsible. Prior to the criminal adjudication, Acme paid $13.7 million in restitution to the customers who had been overcharged.

Deciding before the enactment of the sentencing guidelines, the judge in the criminal case imposed a fine of $6.85 million, roughly half the pecuniary loss suffered by Acme's customers. Under the sentencing guidelines, how-

ever, the results could have been dramatically different. Acme could have been fined anywhere from 5% to 200% the loss suffered by customers, depending on whether or not it had an effective program to prevent and detect violations of law and on whether or not it reported the crime, cooperated with authorities, and accepted responsibility for the unlawful conduct. If a high ranking official at Acme were found to have been involved, the maximum fine could have been as large as $54,800,000 or four times the loss to Acme customers. The following chart shows a possible range of fines for each situation:

What Fine Can Acme Expect?

	Maximum	Miminum
Program, reporting, cooperation, responsibility	$2,740,000	$685,000
Program only	10,960,000	5,480,000
No program, no reporting, no cooperation, no responsibility	27,400,000	13,700,000
No program, no reporting, no cooperation, no responsibility, involvement of high-level personnel	54,800,000	27,400,000

Based on Case No.: 88-266, United States Sentencing Commission, *Supplementary Report on Sentencing Guidelines for Organizations.*

lenol decision," then, is best understood not as an isolated incident, the achievement of a lone individual, but as the reflection of an organization's culture. Without a shared set of values and guiding principles deeply ingrained throughout the organization, it is doubtful that Johnson & Johnson's response would have been as rapid, cohesive and ethically sound.

Many people resist acknowledging the influence of organizational factors on individual behavior—especially on misconduct—for fear of diluting people's sense of personal moral responsibility. But this fear is based on a false dichotomy between holding individual transgressors accountable and holding "the system" accountable. Acknowledging the importance of organizational context need not imply exculpating individual wrongdoers. To understand all is not to forgive all.

The Limits of a Legal Compliance Program

The consequences of an ethical lapse can be serious and far-reaching. Organizations can quickly become entangled in an all-consuming web of legal proceedings. The risk of litigation and liability has increased in the past decade as lawmakers have legislated new civil and criminal offenses, stepped up penalties, and improved support

for law enforcement. Equally—if not more—important is the damage an ethical lapse can do to an organization's reputation and relationships. Both Sears and Beech-Nut, for instance, struggled to regain consumer trust and market share long after legal proceedings had ended.

As more managers have become alerted to the importance of organizational ethics, many have asked their lawyers to develop corporate ethics programs to detect and prevent violations of the law. The 1991 Federal Sentencing Guidelines offer a compelling rationale. Sanctions such as fines and probation for organizations convicted of wrongdoing can vary dramatically depending both on the degree of management cooperation in reporting and investigating corporate misdeeds and on whether or not the company has implemented a legal compliance program. (See the insert "Corporate Fines Under the Federal Sentencing Guidelines.")

Such programs tend to emphasize the prevention of unlawful conduct, primarily by increasing surveillance and control and by imposing penalties for wrongdoers. While plans vary, the basic framework is outlined in the sentencing guidelines. Managers must establish compliance standards and procedures; designate high-level personnel to oversee compliance; avoid delegating discretionary authority to those likely to act unlawfully; effectively communicate the company's standards and procedures through training or publications; take reasonable steps to achieve compliance through audits, monitoring processes, and a system for employees to report criminal misconduct without fear of retribution; consistently enforce standards through appropriate disciplinary measures; respond appropriately when offenses are detected; and, finally, take reasonable steps to prevent the occurrence of similar offenses in the future.

There is no question of the necessity of a sound, well-articulated strategy for legal compliance in an organization. After all, employees can be frustrated and frightened by the complexity of today's legal environment. And even managers who claim to use the law as a guide to ethical behavior often lack more than a rudimentary understanding of complex legal issues.

Managers would be mistaken, however, to regard legal compliance as an adequate means for addressing the full range of ethical issues that arise every day. "If it's legal, it's ethical," is a frequently heard slogan. But conduct that is lawful may be highly problematic from an ethical point of view. Consider the sale in some countries of hazardous products without appropriate warnings or the purchase of goods from suppliers who operate inhumane sweatshops in developing countries. Companies engaged in international business often discover that conduct that infringes on recognized standards of human rights and decency is legally permissible in some jurisdictions.

Legal clearance does not certify the absence of ethical problems in the United States either, as a 1991 case at Salomon Brothers illustrates. Four top-level executives failed to take appropriate action when learning of unlawful activities on the government trading desk. Company lawyers found no law obligating the executives to disclose the improprieties. Nevertheless, the executives' delay in disclosing and failure to reveal their prior knowledge prompted a serious crisis of confidence among employees, creditors, shareholders, and customers. The executives were forced to resign, having lost the moral authority to lead. Their ethical lapse compounded the trading desk's legal offenses, and the company ended up suffering losses—including legal costs, increased funding costs, and lost business—estimated at nearly $1 billion.

A compliance approach to ethics also overemphasizes the threat of detection and punishment in order to channel behavior in lawful directions. The underlying model for this approach is deterrence theory, which envisions people as rational maximizers of self-interest, responsive to the personal costs and benefits of their choices, yet indifferent to the moral legitimacy of those choices. But a recent study reported in *Why People Obey the Law* by Tom R. Tyler shows that obedience to the law is strongly influenced by a belief in its legitimacy and its moral correctness. People generally feel that they have a strong obligation to obey the law. Education about the legal standards and a supportive environment may be all that's required to insure compliance.

Discipline is, of course, a necessary part of any ethical system. Justified penalties for the infringement of legitimate norms are fair and appropriate. Some people do need the threat of sanctions. However, an overemphasis on potential sanctions can be superfluous and even counterproductive. Employees may rebel against programs that stress penalties, particularly if they are designed and imposed without employee involvement or if the standards are vague or unrealistic. Management may talk of mutual trust when unveiling a compliance plan, but employees often receive the message as a warning from on high. Indeed, the more skeptical among them may view compliance programs as nothing more than liability insurance for senior management. This is not an unreasonable conclusion, considering that compliance programs rarely address the root causes of misconduct.

Even in the best cases, legal compliance is unlikely to unleash much moral imagination or commitment. The law does not generally seek to inspire human excellence or distinction. It is no guide for exemplary behavior—or even good practice. Those managers who define ethics as legal compliance are implicitly endorsing a code of moral mediocrity for their organizations. As Richard Breeden, former chairman of the Securities and Exchange Commission, noted, "It is not an adequate ethical standard to aspire to get through the day without being indicted."

Integrity as a Governing Ethic

A strategy based on integrity holds organizations to a more robust standard. While compliance is rooted in avoiding legal sanctions, organizational integrity is based on the concept of self-governance in accordance with a set of guiding principles. From the perspective of integrity,

> # Management may talk of mutual trust when unveiling a compliance plan, but employees often see a warning from on high.

the task of ethics management is to define and give life to an organization's guiding values, to create an environment that supports ethically sound behavior, and to instill a sense of shared accountability among employees. The need to obey the law is viewed as a positive aspect of organizational life, rather than an unwelcome constraint imposed by external authorities.

An integrity strategy is characterized by a conception of ethics as a driving force of an enterprise. Ethical values shape the search for opportunities, the design of organizational systems, and the decision-making process used by individuals and groups. They provide a common frame of reference and serve as a unifying force across different

The Hallmarks of an Effective Integrity Strategy

There is no one right integrity strategy. Factors such as management personality, company history, culture, lines of business, and industry regulations must be taken into account when shaping an appropriate set of values and designing an implementation program. Still, several features are common to efforts that have achieved some success:

□ *The guiding values and commitments make sense and are clearly communicated.* They reflect important organizational obligations and widely shared aspirations that appeal to the organization's members. Employees at all levels take them seriously, feel comfortable discussing them, and have a concrete understanding of their practical importance. This does not signal the absence of ambiguity and conflict but a willingness to seek solutions compatible with the framework of values.

□ *Company leaders are personally committed, credible, and willing to take action on the values they espouse.* They are not mere mouthpieces. They are willing to scrutinize their own decisions. Consistency on the part of leadership is key. Waffling on values will lead to employee cynicism and a rejection of the program. At the same time, managers must assume responsibility for making tough calls when ethical obligations conflict.

□ *The espoused values are integrated into the normal channels of management decision making and are reflected in the organization's critical activities:* the development of plans, the setting of goals, the search for opportunities, the allocation of resources,

the gathering and communication of information, the measurement of performance, and the promotion and advancement of personnel.

□ *The company's systems and structures support and reinforce its values.* Information systems, for example, are designed to provide timely and accurate information. Reporting relationships are structured to build in checks and balances to promote objective judgment. Performance appraisal is sensitive to means as well as ends.

□ *Managers throughout the company have the decision-making skills, knowledge, and competencies needed to make ethically sound decisions on a day-to-day basis.* Ethical thinking and awareness must be part of every managers' mental equipment. Ethics education is usually part of the process.

Success in creating a climate for responsible and ethically sound behavior requires continuing effort and a considerable investment of time and resources. A glossy code of conduct, a high-ranking ethics officer, a training program, an annual ethics audit—these trappings of an ethics program do not necessarily add up to a responsible, law-abiding organization whose espoused values match its actions. A formal ethics program can serve as a catalyst and a support system, but organizational integrity depends on the integration of the company's values into its driving systems.

---

functions, lines of business, and employee groups. Organizational ethics helps define what a company is and what it stands for.

Many integrity initiatives have structural features common to compliance-based initiatives: a code of conduct, training in relevant areas of law, mechanisms for reporting and investigating potential misconduct, and audits and controls to insure that laws and company standards are being met. In addition, if suitably designed, an integrity-based initiative can establish a foundation for seeking the legal benefits that are available under the sentencing guidelines should criminal wrongdoing occur. (See the insert "The Hallmarks of an Effective Integrity Strategy.")

But an integrity strategy is broader, deeper, and more demanding than a legal compliance initiative. Broader in that it seeks to enable responsible conduct. Deeper in that it cuts to the ethos and operating systems of the organization and its members, their guiding values and patterns of thought and action. And more demanding in that it requires an active effort to define the responsibilities and aspirations that constitute an organization's ethical compass. Above all, organizational ethics is seen as the work of management. Corporate counsel may play a role in the design and implementation of integrity strategies, but managers at all levels and across all functions are involved in the process. (See the chart, "Strategies for Ethics Management.")

During the past decade, a number of companies have undertaken integrity initiatives. They vary according to the ethical values focused on and the implementation approaches used. Some companies focus on the core values of integrity that reflect basic social obligations, such as respect for the rights of others, honesty, fair dealing, and obedience to the law. Other companies emphasize aspirations—values that are ethically desirable but not necessarily morally obligatory—such as good service to customers, a commitment to diversity, and involvement in the community.

When it comes to implementation, some companies begin with behavior. Following Aristotle's view that one becomes courageous by acting as a courageous person, such companies develop codes of conduct specifying appropriate behavior, along with a system of incentives, audits, and controls. Other companies focus less on specific actions and more on developing attitudes, decision-making processes, and ways of thinking that reflect their values. The assumption is that personal commitment and appropriate decision processes will lead to right action.

Martin Marietta, NovaCare, and Wetherill Associates have implemented and lived with quite different integrity strategies. In each case, management has found that the initiative has made important and often unexpected contributions to competitiveness, work environment, and key relationships on which the company depends.

Martin Marietta: Emphasizing Core Values

Martin Marietta Corporation, the U.S. aerospace and defense contractor, opted for an integrity-based ethics program in 1985. At the time, the defense industry was under

Strategies for Ethics Management

Characteristics of Compliance Strategy

Ethos	conformity with externally imposed standards
Objective	prevent criminal misconduct
Leadership	lawyer driven
Methods	education, reduced discretion, auditing and controls, penalties
Behavioral Assumptions	autonomous beings guided by material self-interest

Characteristics of Integrity Strategy

Ethos	self-governance according to chosen standards
Objective	enable responsible conduct
Leadership	management driven with aid of lawyers, HR, others
Methods	education, leadership, accountability, organizational systems and decision processes, auditing and controls, penalties
Behavioral Assumptions	social beings guided by material self-interest, values, ideals, peers

Implementation of Compliance Strategy

Standards	criminal and regulatory law
Staffing	lawyers
Activities	develop compliance standards train and communicate handle reports of misconduct conduct investigations oversee compliance audits enforce standards
Education	compliance standards and system

Implementation of Integrity Strategy

Standards	company values and aspirations social obligations, including law
Staffing	executives and managers with lawyers, others
Activities	lead development of company values and standards train and communicate integrate into company systems provide guidance and consultation assess values performance identify and resolve problems oversee compliance activities
Education	decision making and values compliance standards and system

attack for fraud and mismanagement, and Martin Marietta was under investigation for improper travel billings. Managers knew they needed a better form of self-governance but were skeptical that an ethics program could influence behavior. "Back then people asked, 'Do you really need an ethics program to be ethical?' " recalls current President Thomas Young. "Ethics was something personal. Either you had it, or you didn't."

The corporate general counsel played a pivotal role in promoting the program, and legal compliance was a critical objective. But it was conceived of and implemented from the start as a companywide management initiative aimed at creating and maintaining a "do-it-right" climate. In its original conception, the program emphasized core values, such as honesty and fair play. Over time, it ex-

panded to encompass quality and environmental responsibility as well.

Today the initiative consists of a code of conduct, an ethics training program, and procedures for reporting and investigating ethical concerns within the company. It also includes a system for disclosing violations of federal procurement law to the government. A corporate ethics office manages the program, and ethics representatives are stationed at major facilities. An ethics steering committee, made up of Martin Marietta's president, senior executives, and two rotating members selected from field operations, oversees the ethics office. The audit and ethics committee of the board of directors oversees the steering committee.

The ethics office is responsible for responding to questions and concerns from the company's employees. Its network of representatives serves as a sounding board, a source of guidance, and a channel for raising a range of issues, from allegations of wrongdoing to complaints about poor management, unfair supervision, and company policies and practices. Martin Marietta's ethics network, which accepts anonymous complaints, logged over 9,000 calls in 1991, when the company had about 60,000 employees. In 1992, it investigated 684 cases. The ethics office also works closely with the human resources, legal, audit, communications, and security functions to respond to employee concerns.

Shortly after establishing the program, the company began its first round of ethics training for the entire workforce, starting with the CEO and senior executives. Now in its third round, training for senior executives focuses on decision making, the challenges of balancing multiple responsibilities, and compliance with laws and regulations critical to the company. The incentive compensation plan for executives makes responsibility for promoting ethical conduct an explicit requirement for reward eligibility and requires that business and personal goals be achieved in accordance with the company's policy on ethics. Ethical conduct and support for the ethics program are also criteria in regular performance reviews.

Today top-level managers say the ethics program has helped the company avoid serious problems and become more responsive to its more than 90,000 employees. The ethics network, which tracks the number and types of cases and complaints, has served as an early warning system for poor management, quality and safety defects, racial and gender discrimination, environmental concerns, inaccurate and false records, and personnel grievances regarding salaries, promotions, and layoffs. By providing an alternative channel for raising such concerns, Martin Marietta is able to take corrective action more quickly and with a lot less pain. In many cases, potentially embarrassing problems have been identified and dealt with before becoming a management crisis, a lawsuit, or a criminal investigation. Among employees who brought complaints in 1993, 75% were satisfied with the results.

Company executives are also convinced that the program has helped reduce the incidence of misconduct. When allegations of misconduct do surface, the company says it deals with them more openly. On several occasions, for instance, Martin Marietta has voluntarily disclosed and made restitution to the government for misconduct involving potential violations of federal procurement laws. In addition, when an employee alleged that the company had retaliated against him for voicing safety concerns about his plant on CBS news, top management commissioned an investigation by an outside law firm. Although failing to support the allegations, the investigation found that employees at the plant feared retaliation when raising health, safety, or environmental complaints. The company redoubled its efforts to identify and discipline those employees taking retaliatory action

and stressed the desirability of an open work environment in its ethics training and company communications.

Although the ethics program helps Martin Marietta avoid certain types of litigation, it has occasionally led to other kinds of legal action. In a few cases, employees dismissed for violating the code of ethics sued Martin Marietta, arguing that the company had violated its own code by imposing unfair and excessive discipline.

Still, the company believes that its attention to ethics has been worth it. The ethics program has led to better relationships with the government, as well as to new business opportunities. Along with prices and technology, Martin Marietta's record of integrity, quality, and reliability of estimates plays a role in the awarding of defense contracts, which account for some 75% of the company's revenues. Executives believe that the reputation they've earned through their ethics program has helped them build trust with government auditors, as well. By opening up communications, the company has reduced the time spent on redundant audits.

The program has also helped change employees' perceptions and priorities. Some managers compare their new ways of thinking about ethics to the way they understand quality. They consider more carefully how situations will be perceived by others, the possible long-term consequences of short-term thinking, and the need for continuous improvement. CEO Norman Augustine notes, "Ten years ago, people would have said that there were no ethical issues in business. Today employees think their number-one objective is to be thought of as decent people doing quality work."

NovaCare: Building Shared Aspirations

NovaCare Inc., one of the largest providers of rehabilitation services to nursing homes and hospitals in the United States, has oriented its ethics effort toward building a common core of shared aspirations. But in 1988, when the company was called InSpeech, the only sentiment shared was mutual mistrust.

Senior executives built the company from a series of aggressive acquisitions over a brief period of time to take advantage of the expanding market for therapeutic ser-

At NovaCare, executives defined organizational values and introduced structural changes to support those values.

vices. However, in 1988, the viability of the company was in question. Turnover among its frontline employees—the clinicians and therapists who care for patients in nursing homes and hospitals—escalated to 57% per year. The company's inability to retain therapists caused customers to defect and the stock price to languish in an extended slump.

After months of soul-searching, InSpeech executives realized that the turnover rate was a symptom of a more basic problem: the lack of a common set of values and aspirations. There was, as one executive put it, a "huge disconnect" between the values of the therapists and clinicians and those of the managers who ran the company. The therapists and clinicians evaluated the company's success in terms of its delivery of high-quality health care. InSpeech management, led by executives with financial services and venture capital backgrounds, measured the company's worth exclusively in terms of financial success. Management's single-minded emphasis on increasing hours of reimbursable care turned clinicians off. They took management's performance orientation for indifference to patient care and left the company in droves.

CEO John Foster recognized the need for a common frame of reference and a common language to unify the diverse groups. So he brought in consultants to conduct interviews and focus groups with the company's health care professionals, managers, and customers. Based on the results, an employee task force drafted a proposed vision statement for the company, and another 250 employees suggested revisions. Then Foster and several senior managers developed a succinct statement of the company's guiding purpose and fundamental beliefs that could be used as a framework for making decisions and setting goals, policies, and practices.

Unlike a code of conduct, which articulates specific behavioral standards, the statement of vision, purposes, and beliefs lays out in very simple terms the company's central purpose and core values. The purpose—meeting the rehabilitation needs of patients through clinical leadership—is supported by four key beliefs: respect for the individual, service to the customer, pursuit of excellence, and commitment to personal integrity. Each value is discussed with examples of how it is manifested in the day-to-day activities and policies of the company, such as how to measure the quality of care.

To support the newly defined values, the company changed its name to NovaCare and introduced a number of structural and operational changes. Field managers and clinicians were given greater decision-making authority; clinicians were provided with additional resources to assist in the delivery of effective therapy; and a new management structure integrated the various therapies offered by the company. The hiring of new corporate personnel with health care backgrounds reinforced the company's new clinical focus.

The introduction of the vision, purpose, and beliefs met with varied reactions from employees, ranging from cool skepticism to open enthusiasm. One employee remembered thinking the talk about values "much ado about nothing." Another recalled, "It was really wonderful. It gave us a goal that everyone aspired to, no matter what their place in the company." At first, some were baffled about how the vision, purpose, and beliefs were to be used. But, over time, managers became more adept at explaining and using them as a guide. When a customer tried to hire away a valued employee, for example, managers considered raiding the customer's company for employees. After reviewing the beliefs, the managers abandoned the idea.

NovaCare managers acknowledge and company surveys indicate that there is plenty of room for improvement. While the values are used as a firm reference point for decision making and evaluation in some areas of the company, they are still viewed with reservation in others. Some managers do not "walk the talk," employees complain. And recently acquired companies have yet to be fully integrated into the program. Nevertheless, many NovaCare employees say the values initiative played a critical role in the company's 1990 turnaround.

The values reorientation also helped the company deal with its most serious problem: turnover among health care providers. In 1990, the turnover rate stood at 32%, still above target but a significant improvement over the 1988 rate of 57%. By 1993, turnover had dropped to 27%. Moreover, recruiting new clinicians became easier. Barely able to hire 25 new clinicians each month in 1988, the company added 776 in 1990 and 2,546 in 1993. Indeed, one employee who left during the 1988 turmoil said that her decision to return in 1990 hinged on the company's adoption of the vision, purpose, and beliefs.

Wetherill Associates: Defining Right Action

Wetherill Associates, Inc.—a small, privately held supplier of electrical parts to the automotive market—has neither a conventional code of conduct nor a statement of values. Instead, WAI has a *Quality Assurance Manual*—a combination of philosophy text, conduct guide, technical manual, and company profile—that describes the company's commitment to honesty and its guiding principle of right action.

WAI doesn't have a corporate ethics officer who reports to top management, because at WAI, the company's corporate ethics officer *is* top management. Marie Bothe, WAI's chief executive officer, sees her main function as keeping the 350-employee company on the path of right action and looking for opportunities to help the community. She delegates the "technical" aspects of the business—marketing, finance, personnel, operations—to other members of the organization.

Right action, the basis for all of WAI's decisions, is a well-developed approach that challenges most conventional management thinking. The company explicitly rejects the usual conceptual boundaries that separate morality and self-interest. Instead, they define right behavior as logically, expediently, and morally right. Managers teach employees to look at the needs of the customers, suppliers, and the community—in addition to those of the company and its employees—when making decisions.

WAI also has a unique approach to competition. One employee explains, "We are not 'in competition' with anybody. We just do what we have to do to serve the customer." Indeed, when occasionally unable to fill orders, WAI salespeople refer customers to competitors. Artificial incentives, such as sales contests, are never used to spur individual performance. Nor are sales results used in de-

Creating an organization that encourages exemplary conduct may be the best way to prevent damaging misconduct.

termining compensation. Instead, the focus is on teamwork and customer service. Managers tell all new recruits that absolute honesty, mutual courtesy, and respect are standard operating procedure.

Newcomers generally react positively to company philosophy, but not all are prepared for such a radical departure from the practices they have known elsewhere. Recalling her initial interview, one recruit described her response to being told that lying was not allowed, "What do you mean? No lying? I'm a buyer. I lie for a living!" Today she is persuaded that the policy makes sound business sense. WAI is known for informing suppliers of overshipments as well as undershipments and for scrupulous honesty in the sale of parts, even when deception cannot be readily detected.

Since its entry into the distribution business 13 years ago, WAI has seen its revenues climb steadily from just under $1 million to nearly $98 million in 1993, and this is an industry with little growth. Once seen as an upstart beset by naysayers and industry skeptics, WAI is now credited with entering and professionalizing an industry in which kickbacks, bribes, and "gratuities" were commonplace. Employees—equal numbers of men and women ranging in age from 17 to 92—praise the work environment as both productive and supportive.

WAI's approach could be difficult to introduce in a larger, more traditional organization. WAI is a small company founded by 34 people who shared a belief in right action; its ethical values were naturally built into the organization from the start. Those values are so deeply ingrained in the company's culture and operating systems that they have been largely self-sustaining. Still, the company has developed its own training program and takes special care to hire people willing to support right action. Ethics and job skills are considered equally important in determining an individual's competence and suitability for employment. For WAI, the challenge will be to sustain its vision as the company grows and taps into markets overseas.

At WAI, as at Martin Marietta and NovaCare, a management-led commitment to ethical values has contributed to competitiveness, positive workforce morale, as well as solid sustainable relationships with the company's key constituencies. In the end, creating a climate that encourages exemplary conduct may be the best way to discourage damaging misconduct. Only in such an environment do rogues really act alone.

when good people do bad things at work

ROTE BEHAVIOR, DISTRACTIONS, AND MORAL EXCLUSION STYMIE ETHICAL BEHAVIOR ON THE JOB.

BY DENNIS J. MOBERG

The news is full of the exploits of corporate villains. We read about how officials at Lincoln Savings and Loan bilked thousands out of their customers' retirement nest eggs. There are stories of the lies Brown and Williamson Tobacco executives told about the addictive nature of cigarettes and the company's subsequent campaign to destroy whistle-blower Jeffrey Wigant.

Also in the news are the top managers at Time Warner who looked the other way rather than forego millions from the sale of rap music with lyrics that advocated violence directed at women and the police. Such acts are hard to forgive. Scoundrels such as these seem either incredibly weak or dangerously flawed.

Yet not all corporate misdeeds are committed by bad people. In fact, a significant number of unethical acts in business are the likely result of foibles and failings rather than selfishness and greed. Put in certain kinds of situations, good people inadvertently do bad things.

For those of us concerned about ethical actions and not just good intentions, the problem is clear. We must identify the situational factors that keep people from doing their best and eliminate them whenever we can.

From *Issues in Ethics,* Fall 1999, pp. 7-10. © 1999 by The Markkula Center for Applied Ethics at Santa Clara University. Reprinted by permission.

An organizational culture that facilitates work-family balance or encourages employee involvement in the community may move experiences that should not be seen as mere distractions onto the center stage of consciousness.

Problem No.1—Scripts

One factor is something psychologists call scripts. This term refers to the procedures that experience tells us to use in specific situations. When we brush our teeth or congratulate a friend on the arrival of a new grandchild, we probably use scripts.

Unlike other forms of experience, scripts are stored in memory in a mechanical or rote fashion. When we encounter a very familiar situation, rather than actively think about it, we reserve our mental energy for other purposes and behave as though we are cruising on automatic pilot.

In a classic psychological experiment, people approached someone at an office machine making copies and asked, "May I please make just one copy because. . . ." The person at the machine generally complied with this request, but the really interesting finding was that the likelihood of compliance was totally independent of the reasons stated. In fact, superfluous reasons such as "because I need to make a copy" were just as successful as good reasons such as "because my boss told me she needed these right away." Apparently, we have all experienced this situation so often that we don't give the reasons our full attention, not to mention our careful consideration.

One ethical lapse clearly attributable to scripts was Ford Motor Co.'s failure to recall the Pinto in the 1970s. The Pinto was an automobile with an undetected design flaw that made the gas tank burst into flames on impact, resulting in the death and disfigurement of scores of victims. Dennis Gioia, the Ford recall coordinator at the time, reviewed hundreds of accident reports to detect whether a design flaw was implicated. Later, he recalled,

When I was dealing with the first trickling-in of field reports that might have suggested a significant problem with the Pinto, the reports were essentially similar to many others that I was dealing with (and dismissing) all the time. . . . I was making this kind of decision automatically every day. I had trained myself to respond to prototypical cues, and these didn't fit the relevant prototype for crisis cases.

Situations like this occur frequently in the work world. Repetitive jobs requiring vigilance to prevent ethical lapses can be found in quality control, customer service, and manufacturing. In this respect, consider what happened when a nurse with a script that called for literal obedience to a doctor's written orders misread the directions to place ear drops in a patient's right ear as "place in R ear." Good people can inadvertently do *very bad* things.

Scripts may also be at work when we come face to face with those who are suffering. In situations where we observe the pain of those in need, scripts permit us to steel ourselves against feelings of empathy. Most of us have been approached by the homeless on the street, exposed to horrific images on the television news, and asked for donations on behalf of the victims of natural disasters.

According to research at the University of Kansas, scripts allow people to avoid responsibility for the suffering of others in situations when providing help appears costly. In work contexts, this might explain why businesspeople do not always respond philanthropically to documented cases of human suffering. What appears to be calculated indifference may actually not be calculated at all.

Whenever there is repetition, there are likely to be scripts. Accordingly, the best way to eliminate the potential of scripts to result in unethical behavior is to keep people out of highly repetitive situations. Technology can and has been used to eliminate highly routine tasks, but job rotation is also an option. For example, *The Daily Oklahoman* newspaper of Oklahoma City cross-trains most of its editors and schedules them to switch roles often. This helps keep the editors mentally sharp.

One editor who often switches roles from night to night commented: "You're fresh when you come to a particular job. Like last night I did inside [design], and it was a long and torturous night because of the large paper. But then again I turn around and do something thoroughly different tonight, so I don't feel like I'm trudging back to the same old rut again."

Oklahoman News Editor Ed Sargent thinks editing quality has improved because those who switch roles are exposed to the different approaches their colleagues take to the job. "Every editor has different opinions, obviously, about what's a big error and what's a little error," he said. Although the original intent of the role switching was to distribute stress more evenly, a side effect is that the paper is probably less prone to ethical lapses.

Problem No. 2— Distractions

Scripts are cognitive shortcuts that take the place of careful thinking. A similar human tendency is our mindless treatment of distractions. Think for a moment about the last time you drove to a very important meeting. Once there, were you able to recall any details of your journey? Most of us cannot, which demonstrates that when concentrating on completing an involving task, we don't deal well with distractions.

This inattention to what is happening on the periphery can get us into trouble with our spouses and significant others, and it can also result in ethical lapses. In one very telling experiment, divinity students were told that they had to deliver a lecture from prepared notes in a classroom across campus. Half the students were told they had to hurry to be on time, and the other half were told they had more than ample time.

On the way, the students came across a person in distress (actually an actor), who sat slumped motionless in a doorway, coughing and groaning. Shockingly, only 16 of the 40 divinity students stopped to help, most of them from the group that had ample time. To those in a hurry, the man was a distraction, a threat to their focus on giving a lecture. Ironically enough, half of them had been asked to discuss the parable of "The Good Samaritan."

Mindlessness about distractions at work is most pronounced when employees, with limited means of gaining perspective, are encouraged to be focused and driven. The best way to combat this tendency is for senior managers to model the virtue of temperance. If the president of a company is a workaholic, it is difficult to convince employees to be open to problems on the outskirts of their commitments. In contrast, an organizational culture that facilitates work-family balance or encourages employee involvement in the community may move experiences that should not be seen as mere distractions onto the center stage of consciousness.

Moberg Assumes Leadership of Ethics Center

Dennis Moberg was appointed in September as acting executive director of the Markkula Center for Applied Ethics. A professor of management at Santa Clara University, as well as the Presidential Professor of Ethics and the Common Good, Moberg is nationally recognized for his research on business ethics. He has won several awards for undergraduate and graduate teaching.

"With experience as associate dean of the Business School and chair of the Management Department, Moberg has proven administrative and leadership ability," said Don Dodson, vice provost for academic affairs and University planning, when he announced the appointment.

Moberg replaces Thomas Shanks, who will continue with the Center as director of Business and Public Policy Programs, many of which he initiated. "Under Shanks' leadership, the Center has become an important resource for businesses, public policy makers, and nonprofit organizations," Dodson said.

The University is currently conducting a nationwide search for a permanent executive director, expected to take over the helm in fall 2000.

Problem No. 3— Moral Exclusion

A final problem that brings out the worst in good people is the very human tendency to morally exclude certain persons. This occurs when individuals or groups are perceived as outside the boundary in which moral values and considerations of fairness apply. The most striking example occurs during warfare when the citizens of a country readily perceive their enemies in demonic terms. Yet, this tendency to discount the moral standing of others results in us discounting all kinds of people, some of them as close as co-workers and valued customers.

Greater awareness and extensive training have reduced some of the exclusion women and people of color have historically experienced. More work needs to be done in this area, as well as in other equally insidious forms of exclusion.

One way such exclusion shows up is in our use of pronouns. If *we* are in marketing and *they* are in production, the chances are that the distance may be great enough for *us* to be morally indifferent to what happens to *them*. Similarly, if we use stereotypic terms like *bean counter* or sneer when we say *management,* then it is clear that people in these categories don't count.

Not surprisingly, one way to expand the scope of justice is to promote direct contact with individuals who have been morally excluded. One company that applied this notion in an intriguing way is Eisai, a Japanese pharmaceutical firm. In the late 1980s, Haruo Naito had recently become CEO, and his closest advisers expressed concern that his managers and employees lacked an understanding of the end users of Eisai's products.

Hearing this, Naito decided to shift the focus of attention from the customers of his company's products—doctors and pharmacists—to *their* customers—patients and their families. Eisai managers, he decided, needed to identify better with end users and then infuse the insights from this sense of inclusion throughout the organization. This was a revolutionary idea for this company of 4,500 employees, but Naito believed his employees needed a more vivid reason to care deeply about their work.

"It's not enough to tell employees that if they do something, the company will grow this much or their salary will increase this much. That's just not enough incentive," says Naito. "You have to show them how what they are doing is connected to society, or exactly how it will help a patient." Accordingly, Naito decided to send 100 managers to a seven-day seminar: three days of nursing-home training and four days of medical care observation.

These managers were then sent to diverse regions throughout Japan, where they had to deal with different people, many of whom were in critical condition. They met patients with both physical and emotional problems; some of the patients they came in contact with died during their internships.

This pilot program grew to include more than 1,000 Eisai employees. Pretty soon, even laboratory support personnel had to leave their benches and desks and meet regularly with pharmacists and hospital people.

"Getting them out of the office was a way to activate human relationships," says Naito. Another way was to institute hotlines, which have generated product ideas. As a consequence, many new Eisai drugs were produced, including some that have promise in dealing with Alzheimer's disease. Clearly, moral inclusion was stimulated at Eisai at least insofar as the end users of its products are concerned.

Failing to Bother

Jesuit scholar James F. Keenan reminds us that "sinners in the New Testament are known not for what they did, but for what they failed to do—for failing to bother." We are all prone to this failure, but not necessarily because we are sinners. Repetition, distractions, and our natural tendency to exclude those unfamiliar to us cloud our best thinking and forestall the expression of our virtues. We owe it to ourselves to resist these pernicious influences, and we owe it to those in our work communities to help them to do the same.

FURTHER READING

Gioia, D. A. "Pinto Fires and Personal Ethics: A Script Analysis of Missed Opportunities." *Journal of Business Ethics* 11 (1992): 379–389.

Shaw, Laura L., Batson, C. Daniel, and Todd, Matthew R. "Empathy Avoidance: Forestalling Feeling for Another in Order to Escape the Motivational Consequences." *Journal of Personality and Social Psychology* 67.5 (1994): 879–887.

Craig, D. "Cross-training, Rotation Leads to Less Stress." *The American Editor* 788 (January 1998): 16–17.

Opotow, S. "Moral Exclusion and Injustice: An Introduction." *Journal of Social Issues* 46 (1990): 1–20.

Cooper, R. K., and Sawaf, A. *Executive EQ: Emotional Intelligence in Leadership and Organizations.* N.Y.: Grosset/Putnam, 1996.

Acting Executive Director of the Ethics Center Dennis J. Moberg is in the Management Department at Santa Clara University.

If *we* are in marketing and *they* are in production, the chances are that the distance may be great enough for us to be morally indifferent to what happens to *them*.

Mission Driven, Values Centered

In our business, tens of thousands of people depend on our leadership for their livelihood and lives.

WILLIAM W. GEORGE

THE SUBJECT OF BUILDING A mission-driven and values-centered organization is near to my heart. I call this leadership with purpose, meaning leadership with vision, passion, and compassion—vision of what our organizations can become, passion for the people we serve, and compassion for the people with whom we work.

Transcendent leadership envisions a clear mission with purpose and passion and calls upon that purpose and that passion to lead to greater heights. A leadership mission describes the values needed to make it reality, and to set a standard of behavior. Such a mission is not about a code of conduct, rules, systems, and procedures. It is about having a sense of purpose and a set of values that guide our everyday actions.

Values Centered

Patients are the only reason we are in business, and serving them with superior health services at a reasonable cost is our primary objective. The real revolution taking place in this country is not managed care, but patient power. Patients are taking control of their own health care. They are becoming better informed and more proactive. They demand the right to choose their physician and when they leave the hospital, for example, after

giving birth or having a mastectomy. They use the Internet to understand their diseases and the options they face. If they cannot get what they want and need from the health care system, patients are seeking therapies such as herbal medicines, acupuncture, chiropractic services, relaxation therapy, and massage. Often primary care doctors don't know as much about the new treatment methods as their patients do.

Today patients have access to as much current information about their disease as their primary care physician.

The successful hospital organizations of the future—the survivors of the consolidations—will be ones that empower all their employees and the independent physicians to feel passionate about patients, about providing them nurture and care, and insuring that all their patients have an excel-

lent experience that helps restore them to full and active lives.

Implicit in this statement is the presumption that the health care they receive is provided in an efficient and cost-effective manner. I see no conflict between the highest quality health care and the most cost-effective health care.

Mission Driven

How do we get our organizations fully committed and passionate about our missions? How do we get independent people who work with us to buy into the mission?

I believe it starts with the basic reason we come to work every day: We want to serve others and help restore people to full life and health. We aren't there just for the money.

So how do we get this high level of commitment from our employees and stakeholders? I believe it all starts with having a clear mission that includes a clear statement of values. Most organizations have a written mission statement. If you do not, I strongly urge you to get your top team together and write one. That's the easy part. The more difficult part is getting everyone to buy into that mission and values. That takes time and effort, and consistency of action, through bad times as well as good. It only takes one reversal of values at

 From *Executive Excellence*, August 1999, pp. 6-7. © 1999 by Executive Excellence Publishing. Reprinted by permission.

the top when conditions are tough to reverse many years of hard work in setting the standard and the climate. For better or for worse, as leaders we are better known for our deeds than for our words.

The Medtronic Story: A Case History

Let me illustrate how this high commitment and purpose is achieved at Medtronic. We are a $4 billion organization whose major work is designing and manufacturing the finest medical technology products in the world. Our mission is to restore people to full life and health. If we do that well, we will be wildly successful. If we do not, we will fail and eventually cease to exist.

In carrying out our mission, we observe six values: Contribute to human welfare, focused growth, unsurpassed quality, fair profit, personal worth of employees, and good citizenship.

The significant thing about the Medtronic mission statement is that not one word has been changed since our founder, Earl Bakken, wrote it in 1960!

The key to a mission-driven organization is not so much the statement itself, but how it is woven into the daily lives of everyone. Here's how we make the Medtronic mission "come alive" for all our 20,000 employees and everyone who visits or associates with the company:

1. Holiday program. The most important event of the year for us at Medtronic is our annual holiday program, a 40-year tradition. Each December we invite six patients and their physicians to come to Medtronic and tell their personal stories to our employees. After each doctor introduces his or her patients, the patients explain how receiving a Medtronic product has changed or saved his or her life.

2. Medallion ceremony. Another tradition is to meet individually with each new employee and describe the company's history and mission. At the medallion ceremony, we go over the mission, word by word, saying what it means to us. Then we call each employee and give them a medallion with "the rising man," symbolic of the mission, and ask them to make a commitment to the Medtronic mission.

3. Symbols of the mission. At Medtronic we have many symbols of the mission—from the words carved in stone at the base of Earl's statue, to the photos of patients from around the world in our executive area, to the mural of "The Rising Person," to the mission printed in 10 languages, to copies of the mission throughout our facilities.

4. Talking about the mission. To make the mission come alive, we talk about it all the time. I have a monthly breakfast with employees to get feedback on how well we're fulfilling the mission. I send regular e-mails to employees, describing what we are doing to fulfill the mission. At our monthly chairman's briefing and annual shareholders meeting, we talk about the impact of the mission on our customers.

5. Business strategy decisions. The mission is often referred to in business decisions, such as our decision to retain a certain venture, not to acquire another venture, and taking on the FDA because we believed its inaction was harming patients.

6. Quality decisions. The mission is an integral part of our quality decisions. No product can be released to the market until it has been approved by the Medtronic Executive Committee with a formal vote following a quality presentation. The mission was also a factor in our decision to cancel the Parallel heart valve, a decision that cost us $30 million.

7. People decisions. We also refer to the mission in making people decisions such as layoffs and early retirements, as well as ensuring that all employees are shareholders so they can have "a means to share in the company's success."

8. Ethical decisions. The mission weighs heavily on our ethical decisions, such as my decision to terminate the president of Europe for covering up a "promotion fund" for an Italian distributor, or our decision to cease operations at a small acquisition in California where we had uncovered fraud.

9. Profit reinvestment. The mission also led us to reinvest the large patent settlement we received from Siemans rather than taking it to profit. Today those investments are paying off in terms of innovative new therapies.

Does our experience with mission and values relate to yours? You bet it does! We all share common concerns. We are all in a highly competitive environment. And we all have to make the numbers work! Nothing is more important than having a mission-driven, values-centered organization. It is the key to success in any business.

William George is chairman and CEO of Medtronics. This article is taken from Vital Speeches; *www.medtronic.com.*

THE 100 Best Corporate Citizens

Celebrating those companies that excel at serving multiple stakeholders well.

PROJECT DIRECTOR MARJORIE KELLY
ARTICLE BY TOM KLUSMANN
STATISTICAL ANALYSIS BY SANDRA WADDOCK & SAMUEL GRAVE
SOCIAL DATA FROM KINDER, LYDENBERG, DOMINI & CO.

A hopeful metamorphosis is under way in corporate America. Embracing goals beyond the traditional focus on earnings, the best companies are focusing on a host of social issues. They are, in short, serving not only stockholders, but other stakeholders as well. And by stakeholders we mean those with a "stake" in the company: employees, customers, community members, and stockholders. As the performance of our 100 Best Corporate Citizens shows, serving this new community of stakeholders is just good business. One bene-fit, for example, is attracting and retaining employees. As Beth Sawi, chief administrative officer at Charles Schwab, puts it, employees come to Schwab "for something more than just the bottom line."

But Schwab's bottom line is definitely healthy, and that al-lows its positive culture to thrive. This financial services firm headquartered in San Francisco, with $3.9 billion in 1999

This study looks at service to four key **stakeholders:** stockholders, employees, customers, and the community.

revenue, is No. 8 on our list of the 100 Best Corporate Citizens, in part because of financial performance. In 1998 (the latest annual figures available when the analysis was done), total return to investors was an impressive 102 percent. That helped get the firm a rating of 5—on a scale of 1 to 5—in service to shareholders (ratings tracked performance from 1996 to 1998). But Schwab also scored high in service to employees, with a 4.33 score. Excellence in those two areas was the primary reason they scored high overall.

That's typical of companies in this study. It looks at corporate service to four key stakeholder groups (stockholders, employees, customers, and community.) IBM (No. 1 on our list) was virtually alone in serving three groups well: stockholders, community, and employees. More typically, Hewlett-Packard (No. 2) excelled in serving two: community and employees. No company excelled in serving all four, although the top 25 performed at least average in serving all stakeholders.

This study is about good corporate citizenship. We define that as serving a variety of stakeholders well. To put numbers to these judgments, we used data from Kinder, Lydenberg, Domini & Co. (KLD), a social research firm in Boston, which ranks service to stakeholders on a scale ranging from 1, a "major concern"; 3, which is "neutral"; to 5, a "major strength." (For more detail on methodology, see "On the Trail of the Best Corporate Cirizens".)

KLD's research, supplemented by *Business Ethics* interviews, shows a changing corporate landscape. Corporations today simply cannot ignore the social issues in their communities; cannot ignore their employees, with the shortage of skilled staff; cannot neglect the changing needs of their customers; and of course cannot neglect stockholders.

Our study found a myriad of ways America's best corporate citizens serve these stakeholders. While it's difficult to make generalizations about how all of them operate, we can offer a handful of interesting approaches we've observed. Among them:

Having community-service programs be employee-driven, not executive-driven.

In measuring community service, the company ranking second highest is Polaroid, with a score of 4.83. (Whirlpool is No. 1 in community service.) This maker of film and other imaging products, headquartered in Cambridge, Mass., came in No. 37 overall, largely because of lackluster financial return. (In 1998, it lost $51 million on revenues of $1.8 billion.)

One thing innovative at this company is that employees make the decisions on charitable contributions. The Polaroid Foundation, which serves primarily Boston and New Bedford, Mass., has two committees—one for each community—staffed by employees who are overseen by professional staff. Donna Eidson, executive director of the foundation, has one vote like all other members.

The foundation's focus is increasing self-sufficiency among the disadvantaged by building their skills. Eidson gives the example of a single mother who joined a foundation-supported program that helps Latina women assimilate. The woman had moved here from Guatemala twenty years earlier, but hadn't learned English. One day, while working as a house cleaner, she accidentally bumped a button and a computer went on. Not knowing how to turn it off, she waited four hours for the homeowner to arrive home and simply push a button to turn the computer off. She realized, if it were that easy to operate a computer, she could do it.

Today, the woman is fluent in English and proficient in computer skills, and this June she and her daughter will be receiving their high school diplomas. She has plans to become a paralegal aide.

"When you see her, you realize this woman with the right opportunities could have done anything she wanted to," Eidson said. "And yet if she had never learned to speak the language, it wouldn't have happened."

If at Polaroid we see employee involvement in philanthropy, at IBM—the $6.3 billion Armonk, N.Y. computer firm—we see employee involvement in environmental issues. For example, the company gives cash awards to employees for innovative environmental ideas. In some instances, the company has purchased energy from renewable sources, like solar power, at higher rates than other sources.

We might note here that this study's evaluation of community service combines two measures from KLD: community and environment. We considered these the dual aspects of community service.

Taking a rifle-shot rather than a shotgun approach to community service.

In tackling the amorphous area of "education," Hewlett-Packard's three-year-old Diversity in Education Initiative has a pinpoint focus on math and science in four minority communities. This Palo Alto, Calif.-based computer company, with 1998 revenue of $42 billion, was No. 2 on our list. "Rather than work with just one segment of the school population, and watch that segment pass to the next level where there's no program, we pick out a community where we can work with people from elementary to university level," said Roy Verley, director of corporate philanthropy.

The program provides hands-on science kits for elementary and middle-school children, and encourages them to pursue four years of math and science work in high school. There's also the $1.2 million HP Scholar program, now in its third year, which gives 40 high school seniors (ten from each community) $3,000 annual college scholarships. Each student is assigned a mentor, taught how to conduct a job search, and given a paid summer internship at HP.

Cathy Lipe, program manager for education relations in the government affairs department, feels HP is learning as much as the students. "We're learning what it's like to be going through the HP recruiting process and where we have barriers up to the poor," she said.

For Pitney Bowes (No. 12), a Stamford, Conn. business equipment maker with revenues of $4.2 billion, the targeted commitment is to its own community. For nearly 30 years, local economic development has been a part of the firm's corporate culture. Most fundamentally, the company decided to keep its headquarters in a deteriorating section of Stamford's South End, and to work with grassroots organizations to improve the community. The company donated property near its headquarters for an affordable housing complex, and has participated in a down-payment assistance program for home ownership.

Pitney Bowes also supports the grassroots South End Neighborhood Revitalization Zone Initiative, which empowers community residents to make decisions about the neighborhood. "Because a lot of the people who live here are low-income," said Polly O'Brien, director of community affairs, "it's not always easy for them to complain about property owners who don't keep places clean or up to code." The program gives these people voice. "To us, it's very easy to sit and write a check, but it doesn't have the same impact for self-sufficiency as if you partner with people," said O'Brien. "It's really their success."

Encouraging employees to express their individuality.

Melanie Jones, creative manager of public relations at Southwest Airlines (No. 14), said it best: "Individualism is cherished. People are going to work harder if they don't have to be somebody they're not, if they're valued for who they are."

At this $4.1 billion, Dallas,Tex., domestic airline, the corporate culture has a lack of formality and a sense of humor. In making public announcements, for example, flight attendants and customer service agents are encouraged to incorporate humor.

Corporate procedures in general come from the rank and file. "Southwest is known for empowering its people to make the right decision, regardless of what the rules are," Jones said. At almost any meeting, employees from ramp agents to vice presidents have an equal voice in ideas generated. One program that came from employee ideas, for example, is the career development service group, which helps employees assess whether they're on the right career path.

Charles Schwab (No. 8) helps new employees find their right path with a program called Wings, where entry-level employees are rotated to various parts of the company and can apply for jobs in the area they find most interesting. Schwab also offers a no-restrictions sabbatical program, allowing employees to pursue their dreams. For Chief Administrative Officer Beth Sawi, the dream was writing a book. She returned in August 1999 from a sabbatical in Florence, Italy, where she wrote *Coming Up for Air: How to Build a Balanced Life in a Workaholic World*. Every employee at Schwab performing at or above expectations is entitled to a four-week paid sabbatical after five years of service, or eight weeks after ten years.

In a slightly different approach to sabbaticals, Intel (No. 3) offers eight weeks for every seven years of employment. This Santa Clara, Calif., maker of Pentium microprocessors and other computer parts had $26.2 billion in revenue in 1998, and found an impressive $312 million to spend on employee training—including a retraining program that helps employees find new positions within the company.

Finding creative ways to relieve the pressures in employees' lives.

One of the best companies at serving employees is Xerox (No. 6), the document processing products company in Stamford, Conn., which tied for the highest score in the employee category. (The other two highest were Hewlett-Packard and 3Com Corp.)

Among the innovations at the $19.4 billion Xerox is a life-cycle assistance program which, in addition to standard benefits, offers a $10,000 lifetime amount employees can use for things like child care, first-time home buying, and health care for dependents.

UNUMProvident in Portland, Maine, and Chattanooga, Tenn., ranked No. 27 overall, but was tied for fourth place in providing for employee stakeholders. Its business is disability insurance, which makes the company particularly focused on health and wellness. At most of its major locations, its has on-site fitness facilities, offering classes on topics from aerobics to spinning. Fitness professionals are also available for consultations. "If you're experiencing any kind of physical difficulty at work, there's a thorough analysis done not only of your work environment, but your health habits, your eating habits, and your exercise habits," said Catherine Hartnett, director of public relations and issues management. "They really look at the whole person."

Other companies take different approaches to relieving employee stress. Herman Miller (No. 5), the $1.7 billion Michigan furniture maker, takes the unusual step of paying social workers to visit elderly relatives of employees and arrange services. To help employees ease into retirement, Procter & Gamble (No. 4) allows them to work reduced time schedules. This $38.1 billion household products company in Cincinnati, Ohio also allows all employees to take a personal leave of absence without pay, but with benefits, for three months.

Taking a team-based approach to developing products and servicing customers.

Tellabs (No. 7), a telecommunications equipment manufacturer in Lisle, Ill. with $2.3 bil. in 1999 revenue, came in first in serving customer stakeholders, with a score of 5. Given performance like that, it's no accident Tellabs takes an approach to product development that involves all departments in the company. The process is called product realization and it uses "q-gates." This means a product must pass through a number of gates in development. Every product begins as a customer requirement, then passes through gates representing all departments involved in a project's development: sales, customer service, design, manufacturing, quality control, training, and so forth. Sign-off is required at each gate before development can move to the next step, or gate.

Everything emanates from the customer. To keep the pulse of the market, Tellabs has an outside company survey customers periodically and provide a report card. Jim Lauretig, v.p. of strategic quality at Tellabs, notes that throughout the life-cycle of a

Many of these firms have **both** strengths and weaknesses in the same area.

product or service, the needs of the customer may change, so a company must continually adapt.

For Motorola, pleasing the customer means going the extra mile for quality products. It ranked No. 33 overall, but came in second in service to the customer, with a score of 4.67. This Schaumburg, Ill. maker of cellular phones and electronic equipment, with $29.4 bil. in 1998 revenues, has had a quality management program since the 1980s, and has traditionally sought to reduce defects tenfold every two years. Its Six Sigma program, a quality improvement effort, aims for defect-free performance in all areas. Team leaders are trained to analyze processes and identify where defects can be reduced.

The focus on quality at Motorola extends to the environment as well. As part of the quality program, teams throughout the company evaluate ways to improve environmental performance. And all employees must attend a course called Protecting Our Environment.

Showing, in the end, that not even the best corporate citizens are perfect.

For all its strengths in the quality area, Motorola has lost a number of major contracts since 1995 due to service quality issues, according to a May 1998 *Business Week* article. For all its strengths in the area of employee relations and diversity, where the company scored an impressive 4.67, Motorola has no women among senior line executives (though it has two women on its board). Like others, this firm has both strengths and weaknesses in the same area.

And of course, being on the list is no guarantee of strength in all areas. Starbucks (No. 46) scored an admirable 4.5 in service to employees, but came in neutral, with a score of 3, in community service. That's due in part to accusations from community groups—some of whom staged protests at store openings—that Starbucks undermines local businesses and destroys the uniqueness of neighborhoods. On the other hand, in 1998 Starbucks partnered with former pro basketball player Magic Johnson to develop stores in urban areas—where its shops may actually improve neighborhoods.

Business Ethics' 100 Best Corporate Citizens

Rank	Overall rating	Company name	'98 revenues (millions)	'98 net income (millions)	'96–'98 Average Total Return to Shareholders	Community Relations	Employee Relations	Customer Relations
1	4.15167	IBM	$81,667.0	$6,328.0	61.39%	4.50	4.33	3.33
2	4.11000	Hewlett Packard	42,370.0	3,491.0	19.01%	4.33	5.00	4.00
3	4.04500	Intel	26,273.0	6,068.0	69.26%	3.67	4.50	4.00
4	4.04167	Procter & Gamble	38,125.0	3,763.0	32.69%	3.83	4.67	4.00
5	4.02167	Herman Miller	1,766.2	141.8	61.55%	4.00	4.83	3.33
6	4.01833	Xerox	19,449.0	395.0	40.94%	4.17	5.00	3.00
7	3.96000	Tellabs	1,660.1	398.3	57.86%	3.00	3.67	5.00
8	3.93667	Charles Schwab	2,736.2	348.5	86.51%	3.00	4.33	3.67
9	3.87667	Fannie Mae	29,995.0	3,418.0	36.84%	4.00	3.67	4.00
10	3.87000	Times Mirror Company	3,009.1	1,417.3	21.70%	4.33	4.00	4.00
11	3.86333	DeVry Incorporated	420.6	38.8	67.29%	3.00	4.00	4.00
12	3.84000	Pitney Bowes	4,220.5	576.4	45.73%	4.33	4.00	3.00
13	3.83833	Solectron	8,391.4	293.9	66.77%	3.00	4.17	4.00
14	3.83500	Southwest Airlines	4,164.0	433.4	34.14%	3.33	4.50	4.00
15	3.83167	Kroger Company	38,125.0	3,763.0	49.04%	3.83	4.33	3.00
16	3.79333	Compaq Computer	31,169.0	(2,743.0)	64.65%	3.17	3.50	4.00
17	3.79167	Walt Disney Company	23,402.0	1,300.0	17.80%	4.00	3.83	4.33
18	3.79000	Ben & Jerry's Homemade	209.2	6.2	20.20%	4.50	4.50	3.00
19	3.78000	Whole Foods Market	1,567.9	42.2	61.34%	4.17	4.17	3.00
20	3.77833	The Gap	9,054.5	824.5	87.00%	3.50	4.00	3.00
21	3.77667	Texas Instruments	8,460.0	407.0	52.88%	3.00	4.00	4.00
22	3.77500	Medtronic	4,134.1	468.4	39.91%	3.67	3.83	3.67
23	3.76333	Microsoft	11,936.0	3,454.0	86.45%	3.00	4.33	3.00
24	3.74667	Home Depot	30,219.0	1,614.0	63.58%	4.33	2.67	4.00
25	3.73833	Alza Corporation	584.5	112.3	31.82%	3.33	4.17	4.00
26	3.73333	Dollar General	3,221.0	182.0	58.11%	3.50	3.50	4.00
27	3.72667	UNUMProvident	4,641.4	363.4	31.64%	3.50	4.83	3.00
28	3.72000	Tennant Company	389.4	25.3	21.99%	3.17	4.50	4.00
29 (Tie)	3.71333	Ecolab	1,596.6	68.1	36.42%	4.33	3.00	3.67
29 (Tie)	3.71333	Time Warner	14,582.0	168.0	55.86%	4.00	4.00	3.00
31 (Tie)	3.70500	Clorox	4,003.0	246.0	51.36%	4.50	3.33	2.67
31 (Tie)	3.70500	Guidant	1,897.0	(2.2)	97.72%	3.00	3.50	3.50
33	3.69500	Motorola	29,398.0	(962.0)	3.37%	3.17	4.67	4.67
34	3.69000	Nordstrom	5,027.9	206.7	25.56%	3.00	4.67	4.00
35	3.68833	Target (Dayton Hudson)	30,951.0	935.0	65.44%	4.00	3.17	3.00
36	3.68500	New York Times Company	2,936.7	278.9	37.65%	3.33	3.83	4.00
37	3.67833	Polaroid Corporation	1,845.9	(51.0)	(18.13%)	4.83	4.00	4.00
38	3.67333	Sun Microsystems	10,091.0	1,031.3	60.86%	4.00	3.67	3.00
39	3.66667	Dime Bancorp	133.9	19.9	40.22%	3.50	4.50	3.33
40	3.65000	Quaker Oats	4,842.5	284.5	23.68%	4.17	4.17	3.00
41	3.64833	Cisco Systems	12,154.0	2,096.0	83.89%	3.00	4.17	3.00
42	3.64250	SLM Holding Corporation	2,587.6	501.5	36.96%	3.00	4.75	3.00
43	3.64167	Golden West Financial	2,962.5	434.6	21.73%	3.50	4.00	4.00
44 (Tie)	3.62833	Brady Corporation	455.2	28.0	7.00%	4.00	4.50	3.67
44 (Tie)	3.62833	Adolph Coors Company	2,291.3	67.8	46.29%	4.17	3.67	3.00
46	3.61833	Starbucks	1,680.1	101.7	38.87%	3.00	4.50	3.00
47 (Tie)	3.60833	Coca Cola	18,813.0	3,533.0	24.15%	4.17	4.00	3.00
47 (Tie)	3.60833	Wal-Mart	139,208.0	4,430.0	61.81%	3.17	4.33	3.00
49	3.60333	Fifth Third Bancorp	1,912.0	668.0	53.79%	3.33	4.00	3.00
50	3.59250	Granite Construction	1,226.1	46.5	72.46%	3.00	3.25	4.00
51	3.58833	J P Morgan	12,641.0	963.0	14.06%	4.00	4.50	3.00
52	3.57833	American Express	19,132.0	2,141.0	38.40%	3.50	4.00	3.00
53	3.57667	Gillette	10,056.0	1,081.0	25.79%	4.00	3.00	4.00
54	3.57000	A G Edwards	2,240.8	292.1	39.84%	3.00	3.67	4.00
55	3.56333	Oneok	1,842.8	106.4	23.27%	3.83	4.17	3.00
56	3.56000	AT&T	53,223.0	6,398.0	24.37%	3.83	4.17	3.00
57	3.54833	3Com	5,722.0	403.8	11.08%	3.17	5.00	3.00
58	3.54167	Graco	432.2	47.3	32.68%	3.50	3.00	4.00
59	3.53833	MBNA Corporation	3,971.3	776.3	53.34%	4.00	2.83	3.00
60	3.53500	Avery Dennison	3,459.9	223.3	25.01%	3.50	3.33	4.00
61	3.52833	Constellation Energy Group	3,358.1	327.7	9.93%	4.50	4.00	3.00

Rank	Overall rating	Company name	'98 revenues (millions)	'98 net income (millions)	'96–'98 Average Total Return to Shareholders	Community Relations	Employee Relations	Customer Relations
62	3.52667	Cummins Engine	6,266.0	(21.0)	6.50%	4.50	3.83	3.00
63	3.52500	MCN Energy Group	1,880.2	(6.3)	7.39%	3.67	4.50	3.00
64	3.52333	Avon Products	5,212.7	270.0	37.31%	3.50	3.83	3.00
65	3.52000	Merck	26,898.2	5,248.2	33.56%	3.50	4.83	2.00
66	3.51167	Biomet	757.4	116.4	37.72%	3.00	3.50	4.00
67	3.50167	General Mills	6,246.1	534.5	14.07%	4.00	4.17	3.00
68	3.50000	Lucent Technologies	38,303.0	4,766.0	100.43%	2.67	3.67	3.00
69 (Tie)	3.49500	Wachovia Corporation	5,903.8	874.2	28.37%	3.67	2.83	4.00
69 (Tie)	3.49500	Knight Ridder	3,091.1	365.4	20.89%	3.33	3.50	4.00
71	3.49333	FirstFed Financial	303.4	34.6	41.38%	3.17	4.17	3.00
72	3.49000	Dell Computer	18,243.0	1,460.0	232.37%	3.00	3.00	3.00
73	3.48500	Deere & Co	11,750.9	239.2	6.98%	3.33	3.83	4.00
74	3.48000	Reliastar Financial	2,848.2	237.7	30.76%	3.67	3.67	3.00
75	3.47833	Campbell Soup	6,424.0	724.0	28.10%	3.50	4.00	3.00
76	3.47667	Dionex	172.9	28.5	37.58%	3.50	3.50	3.00
77	3.47500	Progressive Corporation	5,292.4	456.7	59.98%	3.00	3.50	3.00
78	3.47000	Baxter International	6,599.0	315.0	21.37%	3.67	4.00	3.00
79	3.46833	Whirlpool	10,323.0	325.0	4.39%	5.00	3.50	3.00
80	3.45333	EMC Corporation	3,791.3	793.4	130.30%	3.00	3.00	3.00
81	3.45000	SBC Communications	28,777.0	4,023.0	29.67%	3.50	3.83	3.00
82	3.44500	Bank Of New York	3,934.0	1,192.0	53.30%	3.33	3.17	3.00
83	3.43833	Energen	497.5	41.4	23.11%	3.83	3.67	3.00
84	3.43750	State Street Corp	2,725.0	436.0	51.61%	3.25	3.50	3.00
85	3.43667	St Paul Companies	9,108.0	89.3	13.12%	4.00	4.00	3.00
86 (Tie)	3.43500	Crown Cork & Seal	8,300.0	105.0	(3.33%)	4.00	3.50	4.00
86 (Tie)	3.43500	SPX Corporation	1,825.4	(41.0)	74.61%	3.50	3.33	3.00
88	3.42667	Modine Manufacturing	1,111.4	73.9	18.02%	3.67	3.00	4.00
89	3.42500	Washington Post Company	2,110.4	417.3	29.20%	3.00	3.17	4.00
90	3.42167	Anheuser-Busch	11,245.8	1,233.3	29.94%	3.67	3.83	2.67
91	3.41833	Church & Dwight	684.4	30.3	27.04%	3.67	3.17	3.33
92	3.41667	Timberland Co	862.2	59.2	40.82%	4.50	2.50	3.00
93	3.41666	Sonoco Products Co	2,557.0	180.0	11.39%	3.67	3.33	4.00
94	3.41665	P N C Bank Corp	5,222.0	1,115.0	25.45%	3.50	3.83	3.00
95	3.41664	TJX Companies Inc	7,949.1	424.2	89.65%	3.00	2.67	3.00
96	3.41663	Tootsie Roll Inds	388.7	67.5	32.29%	3.00	4.00	3.00
97	3.41662	American Waterworks	1,018.0	127.0	24.67%	3.50	3.50	3.00
98	3.41661	CVS Corporation	15,273.6	384.5	62.24%	3.33	3.00	2.33
99	3.41660	Lincoln National	6,087.1	509.8	20.82%	3.67	4.00	3.00
100	3.41659	Alaska Airgroup	1,897.7	124.4	42.65%	3.50	3.50	2.67

Glossary

Rank: overall ranking.

Overall Rating: average of stakeholder categories.

Revenue: taken from the most recently pub-lished annual corporate financial information from Compustat.

Total Return: capital gains plus dividends, an-nual average, 1996–1998.

Community relations: combination of three-year average KLD com-munity relations and environmental measures.

Employee Relations: combination of three-year average KLD em-ployee relations and di-versity measures.

Customer relations: three-year average KLD product rating.

It's also worth noting not all of Wall Street's dar-lings made our list. For example, General Electric—*Fortune's* No. 1 Most Admired Company—failed to make our top 100 because of very low ratings in community and customer areas. That partially due to the company's role in widespread polychlorinated biphenyl (PCB) contamination in Pittsfield, Mass., and elsewhere.

Even our No. 1 company, IBM, with a 4.33 score in service to employees, is not without controversy.

When the company announced changes in its pen-sion plan last year, which would have cut pensions up to 40 percent for long-time employees, CEO Louis Gerstner found himself confronted at the firm's Austin plant in July with a plane circling over-head, dragging a banner that read, "Hey Lou, Thou Shalt Not Steal." The company later reversed itself, restoring many of the benefits that would have been lost. This list, after all, is not the 100 *Perfect* Cor-porate Citizens. It's the 100 *Best* Corporate Citizens.

winery with a
mission

FETZER VINEYARDS HUSBANDS THE EARTH'S RESOURCES

BY MIRIAM SCHULMAN

We are an environmentally and socially conscious grower, producer, and marketer of wines of the highest quality and value.

Working in harmony and with respect for the human spirit, we are committed to sharing information about the enjoyment of food and wine in a lifestyle of moderation and responsibility.

We are dedicated to the continuous growth and development of our people and business.

There are mission statements, and there are missions. Fetzer Vineyards, whose mission statement is reprinted here, appears to have converted what might be just a piece of paper into a real program of action where ethical considerations help guide company policy.

Fetzer President Paul Dolan comments, "When the first words of your mission statement are *environmentally and socially conscious*, it opens up new perspectives on how to operate the entire business."

Environmentally conscious? Fetzer's own acreage is 100 percent certified organic. Under the Bonterra label, the company produces wine made entirely from grapes that are grown without chemical pesticides, herbicides, fungicides, or fertilizers. In addition, the winery's energy-conservation efforts have been so successful that Fetzer won recognition from the White House in 1994.

Socially conscious? As one example, Fetzer offers English as a second language to its Spanish-speaking workers as part of a comprehensive employee-education program.

The ESL program is typical of the way Fetzer operates. Last year, a lab technician with a background in ESL began a pilot project with employees in the winery cellars.

The group met twice a week, half on company time and half on their own time. The project was so successful that a team was set up to assess the ESL needs of other departments, and the winery is now planning a companywide program.

Many divisions at Fetzer have initiated their own socially and environmentally conscious programs. One makes polylaminate, fully recyclable capsules, allowing Fetzer to eliminate the lead capsules traditionally used to cover corks. And Fetzer's Valley Oaks Farm, with its experimental organic garden, regularly donates surplus produce to Plowshares and the Ukiah Food Bank.

Besides instituting socially and environmentally conscious programs in its own facilities, Fetzer has encouraged other companies to go the organic route. Through its Club Bonterra project, Fetzer shares information with its outside growers about organic techniques.

If all this sounds a little too good to be true, the reasoning behind it is hardly warm and fuzzy. Andy Beckstoffer of Beckstoffer Vineyards, a member of Club Bonterra, explains, "It's good business to preserve your land; it's good business to produce a healthy product. We think the more alive the ground and fruit are, the better the varietal character of the wines will be."

Fetzer, the sixth-largest premium winery in the United States, has profited from taking ethical responsibilities seriously, according to Dolan. "That's the way the industry will go, and we'll have been there first," he says.

"The impetus is coming from consumers. In most surveys, 60 to 80 percent of the public say they're interested in the environment."

As for Fetzer's social commitment, the company's director of human resources, Barbara Wallace, says those programs also help the bottom line. "With corporate downsizing and reorganization, many companies are not getting the same sort of loyalty they used to. But our

 From *Issues in Ethics*, Spring 1996, pp. 14–15. © 1996 by the Markkula Center for Applied Ethics. Reprinted by permission.

company feels that developing people's capabilities strengthens the organization. It's a way of creating loyalty."

Not that social responsibility is always profitable. Dolan likes to use the word *sustainable.* "The big question," he says, "is, Will the consumer pay for environmental changes? If we take a position that we will only buy organic fruit, that can be touchy because we don't know what the costs will be. We may have to pay more for the grapes." This would make the product less competitive.

"We need to figure out how to make the changes sustainable," he says; "that is, to make decisions that are both environmentally conscious and economically viable."

Sometimes, the environmentally conscious policies save money. Organic farming, for example, has meant fewer inputs, according to Dolan. "We don't have to use as many chemicals. We don't have to keep driving through the vineyards to check on the chemicals."

Other environmental programs are more of a wash economically. Composting, for example, saves the company money in landfill dump fees, but it exacts more time from employees.

On the social end of things, employee-education programs can be very cost-effective. "The more educated the work force, the better decisions they make," says Dolan. "Our education programs allow us to push decision making down to where it should be—to the fields or the bottling plant or the sales force. That allows us to respond quickly to the needs of the marketplace."

But Fetzer, and its parent company, Brown-Forman, are also committed to social responsibility for its own sake, according to Wallace. "It does help us in the workplace," she says of the English-as-a-second-language program, "but there are so many areas where communication is important—in the family and in the community. Shared understanding between people is important to us."

Miriam Schulman is the editor of Issues in Ethics.

Unit Selections

Key Points to Consider

❖ In what areas should organizations become more ethically sensitive and socially responsible in the next five years? Be specific, and explain your choices.

❖ Obtain codes of ethics or conduct from several different professional associations (for example, doctors, lawyers, CPAs, etc.). What are the similarities and differences between them?

❖ How useful do you feel codes of ethics are to organizations? Explain.

 **Links** **www.dushkin.com/online/**

These sites are annotated on pages 4 and 5.

Business ethics should not be viewed as a short-term, "knee-jerk reaction" to recently revealed scandals and corruption. Instead, it should be viewed as a thread woven through the fabric of the entire business culture—one that ought to be integral to its design. Businesses are built on the foundation of trust in our free enterprise system. When there are violations of this trust between competitors, between employer and employees, or between businesses and consumers, the system ceases to run smoothly.

From a pragmatic viewpoint, the alternative to self-regulated and voluntary ethical behavior and social responsibility on the part of business may be governmental and legislative intervention. From a moral viewpoint, ethical behavior should not exist because of economic pragmatism, governmental edict, or contemporary fashionability—it should exist because it is morally appropriate and right.

This last unit is composed of six articles that provide some ideas, guidelines, and principles for developing the future ethos and social responsibility of business. In the first article, Archie Carroll discusses some of the ethical challenges that will be faced in the new millennium. The second selection, "Old Ethical Principles: The New Corporate Culture," analyzes 10 old ethical principles and applies them to the new corporate culture. In the third article, "Profits From Principle: Five Forces Redefining Business," Bennett Daviss reflects why corporations are finding that social responsibility pays off. Then, "The New Bottom Line" stresses the importance of a business

managing by values and not just by profits. The essay that follows, "The New Workforce," reveals new inroads being made by disabled workers. Finally, in the last article, Marci McDonald describes a new generation of CEOs who are young, wired, and female.

Developing the Future Ethos and Social Responsibility of Business

ETHICAL CHALLENGES FOR BUSINESS IN THE NEW MILLENNIUM: CORPORATE SOCIAL RESPONSIBILITY AND MODELS OF MANAGEMENT MORALITY

Archie B. Carroll

Abstract: As we transition to the 21st century, it is useful to think about some of the most important challenges business and other organizations will face as the new millennium begins. What will constitute "business as usual" in the business ethics arena as we start and move into the new century? My overall thought is that we will pulsate into the future on our current trajectory and that the new century will not cause cataclysmic changes, at least not immediately. Rather, the problems and challenges we face now we will face then. Undoubtedly, new issues will arise but they will more likely be extensions of the present than discontinuities with the past.

As we transition to the 21st century, it is useful to think about some of the most important challenges business and other organizations will face as the new millennium begins. As I write this essay, the public seems to be more concerned with the Y2K problem and whether their computers will keep working, their power will stay on, their investments will be secure, there will be food in the pantry, airplanes will still fly, and that life as we know it will continue as usual. Optimistically, by the time this is published we will all look back and conclude that technology is amazing, humans are survivors, and we will wonder why we got all worked up about Y2K bug in the first place. This is my hope and expectation, so I approach this writing with the optimism that the world will not end in a technological Armageddon but that the transition will be relatively smooth, though perhaps jerky, and that we will return to business as usual soon thereafter.

This raises the question in my mind as to what will constitute "business as usual" in the business ethics arena as we start and move into the new century. My overall thought is that we will pulsate into the future on our current trajectory and that the new century will not cause cataclysmic changes, at least not immediately. Rather, the problems and challenges we face now we will face then. Undoubtedly, new issues will arise but they will more likely be extensions of the present than discontinuities with the past.

Questions have been raised in the past about ethics in business and they will continue to be raised in the future. The public's perception of business ethics has not wavered much over the past 30 years or so and there is no reason to think this will dramatically change. When the Gallup Poll first asked the public to rate the honesty and ethical standards of business executives in 1977, only 19 percent of those surveyed ranked

From *Business Ethics Quarterly*, January 2000, pp. 33-42. © 2000 by *Business Ethics Quarterly*. Reprinted by permission.

them as "very high" or "high." When the same question was asked again in October, 1998, the figure was 21 percent. This is slightly better but statistically insignificant over this period of two decades (*American Enterprise,* March/April 1999). To be sure, some groups of businesspeople rank lower, such as stockbrokers, contractors, real estate agents, insurance and car salesmen, and advertising practitioners, but their numbers are pretty stable over this 30-year period as well. There is not much happening to cause us to think this will change.

There are a number of different ways we could approach this task of thinking about ethical challenges in the new millennium. We could think of them in terms of what new issues will arise or what specific industries will be affected. Such an approach would likely cause us to speculate about the impact of technology—computers, the Internet and World Wide Web, electronic commerce, or genetic engineering and human cloning. *Time* magazine has already hailed the 21st century as the "biotech century" (*Time,* January 11, 1999), so we could easily speculate about the business and ethical implications of this new reality we will face. Alternatively, but related, we could think of specific industries that are likely to pose ethical challenges. This approach, of course, would likely take us into medicine and health care (we do have an aging population), insurance, financial services, and telemarketing, just to mention a few.

Another important point is that all issues and topics will become more global in concern. What were once regional and national concerns have quickly become global concerns. George Soros has outlined the "crisis of global capitalism" (Soros 1999) and this doubtless will carry further ethical implications than we have initially thought.

Another approach to this task would be to look at some enduring or generic management challenges that touch the business sector, business organizations, and managers, for that is an arena which will be vital to business ethics regardless of topic, issue, industry, level of global analysis, and so on. In this connection, I have written about two topics over the past twenty years that touch upon managers and organizations, and I would like to spend the balance of this essay reviewing them and thinking about changes, if any, we are likely to see with respect to them: corporate social responsibility (CSR) and models of management morality.

Trends in Corporate Social Responsibility

Twenty years ago I proposed a definition of corporate social responsibility that has been found useful in thinking about businesses' responsibilities to society and has served as a workable base point in theoretical development and research on this topic (Carroll 1979). The four-part definition held that corporations had four responsibilities to fulfill to society: economic, legal, ethical, and discretionary (later referred to as philanthropic). This definition sought to embrace businesses' legitimate economic or profit-making function with responsibilities that extended beyond the basic economic role of the firm. It sought to reconcile the idea that business could focus either on profits or social concerns, but not both. It sought to argue that businesses can not only be profitable and ethical, but that they should fulfill these obligations simultaneously. Though I have described previously each of these four responsibilities that comprise CSR (1991, 1995), it is useful to briefly recap each as we think about the future.

The *economic responsibility* refers to businesses' fundamental call to be a profit-making enterprise. Though profit making is not the purpose of business (from a societal perspective), it is essential as a motivation and reward for those individuals who take on commercial risk. Though it may seem odd to think of this as a "social" responsibility, this is, in effect what it is. The socio-capitalistic system calls for business to be an economic institution, and profit making is an essential ingredient in a free enterprise economy. While we may think of economics as one distinct element of the CSR definition, it is clearly infused or embedded with ethical assumptions, implications, and overtones.

As we transition to the new millennium, the economic responsibility of business remains very important and will become an ever more significant challenge due to global competitiveness. The new century poses an environment of global trade that is complex, fast-paced, and exponentially expanding into capital, enterprise, information, and technology markets (Kehoe 1998). Hamel and Prahalad (1994) have told us that "competing for the future" will be different. They pose the economic challenges of business as tantamount to a revolution in which existing industries—health care, transportation, banking, publishing, telecommunications, pharmaceuticals, retailing, and others—will be profoundly transformed (p. 30). In addition, these challenges will be global.

In addition to economic responsibilities, businesses have *legal responsibilities* as well, as part of their total corporate social responsibility. Just as our society has sanctioned our economic system by permitting business to assume the economic role of producing goods and services and selling them at a profit, it has also laid down certain ground rules—laws—under which business is expected to pursue its economic role. Law reflects a kind of "codified ethics" in society in the sense that it embodies basic notions of fairness or business righteousness, at least as agreed upon by our legislators. As Boatright has concurred, business activity takes place within an extensive framework of law, and all business decisions need to embrace both the legal and the economic though he agrees that the law is not enough (1993, p. 13). In the 21st century, as we usher in the millennium, we will likely see the continuing expansion of the legal system. There will be no relief in sight as the growing number of lawyers being produced annually in our nation's law schools will ensure that the supply will drive the demand. There is no diminishment in Congress of legislators with law degrees. As long as these individuals continue to be instrumental in controlling our legal system, things may well get more litigious rather than less so. Factors in the social environment such as affluence, education, and awareness will continue to produce rising expectations, an entitlement mentality, the rights movement, and a victimization way of thinking. All of these feed into and drive a litigious society (Carroll 1996, pp. 10–16). Many laws are good and valid and reflect appropriate ethical standards, however, and we will continue to see the legal responsibility of business as a robust sphere of activity.

In addition to fulfilling their economic and legal responsibilities, businesses are expected to fulfill ethical responsibilities as well (Carroll 1979). Ethical responsibilities embrace those activities, practices, policies, or behaviors that are expected (in a positive sense) or prohibited (in a negative sense) by societal members though they are not codified into laws. Ethical responsibilities embrace a range of norms, standards, or expectations of behavior that reflect a concern for what consumers, employees, shareholders, the community, and other stakeholders regard as fair, right, just, or in keeping with stakeholders' moral rights or legitimate expectations.

As we transition to the new millennium, this category of CSR will be more important than ever. Business has embraced the notion of business ethics with some conscious degree of enthusiasm over the past decade, and this trend is expected to continue. Organizations such as the Ethics Officers Association and Business for Social Responsibility provide testimony to the institutionalization of this quest. Another statistic is relevant and impressive: corporations now spend over $1 billion per year on ethics consultants (Morgan and Reynolds 1997). A major research firm, Walker Information of Indianapolis, Indiana, markets new and innovative products: business integrity assessments and stakeholder management assessments, side-by-side with more traditional products such as customer satisfaction studies. What was once relegated to writings in obscure academic journals has now made the transition into practitioner books by the dozens. One such example is *The Ethical Imperative* (1998) by consultant John Dalla Costa, wherein he argues that ethics is becoming the defining business issue of our time, affecting corporate profits and credibility, as well as personal security and the sustainability of a global economy. He argues that by conservative estimates yearly losses to corporations due to unethical behavior equal more than the profits of the top forty corporations in North America and that such economic waste and moral loss requires more than a PR Band-Aid.

But there is a possible down side to this obsession that we should be sensitive to as the ethics industry grows and matures and we move into the new century. Morgan and Reynolds (1997) have argued that for two decades now we have engaged in "a vast campaign to clean up our ethical act" in the workplace, politics, and communities. We have crafted mountains of regulations, created vast networks of consultants and committees, and have made terms such as "conflicts of interest" and "the appearance of impropriety" part of our everyday language. However, they argue, the public's confidence in business people and politicians to "do the right thing" has plummeted to an all-time low. They claim we have made legitimate ethical concerns into absurd standards and have wielded our moral whims like dangerous weapons. We have obscured core truths. Now, inflated misdemeanors are the stuff by which careers and reputations are ruined. In this climate, real integrity has been lost to this obsession with wrongdoing.

In summary, they have argued that the ethics wars have "undermined American government, business, and society." As we move into the early 2000s, their concerns pose some serious problems for thought and reflection.

The fourth part of the CSR definition is the discretionary, or philanthropic, responsibility. Whereas the economic and legal accountabilities are required of business and ethical behaviors, policies, and practices are expected of business, philanthropy is both expected and desired. In this category we include the public's expectation that business will engage in social activities that are not mandated, not required by law, and not generally expected of business in an ethical sense, though some ethical underpinnings or justification may serve as the rationale for business being expected to be philanthropic. The subtle distinction between ethical and philanthropic responsibilities is that the latter are not expected with the same degree of moral force. In other words, if a firm did not engage in business giving to the extent that certain stakeholder groups expected, these stakeholders would not likely label the firm as unethical or immoral. Thus, the philanthropic expectation does not carry with it the same magnitude of moral mandates as does the ethical category. Examples of philanthropy might include business giving, community programs, executive loan programs, and employee voluntarism. I have depicted the normative prescription of philanthropy to "be a good corporate citizen." This, however, is a narrow view of corporate citizenship. On another occasion, I proposed a wider view by portraying all four of the CSR categories to constitute the "four faces of corporate citizenship" (Carroll 1998). Upon deeper reflection, I came to think that a wider view which included being profitable, obeying the law, being ethical, and "giving back" to the community, was more fully reflective of what corporate citizenship was all about.

As we transition to the 21st century, I expect the current trend toward "strategic philanthropy" to remain the guiding philosophy. Businesses will continue to strive to align their philanthropic interests with their economic mandates so that both of these objectives may be achieved at the same time. One of business's most significant ethical challenges will be to walk the fine line between conservative and liberal critics of its philanthropic giving. It is becoming increasingly difficult to direct corporate philanthropy without being offensive to some individual or group. Jennings and Cantoni (1998) provided several vivid illustrations of how this might happen. Apparently, retailer Dayton-Hudson made a contribution to Planned Parenthood only to find right-to-lifers outside its stores cutting their credit cards. They did an about-face and made contributions to right-to-life groups only to subject themselves to pro-choice protestors. In other illustrations, U.S. West gave money to the Boy Scouts of America and was flogged by gay-rights activists. Levi Strauss withdrew support from the Boy Scouts, and drew a backlash from religious leaders. This type of dilemma will pose significant and continuing problems for businesses in the future as our special-interest society flourishes.

In summary, as businesses, in their quest to be socially responsible, seek to concurrently (1) be profitable, (2) obey the law, (3) engage in ethical behavior, and (4) give back through philanthropy, they will face new and continuing ethical challenges in the new millennium. I have only touched on some of the relevant issues, but they will doubtless extend beyond what I have chosen to discuss here.

Models of Management Morality

In 1987, I embarked on a "search for the moral manager." Pertinent questions then and now included "are there any?" "where are they?" and "why are they so hard to find?" (Carroll 1987). The thesis of my discussion was that moral managers were so hard to find because the business landscape was so cluttered with immoral and amoral managers. At that time I articulated three models of management morality: Immoral Management, Moral Management, and Amoral Management. The purpose of describing these three moral types was to delineate, define, and emphasize the amoral category and to provide models of management morality that I thought would better convey to businesspeople the range of moral types in which managerial ethics might be classified. I believed that through description and example managers would be able to better assess their own ethical behaviors and motivations and that of other organizational members as well—their supervisors, subordinates, and colleagues. I was moved to emphasize the Amoral Management category by virtue of my observational world that did not seem to fit under the category of Immoral Management. As I recap each of these moral types, I will comment on their relevance as we transition into the 2000s. Immoral and Moral Management are easier to describe and are more traditional, so I will start with them.

Immoral Management (or Managers) is a good place to start, for without them we would have no field known as business ethics. Positing that unethical and immoral are synonymous in the organizational context, I defined Immoral Management as that which is not only devoid of ethical principles or precepts but also positively and actively opposed to what is right or just. In this model, management decisions, actions, and behavior imply a positive and active opposition to what is ethical or moral. Decisions here are discordant with ethical principles and the model implies an active negation of what is moral. Management motives are selfish. They are driven by self-interest wherein management cares only about itself or about the organization's gains. The goal is profitability and success at any price, and legal standards are seen as barriers that must be overcome. The Immoral Management strategy is to exploit opportunities and cut corners wherever it is helpful (Carroll 1987, 1991). In short, the Immoral Managers are the bad guys. It is doubtful that ethics education or more ethical organizational climates will change them.

As we enter the new millennium, I have no strong reason to argue that this group will change significantly. There are still immoral managers and they will likely always be with us. If the initiatives of business ethics scholars, teachers, and consultants have had any impact, combined with initiatives from

the business community itself, it is logical to argue that they will be a diminishing if not a vanishing breed.

By contrast, *Moral Management (or Managers)* represents the exemplar toward which I could well argue our teaching and research is directed. That is, as educators and business leaders, we are striving to create Moral Managers. John Boatright, in his 1998 presidential address to the Society for Business Ethics, spoke of a Moral Manager Model, wherein the manager both acted and thought morally, and Boatright concurred that the goal of business ethics is to turn out moral managers. In Moral Management, business decisions, attitudes, actions, policies, and behavior conform to a high standard of ethical, or right, behavior. The goal is conformity to lofty professional standards of conduct. Ethical leadership is commonplace and represents a defining quality. The motives of Moral Managers are virtuous. The motives are directed toward success within the confines of the law and sound ethical precepts (e.g., fairness, justice, due process). The goal of Moral Management is success within the letter and spirit of the law. The law is regarded as a minimum and the Moral Manager prefers to operate well above what the law mandates. The strategy is to live by sound ethical standards and to assume ethical leadership. If Immoral Managers were the bad guys, Moral Managers are the good guys.

There seems to be an inclination toward emphasizing Moral Management as we move into the new century and millennium. Obviously, it is the underlying premise or implicit goal of the business ethics field and much of its literature. For example, Moral Management is similar to Paine's "integrity strategy" in which she argues that ethics should be the driving force of the organization (Paine 1994). The model fits well with Ciulla's and Gini's discussions of ethics as the heart of leadership (Ciulla 1998, Gini 1998), and it is consistent with Aguilar's recommendations for leadership in ethics programs that can contribute substantially to corporate excellence (Aguilar 1994). The Moral Management model follows logically with Wilson's "moral sense" (1993), and is the underlying model for ethical leadership in Hood's "heroic enterprise" (1996). Moral Management is harmonious with Badaracco's belief that executives can use defining moments as an opportunity to redefine their company's role in society (1998). Finally, it must be argued that the Moral Manager is the prototype for "understanding stakeholder thinking" (Nasi 1995) and for managing "the stakeholder organization" (Wheeler and Sillanpaa 1997). Like the other models, the trends here are global (Carroll and Meeks 1999). All of these writings, and many others, suggest a bright future for the Moral Management Model and its associated characteristics.

The third conceptual model is *Amoral Management (or Managers)*. I distinguish between two types of amoral managers—those that are intentional and those that are unintentional. *Intentional Amoral Management* is characterized by a belief that moral considerations have no relevance or applicability in business or other spheres or organizational life. Amoral management holds that management or business activity is outside of or beyond the sphere in which moral judgments apply. These managers think that the business world and the moral world are two separate spheres and never the twain should meet. Intentional Amoral Managers are a vanishing breed as we enter the new millennium. We seldom find anymore managers who think compartmentally in this way. There are a few left, but those who are left seem reluctant to admit that they believe in this way. I do not anticipate that they will be as much of a problem in the next century. Richard De-George (1999) also has been concerned with this group in his discussions of the myth of amoral business in several editions of his *Business Ethics* textbook. As he points out, most people in business do not act unethically or maliciously; they think of themselves, in both their private and their business lives, as ethical people. They simply feel that business is not expected to be concerned with ethics. He describes them as amoral insofar as they feel that ethical considerations are inappropriate in business—after all, business is business (p. 5).

On the other hand, there is *Unintentional Amoral Management,* and it deserves closer scrutiny. These managers do not factor ethical considerations into their decision making, but for a different reason. These managers are well-intentioned but are self-centered in the sense that they do not possess the ethical perception, awareness, or discernment to realize that many of their decisions, actions, policies, and behaviors have an ethical facet or dimension that is being overlooked. These managers are ethically unconscious or insensitive; they are ethically ignorant. To the extent that their reasoning processes possess a moral dimension, it is disengaged. Unintentional Amoral Managers pursue profitability within the confines of the letter of the law, as they do not think about the spirit of the law. They do not perceive who might be hurt by their actions.

The field of managers to whom the Unintentional Amoral Management characteristics apply is large and perhaps growing as the new decade arrives. These managers are not hostile to morality, they just do not understand it. They have potential, but have not developed the key elements or capacities that Powers and Vogel (1980) argue are essential for developing moral judgment. Key among these capacities are a sense of moral obligation, moral imagination, moral identification and ordering, moral evaluation, and the integration of managerial and moral competence. The good news is that this is the group that should be most susceptible to learning, changing, and becoming Moral Managers. Of the three moral management models presented, I would maintain that the Unintentional Amoral Managers probably dominate the managerial landscape. An alternative view is that within each manager, each of the three models may be found at different points in time or in different circumstances, but that the Amoral Management model's characteristics are found most frequently. If these are correct assessments, this represents a huge challenge for business ethics educators, consultants, and organizations seeking to brink out the Moral Management model in the new millennium.

Conclusion

There will be many challenges facing the business community and organizational managers as we transition into the new millennium. Many industries and business sectors will be affected. Products and services as well as channels of distribution may be revolutionized and with these changes will come the usual kinds of ethical issues that commercial activity inevitably generates. Though it is impossible to predict all the arenas that will be affected, the safest conclusion is that many of the issues we have faced in the latter half of the twentieth century will endure for some time to come. Corporate social responsibility will continue to be a meaningful issue as it embraces core concerns that are necessary to the citizenry and business alike. Companies will be expected to be profitable, abide by the law, engage in ethical behavior, and give back to their communities through philanthropy, though the tensions between and among these responsibilities will become more challenging as information technology continues to push all enterprises toward a global-level frame of reference and functioning.

With respect to the three models of management morality, it is expected that Immoral Management will diminish somewhat as values and moral themes permeate and grow in the culture and the commercial sphere. Immoral Management will become an endangered species but will not disappear. Greed and human nature will ensure that Immoral Managers will always be with us. Our goal will be to minimize their number and the severity of their impact. The Moral Management model will grow in importance as an exemplar toward which business and organizational activity will be focused. The great opportunity will be in the vast realms of Unintentionally Amoral Managers. As the public and many private schools and educational systems continue to eliminate a concern for virtue and morals from classroom teaching, or alternatively, promote values clarification or ethical relativism, a ready supply of amoral young people entering business and organizational life will be guaranteed. In recent years, however, there have been the beginnings of a moral awakening in society, and I would like to believe that this optimistic paradigm will succeed, grow, and survive, but it will be facing major obstacles. At best, unintentional amorality will continue to be with us, and thus we ethics professors and consultants will continue to be employed and to have a challenging task ahead of us as the new millennium arrives.

Bibliography

Aguilar, Francis J. 1994. *Managing Corporate Ethics.* New York: Oxford University Press.

American Enterprise. 1999. "Opinion Pulse." May/June, p. 90.

Badaracco, Joseph L., Jr. 1998. "The Discipline of Building Character." *Harvard Business Review,* March–April, pp. 115–124.

Boatright, John R. 1993. *Ethics and the Conduct of Business.* Englewood Cliffs, N.J.: Prentice-Hall.

Boatright, John R. 1998. "Does Business Ethics Rest on a Mistake?" San Diego: Society for Business Ethics Presidential Address, August 6–9.

Carroll, Archie B. 1979. "A Three-Dimensional Conceptual Model of Corporate Social Performance." *Academy of Management Review* 4: 497–505.

_____. 1987. "In Search of the Moral Manager." *Business Horizons,* March–April. pp. 7–15.

_____. 1991. "The Pyramid of Corporate Social Responsibility: Toward the Moral Management of Organizational Stakeholders." *Business Horizons* 34: 39–48.

_____. 1995. "Stakeholder Thinking in Three Models of Management Morality: A Perspective with Strategic Implications." In *Understanding Stakeholder Thinking,* ed. Juha Nasi. Helsinki: LSR-Publications, pp. 47–74. Also in Clarkson 1998, pp. 139–172.

_____. 1996. *Business and Society: Ethics and Stakeholder Management,* 3rd ed. Cincinnati: South-Western College Publishing/International Thompson Publishing.

_____. 1998. "The Four Faces of Corporate Citizenship." *Business and Society Review* 100/101: 1–7.

_____ and Meeks, Michael D. 1999. "Models of Management Morality: European Applications and Implications." *Business Ethics: A European Review* 8, no. 2: 108–116.

Clarkson, Max B. E., ed. 1998. *The Corporation and its Stakeholders: Classic and Contemporary Readings.* Toronto: University of Toronto Press.

Ciulla, Joanne B. 1998. *Ethics, the Heart of Leadership.* Westport, Conn.: Praeger.

Costa, John Dalla. 1998. *The Ethical Imperative: Why Moral Leadership is Good Business.* Reading, Mass.: Addison-Wesley.

DeGeorge, Richard T. 1999. *Business Ethics.* 5th ed. Upper Saddle River, N.J.: Prentice-Hall.

Gini, Al. 1998. "Moral Leadership and Business Ethics." In *Ethics, the Heart of Leadership,* ed. Joanne Ciulla, pp. 27–45.

Hamel, Gary and Prahalad, C. K. 1994. *Competing for the Future.* Boston: Harvard Business School Press.

Hood, John M. 1996. *The Heroic Enterprise: Business and the Common Good.* New York: The Free Press.

Isaacson, Walter. 1999. "The Biotech Century." *Time,* January 11, pp. 42–43.

Jennings, Marianne and Cantoni, Craig. 1998. "An Uncharitable Look at Corporate Philanthropy." *Wall Street Journal,* December 22, p. A8.

Kehoe, William J. 1998. "GATT and WTO Facilitating Global Trade." *Journal of Global Business,* Spring, pp. 67–76.

Morgan, Peter W. and Reynolds, Glenn H. 1997. *The Appearance of Impropriety: How the Ethics Wars Have Undermined American Government, Business, and Society.* New York: The Free Press.

Nasi, Juha, ed. 1995. *Understanding Stakeholder Thinking.* Helsinki, Finland: LSR Publications.

Paine, Lynn Sharp. 1994. "Managing for Organizational Integrity." *Harvard Business Review,* March–April, pp. 106–117.

Powers, Charles W. and Vogel, David. 1980. *Ethics in the Education of Business Managers.* Hastings-on-Hudson, N.Y.: The Hastings Center, pp. 40–45.

Soros, George. 1998. *The Crisis of Global Capitalism.* New York: Public Affairs.

Wheeler, David and Sillanpaa, Maria. 1997. *The Stakeholder Corporation.* London: Pitman Publishing.

Wilson, James Q. 1993. *The Moral Sense.* New York: The Free Press.

Old Ethical Principles

THE NEW CORPORATE CULTURE

Address by WILLIAM J. BYRON, *S. J., Distinguished Professor of Management, McDonough School of Business, Georgetown University, Washington, D.C.*
Delivered to the Annual Luncheon of the Duquesne University NMA Students Association, Pittsburgh, Pennsylvania, April 21, 1999

It would be an interesting exercise if you attempted, right now as I begin to address the topic, "Old Ethical Principles for the New Corporate Culture," to jot down on a notepad (on a mental notepad, at least) what you would regard as old or "classic" ethical principles—the time-honored, enduring principles that should always be there to guide the business decision maker.

I've come up with ten and will attempt to apply them to the new corporate culture. Without waiting for you to give me yours, I'm going to proceed to list mine. Here they are: (I) the principle of human dignity; (II) the principle of participation; (III) the principle of integrity; (IV) the principle of fairness (justice); (V) the principle of veracity; (VI) the principle of keeping commitments; (VII) the principle of social responsibility; (VIII) the principle of subsidiarity; (IX) the principle of pursuit of the common good; and (X) the ethical principle of love.

Principles are initiating impulses—they are internalized convictions that produce action. Principles direct your actions and your choices. Your principles help to define who you are. Principles are beginnings, they lead to something.

How do the old ethical principles outlined above play themselves out today in the new corporate culture? First a word about both "culture" and what is new in the "new" corporate culture.

A culture is a set of shared meanings, principles, and values. Values define cultures. Where values are widely shared, you have an identifiable culture. There are as many different cultures as there are distinct sets of shared meanings, principles, and values. This is not to say that everyone in a given culture is the same. No, you have diversity of age, wealth, class, intelligence, education, and responsibility in a given culture where diverse people are unified by a shared belief system, a set of agreed-upon principles, a collection of common values. They literally have a lot in common and thus differ from other people in other settings who hold a lot of other things in common. You notice it in law firms, hospitals,

colleges, corporations—wherever people comment on the special "culture" that characterizes the place.

The old corporate culture in America was characterized by values like freedom, individualism, competition, loyalty, thrift, fidelity to contract, efficiency, self-reliance, power, and profit. If not controlled by self, or by social norms, or by public law, pursuit of some of these values could be fueled by unworthy values like greed and the desire to dominate. You have to remember that for some people greed is a value (a supreme value!), so is revenge; the list of negative destructive values could run on.

The new (or newer, or most recent) corporate culture is defined by many, but not all, of these same values, although they are interpreted now somewhat differently. And there are some new values emerging in the new corporate context. Think of this new context in terms of what might be called the new corporate contract.

What was once presumed to be a long-term "relational contract" can no longer be relied upon to sustain an uninterrupted employment relationship over time. What brings employees, even managerial employees, and their employers together in corporate America is now more of a 3 transactional contract; the transaction and the concomitant employment may be short-lived. Both parties to the employment transaction (the new corporate contract) negotiate the arrangement in a new way. The middle manager, for example, wanting to be hired says, in effect, "If you hold me contingent, I'll hold you contingent." He or she will settle in, but not too comfortably; other options will always be explored, front-end financial considerations will be more important than they were in more stable times, and severance packages will be filled and neatly wrapped before the job begins. Not only will other options be considered as the ink is drying on the new employment contract, but actual offers will be entertained at any time.

Another term for this approach is free-agent management. The free agent will not jump unless a safe landing is assured, and he or she is well aware that the best way

From *Vital Speeches of the Day*, July 1, 1999, pp. 558-561. © 1999 by City News Publishing Company, Inc. Reprinted by permission of *Vital Speeches of the Day* and the author.

to get a new job is to be effective, and appear to be content, in the old one. But contingency, not loyalty, is the thread that ties the contracting parties together today. Let me continue the comparison now with the way things used to be.

Whereas the old (say, fifty years ago) corporate culture would tolerate an employer's not looking much beyond the interests of a firm's shareholders, the new corporate culture is growing comfortable with the notion of "stakeholder" and sees an ethical connection between the firm and not only its shareholders, but all others who have a stake in what that firm does: Employees, suppliers, customers, the broader community, and the physical environment, to name just a few. The corporate outlook is more communitarian, more attentive to the dictates of the common good. There was some of this in the past, a "social compact" between employer and employee that was somewhat paternalistic and relatively free of both the deregulation and foreign competition that have caused much of the present economic dislocation in America, but the dominant value of the old corporate culture was individualism, not communitarianism. There is evidence now that individualism is again on the rise. As that happens, you have to begin to wonder about the fate of a few of those "old" ethical principles.

What is "new" in the new corporate culture is more easily examined these days through the lens of employment contracts (written or unwritten). People have been getting fired since hired hands were first employed to extend an owner's reach and productivity. But now there is something new in the old reality of layoff or separation from payroll. In that "something new" lies the difference between firing and downsizing. There is more to the difference than a simple distinction between blue and white collars. Today's wilted white collars were never so plentiful, and their wearers' hopes for quick and permanent reinstatement have never been so thin.

Typically, organizations are "downsized" at the end of a process that has come to be known as delayering, restructuring, or reengineering. The machine-tool metaphors veil the psychological pain felt by men and women who are set adrift. Not all that long ago, those who bounced back quickly were leaving organizations that were not shrinking, just experiencing turnover. This was before the days of what the Economist of London, in describing the contemporary American economy, called "corporate anorexia."

Multiplication of managerial positions was then taken for granted as technology developed, markets expanded, and the economy grew. Now technology keeps on expanding, many old markets (and lots of new ones) continue to grow along with the economy. But layers of management, like so many rugs, are being pulled out from under the well-shod feet that, until recently, walked with confidence along the corridors of corporate America. Now they are out and looking—many could be looking for quite awhile unless they understand themselves and the new corporate culture. As their organizations shrink, displaced managers themselves have to expand personally. They have to enlarge their outlook and their personal ensemble of employable skills.

Now with all of this said, I want to line up the old ethical principles over against the ethical challenges presented by this new corporate culture.

I. The Principle of Human Dignity. This is the bedrock principle of both personal and social ethics. In the new corporate culture, human dignity is taking a beating. In some corporations, workers at all levels are being treated as if they were disposable parts. Although employees will, regrettably, but for sound economic reasons, continue to be separated from their jobs, they must never be viewed by those making the downsizing decisions as disposable parts.

II. The Principle of Participation. Every human person in any workplace has a right to have some say in the decisions that affect his or her livelihood. To be shut out of all discussion is to be denied respect for one's human dignity. The ethical thing to do in this new corporate culture, in cases either of layoff or of career continuation in the same organization, is to involve the employee in planning and in the execution of the plan. This means preparation for separation, should that have to happen; it also means enhancing the "value added" potential and the productivity of employees who will remain.

III. The Principle of Integrity. Honesty is always the best policy on both sides of the employer-employee hyphen; it is also the best policy to guide relations with all the organization's stockholders.

It is one thing to take severe measures to guarantee the survival of the enterprise, it is quite another to deceive others and even worse to reduce employment in order to improve a balance sheet or boost a stock price. After downsizing, some who remain and occupy positions of power at the top of the organization will benefit economically; they should be honest about the extent of that benefit and the uses they intend to make of what might well be regarded as a windfall.

IV. The Principle of Fairness (Justice).

Everyone knows what fairness is. At least we think we know, and we are usually convinced that we are absolutely right. We just know it! Sometimes, a few additional facts or the recognition of our own biases will prompt us to reset our fairness clock, but we have a way of just knowing when unfair treatment occurs.

A strong sense of justice will safeguard a person of integrity from violating any trust. If no trusts are violated, if no injustice is involved, a downsizing in response to economic necessity can be justified. But there is such a deep feeling of injustice, of unfair treatment, in so many downsized corners of our new corporate culture that those in control must examine their corporate conscience for evidence of injustice done to millions of separated employees in recent years.

V. The Principle of Veracity.

Why "veracity" when you've just noted that "integrity" belong on your list? Integrity means living truthfully, while veracity, of course, means speaking truthfully.

Veracity is truthfullness, and the truth will always set you free. There may be unpleasant consequences for you if you tell the truth. But, as the saying goes, "the truth will always out," and the truth teller will always have a place to stand, a soul to claim, and a peace of mind that can never be taken away. Truth not just when convenient, truth in all circumstances is the only compass that works in an age of ambiguity. Truth telling, as difficult as it may be at times, is the only way to preserve an ethical corporate culture.

VI. The Principle of Keeping Commitments. Here again the issue of trust is in the foreground. Inevitably, when journalistic accounts of the new corporate culture touch upon the human side of downsizing, you will read that corporate loyalty is a thing of the past. Corporations no longer keep their commitments, the story usually goes. And often that is exactly the case.

Commitments are the cement of social relationships. If commitments are kept in the workplace, morale and a sense of security will be high. If a firm simply cannot make commitments to its employees, uncertainty, anxiety, and the individual's commitment to self-preservation will increase in the best of hearts and the best of workplaces. Since fewer and fewer firms are able in this new corporate culture to promise permanent employment, closer and completely honest communication is all the more necessary if trust is to be preserved in the workplace.

VII. The Principle of Corporate Social Responsibility. This principle relates to the economic, the legal, the ethical, and the positive discretionary or philanthropic categories of a firm's behavior. The good corporate citizen will make a profit and abide by the law. Just to remain within the law, however, is not the sum and substance of corporate responsibility; not everything that is required by ethics is also required by law.

Corporate ethical responsibility stretches all the way from respect for individual human dignity (in employees, customers, suppliers, colleagues, competitors) all the way out to respect for the physical environment that is necessary to sustain life on this planet.

Countless ethical considerations come to mind in the context of downsizing and this new corporate culture of economic uncertainty and contingent employment. One that I see as crucial belongs in the category of "employability" and applies to both employer and employee. Keeping an employee employable is an ethical responsibility of both employer and employee in the new corporate culture.

In a knowledge economy (not simply an "information economy") like ours in this new corporate culture, the ethical imperative points not only to the care of casualties, but also to the advancement of education for the cultivation of new ideas, new creativity, new technology, new products, services, and eventually, jobs.

VIII. The Principle of Subsidiarity. Those who say the care of economic casualties and the creation of jobs should be "left to government," risk violating the principle of subsidiarity, which would allow neither decisions nor actions at a higher level of organization that could be taken just as effectively and efficiently at a lower level. This principle would push decision making down to lower levels, but sometimes government must act in the interest of the common good. And there will be instances when only government can address an issue properly and effectively.

The principle of subsidiarity should also apply in private sector organizations, in ordinary workplaces. This ties in with the principle of participation and, as is so often the case, is reducible to the principle of human dignity. Individuals are not to be ground under by impersonal, anonymous decision makers at higher levels in the organization.

IX. The Common Good Pursuit of the Common Good is a basic principle of ethical behavior; it is a bedrock principle like the principle of human dignity. Without it, social chaos would prevail. The "Common Good" is a catch-all phrase that describes an environment that is supportive of the development of human potential while safeguarding the community against individual excesses. It looks to the general good, to the good of the many over against the interests of the one.

It is important that there be agreement in the community that the common good should always prevail over individual, personal interests. To promote and protect the common good is the reason why governments exist—a point worth noting here just after a discussion of the principle of subsidiarity, the principle that has a way of keeping government in its proper place.

X. Love. One reason why the old ethical principles have continuing relevance in this new corporate culture, is the fact that they are rooted in a human nature that does not change all that much from age to age. Underlying human nature in any circumstance is the law of love. The challenge today is not to find a replacement for the law of love, which is always applicable, of course, to God, self, family, neighbor, and workplace associates, the challenge is just to let love happen in this new, but still very human corporate culture. The challenge is also there to be clear about the meaning of love; it means sacrifice, the willingness to be and do for others.

Now go back to your mental notepad and compare the "old" ethical principles you listed there with the ones outlined in this presentation. It would be regrettable, wouldn't it, if all those old principles just grow older as newer and greater challenges appear in the corporate culture and in the other activity centers of contemporary American life. That could happen. It will certainly happen if those who still recognize the old principles do nothing to apply them.

Profits from Principle

Five Forces Redefining Business

By Bennett Daviss

Corporations are finding that social responsibility pays off. This realization will change the very nature of business.

Ray Anderson built Interface, Inc., a billion-dollar international carpet manufacturer based in Atlanta, on a simple precept: A corporation's purpose is to earn a good return for shareowners while complying with the law. Then, in 1994, during a struggle to regain lost market share and shore up his company's sagging stock price, Anderson read eco-entrepreneur Paul Hawken's book, *The Ecology of Commerce,* which documents industry's profligate squandering of natural resources and sketches a vision of environmentally sustainable business.

Anderson took it personally. His company was chewing up more than 500 million pounds of raw material each year and excreting more than 900 tons of air pollutants, 600 million gallons of wastewater, and 10,000 tons of trash.

Reading the book was Anderson's epiphany—"a spear in my chest"—the CEO recalls. It also put a spur in his backside: Anderson set out to make his corporation's 26 factories

on four continents the world's first environmentally sustainable manufacturing enterprise, recycling everything possible, releasing no pollutants, and sending nothing to landfills. "We're treating all fossil fuel energy as waste to be eliminated through efficiencies and shifts to renewable energy," he says.

Idealistic? Definitely. Unbusinesslike? Definitely not.

"In just over two years, we've become 23% more efficient in converting raw stuff into sales dollars—and we've only scratched the surface," Anderson notes. That efficiency has cut not only waste, but also a cumulative $40 million in costs. The savings, which were projected to grow to $76 million by the end of 1998, helped Interface make the winning low bid in 1997 to carpet The Gap Inc.'s new world headquarters in San Francisco. The Gap invited Interface to bid specifically because of the carpet company's environmental initiatives.

"We've found a new way to win in the marketplace," Anderson believes, "one that doesn't come at the expense of our grandchildren or the earth, but at the expense of the inefficient competitor."

Anderson's crusade is one example among countless others proving a new rule in business: Profits and social responsibility are becoming inseparable.

Helping Workers Work

Just ask Donna Klein, director of work/life initiatives for Washington, D.C., based hotelier Marriott International. Her industry depends on the low-wage workers who change sheets and scrub tubs. They often live below the poverty line and spend less than a year on the job.

The company couldn't afford to simply hike wages in an effort to retain more of its approximately 150,000 low-wage workers. Casting about for a way to reduce turnover, and thereby the extra costs involved

Originally appeared in the March 1999, issue of *The Futurist,* pp. 28-32. © 1999 by Bennett Davis and the World Future Society, 7910 Woodmont Avenue, Bethesda, MD 20814; http://www.wfs.org/wfs. Reprinted by permission.

in training and supervising new employees, Klein discovered that the workers were usually driven from their jobs by personal problems: domestic violence, scrapes with immigration authorities, becoming homeless, or an inability to master English, among others. Supervisors reported spending as much as half their working time trying to help employees straighten out their personal lives.

In 1992, Klein set up a 24-hour, multilingual hotline staffed by trained social workers whom hotel employees could call for help and referrals to aid agencies. By 1997, the project had cut Marriott's turnover to 35%, compared with the hotel industry's average of 100% or more.

The hotline is handling more than 2,000 employee calls each year. "It costs well over $1 million a year to run it, but it saves us more than $3 million a year in hiring, training, and other costs," Klein says. In 1997, Klein's office documented 600 cases in which the hotline was the key factor that kept an employee from quitting, saving an estimated $750,000 for that year, she reports. "We've documented increases in productivity, morale, and better relations with managers and co-workers as a result of the hotline. But we're not able to quantify the gain in managers' time. The hotline frees them to focus on customer service instead of employees' problems."

Such examples are legion. After the Malden Mills factory in Lowell, Massachusetts, burned during the

INTERFACE, INC.

Ray Anderson of Interface saved his carpet manufacturing company $40 million through measures such as recycling and cutting waste.

Skylights supply daytime lighting at Interface's new plant.

INTERFACE, INC.

1995 Christmas season, owner Aaron Feuerstein continued to pay workers' salaries and benefits until a new plant was built. In the new factory, worker productivity reportedly improved by 25% and quality defects have dropped by two-thirds. Although some of the gains are attributable to newer equipment, Feuerstein believes it's "a direct result of the good will of our people." San Francisco's Thanksgiving Coffee Company invests a share of its revenues in community development among the Central American villages that grow its beans, ensuring loyal suppliers and reasonable prices during times of small harvests. Mercedes-Benz has designed its new S-class sedans and 500/600SEC luxury coupes to be entirely recyclable, giving it and its dealers a new source of low-cost used parts.

The evidence that social responsibility swells profits appears in studies as well as stories. Returns for the Domini 400 Social Index—a roster of 400 publicly traded, socially responsible firms tracked by the Boston investment advisory firm of Kinder,

Lydenberg, Domini & Co.—have outpaced those for the Standard & Poor's 500 for each of the last three years. In 1992, UCLA business professor David Lewin surveyed 188 companies and found that "companies that increased their community involvement were more likely to show an improved financial picture over a two-year time period." A 1995 Vanderbilt University analysis found that in eight of 10 cases low-polluting companies financially outperform their dirtier competitors. And the U.S. General Accounting Office reports that employee stock-option plans and participatory management schemes hike productivity an average of 52%.

"We're going through a mind-change," says Marjorie Kelly, editor of the Minneapolis-based *Business Ethics* magazine. "Most of us still carry around the subliminal idea that ruthless behavior beats the competition and good behavior is money out of pocket. But the data shows that the traditional idea is wrong. Social responsibility makes sense in purely capitalistic terms."

Five Forces Redefining Business

Conservative economists, most notably Nobel laureate Milton Friedman at the University of Chicago, have long argued that the sole mission of a corporation is to maximize profits for the benefit of shareholders and that spending on social causes violates that prime directive. But the new marketplace is proving that profits can best be maximized by embracing, rather

than forswearing, social concerns. The idea that profitability and social awareness are not antagonistic but interdependent redefines the purpose of business.

Five forces are converging to shape business's new social imperative: consumer conscience, socially conscious investing, the global media, special-interest activism, and expectations of corporate leadership.

1 First, today's consumers have learned by experience that societies and economies—like nature—are closed systems. Automobile exhaust doesn't disappear into the sky; it transforms the atmosphere and consequently our climate. When employers don't make health insurance available to workers, the cost of health care for those workers isn't saved, but is shared among all of us in higher health-care costs and taxes that support public emergency rooms.

Two decades ago, if a company made cars with exploding gas tanks or marketed U.S.-banned pesticides

INTERFACE, INC.

Reflective surfaces on the outside of Interface's new plant minimize the need for air conditioning, thereby reducing the company's energy consumption.

in Third World countries, it could view these as purely financial issues. Then, as the flower children of the 1960s became the consumers of the 1980s, such issues were recast in a moral light. Those consumers began speaking out—with their voices, their votes, and their wallets.

The result: By 1992, a survey by the Public Relations Society of America identified social-issues marketing—that is, celebrating a company's commitment to public issues as well as to its products and customers—as the leader among the industry's 10 hottest trends. The same year, the quarterly *Business and Society Review* reported in its summer issue that "corporate social responsibility is now a tidal wave of the future."

"People judge corporations today by their social performance as much as by their financial performance— their impact on the environment, their role in aggravating or relieving social problems," explains Richard Torrenzano, president of the Torrenzano Group, a New York consulting firm. "People indicate by their purchases not just the value of a product or service, but how they view the company's role in their communities." Because ethical probity shapes consumer choices, a company's deportment has become a crucial bottom-line concern.

For example, a 1980s boycott of Burger King for its use of beef raised on pasture slashed from South American rain forests damaged sales enough to force the company to change its purchasing habits. On the other hand, New Hampshire's Stonyfield Farm yogurt company has been able to expand its share of the stagnant retail yogurt market by touting its steady financial support for organic and family farms.

2 Consumers' new conscience has complemented, and cultivated, the second factor—the rise of socially conscious investing. The movement gained momentum during the 1970s and 1980s as institutions and investment funds were pressured to shed their South African holdings to protest apartheid. According to the Social Investment Forum, a New York-based nonprofit information clearinghouse, in the last 10 years the value of U.S. socially aware investments has grown from $50 billion to more than $500 billion and is one of the financial industry's strongest growth areas.

"If I don't invest in companies with actual or potential social and environmental liabilities, I'm reducing my risk of owning a company that suddenly owes huge fines or settlements in damage suits," says Hugh Kelley, president of the Social Responsibility Investment Group, an Atlanta advisory firm. Neither will his companies be rocked by boycotts and bad publicity. "Those kinds of problems go right to the bottom line."

3 Those potential problems are exacerbated by the third factor: a competitive, unsparing, and technologically endowed media—especially television—that makes once-abstract concepts like global warming or sweatshop labor personal to consumers. Once discovered, a company's ethical lapse can now be flashed to

> **A company's deportment has become a crucial bottom-line concern.**

news outlets and brokerage firms globally before a CEO can hurry back from lunch. "Journalists today are much more sophisticated," Torrenzano adds. "They ask tougher questions, and they give no slack when someone has a problem. It motivates companies."

4 Fourth, zealous special-interest groups have become deft at using the media to link corporate practices with social and environmental problems and solutions. Burger King's troubles began in 1986 when the upstart Rainforest Action Network called on the world to boycott the chain, claiming it used "rain-forest beef" grazed on pastures carved from South America's imperiled tropical forests. At first, the company ignored the allegation. Within two years, Whopper sales slumped— as much as 17% by some reports— and the burger giant capitulated with a statement forswearing ecologically incorrect meat. "Activists are becoming increasingly effective in forcing corporations to cooperate in their vision of social change," noted the late Rafael Pagán, a pioneering corporate social-policy adviser.

5 Fifth, the public is transferring its expectations of leadership in solving social problems from government to business. Over the past two decades, the failure of federal "Great Society" programs and increasing partisan gridlock has exacerbated public demand for action against society's lingering ills. As a result, while Congress dithers, commercial firms pressured by consumers' new concerns are enacting social policy ranging from environmental cleanup to flexible work policies, from Third World economic development to new product safety standards. By those actions, companies not only gain a competitive edge but also ratify a new moral compact between business and society.

Increasingly, companies are embracing that new compact deliberately. The San Francisco-based group Business for Social Responsibility has grown from 45 members in 1993 to more than 1,400 today. "The companies joining the group aren't just the Ben and Jerrys of the world," says charter member Gary Hirshberg, co-founder of Stonyfield Farm. "We're getting divisions of Kraft, the Fortune 500, and investment bankers out to make a killing who recognize that this is the way to success. We don't just have the oddball New Age companies any more. We've got the suits." BSR's members now include giants such as General Motors and Coca-Cola and boast combined annual sales of more than $1 trillion—a seventh of the entire U.S. economy.

"These companies aren't joining just to say they're members," says Cliff Feigenbaum, editor and publisher of the *Green Money Letter*, a quarterly newsletter tracking the new business conscience. "They're joining because they want help."

Drawing a New Balance

Companies that venture into this new territory are learning that profiting by principle demands an unequivocal commitment to both conscience and cash flow. But the new compact also is forcing companies to calibrate a new and delicate—even precarious—balance between the two. Consumers United Insurance Company and The Body Shop have provided object lessons.

Founded in 1969, Consumers United was a company ahead of its time. It offered unisex insurance rates and covered policyholders' unwed domestic partners before either became a public issue. Founder Jim Gibbons turned full ownership of the firm over to the employees, who controlled corporate policy and could overrule his decisions with a majority vote. The wage structure ensured that the lowest-paid worker would be able to support a family of four. This experiment in controlled chaos thrived, and by 1986 the company managed $47 million in invested assets.

Gibbons deployed his clients' funds with the same earnest idealism with which he managed the company. The firm bought 26 vacant acres in Washington, D.C., and built low-income housing. It funded a local youth group and promised each of the 70 children who joined that, if they stayed drug-free and didn't make babies, Consumers United would pay their way through college.

Such largesse drew the attention of insurance industry regulators in Delaware, the state in which Consumers had incorporated. The regulators weren't convinced that big-hearted gestures such as paying poor kids' college bills guaranteed enough future cash to pay claims. Finally convinced that Gibbons wasn't being prudent enough with policyholders' money, the regulators felt they had no alternative but to seek a court order declaring Consumers insolvent. In 1993, the state seized control of its assets and shut the company down. "It provides a cautionary tale for any business that pays more attention to its social mission than to its bottom line," *Business Ethics* writer Bill Gifford noted in an obituary article.

If Consumers did too much of a good thing, The Body Shop did too little. In the 1980s, promotional materials for the British-based bodycare products company featured photos of co-founder Anita Roddick sitting in rain-forest clearings dickering with natives to buy their renewable products. It avowed that none of its products were tested on animals. Body Shop catalog covers promoted progressive causes. Roddick and husband Gordon became celebrated symbols of business with a conscience.

Then, in 1994, a six-page expose in the pages of *Business Ethics* detailed evidence that native peoples supplied less than 1% of the company's raw materials, that many of its ingredients were being tested on animals (although not by The Body Shop itself), and that its "natural" products included generous amounts of petroleum. The article also hinted that the corporation's well-publicized concern for social betterment was prompted as much by greed as by conscience. After the public glimpsed the gap between rhetoric and reality, the company's stock prices plunged and sales slumped.

"They were making claims that didn't exactly match their practices, and it came back to bite them," says Dan McKenna, president of Principle Profits Asset Management in Amherst, Massachusetts, an invest-

ment advisory firm serving the socially conscious. "They saw their financial position suffer when the reality didn't live up to the image."

Shoe giant Nike is busy teaching itself a similar lesson. Widely accused of using child labor in Third World sweatshops to make its high-priced sneakers, the company has launched a number of initiatives to improve the lot of foreign workers. In October 1996, Nike tried to polish its image by releasing an independent study showing that its workers in Indonesia and Vietnam were buying VCRs and otherwise living well. Three weeks later, an audit by accounting firm Ernst & Young detailing unsafe working conditions in one of Nike's Vietnamese factories made the front page of the *New York Times*. According to one report, in 1996 Nike paid Michael Jordan more for his endorsement—at least $30 million—than it did its 19,000 non-U.S. factory workers combined.

"That can be read as a statement of the way Nike balances marketing with human dignity," McKenna says. "It seems that Nike hasn't yet committed to the full meaning of social responsibility."

Business Ethics editor Marjorie Kelly agrees. "Social responsibility can't follow the catalytic converter model," she admonishes. "In a car, you can leave the engine unchanged and just bolt on a new part to take out the pollutants. But in a business you can't just open an ethics office down the hall and leave the company's culture and practices unchanged. A genuine commitment to social responsibility transforms not just what a company does, but also how it thinks."

What's Ahead: Four Trends

That commitment will continue to be tested in the next decade. Today's demands and pressures for corporate social leadership are redrafting the tacit contract between business and society. Four trends are shaping the terms of the new covenant:

1. Good works and financial gain must balance. During the cash-rich 1980s, socially involved corporations and pressure groups coined the term "the double bottom line" to describe a company's attempts to better its profits and its community at the same time. But the '80s are over and the double bottom line still has to be derived from a single balance sheet. In the future, each company will define its social role in terms of self-interest and fund good works only to the extent that the company gains financially from them.

For those reasons, social and environmental initiatives will focus largely within companies themselves. For example, a corporation may be willing to underwrite an alternative-energy program, but only in its own factory and only if the scheme doesn't add to costs, compromise product quality, or lengthen delivery times. A proposal for an on-site day-care center, flextime program, or employee gym will win favor only by showing evidence that it will reduce turnover and absenteeism enough to pay its own way.

Privately owned companies will have more flexibility but still must align social programs to profits. Stonyfield Farm plants forests to offset its factory's carbon-dioxide emissions—an investment that also strengthens its brand identity and consumer loyalty in an increasingly competitive industry.

2. Activists gain leverage by becoming advisers, not adversaries. Because financial self-interest will circumscribe corporations' social initiatives, the role of the activist is expanding from adversary to adviser. As long as there are corporations, there will be a place for corporate watchdogs. But in the years ahead, activists will gain greatest leverage by working directly with companies to help executives make the links between profit and social and environmental probity—helping them see the connections between life-cycle product engineering and cost cut-

ting, or between better treatment of workers and money saved from turnover, lawsuits, boycotts, government fines, and public-relations expense. Adversarial groups will still prod with sticks, but activist-advisers will entice companies by dangling the carrots of cost savings and competitive advantage.

3. Corporations will be audited socially just as they now are financially. Progressive companies have begun to hire specialized consultants to rate their social and environmental performance; in the future, shareholders and activists will place all corporations under greater pressure to open their doors to these outside consultants. The ISO 9000 standards for industrial quality management, pro-mulgated by the International Organization for Standardization (ISO), sparked the ISO 14000 standards for environmental systems management. Recently, the Council on Economic Priorities promulgated the SA 8000 standards (for "social accountability"), setting forth criteria by which companies' treatment of domestic and foreign workers can be assessed, rated, and publicized. Look for outside social and environmental auditing to become a new norm as companies seek to ingratiate themselves with savvy and discerning consumers.

4. Corporate social identity will be as important as brand identity. As people come to expect corporations to take a larger social role, companies will develop a social identity that consumers respond to as strongly and readily as they do a brand identity.

That shift links a corporation's behavior to its product image and, therefore, to its profits. When Texaco's corporate culture was accused of racial prejudice, millions of people boycotted the firm's gas stations. After Johnson & Johnson's open, thorough, and cooperative response to deadly tamperings with its Tylenol tablets, the pain remedy actually increased its market share.

As these and other companies have learned, a corporation will not be able to choose whether to have a social identity; the public will fashion one for it based on a company's social and environmental actions—or lack thereof. Companies sculpt brand identities by manipulating images in the public mind, but businesses will find their social identity harder to control. There are too many prying journalists, activists, and shareholders to avoid.

As companies learn that social or environmental gaffes gnaw at profits, they also will realize that there is only one way to guard against the financial losses that these kinds of blunders can lead to. Companies must "walk the talk": From the boardroom to the loading dock, they must adopt policies and practices that enact the new, nobler norms of corporate conduct that corporate precedents and public expectations are imposing.

Traditionalists have long argued that business's only social obligation is to maximize profit. The new social contract between business and society inverts that principle: In the new century, companies will grow their profits only by embracing their new role as the engine of positive social and environmental change.

About the Author
Bennett Daviss is an independent journalist who writes, speaks, and consults on education reform, socially responsible business, and other issues of sustainability. His articles have appeared in more than 40 magazines on four continents. With Nobel physicist Kenneth Wilson, he is co-author of the book *Redesigning Education*. His address is Walpole Valley Road, Walpole, New Hampshire 03608.

Portions of this article first appeared in *Ambassador Magazine*. Reprinted courtesy of *Ambassador Magazine* and Trans World Airlines.

The New
BOTTOM LINE

The "one minute manager" tells entrepreneurs what it takes to have a successful company.

BY KEN BLANCHARD

ILLUSTRATION © BRIAN RASZKA

WOULDN'T IT BE GREAT if you could give your business the gift of a magnificent and promising future while also discovering a way for all your employees to be satisfied? You can—with a little work.

Boosting your business *and* satisfying employees means changing the way you do business. It means implementing a broader approach that builds on the foundation of an effective organization—namely, its mission and values.

Rather than focusing solely on results, winning companies first emphasize values—the beliefs and attitudes that you, as the business owner, have about your employees, customers, quality, ethics, integrity, social responsibility, growth, stability, innovation and flexibility. Managing by values—not by profits—is a powerful process that will set your business on the path to becoming what I call a "Fortunate 500" company.

■ FORTUNE TELLING

What is a Fortunate 500 company? Over the past few years, my colleagues and I have devoted significant time to defining exactly that. So far, we've identified the following 10 characteristics:

I. Vision. Fortunate 500 companies have a clear vision that stems from the business owners as to what they are about and what they want to be. That vision is communicated to all employees and used daily as a basis for decision-making.

From *Entrepreneur* magazine, February 1998, pp. 127–131. © 1998 by Entrepreneur Media Inc. Reprinted by permission.

2. Empowerment. Employees are treated as partners in the business–not just cogs in the machine. Business owners and managers expect a lot from every employee, and in return, they help employees do their jobs with minimal barriers. You can expect your employees to constantly learn and grow–as long as you back up your expectations with solid training and career development options to facilitate that growth.

3. Performance. Employee performance is measured and monitored in a way that encourages your employees to give their best. Set performance goals and routinely provide feedback to let your workers know how they're doing.

4. Team approach. Employees are organized into teams to find the best means to solve problems, build morale and achieve company goals.

5. Customer service. Customers are treated as the most important part of the business–which they are.

6. Quality. The business prides itself on producing high-quality goods and services and never letting standards slip. Your company's long-term success depends largely on its long-term reputation, so make it a priority to build exceptional products.

7. Communication. This is the oil that keeps the company running smoothly. Make sure the doors are open for employees to communicate in any direction within the company.

8. Ethics. The company expects all employees to be ethical.

9. Wellness. The business is concerned about the wellness of its employees. Healthy employees are more energetic–and less absenteeism means higher productivity.

10. Profit. The company is profitable–but it does not treat this as its sole purpose for existing.

■ GETTING THERE

Any company can be a Fortunate 500–if it can keep employees and customers happy and make money. Businesses driven by these values possess a certain operating philosophy. The work environment is fulfilling, customers are "raving fans," and share-holder value is enhanced. Your company can become a Fortunate 500 company by identifying and communicating core values, and aligning values and practices.

✔ *Identifying core values.* Managing by values begins when you identify a set of operating values. Many companies claim they have core values, but typically what they're referring to are generic beliefs: having integrity, making a profit, responding to customers and so on. These values only have meaning when they're defined in terms of how people behave and are ranked to set priorities.

For example, Disney's core values for its theme parks are, in order of importance, safety, courtesy, the show (performing according to a role's requirements) and efficiency. If these values had not been ranked, employees would have been left to decide which was most or least important.

Today, your company must know what it stands for. Values-based business behavior is no longer simply an interesting option–it's crucial to your survival. Once you understand your mission and values, you have a strong basis for evaluating your practices and aligning them accordingly.

✔ *Communicating core values.* First, make sure your chosen values are clear to all stakeholders–employees, customers, suppliers, stockholders and the community. Look at Norstan Inc., a telecommunications company in Minneapolis, for example. Rapid growth and a series of acquisitions had made the company diverse, and it needed a binding force to pull it together. The company determined its core values were to be ethical, responsive and profitable. It then defined these values in terms of its major stakeholders:

"Norstan is a full-range provider of integrated voice, data and video solutions that satisfy both today's and tomorrow's business needs. Through ethical, responsive and profitable actions, Norstan will provide a fulfilling work environment for our employees, legendary service for our customers, enhanced value for our shareholders and a spirit of shared responsibility with our community."

✔ *Aligning values and practices.*

Once you articulate the values, make sure they are actually put into practice. Are you ready to walk the walk? Aligning your behavior with the values you've set is inherent in the concept of the Fortunate 500 company. "Do as I say but not as I do" will get you nowhere with employees–and defeats the purpose of working toward a values-led company.

Norstan found that aligning its values was a challenge. To help ease the process, the company set up a helpline for employees to air ethical concerns anonymously. Training sessions were offered to all employees. Key responsibility areas were defined, and leadership styles became part of the performance planning process. Employee committees were organized to recognize peers, and the company set up a program to recognize long-term outstanding performers.

Employees were not the only ones to benefit. Surveys showed an increase in customer satisfaction–from 86 percent in fiscal year 1988 to 94 percent in fiscal year 1997. Norstan's earnings per share have grown at a compound annual rate of 17 percent since 1994.

Achieving excellence and becoming a Fortunate 500 company comes more from managing the journey than just announcing the destination. Too often, changes are announced by managers who revert to a "leave alone" leadership style–and later wonder why nothing happens.

While one company's path to managing by values will differ from another's, to make the journey smooth and successful, there are seven basic steps all companies should follow. The first five involve diagnosis; the last two involve implementation.

I. Articulate values. Establish a clear set of values. This includes descriptions of how each value would be practiced every day, as well as a way to measure each practice on an ongoing basis. For example, if one of the desired values was "outstanding customer service," this could translate into employees going out of their way every day to help customers.

2. Identify and describe key business practices. Evaluate your business to determine a baseline of company operations. This information would come from various sources, including interviews, historical documents and so on.

3. Compare values with practices. Does your company practice what it preaches? This is crucial to building credibility among customers *and* employees. After all, if your employees see you tout honesty and then watch you mislead customers, how can you expect them to believe in your mission and values? It's helpful to obtain additional feedback from other sources such as focus groups and employee and customer surveys.

4. Establish priorities for realignment. Once you've seen where your values and practices are not in sync, set priorities for aligning them.

5. Recommend changes and an implementation strategy. The strategy should incorporate a vision of how your business will continually change as new priorities dictate and should include an implementation timeline.

6. Make changes. This will take some serious effort—from you and your employees—over a period of several years. Outside expertise may be helpful in specific areas, such as management training, performance management, team-building, customer responsiveness, and reward systems.

7. Monitor progress. Finally, measure the company's ongoing progress. This encourages everyone to stay involved and can alert you to the potential need for midcourse corrections.

■ MANAGING THE JOURNEY

Making changes in your company is an important step. But to manage the journey over the long-term, four systems should be in place:

✔ *Accountability system.* Everyone needs to know whose responsibility it is to do what. The primary reason change often doesn't last is people don't know what's expected of them.

✔ *Information system.* Too often in business, only financial data is gathered—and then it is distributed only to management. Other key indicators that relate to performance areas also need to be tracked. Information on performance has to be made available to those people who can best use it—those doing the work.

✔ *Feedback system.* It's difficult for employees to improve their performance if they don't have a clue how they're doing.

✔ *Recognition system.* For change to last, good performance must be acknowledged. If current performance is below expectations, you must reprimand or provide training as needed.

■ WAY TO GO

A Fortunate 500 company is driven by values—not results. When values prompt change, every employee is involved and customers will benefit. But keep in mind the journey is never complete—one never achieves perfect alignment of values with practices in a company—just as one never truly achieves excellence. Yet the journey is well worth taking.

Ken Blanchard, Ph.D., is chair of Blanchard Training & Development Inc. in San Diego, California, and author of The One Minute Manager *(William Morrow & Co.) and* Managing by Values *(Berrett-Koehler).*

THE NEW WORKFORCE

A tight labor market gives the disabled the chance to make permanent inroads

The Gap's emporium of affordable chic in midtown Manhattan throbs with New Economy action. Salesclerks sporting headsets race across the store to wait on tourists and time-starved New Yorkers. Stockboys heave huge boxes overflowing with clothes. At the center of this retail hubbub is Gap's "wild man in a wheelchair," supersalesman Wilfredo "Freddy" Laboy, a fast-talking, goateed 36-year-old who lost his legs when he fell off a freight train at age 9. Freddy dances across the store, popping wheelies and spinning himself around to the bouncy pop music. Little kids stare as he hops off his chair and onto the floor to grab a tangerine-colored T-shirt and then pulls himself up on his stump to reach for another pair of khakis. Instead of using the elevator, he prefers to horrify colleagues by scooting himself down the stairs. "It's faster," he says.

Freddy loves the Gap, and the Gap loves Freddy. But just six months ago, the story was altogether different. An amateur wheelchair basketball star who pulled himself through the New York City Marathon, Freddy was used to letting nothing stand in his way. But even with New York City's unemployment level at record lows, he couldn't find a job. Once prospective employers caught sight of his legless torso, they lost interest. Still, on a whim, Freddy wheeled himself into the Gap last October. To his astonishment, they hired him. "I finally got accepted somewhere because they didn't just see the wheelchair," says the married father of three. "They saw me."

Freddy may well be at the cusp of a huge change rocking the world of the workplace, marking the first time in history that people with disabilities have been poised to enter Corporate America en masse—many of them with the help of wheelchairs and seeing-eye dogs.

Facing the worst labor shortage in modern history, recruiters are tapping the kinds of workers they would have easily blown off just 10 years ago: prepubescent wireheads, grandmothers—even convicted murderers. Next up are the disabled, who may prove to be the last great hope— if only because they're the only labor pool that hasn't been completely drained. At the same time, groundbreaking technology is creating ways for people with disabilities to better perform jobs, helping to erase the deep divisions that once existed between them and everybody else.

HELPFUL COMPUTERS. Sure, a few companies have a long record of hiring workers with disabilities. In the 1980s—still the Dark Ages of the movement—Marriott International Inc. was doing the unheard-of: paying adults with Down's Syndrome $7 an hour to work 40 hours a week cleaning rooms and sweeping floors. But that was the exception. Despite the Americans With Disabilities Act (ADA), passed a decade ago this July, only 25% of the country's 15 million disabled who are also of working age are employed. Of the 75% who aren't working, Harris Polls indicate that two-thirds of them wish they could be. Says Paul H. Wehman, director of the rehabilitation research center at Virginia Commonwealth University: "The dirty little secret of the welfare-to-work movement is that people with disabilities got left out."

That may be about to change. Never before has it been so easy and made so much economic sense for companies to invest in workers with disabilities by making accommodations for them. "We can use new technologies to contribute to society in ways that weren't really possible when I started 25 years ago," says Michael Coleman, IBM's vice-president for global operations. Coleman, who lost both his hands in Vietnam when he was trying to defuse a bomb, is IBM's top-ranking disabled worker. He is also chairing the company's task force to find ways to employ more workers with disabilities.

Crestar Bank has already found ways to make that happen. New-fangled voice-activated technology means that callers to the bank never know that customer-service representative Chris Harmon is a quadriplegic. He is so disabled that the recruiter who hired him had to stick a pen in his mouth so he could sign the employment application. At the company's Richmond (Va.) call center, he simply tells his computer what to do and the information appears on the screen in a flash.

Crestar is one of a growing list of businesses that is mining the ranks of the disabled to solve labor crises they say would otherwise have been catastrophic. Turns out that what began as a last-ditch maneuver to stem this worker draught has yielded an unexpected boon that veteran employers of people with disabilities have long known about: The disabled are often more proficient, productive, and efficient than "normies," according to researchers.

A 30-year study by DuPont revealed that job performance by workers with disabilities was equal to or better than fully functioning peers. The disabled had a 90% above-average job performance, with safety and attendance records that were far above the norm, too. Perhaps most enticing to human-resource heads pulling their hair out over the dot-com-induced worker exodus is the fact that people with disabilities can often be far more loyal to the employers who gave them a break and are therefore less likely to be lured away by a boss dangling a bigger paycheck.

"AT A LOSS." But until recently, the disabled were actually penalized for finding a job because even a minimum-wage gig flipping burgers or mopping floors meant the automatic loss of Medicaid benefits. That huge barrier to employment fell in December when President Clinton signed the Workers Incentives Improvement Act, clearing the path for states to change Medicaid laws to let the disabled hang on to much-needed benefits while entering the workforce.

The move comes none too soon. Already, temporary agency Manpower Inc. is raiding the ranks of the disabled to fill its employee rolls. The National Disability Council reports a 50% jump in requests for workers with disabilities from companies as diverse as Merrill Lynch & Co. and Microsoft Corp.

In fact, Microsoft is so eager to hire such workers that the software company is spearheading the Able to Work program, a consortium of 22 businesses scrambling to find the best ways to place disabled people in jobs. Says Microsoft's director of diversity, Santiago Rodriguez: "Until now, the whole country has been at a loss as to how to do this."

To many advocates for the disabled, this confusion is a disappointment. The ADA was passed with great hopes of creating jobs and access for America's disabled population of 54 million. It prohibited employers from refusing to hire qualified applicants

WHERE THE DOOR IS OPEN
Some companies that offer job opportunities for the disabled

BOOZ, ALLEN & HAMILTON Advanced policies for employees with AIDS. Has National Task Force on Disability.

CATERPILLAR Sponsors Special Olympics and is considered a model of high-tech accessibility.

CHARLES SCHWAB Founder Charles Schwab has dyslexia, and his sensitivity to the issue pervades the organization. Special efforts to recruit people with disabilities, especially the blind.

CRESTAR BANK Offers disabled customers special services and recruits disabled workers through partnerships with the Virginia Rehabilitative Services Dept. and the National Association of the Deaf.

FORD MOTOR Staged commitment to including people with disabilities— works with more than 100 local diversity councils.

HONEYWELL Participant in Able to Work program, a consortium of 22 companies that finds ways to employ the disabled. Good track record on turning its own high-tech innovations into perks for employees with disabilities.

IBM Aggressive recruiter of disabled workers, including students.

JOHNSON & JOHNSON Runs a comprehensive disability management program that helps employees return to work after they have been disabled.

MICROSOFT Took the lead in establishing Able to Work program last year.

WELLS FARGO Long legacy of hiring and training disabled workers.

ENABLING TECHNOLOGIES

A quarter of a century ago, only the exceptional employer hired a person with a disability. Most execs felt the disabled worker would flounder at even the simplest of tasks. And change has been slow. Even today, only 1 in 4 disabled adults have jobs—despite strong laws prohibiting employment discrimination and the tightest job market in modern history.

But a revolution in the development of specially adapted machines—known as assistive technology—is creating some dramatic changes. Spearheaded by the likes of Microsoft, Intel, Pitney Bowes, Toshiba, IBM, and Apple Computer, as well as niche players such as Human-Ware and Dragon Dictate, this effort includes new products that can help disabled people better see a computer screen, hear a telephone call, talk to others when they lack speech, and do word processing when they cannot type. "Accessibility is a fundamental part of our software design process," says Microsoft Corp. Chief Executive Steven A. Ballmer.

These breakthroughs expand the universe of opportunity for the 54 million disabled people in the U.S.—a group the Americans with Disabilities Act defines as having a physical or mental impairment that limits life's major activities. Companies that make these products are banking not only on an exploding market for the disabled but also on an aging workforce. As baby boomers grow older, they are discovering that one-third of all Americans will have a disability at some point in their adult lives. As they remain in the workforce longer, they, too, will benefit from the innovations being cranked out today. Over time, the new technologies could make the workplace of the 21st century a lot more diverse.

Assistive-technology gadgets range from the most basic to machines worthy of a William Gibson sci-fi novel. Among them: computers displaying information in extremely large print for the sight-impaired or in braille formats for the blind; software that converts text into computer-synthesized speech; telecommunications relay products for the deaf that allow them to read what is spoken on the other end of the phone; improved prosthetics that replace a lost limb; and eye-gaze programs that allow paralyzed individuals to type on a computer screen simply by gazing at different points on the monitor.

All this hasn't been lost on companies looking to find fresh talent and keep the people they already have. After Joseph Martin, special counsel to Bank of America, was diagnosed with Lou Gehrig's disease in 1994, the company purchased the $16,000 Eyegaze System made by LC Technologies Inc. to enable him to keep working even though he had lost control of his arms and legs.

Simply by looking at control keys displayed on a computer monitor, Martin is able to direct a laser beam to various points on the screen. The laser prompts commands, whether to type a letter or a number. This enables him to dial a phone number, operate a PC, or log on to the Internet. All he needs is control of one of his eyes and the ability to keep his head still. For giving speeches, Martin downloads what he has written to a portable voice synthesizer made by Sentient Systems. He operates the voice synthesizer with a simple click-switch with the help of one finger on his hand that he can still move around.

Phone services are also taking on new dimensions. Deaf author Frank Bowe, who writes about the disability movement, does his research and interviews with a telecommunications device for the deaf (TDD). These kinds of interpretive and speech-to-speech services that enable communication between a deaf and hearing person now offer special operators who will read the message typed by a deaf person to a hearing person who doesn't have a TDD. Bowe uses coded signals transmitted through a wire or radio communications systems to type in a telephone number. The message is relayed by liquid-crystal display to the operator. Bowe then types in his message, and the operator makes the call. TDDs can now store messages, record them, and leave them. There are even wireless TDDs that perform like cell phones. Then there's voice recognition technology, which is still plagued with glitches, though systems are improving every year. When it's running smoothly and widely available, this innovation will go a long way toward empowering those with disabilities to compose on a PC using their own voices.

Even the good old photocopying machine is getting a disability face-lift. One of the most versatile products in years is Pitney Bowes Inc.'s Universal Access Copier System. The sleek, braille-labeled machine is outfitted with speech recognition and has oversize graphic-user interface and copy selector buttons that can be controlled with a mouse, fingers, or pointing stick. For wheelchair users, the copier is lower to the ground than conventional machines, making it a cinch to wheel right up to.

NET POWER. Of all the new technologies, though, it's the Internet that has the greatest potential for empowering the disabled in ways never before imagined. MCI WorldCom Inc. Senior Vice-President Vinton Cerf, who is partially deaf and is one of the founding fathers of the Net, anticipates the day when people with poor sight will be able to navigate an audio page that in some respects will be better than today's visual page. "The potential is there," says Cerf. For people with cognitive impairments, such as learning disabilities, the Net will soon offer simpler appliances that require less technical knowhow than what's required today to boot up a typical PC.

The bottom line: The Internet and other technologies are removing many of the can'ts that kept disabled people out of the office for so long. For worker-starved companies, the breakthroughs come not a moment too soon.

By John Williams in Washington

---

who also had disabilities. It also mandated that the disabled have access to telecommunications equipment and public transportation.

But the barriers standing between most people with disabilities and a good, solid job haven't exactly been wiped out by employee sensitivity training courses and curb-cut accessible sidewalks. Those and other strides have helped, but problems still abound. Cities such as Chicago and New Orleans face lawsuits for failing to bring their public transportation systems into compliance.

There are also, disability advocates say, still too many lawsuits like the one brought on behalf of a mentally retarded janitor, Don Perkl, who loved scrubbing toilets for Chuck E. Cheese in Madison, Wis. A district manager, a lawsuit alleges, fired him after saying "we don't hire people like that." The pizza parlor's local manager and two other employees quit in protest because they claimed the perennially upbeat Perkl was do-

ARTIFICIAL EYES, TURBINE HEARTS

Mechanical body parts could someday make disabilities irrelevant in the workplace

Getting a makeover is about to take on a whole new meaning. In the not-too-distant future, doctors will be able to do as much under the skin as beauticians now do on top. For the many people with disabilities or chronic diseases, technology is on the verge of unlocking a whole new world.

Scattered across the globe, dozens of research teams are working on computer chips that will be implanted in the brain or spinal cord to give artificial vision to the blind, hearing to the deaf, and speech to the victims of stroke. Other laboratories and companies are developing products that will regulate bladder function for the incontinent, restore movement to the paralyzed, and give back muscle control to people with amyotrophic lateral sclerosis (ALS, or Lou Gehrig's disease). Artificial kidneys and blood vessels are being tested in several labs, including the McGowan Center for Artificial Organ Development at the University of Pittsburgh. At the University of New Mexico's Artificial Muscle Research Institute, scientists are developing polymer-metal composites that could serve as replacement muscles for patients suffering such afflictions as muscular dystrophy.

SILICON RETINAS. Name almost any disability, and there's probably research under way to overcome it. Most magical of all, though, is the drive to restore vision in the blind. Already, Dr. Mark S. Humayun, a researcher at Johns Hopkins University Medical Institutions in Baltimore, has implanted light-sensitive chips in the eyes of some 15 patients. These tiny silicon retinas provide a very crude, 15-pixel image. A somewhat better, 64-pixel image is provided by an artificial-vision system that relays scenes from a miniature videocamera to a small electronic-circuit card inside the skull of Jerry . . . (He asks that his last name not be used.) Jerry's vision system was developed over four decades by William H. Dobelle, CEO of Dobelle Institute Inc. in Commack, N.Y. "My next version will be better still," he says—with 512 pixels. Still, that's a far cry from the hundreds of thousands of pixels on a TV screen or computer monitor.

Image quality will keep getting better as semiconductor technology continues to pack silicon chips with more power. In 10 years it might be good enough that

users will blend into the crowd. In 20 years, the acuity of artificial vision might rival that of a biological eye, says Dr. William J. Heetderks, head of a National

Institutes of Health program focused on developing electronic implants. In fact, fully functioning artificial eyes should be ready by 2024, predicts Ian D. Pearson,

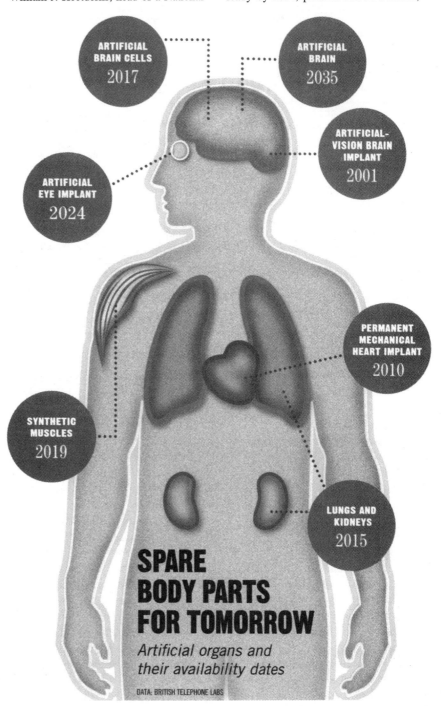

ARTIFICIAL BRAIN CELLS 2017

ARTIFICIAL BRAIN 2035

ARTIFICIAL-VISION BRAIN IMPLANT 2001

ARTIFICIAL EYE IMPLANT 2024

PERMANENT MECHANICAL HEART IMPLANT 2010

SYNTHETIC MUSCLES 2019

LUNGS AND KIDNEYS 2015

SPARE BODY PARTS FOR TOMORROW

Artificial organs and their availability dates

DATA: BRITISH TELEPHONE LABS

LAUREL ALLEN/BW

a researcher at British Telecommunications PLC's BT Laboratories in England.

Long before then, other manmade body parts will be helping people to overcome disabilities. Artificial hearing implants, offering better sound than today's cochlear implants, may arrive sooner—perhaps within a year. Electronic implants to stimulate the muscles in paralyzed limbs should be ready by 2002, says Pearson of BT labs. Artificial lungs and kidneys may follow by 2015, although some researchers optimistically predict 2010, when a permanent artificial heart may be ready.

Advanced prototypes of all these spare body parts already exist in research labs. The history of such efforts, after all, goes back almost six decades to the kidney dialysis machine, which was invented in 1943 in the Netherlands by Dr. Willem J. Kolff. Known today as the father of artificial organs, he came to the U.S. in 1950, developed an artificial heart at the Cleveland Clinic in the mid-1950s, and in the 1960s formed an artificial-organ research program at the University of Utah. Many others followed; Dobelle, for one, started his artificial vision work under Kolff's tutelage.

Probably the Utah group's most famous product was the Jarvik heart, named after Robert K. Jarvik, who developed the original design in the late 1970s while he was an engineering student at Utah—building on the work of at least 147 of Kolff's students. Since then, mechanical-heart designs have leaped into the Space Age. Several of the latest versions have tiny turbines for pumping blood—borrowed from the turbines that pump fuel in the Space Shuttle. Supercomputer simulations at NASA and the Pittsburgh Supercomputing Center honed the turbine designs to make them superhumanly efficient. For now, these pumps are used only as "bridge" devices to sustain a patient until a human heart is available for transplant. But researchers are confident they'll eventually be permanent replacements.

Moreover, artificial organs no longer need a connection through the skin to an outside power source. In 1991, researchers at the University of Ottawa Heart Institute developed a so-called inductive system that "broadcasts" electrical power through the skin. Patients can move about freely using a battery pack. A similar system also transmitted signals through the skin, activating an artificial-vision brain implant. So blind people may not need a hole in their head like Jerry has.

Americans who want Dobelle's system may have to fly to Zurich, where he has a clinic. Stringent U.S. Food & Drug Administration safety rules make it uneconomical to introduce artificial-organ technology at home, he says.

That's why Dr. Bartley P. Griffith, director of Pittsburgh's McGowan Center for Artificial Organ Development, will head to Israel to perform the first human implant of a new turbine heart. "The U.S. standard is that we're not going to use devices that might do harm, no matter how gravely ill the patient is," he says. To Kolff, who's now 89, that doesn't make sense, and he has been lobbying Washington for a change. Some 95,000 people will die this year "without a chance," he laments, because only a couple thousand donor hearts will probably be available. Dr. Steven J. Phillips, an assistant research director at the National Institutes of Health, also believes the FDA could ease up. "Europe's safety record with our new devices is actually better than our own—and they're saving more lives," he notes. He also worries about so much of the research migrating to Europe because of its encouraging climate.

Yet ultimately, most of these gadgets may be replaced. Biotech engineers will figure out how to tinker with genes and prevent or cure blindness, heart disease, and other afflictions. But it won't happen for at least 20 years, says Griffith. That leaves a big gap for mechanical body parts to fill. Soon, "making a new you" could take on a whole new meaning.

By Otis Port in New York

---

ing such a stellar job. Last year, a jury in federal court in the Western District of Wisconsin agreed with them, slapping the company with $13 million in punitive damages—the largest ADA award ever for a single plaintiff. A judge is still reviewing the jury's verdict. Chuck E. Cheese claims that Perkl "wasn't dismissed due to his disability but because he couldn't perform the job," says company spokesman Jon Rice.

LAWSUITS ON THE FRINGE.
Plenty of other lawsuits brought under the ADA have caused critics to question its scope. Some worry that the act is not broad enough, pointing to a recent Supreme Court ruling that established that people with treatable disabilities don't qualify for protection. Others say the ADA is straying into the realm of the absurd, noting such cases as the employee with bad body odor who argued she should be protected from getting fired because her glandular problem qualified her as disabled.

But most of the country's workers with disabilities face challenges that are far more clear-cut: They are deaf, blind, paralyzed, or emotionally impaired. Some have been burdened with disabilities since they were born. Others, like Booz, Allen & Hamilton Inc. principal Jeffrey Schaffer, are new to the minority—a group that one in three people will be a part of during their lives. Three years ago, Schaffer's car was in a head-on collision with another vehicle that swerved into his lane on a windy back road in West Virginia. It took paramedics an hour to cut him from the wreckage.

After learning he would be confined to a wheelchair, Schaffer says, the thought of returning to work was the thing that kept him going. "Getting back to work was critical to my sense of well-being," says Schaffer from the bed of a hospital where he has just undergone his sixth operation since the accident. "Work end sup being a defining characteristic for self-worth."

For worker-starved companies, spreading that kind of self-worth around is looking more and more like the only answer to today's labor-shortage woes. Still, the real test will be when the economy cools and companies can afford to get picky about choosing between applicants with disabilities and everyone else. By then, though, it may be a lot harder to tell the difference.

By Michelle Conlin in New York

A Start-up of Her Own

Meet the new generation of American CEOs:
They're young, wired, fearless—and female

BY MARCI MCDONALD

It is not your usual girls' night out. By 6 p.m., when most employees have already fled a corporate steel-and-glass low-rise in Redwood Shores, Calif., a dozen women are just drifting into a borrowed second-floor boardroom for their semimonthly get-together. Sporting everything from tailored power suits to jeans, they pick up Styrofoam cartons of Chinese takeout and settle around the oval conference table to catch up on each other's news. Marianne van Gelder, a single mother and recent law school graduate, can hardly wait to report her latest coup. "This week was just awesome," she enthuses. "Tomorrow I see my $10 million guy."

In another era—say, even five whole years ago—her audience might have concluded that van Gelder had just landed a hot date with a sugar daddy. But in this room, when the subject turns to courtship, the women mean their own wooing of "VCs"—which, for the uninitiated, means venture capitalists, not Viet Cong. For van Gelder, who heads her own E-commerce start-up, AnWang Enterprises, the next day's rendezvous is her chance to pitch one of Silicon Valley's leading firms for $10 million in second-round funding. Listening to that news, the boardroom breaks out in the kind of admiring oohs and applause once reserved for a debutante showing off a high-watt diamond. Welcome to girl talk in the new millennium, where budding

**Kim Fisher, CEO of AudioBasket, calls herself a "born entrepreneur."
As a child, she sold hand-decorated lunch bags at school. After getting her M.B.A., she helped set up an Internet portal in Lithuania.**
"What's important to me is really building something."

female entrepreneurs would rather chat about boosting the bottom line of their businesses than updating their hairstyles. For these aspiring tycoons, dishing the dirt means getting the lowdown from that night's guest CEO on when to demand a nondisclosure agreement. The evening is the fourth in a six-part training series sponsored by the San Mateo, Calif.-based Forum for Women Entrepreneurs, one of a handful of organizations that have banded together in an effort to put more women into the driver's seat of the "new economy." Although the movement so far is small, its aims are by no means modest. "We didn't want women to be doing nail salons," says Denise Brosseau, the forum's executive director. "We wanted them to be thinking about joining the *Fortune* 500."

Across the country, Brosseau and a group of private foundations—some funded by the first generation of Silicon Valley's female millionaires—are tackling one of the last frontiers of the women's movement: boosting a new generation of female entrepreneurs into the country's loftiest economic circles. In doing so, they are accelerating a trend that has already begun to change the face of American business. During the past decade, women have been starting their own companies at nearly twice the national average and now own 38 percent of all U.S. firms. Since 1987, the number of female-owned ventures has doubled from 4.5 million to 9.1 million, according to the National Foundation for Women Business Owners (NFWBO).

No longer sidelines. Once, the majority of those businesses were dismissed as minor-league operations. But over the past three years, their staff and revenues have skyrocketed. By 1999, female-owned companies employed more than 27 million Americans—nearly 9 million more than in 1996—and their annual sales had risen from $2.3 trillion to $3.6 trillion. "Quite clearly, these aren't women who just want to stay home and start a little something on the side," says NFWBO Executive Director Sharon Hadary. "Their businesses are getting bigger and more substantial."

That shift in scale is largely the result of an influx of female CEOs of the Internet gen-

eration. Young, tech-smart, and armed with both impressive credentials and chutzpah, they aren't content to work their way up through the corporate ranks and await the keys to the executive suite. After all, despite the hoopla capping Carly Fiorina's appointment as CEO of Hewlett-Packard last year, she remains one of only three women heading a *Fortune* 500 corporation.

Instead, women are hitching their fortunes to the entrepreneurial zeitgeist in the air, writing their own business plans and appointing themselves president, CEO, and chairwoman of the board. "The new generation of women entrepreneurs that I see have not even tested the corporate waters," says Myra Hart, a professor of entrepreneurship at Harvard Business School. "They're going straight out on their own. The economic environment is better for women than it ever has been."

One reason is the emergence of the Internet economy. Originally, the high-tech revolution centered on semiconductor makers and hardware know-how, a traditional male stronghold. But five years ago, the commercialization of the Internet brought a demand for marketing savvy and consumer service—fields in which women have long flourished. "Now you can take a retail idea, put it on top of the Internet, and build a huge business," says Hart. "For the first time, really big deals were open to women."

These days the media regularly offer up inspirational images of those self-made moguls: Meg Whitman building eBay into a multimillion-dollar online flea market and Martha Stewart wowing Wall Street with her artfully crafted stock offering, served up along with cocktails and canapés. As Hart points out, "The role models for entrepreneurs have become almost as popular as basketball stars."

Even for a 29-year-old techno-wizard like Krishna Subramanian, who holds a master's degree in computer science and five patents from Sun Microsystems' labs, those celebrity role models have proved oddly reassuring. Last year, when she left Sun to co-found Kovair, a San José-based Web platform for managing E-business clients,

she found comfort in the notion that other unlikely women had transformed themselves into new-economy deal makers. "When you see more women running big companies, it seems more doable," she says. "And it's changed other people's perception of whether women can do the job."

In a sleek loft development in San Francisco's trendy South of Market district—known here as start-up central—one sculpture strikes a strangely plaintive note. Over a fireplace, a foot-high pink papier-mâché dress, complete with prim pleated skirt, sports a caption reading, "I Hope He Calls Me Tomorrow." That tribute to decades of helpless feminine longing stands in ironic counterpoint to the can-do determination of the dozen resident entrepreneurs currently ensconced in the Women's Technology Cluster.

High-tech incubator. Founded last year by Catherine Muther, 52, a former vice president of marketing at Cisco Systems, the cluster is a monument to mentoring: the first high-tech incubator focused exclusively on fostering female-run firms. Initially financed by Muther's Three Guineas Fund—a private foundation named after a Virginia Woolf essay—it provides loft space, advice, and expert round tables for 10 to 13 burgeoning businesses at any given time.

Muther's theory was that the incubator's sense of community and its visiting cast of experts could make up for the financial networks that most women entrepreneurs lack as they set out to join the dot-com gold rush. "We're interested in Internet companies because that's where the new wealth is being created," says Margarita Quihuis, the cluster's 38-year-old director. "And our mission is to make sure women get their share."

Until now, their pickings have been slim. In a survey of 100 Internet-related companies released last month, Spencer Stuart, an executive search firm, found only 3 percent of them had female directors. By contrast, 84 percent of *Fortune* 500 companies boasted at least one woman on their boards.

With an eye to changing the dynamic, she and Muther screen every applicant in a grueling good cop-bad cop interview routine. "We see how they respond to pressure," Quihuis says. "If they go in front of a venture capitalist, they're going to get hammered." One team's business plan looked promising on paper. "But they came in and they immediately cratered," she recalls. "You could tell from the body language and the slumped shoulders that they didn't have what it takes."

Once CEOs pass muster, they can stay at the cluster until their companies grow beyond an informal 30-employee limit. Then, as Quihuis puts it, "We kick them out of the nest." Already, four of the cluster's firms have graduated in the past six months. And scheduled for the boot by September is Lev-

Pamela Kleier, 46, CEO of c-z.com, a Kentucky-based construction materials Web site, raises venture capital while husband Glenn writes novels and looks after their sons. She feels discrimination not as a woman but as a Southerner.
"There's geographic bias in the dot-com world."

elEdge.com, the brainchild of 38-year-old Lisa Henderson. A spiky-haired blond who grew up poor but athletic, Henderson got into Missouri's Lindenwood University through a fluke. Watching a college soccer game when she was a high school senior, she was asked to sub for an absent player. She scored two goals, landing herself an athletic scholarship. After graduation and six years in marketing at Ralston Purina, Henderson realized the Internet could offer other young athletes the future she once kicked open for herself. At lunch with Muther last fall, she plotted out her dream on a paper napkin: a database that would democratize college recruiting by tracking the performance of America's 10 million high school athletes. "I thought technology could be the great equalizer to get kids noticed," she says.

In April, she launched LevelEdge.com at the National Collegiate Athletic Association finals, and 3,000 coaches signed up. That same week, she wrapped up $4 million in first-round financing from investors, including Goldman Sachs and former tennis star Billie Jean King. But for Henderson, the most moving vote of confidence came in a personal check from one of her former bosses, Carol Bartz, CEO of San Raphael-based Autodesk. "I got two slides into my presentation," Henderson recalls, "and she said, 'I love it. I know you have the drive to succeed. Let me introduce you to whoever I can.'"

That sort of mentoring is precisely what Muther hopes to encourage as she rolls out plans for a series of similar Women's Technology Clusters in high-tech hubs from Seattle and Austin to the suburbs of Washington, D.C., over the next two years. But she has not left that philanthropic impulse entirely to chance. The price for enlisting in her incubator is to hand over 2 percent of each company's worth. For Muther, the point is not to build a fat stock portfolio but to ensure that the cycle of philanthropy carries on. "It's not enough to make money," Quihuis says. "You have to give back."

In the conference room at Oracle Corp.'s headquarters in Redwood Shores last January, Kim Fisher had no time to savor her status as a pioneer. Only minutes before the 31-year-old CEO of AudioBasket was scheduled to make her pitch at Springboard 2000—a landmark venture-capital fair focused exclusively on women-run firms— Fisher realized she couldn't carry all her props on stage. With her arms already full

of magazines and newspapers intended to illustrate the information overload her customized audio-news service would supplant, she had no way to illustrate its range of unique delivery, from cellphone to Palm III. Then she hit upon the notion of clipping those devices to her belt. Fisher was well into her 17-minute pitch when she saw she was winning the attention of the 225 assembled venture capitalists in a way she had not intended. "I started unbuttoning my jacket," she says, "and people thought I was doing a striptease."

Despite that blip, Fisher was among the stars of Springboard 2000. Co-sponsored by the Forum for Women Entrepreneurs and the Washington-based National Women's Business Council, the all-day event was designed to smash the single biggest barrier for women entrepreneurs in the new economy: their access to the megabucks of venture capital. To some like Deborah Naybor, who runs a land-surveying company outside Buffalo, the problem was a familiar story. A decade ago, she faced banks wary of granting women small-business loans. One gave her 30 days to pay back $70,000.

Now, banks have come around, but women are getting short shrift from venture capitalists. As a recent study led by Candida Brush of Boston University showed, out of the total venture funds invested last year—an estimated $20 billion—only 4 percent went to women.

"The venture world is probably the ultimate old-boys network," acknowledges Jay Hoag, the managing partner of Technology Crossover Ventures, based in Palo Alto, Calif. "Until a few years ago, you'd go to a venture capital event, and it was all guys." Over the past five years, more firms like his have welcomed female partners, with a predictable result. This spring, Hoag was surprised to learn that eight of the 40 companies his fund had backed were headed by women.

But in a field that boasts 2,375 men, the arrival of an estimated 100 women partners meant that less than 4 percent of the community was female. "There's still a lot of venture firms that are strictly male," says Susan Mason, one of three female partners

at Onset Ventures in Menlo Park, Calif. "And they're proud of it."

Five years ago, Sona Wang, a Chicago venture capitalist, co-founded the first woman-focused fund, Inroads Capital Partners in Evanston, Ill., which targeted companies in technology and health care. "We're in a time when the constant challenge is to find more attractive projects," she says. "Yet there was this whole other market not being tapped." Since then, a half dozen other women's venture firms have emerged. But they still represent a tiny fraction of the entire venture-capital industry.

Wang and others knew more-radical measures were needed. One problem was the insider nature of the venture community, which operates on a complex web of personal ties. "A typical venture firm gets 5,000 business plans a year," explains Quihuis. "So they have this triage: never accept a proposal over the transom. You have to come in pre-screened—through an attorney, an accountant, or someone in their circle. Women have not had access to those networks, nor did they understand that's how it worked."

Muther proposed demystifying the process with the first-ever women's venture fair, patterned after celebrated high-testosterone events run every year in Silicon Valley by *Red Herring* magazine and Garage.com. Her Three Guineas Fund seeded the project, which cost an estimated $500,000. Issuing an appeal for promising business plans from women CEOs over the Internet, Springboard's organizers were swamped with over 300. They whittled that list down to 27—among them Fisher's AudioBasket. Each was promised 17 minutes to make her case to 225 leading venture capitalists. To make sure those 27 were up to par, the organizers hired Kim Marinucci, whose Winning Pitch specialized in honing venture presentations. "There's a style thing—physical presence, how to stand," Quihuis explains. "When women get nervous, we get the Minnie Mouse voice."

Three months later, 26 of the 27 Springboard presenters have received funding worth an estimated $100 million, plus strategic partnerships. "They were fighting off investors," says Amy Millman of the National Women's Business Council.

So successful was Springboard 2000 that follow-up events are already scheduled across the country over the next six months, beginning in Washington, D.C., next fall. And last month, a New York version, billed as "The Women of Silicon Alley Summit," showcased 21 female entrepreneurs—including Pamela Kleier, CEO of c-z.com, a Kentucky-based Web site featuring construction materials. For Kleier, the event helped counter the discrimination she felt from venture capitalists—not as a woman, but as a Southerner. "There's a geographic bias in the dot-com world," she says. "If it doesn't happen on the West Coast, it's probably not a valid concept."

Still, in the wake of the high-tech market meltdown in recent weeks, some women worry that, at the very moment they are finally landing invitations to the inner sanctums of venture capital, the party is winding down. "It will become more competitive to get that cash," concedes venture capitalist Mason. "The numbers will go down—but not just for women."

Quihuis argues that the new climate may, in fact, play in women's favor. "There was a good deal of get-rich-quick going on," she says. "But women are very conservative. They want to build something real." Fisher, who earned her M.B.A. from Berkeley in 1994, agrees. "People are going to be more selective about where they put their money," she says, "and I kind of like that. Having gone to business school before all this happened, I kind of thought [profitability] was supposed to be your goal. "

Eight months ago, Menekse Gencer looked around her Los Angeles office and found she didn't care for the long-term view. Barely a year after earning her M.B.A. from Pennsylvania's Wharton School of Business, she had landed a consulting job at PricewaterhouseCoopers. Although she had no complaint about her assignments or six-figure salary, she recoiled from the women she saw in upper management. "Frankly, they just seemed miserable," she recalls. "I said to myself, 'I don't want that to be me.' "

In October, Gencer resigned to join two former Wharton classmates as a co-founder of Vistify, a deco-styled Internet appliance intended to simplify household E-commerce. As her example shows, the flip side of women's mass migration to entrepreneurship is their mass exodus from corporate Amer-

ica. For some consulting firms like Deloitte & Touche—where women were once leaving at twice the rate of men—that exodus became so critical that it prompted a radical rewrite of promotion and family-leave policies. And in the tightest labor market in postwar memory, it has added to the thorny task of recruiting women for top management. "There's a huge shortage of talent," says Jeffrey Christian, the Cleveland-based headhunter who found Fiorina for Hewlett-Packard. "There aren't enough good women to go around."

The National Foundation for Women Business Owners reports that women are decamping from corporations out of growing frustration over their treatment. But Gencer, at 28, doesn't share that complaint. For her and others, the tales of thwarted ambition told by older women entrepreneurs seem alien and exotic—a symptom of a yawning generational divide. "Today, young women are much more confident, not only in their own abilities," says Hart, "but about their place in the business world."

There are also more women with M.B.A.'s and high-tech degrees. In 1997, 34 years after the first woman graduated from Harvard Business School, women earned 39 percent of all graduate business and management degrees. JoMei Chang, 47, the CEO of Vitria Technology—a $5 billion company specializing in applications integration software—has watched the ranks of women in high tech grow as well. In 1984, when she arrived at a small Silicon Valley start-up called Sun Microsystems with a Ph.D. in database management from Purdue, she found herself the only female engineer on a 20-person team. By last year, when she was asked back to speak, her hosts couldn't tell her how much those ranks had swelled. "There were so many, they couldn't count." In her own case, she says, "I never let the fact of my gender or race become an issue."

Today, the greatest challenge to women entrepreneurs—after finding capital—is as old as biology itself: the difficulty of juggling both a fledgling company and a fledgling family. Heather Blease, 37, who founded EnvisioNet (which provides techni-

cal support for the Microsoft Network) in Brunswick, Maine, five years ago, can speak to those conflicting tugs. At a time when her company was exploding from three to 1,500 employees, she was changing diapers for three toddlers under 6. Leaving for one pivotal fundraising trip to the West Coast, she was kissing her second son goodbye when he demanded, "Mommy, do you love your company more than me?" She got over that moment—"You just have to," she says—and has gone on to build Maine's fastest-growing company.

But no female entrepreneurs pretend that such warring demands are without a price. "It's not easy," says Sandra Kurtzig. the 51-year-old founder of the Ask Group, a manufacturing software system that was once the country's second-largest woman-led firm. Kurtzig recalls her mother phoning to scream at her, "How can you fly off when your son has measles?" And she admits her work played no small part in her divorce. Still, she now urges young women M.B.A. students to "Go for it. Just be willing to take the same amount of risks as men."

In fact, she offers the prospect of a future payoff. At a time when some women are grappling with empty-nest syndrome, her oldest son has just asked her to join him as a partner in a start-up. "Now my kids need me in a different way," she says. "And the more mothers that are working, the better effect it will have on their sons' hiring women in business."

Two years ago, a pair of female students at Harvard Business School asked Hart, one of the four co-founders of the Staples office empire, to add a course on entrepreneurship for women to the curriculum. "They saw entrepreneurship as a career choice that was much more compatible with raising children than corporate life," she recalls. But after hearing horror stories from some of the country's top women CEOs, many revised their opinion. Now, Hart says, unlike earlier generations, they look at starting their own businesses as "one among a number of career choices. There's a feeling you can have it all—and you don't have to do it all at once, or at the same time."

At the Women's Technology Cluster, Meneske Gencer shares that view. As a single woman without children, like most of the new generation of female entrepreneurs, she hasn't yet had to figure out how she'll juggle family and her start-up, but she's confident she will. "Today, you think, 'Thank God, women don't have to be one thing or another—a businesswoman or a mother,' " she says. "If women are the CEOs, they can make it OK to be both." Sharon Hadary of the National Foundation for Women Business Owners agrees. "The rules for business are being rewritten even as we speak," she says. "And what's become clear now is that women will have a role in rewriting them."

Test Your Knowledge Form

We encourage you to photocopy and use this page as a tool to assess how the articles in **Annual Editions** expand on the information in your textbook. By reflecting on the articles you will gain enhanced text information. You can also access this useful form on a product's book support Web site at ***http://www.dushkin.com/ online/.***

NAME: _____   DATE: _____

TITLE AND NUMBER OF ARTICLE: _____

BRIEFLY STATE THE MAIN IDEA OF THIS ARTICLE: _____

LIST THREE IMPORTANT FACTS THAT THE AUTHOR USES TO SUPPORT THE MAIN IDEA:

_____

WHAT INFORMATION OR IDEAS DISCUSSED IN THIS ARTICLE ARE ALSO DISCUSSED IN YOUR TEXTBOOK OR OTHER READINGS THAT YOU HAVE DONE? LIST THE TEXTBOOK CHAPTERS AND PAGE NUMBERS:

_____

LIST ANY EXAMPLES OF BIAS OR FAULTY REASONING THAT YOU FOUND IN THE ARTICLE:

_____

LIST ANY NEW TERMS/CONCEPTS THAT WERE DISCUSSED IN THE ARTICLE, AND WRITE A SHORT DEFINITION:

_____

ANNUAL EDITIONS revisions depend on two major opinion sources: one is our Advisory Board, listed in the front of this volume, which works with us in scanning the thousands of articles published in the public press each year; the other is you—the person actually using the book. Please help us and the users of the next edition by completing the prepaid article rating form on this page and returning it to us. Thank you for your help!

ANNUAL EDITIONS: Business Ethics 01/02

ARTICLE RATING FORM

Here is an opportunity for you to have direct input into the next revision of this volume. We would like you to rate each of the 49 articles listed below, using the following scale:

1. **Excellent: should definitely be retained**
2. **Above average: should probably be retained**
3. **Below average: should probably be deleted**
4. **Poor: should definitely be deleted**

Your ratings will play a vital part in the next revision. So please mail this prepaid form to us just as soon as you complete it. Thanks for your help!

We Want Your Advice

RATING

ARTICLE

1. Thinking Ethically: A Framework for Moral Decision Making
2. The Sears Lectureship in Business Ethics at Bentley College—Ethics: The Way to Do Business
3. Defining Moments: When Managers Must Choose Between Right and Right
4. Doing Well by Doing Good
5. Ford-Firestone Lesson: Heed the Moment of Truth
6. Why Character Counts
7. Is Your Office Killing You?
8. Electronic Communication in the Workplace—Something's Got to Give
9. Religion in the Workplace
10. Cyber Crime
11. The Anatomy of Fraudulent Behavior
12. Dirty Money Goes Digital
13. Harassment Grows More Complex
14. Tales From the Front Line of Sexual Harassment
15. What Minority Employees Really Want
16. Silver Lining
17. Sorrow and Guilt: An Ethical Analysis of Layoffs
18. Alternatives to Downsizing
19. Blowing Whistles, Blowing Smoke
20. Columbia/HCA Whistle-Blowers to Fight for Gold
21. Leaders as Value Shapers
22. Motivating Moral Corporate Behavior
23. 3M's Big Cleanup
24. The Parable of the Sadhu
25. Work & Family: Family-Friendly CEOs Are Changing Cultures at More Workplaces

RATING

ARTICLE

26. The Greening of Corporate America
27. The Elephant at the Environmental Cocktail Party
28. Trust in the Marketplace
29. Virtual Morality: A New Workplace Quandary
30. Online Privacy: It's Time for Rules in Wonderland
31. Values in Tension: Ethics Away From Home
32. Global Standards, Local Problems
33. The Environment of Ethics in Global Business
34. The Caux Round Table, Principles for Business: The Rise of International Ethics
35. Sweatshops: No More Excuses
36. Companies Are Discovering the Value of Ethics
37. Ethics in the Public Eye
38. The Company Simply Refused to Pay
39. Managing for Organizational Integrity
40. When Good People Do Bad Things at Work
41. Mission Driven, Values Centered
42. The 100 Best Corporate Citizens
43. Winery With a Mission
44. Ethical Challenges for Business in the New Millennium: Corporate Social Responsibility and Models of Management Morality
45. Old Ethical Principles: The New Corporate Culture
46. Profits From Principle: Five Forces Redefining Business
47. The New Bottom Line
48. The New Workforce
49. A Start-Up of Her Own

(Continued on next page)

NO POSTAGE
NECESSARY
IF MAILED
IN THE
UNITED STATES

BUSINESS REPLY MAIL
FIRST-CLASS MAIL PERMIT NO. 84 GUILFORD CT

POSTAGE WILL BE PAID BY ADDRESSEE

**McGraw-Hill/Dushkin
530 Old Whitfield Street
Guilford, CT 06437-9989**

ABOUT YOU

Name   Date

Are you a teacher? ☐   A student? ☐
Your school's name

Department

Address   City   State   Zip

School telephone #

YOUR COMMENTS ARE IMPORTANT TO US !

Please fill in the following information:
For which course did you use this book?

Did you use a text with this *ANNUAL EDITION*? ☐ yes ☐ no
What was the title of the text?

What are your general reactions to the *Annual Editions* concept?

Have you read any particular articles recently that you think should be included in the next edition?

Are there any articles you feel should be replaced in the next edition? Why?

Are there any World Wide Web sites you feel should be included in the next edition? Please annotate.

May we contact you for editorial input? ☐ yes ☐ no
May we quote your comments? ☐ yes ☐ no